Vigilante Politics

Dane Archer

Richard Maxwell Brown

Kanti C. Kotecha

William P. Kreml

Richard Ned Lebow

Gary T. Marx

Ali A. Mazrui

Fred R. von der Mehden

Christian P. Potholm

H. Jon Rosenbaum

Edward Schneier

Peter C. Sederberg

R. Lance Shotland

Edward Stettner

James L. Walker

Vigilante Politics

H. Jon Rosenbaum
and
Peter C. Sederberg
Editors

University of Pennsylvania Press / 1976

Contents

Preface vii

PART I: THEORETICAL PERSPECTIVES
  1. Vigilantism: An Analysis of Establishment Violence
     H. Jon Rosenbaum and *Peter C. Sederberg* 3
  2. Spontaneous Vigilantism: A Bystander Response to
     Criminal Behavior
     R. Lance Shotland 30
  3. The Vigilante Personality
     William P. Kreml 45
  4. Vigilantism and Political Theory
     Edward Stettner 64

PART II: AMERICAN PERSPECTIVES
  5. The History of Vigilantism in America
     Richard Maxwell Brown 79
  6. White Collar Vigilantism: The Politics of
     Anti-Communism in the United States
     Edward Schneier 110
  7. Community Police Patrols and Vigilantism
     Gary T. Marx and *Dane Archer* 129
  8. Vigilantism and the American Police
     Kanti C. Kotecha and *James L. Walker* 158

PART III: COMPARATIVE PERSPECTIVES
  9. Comparative Vigilantism: The United States
     and South Africa
     Christian P. Potholm 175
  10. Black Vigilantism in Cultural Transition: Violence
      and Viability in Tropical Africa
      Ali A. Mazrui 194
  11. "Pariah" Communities and Violence
      Fred R. von der Mehden 218

12. Vigilantism in Northern Ireland
    Richard Ned Lebow 234
PART IV: CONCLUSIONS
13. Vigilante Politics: Concluding Observations
    Peter C. Sederberg and *H. Jon Rosenbaum* 261

Contributors 274
Index 279

Preface

Jim Phelps outlines the tactics needed to accomplish the latest assignment of his "Impossible Mission Force (IMF)": breaking and entering, electronic surveillance, sabotage and seduction. Why has the government turned to the IMF? Simply because "conventional law enforcement agencies" have been unable to complete the task and help is needed from an organization not bound by the rules governing "conventional" law enforcement. Of course, if the IMF is discovered, the "Secretary" will disavow any knowledge of their activities.

Gordon Liddy outlines for Attorney General John Mitchell the tactics he feels are necessary to accomplish his assignment: breaking and entering, electronic surveillance, sabotage and seduction. Why has the Committee to Re-elect the President turned to Liddy and his coterie of ex-CIA agents? Simply because "conventional law enforcement agencies" cannot be sufficiently exploited to undermine the Democratic Party and secure the election of Richard Nixon. Of course, when Mr. Liddy and his operatives were discovered, the attorney general disavowed any knowledge of their activities.

In the popular movie *Death Wish*, mild-mannered architect Paul Kersey (Charles Bronson) turns into an avenging angel after the murder of his wife and rape of his daughter. Ferreting out New York City's muggers, he proceeds to gun them down, thereby lowering the film city's crime rate and providing tension-release for its frustrated real-life inhabitants.

Not all the frustrations of the citizens of New York are released through fantasy projections. On July 20, 1973, after witnessing a shooting incident on West 134th Street, about one hundred locals set upon the perpetrator and beat him senseless.

In another movie, *Gordon's War*, a Vietnam veteran organizes a group of his buddies and goes after the drug dealers in Harlem. Again, film fantasy found an echo in reality, for in the fall of 1974 three men from the Bronx declared their own private war on the addicts using a vacant apartment in their neighborhood as a "shooting gallery." One drug suspect was beaten to death with a wrench, broken bottle, and metal pipes.

The similarities between the real and the fictionalized acts of violence are striking, and examples of other parallels could be developed. They are not, of course, directly linked to one another; rather, all reflect an apparent resurgence of vigilantism in America. The tradition of violent self help is a well established one in the political history of the United States, and film and novel audiences have been entertained for decades by the antics of frontier vigilantes, as well as the rugged private enforcers like Mike Hammer, Sam Spade, and Phillip Marlowe. Recently, however, vigilante action, both real and fictional, appears to be turning more frequent and violent. The frustrations bred by a rising crime rate and a decay in the basic norms of political civility and trust in government led even former Attorney General William Saxbe to warn of still further increases in the defensive violence of an outraged citizenry.

Various forms of dissident violence, from common crime to revolutionary war, have received considerable attention in recent years from both the general public and the scholarly community. The literature devoted to vigilantism (or "establishment violence"), however, has been largely restricted to a few historical studies and radical tracts which condemn all government coercion as violence. Therefore, in an attempt to help fill this void, this volume is dedicated exclusively to the consideration of vigilante politics. It is hoped that this multidisciplinary effort, which contains contributions by historians, political scientists, sociologists, and psychologists, will lead to a greater understanding of vigilantism and encourage others to continue to explore this subject.

We have performed four tasks in preparing this book. First, we wrote chapter 1 which is designed to be exploratory, suggestive, and provocative. Second, we then selected the scholars that have contributed all but one of the book's remaining chapters and distributed the introductory chapter to them. In view of the wide variety of the topics treated, each author was left to his own discretion as to how closely he wished to comply with the format and vocabulary employed in our chapter.

It has been extremely gratifying to be able to assemble such a distinguished group of contributors. The authors have studied their subjects in depth; several of them either have published or have publications in press on the subjects discussed in their essays. However, eleven of the thirteen chapters were written specifically for this volume. Chapter 1, while prepared by the editors with this book in mind, first appeared in *Comparative Politics*. Chapter Six was originally published by the *American Behavioral Scientist* but has been lengthened and extensively revised for this volume. We wish to thank the publishers of these journals for permission to republish these pieces.

The essays in the volume appear in substantially the form in which they were submitted by their authors. In completing our third task, we confined ourselves to standardizing spelling and citations in order to attain as much consistency as possible throughout the collection. In no case was the content of the essays altered in any significant way; the essays must stand, then, on their own merits.

Finally, in the last chapter, we have attempted to respond to some of the criticisms of the introductory chapter by the other authors. We also have sought to explain or reconcile many of the seemingly conflicting conclusions reached by the contributors.

The volume is organized in three parts. Part I is devoted to theoretical perspectives. Chapter 1, by the coeditors, seeks to make a contribution to the understanding of vigilantism through: (1) a preliminary investigation of the conditions likely to produce vigilante action; (2) the development of a typology of vigilantism; and (3) a discussion of the effects of vigilantism on the creation and maintenance of a stable sociopolitical order. In chapter 2, R. Lance Shotland discusses spontaneous vigilantism, the act by a group of bystanders of not only apprehending a suspected wrongdoer but instantly meting out punishment and retribution which fall outside of the normal judicial process. Chapter 3, by William P. Kreml, analyzes the vigilante personality, and chapter 4, by Edward Stettner, considers the relationship between vigilantism and the normative concerns of political theorists.

Part II is devoted to a discussion of vigilantism in the United States and begins with a survey of the history of American vigilantism by Richard Maxwell Brown in chapter 5. In chapter 6, by Edward V. Schneier, Jr., it is demonstrated how subtle forms of vigilantism have permeated the country's culture and perverted its political system. This is followed by an examination of community police patrols by Gary T. Marx and Dane Archer and an evaluation of police vigilantism by Kanti C. Kotecha and James L. Walker in chapters 7 and 8.

Part III places vigilantism in a comparative perspective. Chapter 9 by Christian P. Potholm compares vigilantism in the United States and Southern Africa. In chapter 10 Ali A. Mazrui examines black vigilantism in tropical Africa, and in chapter 11 Fred R. von der Mehden discusses the application of vigilantism against *pariah* communities in Asia and Africa. This part of the volume concludes with a discussion by Richard Ned Lebow in chapter 12 of vigilantism, both past and present, in Ireland.

Part IV, chapter 13, contains the volume's conclusions. A summary of its contents already have been provided.

Aside from the general reader, this book should be of interest to those studying the history, sociology, politics, or psychology of violence. It also should prove useful in courses dealing with law enforcement, the administration of justice, and social change.

We are grateful for the editorial assistance of Margaret C. Bayldon and A. Denman Pierce-Grove. We also wish to express our appreciation to the

University of South Carolina Research and Productive Scholarship Fund for a grant used for the preparation of the index. Finally, thanks are due to our wives, Betsey R. Rosenbaum and Nancy B. Sederberg, for their encouragement, forbearance, and recommendations.

H. Jon Rosenbaum
New York, New York

Peter C. Sederberg
Columbia, South Carolina

Part I:

Theoretical Perspectives

Chapter One

Vigilantism: An Analysis of Establishment Violence

H. Jon Rosenbaum and Peter C. Sederberg

During the past decade a significant number of scholars have investigated the nature, causes, and prevention of social and political violence. Their primary interest, motivated perhaps by observations of revolutionary war in Asia and social turmoil in the United States, has been the study of violence aimed at changing the established order. Some of these scholars have developed sophisticated causal models in an attempt to identify the conditions which lead people to turn to violence as a means of transforming political systems.[1]

Although the prevailing concern with revolution is understandable, it obscures a second form of violence—that designed to maintain the established socio-political order. The identification of this type of violence is related to the distinction commonly made between the "legitimate" coercion exercised by the regime and the "illegitimate" coercion engaged in by private individuals. The latter private coercion exceeds the boundaries set by the political system; an example may be seen in the difference between legitimate parental discipline and child brutality.

Illegitimate coercion directed by private persons against one another or

---

*The original version of this article first appeared as "Vigilantism: An Analysis of Establishment Violence," by H. Jon Rosenbaum in *Comparative Politics* 6, no. 4 (July 1974): 541-571.

1. Hannah Arendt, *On Revolution* (New York: Viking, 1965); James C. Davies, ed. *When Men Revolt and Why* (New York: Free Press, 1971); Ted Robert Gurr, *Why Men Rebel* (Princeton: Princeton University Press, 1970); Chalmers Johnson, *Revolutionary Change* (Boston: Little, Brown, 1966); Carl Leiden and Karl M. Schmitt, *The Politics of Violence: Revolution in the Modern World* (Englewood Cliffs: Prentice Hall, 1968); Nathan Leites and Charles Wolf, Jr., *Rebellion and Authority* (Chicago: Markham, 1970); H. L. Nieburg, *Political Violence* (New York: St. Martin's, 1969); Martin O. Oppenheimer, *The Urban Guerrilla* (Chicago: Quadrangle, 1969); Eric R. Wolf, *Peasant Wars of the Twentieth Century* (New York: Harper and Row, 1969). On causal models, see especially the studies by Gurr and Johnson cited above.

against the regime may be defined as violence.[2] The exercise of coercion by the regime is also generally viewed as regulated by these formal boundaries. The boundaries are, of course, flexible; and at times of severe social disruption, such as internal war, they may be nearly nonexistent. Except for the extreme case of a regime based solely on force, some rules defining procedures and limits of the exercise of coercion by the regime or groups acting in its behalf are generally recognized. When individuals or groups identifying with the established order defend that order by resorting to means that violate these formal boundaries, they can be usefully classified as vigilantes.

Admittedly, vigilantism tends to connote rowdy cowboys lynching an unfortunate horse thief. It is commonly summarized as "taking the law into one's own hands." Yet, generalizing from the specific phenomenon, vigilantism is simply establishment violence. It consists of acts or threats of coercion in violation of the formal boundaries of an established sociopolitical order which, however, are intended by the violators to defend that order from some form of subversion.[3] Vigilantism, then, is considerably more inclusive than the summary "justice" dispensed by angered crowds against "criminal" elements. Thus, it is deserving of serious study. This chapter seeks to make a contribution to the understanding of establishment violence through: (1) a preliminary investigation of the conditions likely to produce vigilante action; (2) the development of a typology of vigilantism; and (3) a discussion of the effects of vigilantism on the creation and maintenance of a stable sociopolitical order.

THE NATURE AND CAUSES OF VIGILANTISM: A PRELIMINARY STATEMENT

Acts of sociopolitical coercion—as opposed to those of purely expressive destructiveness—can be placed on a continuum of intentionality, depending on whether they are primarily directed at the creation, maintenance, or restoration of a distribution of values. Coercive acts may also be ranked—at least conceptually—according to their relative intensity.[4] Though most large-

2. Warren F. Ilchman and Norman Thomas Uphoff, *The Political Economy of Change* (Berkeley and Los Angeles: University of California Press, 1971), pp. 70-71. The definition of legitimacy implied here is legalistic. Coercive acts are intended to damage a person or his values.

3. The implication of this approach is that, in order to understand the meaning of a violent act, it is necessary to assess the intentions of the perpetrator. Intentionality is inferred from the judicious evaluation of what actors say they are doing as well as by observation of their acts. See Alfred Schutz, *The Phenomenology of the Social World*, trans. George Walsh and Frederick Lehnert (Evanston: Northwestern University Press, 1967). For an interpretation of how the problem of intentionality can be reconciled with the essentially positivist methods of social science, see Peter C. Sederberg, "Subjectivity and Typification: A Note on Method in the Social Sciences," *Philosophy of the Social Sciences* 2 (June 1972): 167-76.

4. Intensity, as it is used here, is a multidimensional aggregate including such factors as: the degree of damage done to a person's value position; the degree of due process in carrying out the act; the proportionality between the damage inflicted and the act being punished; and the numbers affected by a given coercive act.

scale, enduring social systems possess formal boundaries which approximately delineate between allowable coercion and "violence," the apportionment of legal coercion is not neutral. Rather, such coercion tends to be predominately supportive of the status quo. Indeed, when coercive acts increase in intensity or when a more radical redistribution of values is attempted, the probability that such acts may violate these boundaries also rises, other things being equal. Violence aimed at the redistribution of values may be identified as either "revolutionary" or "reactionary," while violence directed at value maintenance may be termed "vigilante." Figure 1 provides an idealization of these relationships.

Systems, of course, differ with respect to formal boundary definition. Some may allow nearly all coercive acts that are primarily supportive of the existing distribution (Figure 1, a); others may not only strictly limit maintenance coercion, but may also allow some forms of redistributive coercion (Figure 1, b). The difference between an "open" and "closed" society may be more accurately characterized in terms of the allowable range of coercion as well as the limits on intensity, rather than the usual consensus/coercion dichotomy.[5] In any case, the potential for vigilante violence is greater in "b" than in "a" because of the extensive restraints placed on maintenance coercion. Figure 1 also suggests that vigilante violence can merge into either form of redistributive violence, though certain modal characteristics may be distinguished.

Since vigilantism is one form of violence, much of what has been written concerning violence generally may be applicable to the analysis here. In a commendable synthesis, Ted Robert Gurr has devised a complex causal model of the determinants of the magnitude of political violence.[6] Although Gurr is basically searching for answers to the question of "why men rebel," he furnishes several suggestive approaches to the understanding of vigilante violence.

The potential for violence, in Gurr's analysis, is fundamentally linked to the intensity and scope of feelings of "relative deprivation." These feelings in turn are related to the extent to which "value expectations" exceed "value capabilities."[7] In the special case of vigilante violence, a singular type of deprivation appears to be operative: "decremental deprivation."[8] This occurs when value expectations of groups remain fairly constant, but perceived value

---

5. Similarly, in an "open" society conflict within certain limits would be tolerated and regulated rather than repressed. The toleration of conflict may be an index of the stability of a society. See Lewis Coser, *The Functions of Social Conflict* (New York: Free Press, 1956), pp. 81-85.

6. Gurr, *Rebel,* especially Chap. 10, pp. 317-59.

7. "The *value expectations* of a collectivity are the average value positions to which its members believe they are justifiably entitled." "The *value capabilities* of a collectivity are the average value positions its members perceive themselves capable of attaining or maintaining." Ibid., p. 27.

8. Ibid., pp. 46-50.

Figure 1   The "Field" of Coercive Acts

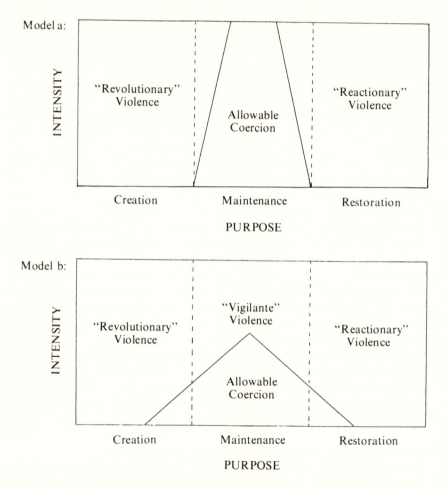

Note: These idealizations are illustrative, not exhaustive.

capabilities decline. The more precipitous this decline, the greater potential for violence by the "deprived" groups.

From this perspective, the social context of vigilantism consists of certain groups that believe they possess a vested interest in the preservation of the current distribution of values. In short, they compose an establishment, though not necessarily an elite. Moreover, they usually regard the formal political order so constituted as to protect this distribution. Government, then, is viewed as the superstructural manifestation of the dominant value system of the social base (with apologies to Marx). The value expectations of these groups are relatively stable, and the state is generally seen as an important contributor to their value capabilities.

In every society, however, there are other groups that have a latent—if not a manifest—interest in altering the status quo, whether through criminal violence, reform, or revolution.[9] In certain circumstances, a peaceful, partial redistribution of values may be possible. Where it is not, these discontented groups, depending among other things on their feelings of relative deprivation, may resort to more threatening challenges to the existing distribution. From the point of view of the challenged groups, a primary function of government is to control these dissidents. Most governments, however, are bound by certain rules regulating the threat or use of the instruments of social control, although these rules may be regarded by some establishment groups as hampering the government's effectiveness.

Other sources of discontent arise if the government's formal goal achievement is being frustrated by corruption or other causes of inefficiency. Establishment groups, then, may view their value capabilities as a diminishing asset. Under these conditions, the inclination to take defensive action in violation of the system's formal rules will increase. This action, nevertheless, is believed to be fundamentally supportive. A basic relationship can be hypothesized from the above analysis: *the potential for vigilantism varies positively with the intensity and scope of belief that a regime is ineffective in dealing with challenges to the prevailing socio-political order.*[10]

As with the likelihood of violence in general, the probability of vigilantism is directly related to the scope and intensity of the normative and utilitarian justifications for political violence.[11] Thus, dissident and establishment violence may be nurtured by the same systemic values. Gurr, moreover, considers two additional variables to be important determinants of the magnitude of *dissident* violence: (1) the balance of dissident and regime coercive control, and (2) the balance of dissident and regime institutional support.[12] Neither of these variables seems to be of direct relevance to this analysis, though they undoubtedly affect the establishment groups' feelings of relative deprivation. Two factors of possible importance, however, are suggested: the coercive capability of the formal state apparatus vis-a-vis the vigilantes, and the amount of social support for those who engage in acts of established violence. *The magnitude of vigilante violence appears negatively related to the ability (both objective capability and "will") of the regime to defend its formal boundaries against this type of breeching and positively*

9. Ralf Dahrendorf, *Class and Class Conflict in Industrial Society* (Stanford: Stanford University Press, 1959).

10. Compare this special statement of the VE/VC gap with Gurr, *Rebel,* pp. 24ff. The intensity of these feelings, in turn, would be related to the importance to the established group of the values threatened.

11. Ibid., pp. 155-231.

12. Ibid., pp. 232-316.

related to the scope and coherence of social support for the vigilante movement.

One might expect a regime to be less willing to impose severe sanctions on those who seem basically supportive, even though formally violating its rules, especially if the vigilantes appear to have the support of "core" establishment groups in the community.[13] Officials are also more likely to tolerate acts seen as relatively minor violations of the boundaries; in other words, the more extreme the violation, the more likely the official response. Moreover, if a regime is ineffective in deterring the dissidents who originally contributed to the potential for vigilantism, it may also lack the capability to deter the vigilantes. If community support is low, however, the number of people willing to engage in "vigilantics" will be correspondingly limited, and the formal institutional efforts to maintain due process will be reinforced rather than frustrated. The preceding discussion can be schematically illustrated by the preliminary causal framework in Figure 2.

The framework of analysis developed here is relatively simple and certainly

Figure 2 Hypothesized Framework of the Determinants of Establishment Violence (cf. Gurr, p. 320)

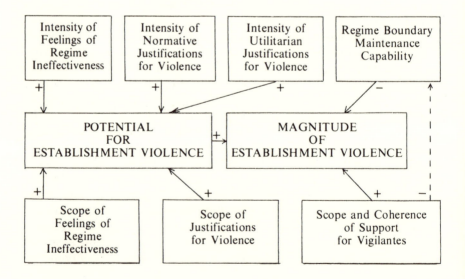

13. Richard Maxwell Brown notes that vigilantism has received community support throughout American history for a number of reasons: popular sovereignty, which gave the people the right to take the law into their own hands; localism, which prompted neighborhood courts and executioners; the desire for economy in law enforcement; and the wish for more effective norm enforcement. See Brown, "Legal and Behavioral Perspectives on American Vigilantism," *Perspectives in American History* 5 (1971): 106-16.

could be elaborated further. Indeed, Gurr adds many supplementary hypotheses which might be adapted to fit this special case. These deal with the determinants of the decline in value capabilities, in this case, the causes of perceived regime ineffectiveness, and of the intensity and scope of the justifications for political violence. Further examination of the regime's boundary maintenance ability and the social support for the vigilantes could be undertaken in addition. Such elaboration, however, would necessitate going far beyond the limits of this preliminary investigation.

As with any framework, the distinctions drawn tend to deteriorate when applied to the actual social world. In this case, the major problem lies with the concept of the establishment groups' perception of declining governmental effectiveness. This could result from actual decay or simply because the formal institutions are no longer representing previously established value positions; that is, the problem is one of a formally sanctioned redistribution of values, not of ineffectiveness. This can occur particularly when a subsystem establishment differs substantially from that of the larger system of which it is a part. Under these circumstances, vigilantism begins to shade into forms of dissident violence. Several such marginal cases are discussed in the typology of establishment violence presented in the following section.

Another problem concerns the identification of the establishment and the status quo. When the metamorphosis of a society is prolonged, dual establishments coexist uncomfortably. The old establishment tries to protect its remaining value capabilities, while the new establishment attempts to consolidate and improve its position. When societal change occurs unevenly, it becomes nearly impossible to determine just which establishment represents the national status quo.

During the Salvador Allende years (1970—1973), for instance, the Chilean economic and political systems were transformed at different rates. Mapuche Indians and other peasants seized farms and workers took control of private industries. The traditional establishment used violent means to protect or regain possession of properties. Seizures often occurred with the tacit consent or support of the Allende administration, and the government refused to allow the police or soldiers to dislodge the workers and peasants. Allende did not favor the seizures, however, and the courts frequently ordered the return of the properties to their former owners. It was difficult, therefore, to ascertain just who were the vigilantes. Were the workers and peasants vigilantes or revolutionaries? Or was the old establishment engaged in counter-revolutionary violence or vigilantism?

A TYPOLOGY OF VIGILANTISM

Vigilantism covers a wide range of violent acts merging, on the one hand, into forms of dissident violence, and, on the other, into the legal exercise of physical coercion by a regime or its representatives. Several basic types of this variegated phenomenon can be analytically distinguished, however. Fundamentally, these are related to the intended purposes of vigilante action. Three such purposes appear to predominate: crime control, social-group control, and regime control. Within these three categories, it is often useful to divide the participants in vigilante action into private and public persons. The latter are those who perform recognized public roles, such as policemen. As with any typology, the categorization oversimplifies reality, for human beings can have multiple purposes for their actions and can fill multiple roles which overlap rather than neatly compartmentalize. But by investigating the ramifications of this typology, a more systematic comprehension of vigilante action is possible. While no exhaustive historical or contemporary survey can be made, specific examples are used to illustrate each of the identified types.

CRIME-CONTROL VIGILANTISM

This is directed against people believed to be committing acts proscribed by the formal legal system. Such acts harm private persons or property, but the perpetrators escape justice due to governmental inefficiency, corruption, or the leniency of the system of due process. This form of establishment violence, engaged in by private persons, is the kind most commonly associated with vigilantes. Indeed, American history is replete with examples of private groups restoring "law and order"where is has broken down or establishing it in areas into which the government's formal apparatus of rule enforcement has not yet effectively extended.[14] This action has often been organized and led by representatives of the higher socioeconomic classes in the crime-plagued community, though the followers have tended to represent broader class backgrounds.[15]

Crime-control vigilantism initiated by private persons can occur in any society where the government is believed to be ineffectual in protecting persons and property. One of the more prominent contemporary illustrations is that of the *Esquadrão da Morte* (Death Squad) in Brazil. These self-appointed interpreters of the law, thought to be mainly off-duty policemen, have executed an estimated five hundred to twelve hundred people. According to spokesmen claiming to be *Esquadrão* members, the death squads have been taking these actions because of the inefficiency of Brazil's established judicial institutions. The spokesmen claim that apprehended criminals are permitted to go free for long periods while awaiting trial by the authorities. *Esquadrão* members, additionally, feel that most criminals cannot be or are not being rehabilitated. For these reasons, the squads believe that they are performing a

---

14. For a compact history of American vigilante movements, see Brown, "The American Vigilante Tradition," in Hugh David Graham and Gurr, eds. *The History of Violence in America* (New York: Bantam, 1969), pp. 154-217.
15. Ibid., pp. 192-96.

service for the nation by executing people suspected of being habitual criminals. Evidently many Brazilians are in agreement with this appraisal. In a 1970 public opinion study, for example, 60 percent of the Sao Paulo residents polled claimed that they favored the existence of the *Esquadrão da Morte*.[16]

While Brazilian crime-control vigilantes specialize in the elimination of petty thieves and hardened criminals, particularly narcotics dealers and assassins of policemen, vigilantes in neighboring Argentina are engaged in debt collection. An Argentine group, The Gentlemen, was founded in 1971, stimulated by the belief that the judicial procedures were inadequate and that habitual debtors had to be forced to meet their obligations. Although indebtedness is considered a civil offense in most countries, including Argentina, the economic instability of their country presumably led the Argentine vigilantes to feel that large debtors are criminals.[17]

Other interesting examples of this type of vigilantism have occurred in American urban ghettos. In Chicago an organization called the "Afro-American Group Attack Team" is attempting to rid the community of drug dealers.[18] Similar groups are operating in New York, where it has been reported that ten drug pushers were executed during an eighteen-month period by black and Puerto Rican vigilantes, and in Washington, where the "Spades Unlimited" are trying to make it "dangerous" for dope peddlers to trade.[19] The primary causes of these activities are disillusionment with the government's ability to enforce the laws and, apparently, the belief that the police are corrupt.[20] These cases are examples where groups normally classified as potential participants in dissident violence share certain values with the established legal system and are attempting to extend the enforcement of these shared norms into their neglected communities.

Though crime-control vigilantism is usually associated with private persons, the occupational origin of many *Esquadrão* members suggests that law-enforcement officials may also engage in establishment violence in the fulfillment of their regular duties. Most simply, this occurs when excessive physical compulsion is used by a policeman in apprehending a criminal. Of course, the line between justifiable and excessive coercion is fine. Enough evidence has been gathered, however, to suggest that police violation of

16. "Justica e feita," *Veja,* no. 99 (July 29, 1970): 26-32.
17. H. J. Maidenberg, "Novo 'terror' vai ao ataque," *Estado de Sao Paulo* (July 25, 1971): 9.
18. "Chicago's Black Vigilantes," *Newsweek* (September 27, 1971): 75ff.
19. William Raspberry, "War on Drug Dealers," *Washington Post* (February 9, 1972): A15. Columnist Raspberry has observed that the results of these attitudes are that "the word is seeping through black ghettos that vigilante action—up to and including 'elimination'—may be the only way to halt the growing use of heroin among black youths." Incipient vigilante groups are also forming in many white communities. See Brown, pp. 201-8.
20. A fuller discussion of American crime control groups is contained in Gary T. Marx and Dane Archer, "Citizen Involvement in the Law Enforcement Process," *American Behavioral Scientist* 15 (September/October 1971): 52-72.

formally guaranteed rights occurs in the United States and elsewhere.[21] Not uncommonly, the rules governing the official application of physical coercion are castigated as "handcuffing" the police and preventing them from carrying out their crime-control responsibilities effectively.[22]

Excessive police coercion is generally considered the result of individual deviation. A regularized policy to violate formal guarantees, such as the unauthorized surveillance of suspected criminal elements, is not too difficult to imagine. The discussion of such "official vigilantism" will be continued later.[23]

SOCIAL-GROUP-CONTROL VIGILANTISM

Establishment violence directed against groups that are competing for, or advocating a redistribution of, values within the system can be considered social-group-control vigilantism. This is based on the recognition that not all violence perceived as supportive of the status quo is exercised against "normal" criminal activity. Rather, illegal coercion is often the response of those who feel threatened by upwardly mobile segments of society or by those who appear to advocate significant change in the distribution of values. Group-control vigilantism can easily lapse into a form of reactionary violence as the formal political system becomes supportive of a new distribution of values. But unlike threats to the established order from simple criminal elements, it may be possible to satisfy both the threatening and established groups through a partial redistribution. If the situation is viewed as essentially "zero-sum," however, the potential for this type of vigilantism probably increases.

The diverse manifestations of this form of vigilantism may be roughly distinguished according to whether the identity of the target group is basically communal (i.e., having a primordial characteristic such as race, religion, caste, tribe, and the like), economic, or political. Violence intended to regulate *pariah* communal groups constitutes the first subtype. Unlike crime-control vigilantism, this form of establishment violence often appears rooted less in government ineffectiveness per se than in the irrelevance of formal avenues of

21. See Theodore L. Becker and Vernon G. Murray, eds. *Governmental Lawlessness in America* (New York: Oxford University Press, 1971), pp. 3-90. The widely publicized excesses of some federal and local narcotics agents provide dramatic illustrations of the potential for police violence in crime control. See "Terror in the Night—In the U.S.," *New York Times* (July 1, 1973): Section E, p. 6.

22. For a description of an attempt to control the police and the response it created, see "The Gain Mutiny," *Newsweek* (December 27, 1971): 35.

23. The popular television show, "Mission Impossible," deals with the fight against organized crime. The "Impossible Mission Force" is actually nothing more than a glorification of official vigilantism. Members are obviously under contract to the government and each week they bring to justice those villains who slip through the loopholes of due process which frustrate "conventional law enforcement agencies." A number of recent movies, interestingly, also deal rather sympathetically with police violence, for example, *Dirty Harry* and *The French Connection*.

redress. Other contributing factors should not be underestimated, however, for certain communal groups often expect the government to protect their interest through formal procedures. A case in point is that certain Islamic groups in predominantly Moslem countries advocate the creation of an Islamic constitution.

The catalyst for communal vigilantism is usually the attempt of a low-ranked group to rise above its socially prescribed position. Low status "jatis" in India have often met violent resistance to their attempts to raise their ritual status. Mandelbaum, for example, relates how "the Noniyas, the earth workers, of Senapur village and vicinity decided at a meeting in 1936 to put on the sacred thread to show that they were really Chauhans by caste and Kshatriyas in varna. When some of them did so, the dominant landowners beat them, tore off the sacred thread, and imposed a collective fine on the whole Jati group."[24] While such a response was not necessarily illegitimate in traditional village India, private violence to protect the established caste hierarchy could probably be considered vigilante in nature from the perspective of the more secular imperial and independence governments.

Much of the anti-black violence in the United States exhibits the characteristics of communally based vigilantism. The early Ku Klux Klan was, in part, intended to terrorize Negroes back into their "proper position" after the upward mobility they experienced during the Reconstruction.[25] Morris Janowitz notes that some of the race riots that occurred in the first quarter of the twentieth century expressed the desire of certain elements of the white community "to 'kick the Negro back into his place.' "[26] Such sentiments probably continue to contribute to white violence against blacks, such as the anti-busing incidents in Pontiac, Michigan, in 1971.[27] In some outbreaks of anti-black violence in the United States, establishment violence in the local or regional subsystem may be considered reactionary violence in the context of the national system.

Racial vigilantism is not confined to the United States. The position of the overseas Chinese community in Southeast Asia is quite tenuous, and the Chinese often suffer violence at the hands of the dominant ethnic group. In

24. David G. Mandelbaum, *Society in India, Continuity and Change* (Berkeley and Los Angeles: University of California Press, 1970) 2: 477-78.
25. For a fuller discussion of the Ku Klux Klan, consult the following: David Chalmers, *Hooded Americanism* (New York: Doubleday, 1965); Stanley Frost, *The Challenge of the Klan* (Indianapolis: Bobbs Merrill, 1924); Emerson Loucks, *The Ku Klux Klan in Pennsylvania* (New York: Telegraph Press, 1936); and William Randel, *The Ku Klux Klan, A Century of Infamy* (New York: Chilton, 1965).
26. Morris Janowitz, "Patterns of Collective Racial Violence," in Graham and Gurr, eds., *History of Violence*, p. 416.
27. Another example of northern vigilantism designed to prevent the upward mobility of blacks occurred prior to the election of the first black mayor of Newark, New Jersey, Kenneth Gibson. With the political power of the Italian community in jeopardy, a vigilante group was organized by Anthony Imperiale. This group's activities have been investigated by journalist Ron Porambo in *No Cause for Indictment* (New York: Holt, Rhinehart and Winston, 1972).

May 1969, for example, communal tensions in Malaysia exploded into several weeks of bloody riots. The official estimate of the total killed was placed at two hundred, predominantly Chinese. In Malaysia, where no communal group possesses a majority, the dominant Malays resist relinquishing significant control of the system to the Chinese community, whereas the Chinese will not submerge their culture into that of the Malay.[28] This type of vigilantism is similar to that manifested by some tribal violence in Africa. The anti-Ibo attacks in northern Nigeria in May and September 1966 were rooted in resentment against the economic inroads the industrious Ibos had made in the north.

Social-group-control vigilantism may also be employed when religious values are threatened by the spread of secularism, heresy, or competition with another faith. These forces contributed to the ascendance of vigilantism in Egypt during the 1930s. Repelled by their countrymen who spurned religious orthodoxy and adopted Western culture, the Society of the Muslim Brothers fought moral decay in Egypt during that period by practicing vigilantism in the name of Islam and morality.[29] Similar violence has been exercised against heretical sects by orthodox Muslims in Pakistan.[30] And in Northern Ireland, the Catholic minority has been periodically victimized by the violence of the dominant Protestants.[31]

Although in the cases of communal vigilantism just cited the participants were generally private persons, supervisory officials often appeared to be tolerant of the violence of dominant groups. Malaysian troops and police were accused of dealing quite harshly with the Chinese community, for example, while doing little to restrain the Malays.[32] Janowitz reports that in the Chicago race riots of 1917 and 1919, the police were deficient in their attempts to protect black enclaves from white violence, and even "occasionally assisted the white rioters."[33] Similarly, in Northern Ireland the Protestant B Specials, a branch of the police force, often abused Catholics before the former were dissolved by British authorities. Thus, although the formal system is supposedly evenhanded in enforcing the law, the occupants of official positions may identify with the dominant communal groups and essentially support their efforts to maintain the status quo.

At times, official support of one side in a communal struggle may extend

28. Gerald P. Dartford, "Crisis in Maylasia," *Current History* 57 (December 1969): 354.
29. Richard P. Mitchell, *The Society of the Muslim Brothers* (London: Oxford University Press, 1969).
30. Khalid Bin Sayeed, "Islam and National Integration in Pakistan," in Donald E. Smith, ed. *South Asian Politics and Religion* (Princeton: Princeton University Press, 1966), pp. 402-05.
31. Tim Coogan, *The I.R.A.* (New York: Praeger, 1970). Catholic counteraction would be a case of dissident violence. IRA coercion within the Catholic community constitutes an interesting marginal case. One might consider such action vigilantism, but one could also argue that the IRA constitutes the "legitimate" authority in a dissident community.
32. Dartford, "Crisis," p. 354.
33. Janowitz, "Patterns," p. 417.

beyond individuals. The results may range from biasing the manner in which these individuals fulfill their duties to an apparently deliberate policy of illegal regime coercion of deviant communities. At its extreme, this "official vigilantism" in violation of the regime's own formal standards becomes a program of terror.[34] A recent example of official vigilantism against a communal group striving for a redistribution of political and economic values is that of the West Pakistani pogrom against the Bengalis. This was an attempt by the dominant groups of the country to preserve their position from the threat of the Awami League, even though the League had triumphed in the election sponsored by the regime. The history of governmental coercion of the American Indian in violation of a series of treaties supplies another example of official vigilantism in the area of communal group control.

Communal vigilantism is not the only form of establishment violence intended to control threatening social groups. The history of American and foreign labor movements, for example, has been repeatedly punctuated by both dissident union violence and clear violations by employers of existing rules governing the application of coercion.[35] Such employer vigilantism has often enjoyed the tacit protection of the regime. In the first two decades of this century, the radical Marxist position of the IWW provoked vigilante violence that included official complicity.[36]

The upward mobility of peasant groups may inspire a violent reaction. Armed seizures by peasants of farms in Chile's lake region during the Allende era, for example, stimulated landowners to take defensive action. Armed vigilance committees were formed to prevent seizures and evict the invaders. Although the regime of the late President Salvador Allende Gossens was Marxist, the land seizures did not have the official approval of the government, which preferred to revolutionize agriculture through legal channels.[37]

Finally, individuals and groups espousing dissident political views have often suffered the loss of their formally guaranteed rights. In some cases, such as the Chicago Democratic Convention riots of 1968, the police seemed simply out of control.[38] Other contemporary occurrences, however, appear to

34. "Terror," as it is used here, must be distinguished from the violence of internal war. Vigilante terror is carried out against relatively unresisting communities, in an attempt to crush them before they become a serious threat. As in Bengal, a program of vigilante terror may stimulate resistance.

35. Philip Taft and Philip Ross, "American Labor Violence: Its Causes, Character, and Outcome," in Graham and Gurr, eds., *History of Violence,* pp. 281-395.

36. Lynne B. Iglitzin, *Violent Conflict in American Society* (San Francisco: Chandler, 1972), p. 120.

37. Juan de Onis, "In the Chilean Lake Country, Political Crosscurrents Are Aswirl," *New York Times* (March 27, 1972): 18. This case illustrates certain ambiguities caused by a change in regime, for one could argue that the peasants were the viglantes, "defending" the newly established status quo.

38. Walker Commission Report, *Rights in Conflict* (New York: E. P. Dutton, 1968).

be more deliberate policies by some sectors of the regime's apparatus to violate dissident rights, such as in the killing of Fred Hampton and Mark Clark in Chicago in 1969.[39] Official vigilantism is common in more authoritarian regimes; it ranges from terror and torture in Brazil and Greece to the subtle evasion of defendant rights through insanity proceedings in the Soviet Union. In such cases, the regime's formal channels of rule enforcement are probably considered both ineffective and, perhaps, too lenient.

On a more abstract level, authoritarian elements may consider "democratic" guarantees as hindrances in dealing with revolutionary, or even reformist, movements. Such was evidently the case after the October 1968 student riots in Mexico City. Certain important members of the dominant Mexican political party, the *Partido Revolucionario Institucional,* apparently participated in the creation of youth combat groups, known as the *Halcones* (Falcons), organized to prevent future student riots and to "maintain order." On June 11, 1971, ten thousand university students supporting a strike were attacked by several hundred Falcons armed with bamboo staves, pistols, automatic rifles, and submachine guns.[40]

Some politically motivated vigilantes enjoy the sympathy, and even support, of their national governments, or these governments pretend to be unaware of their activities. During 1971, for example, the Balaguer regime in the Dominican Republic refused to admit that a vigilante group known as the "Band" was terrorizing individuals suspected of leftist leanings. Yet the Band was reputed to have murdered at least fifty leftist opponents and beaten and harassed others.[41]

Likewise, during the 1930s Hitler secretly used the S.A. Brown Shirts) to destroy his political enemies. Although these acts were clearly illegal, Jews were arrested and interned, synagogues destroyed, and the "insane" liquidated as a result of "mercy killings." All of this was attributed to the spontaneous wrath of the people.

---

39. Lillian S. Calhoun, "The Death of Fred Hampton," in Becker and Murray, eds., *Governmental Lawlessness,* pp. 34-47.

40. Conrad Manley, "Massacre by Falcons Unsolved," *Times of the Americas* (February 6, 1972): 8. Other examples of vigilantism against "subversive" political groups abound in Latin America and elsewhere. In Argentina, the *Comando de Represion de Actividades Rediciosos,* founded in 1970, threatened to take vengeance against people who killed policemen or participated in revolutionary activities. Other similar groups in Argentina are the Organized National Argentine Movement (MANO) and the Anti-Communist Group (GRACO). Guatemalan political vigilante groups include the New Anti-Communist Organization (NOA), the National Resistance Front (FRN), the Anti-Communist Command of Guatemala (CADEG), and the *Ojo por Ojo* ("Eye for an Eye"). The Death Squadron in Bolivia, unlike its Brazilian namesake, is primarliy concerned with controlling revolutionaries who threaten the stability of the current regime. In Indonesia, a group of students protesting Mrs. Suharto's plán for an amusement park were attacked by a group of young men, and four were shot.

41. Alan Riding, "Armed Band Said to Terrorize Leftists in Dominican Republic," *New York Times* (August 28, 1971): 2. Reportedly the Band was created by national police chief Major General Perez y Perez and was composed of approximately 400 members, mainly youths. Additional members were recruited by coercion from the ranks of the leftists. Raids were also conducted in slum areas where the government's policies were opposed.

Vigilantism of a political nature may persist despite repudiation by the central government when local governmental officials conspire with the vigilantes. In the larger developing countries the central government may be unable fully to eradicate vigilante activities supported by civilian or military leaders on the local level. While the Medici regime in Brazil may be opposed to torture, for example, it has not been completely successful in ending this practice. Total control from the center is nearly impossible in such a mammoth developing nation, and even if the government is sincere in its abhorrence of torture, it may not be capable of enforcing its will locally.

REGIME-CONTROL VIGILANTISM

The examples of crime and social-group-control vigilantism are cited simply for illustration; undoubtedly, they could be multiplied many times. For the most part, they concern the use of violence by established groups to preserve the status quo at times when the formal system of rule enforcement is viewed as ineffective or irrelevant. Essentially, the violence is directed outward against the threatening elements in society. Government ineffectiveness, however, suggests that vigilante action may be directed against the regime itself, if the established sectors find the lack of capabilities too frustrating. Regime-control vigilantism, then, is establishment violence intended to alter the regime, in order to make the "superstructure" into a more effective guardian of the "base."

The borderline between regime-control vigilantism and redistributive dissident violence can be quite fine. Nevertheless, certain cases of violence directed against a particular institutional order or its personnel do little to alter the fundamental power relationships. From this point of view, political officeholders and even constitutions exist at the discretion of powerful social and political groups. While it is conceivable that private individuals or groups as such may engage in this type of action, the vigilantes generally either occupy official positions (e.g., in the army or the bureaucracy) or have powerful official allies. However, the political assassinations which proliferate during Philippine election campaigns may be examples of private persons engaging in this type of vigilantism. In addition, private organizations may be involved in regime-control vigilantism. For example, Costa Rica's *Movimiento Costa Rica Libre,* a group largely composed of a middle- and upper-class membership and led almost exclusively by successful businessmen, has long maintained a paramilitary force to be used in the event the regime requires controlling.[42] Likewise, the American Minutemen are a potential regime-control vigilante group, although they and the *Movimiento Costa Rica Libre,* like many organizations considered in this study, have several functions in addition to vigilantism.

The coups d'etat that erupt periodically in some essentially conservative

42. This information was provided by private informants in Costa Rica.

Latin American countries certainly constitute cases of political violence, but not of a redistributive sort. The ruling classes' position is seldom disturbed, though selected individuals might be exiled. Such "conservative coups" are simply establishment violence against a formal political order judged to have outlived its usefulness. They are a potentiality in any system where the military considers itself the final arbiter of the "true" constitution. Even the intervention of Ayub Khan in Pakistan in 1958 hardly altered the underlying power structure, though the activities of various politicians were temporarily proscribed. Coups d'etat in Thailand, Brazil, and Argentina may provide other examples of this type of regime-control vigilantism.

Some coups undoubtedly bring about significant alterations in the social base. One of these was Nasser's seizure of power in Egypt. Others may be reactionary, in the sense that previously disestablished groups regain their former position. The ultimate outcome in Ghana after the coup of 1966 approximates this result.[43] Some, however, constitute extralegal establishment violence against the formal instruments of government, and as such can be considered regime-control vigilantism.

An interesting marginal subtype of regime-control vigilantism exists also. The discussion so far has tended to treat the establishment as a relatively cohesive sector. While such simplification is heuristic, it obscures possible deep divisions among the groups included in the establishment. Consequently, one establishment group may use extralegal coercion as a means of reducing or eliminating another group's relative power position. In some sense, such action would alter the status quo, but it cannot be facilely equated with the types of action commonly considered dissident. Such violence characterizes aspects of Stalinist terror against elements of the party, state, and military apparatus. A more recent example may be Mao's attempt to revitalize the revolution in China and to control or reduce the power of the state and party bureaucracies. Finally, the criminal activities of those involved in the Watergate operation, though rationalized in terms of the need to control radical dissidents, were in part directed against a sector of the American political establishment, the Democratic party.[44] Insofar as radicals were the target, these actions are an example of the political subtype of social-group-control vigilantism.

The typology developed here certainly does not completely encompass the complexity of establishment violence. Yet it does provide a preliminary framework for the categorization of types of vigilante behavior. Figure 3 diagrams the basic divisions of the typology.

There are of course some vigilante groups that may be properly characterized as conforming to more than one of the categories in the

43. K. A. Busia and other members of the old "Anglo-African" elite in Ghana, who were eclipsed after Nkrumah's rise to power, regained their position subsequent to his ouster.
44. J. Anthony Lucas, "The Story So Far," *New York Times Magazine* (July 22, 1973): *passim.*

typology. Rabbi Meir Kahane's Jewish Defense League (JDL) patrols transitional neighborhoods in order to prevent crimes against Jews, but it could also be considered a social-group-control vigilante group because it protects the Jewish establishment in areas where blacks are becoming the majority.[45] Other vigilante groups are dynamic. The Society of the Muslim

Figure 3 A Typology of Vigilantism

PURPOSE

		Crime Control	Social Group Control	Regime Control
PARTICIPANTS	Private	"Normal" Vigilantism: South Carolina Regulators; *Esquadrão da Morte*	Violence against pariah communal, economic and political groups	Some political assassinations
	Public	Excessive police coercion against criminal suspects	Regime terror	"Conservative" *coups d'état*

Brothers in Egypt and the White Hand of Guatemala began their existences as social-group-control vigilante organizations, but eventually undertook regime-control activities.

VIGILANTISM AND THE CREATION OF A STABLE SOCIOPOLITICAL ORDER

The potential for establishment violence is directly related to the degree to which those who have a vested interest in the status quo feel that the formal institutions of boundary maintenance are ineffective in protecting their interests. Essentially, it is a conservative phenomenon. Ultimately, therefore, an evaluation of vigilantism must be grounded in judgments as to the value of the social order being conserved. Secondarily, however, one might ask if vigilantism is an efficacious strategy for stabilizing a sociopolitical order and, if so, under what conditions. The answer to this question can be obtained through an understanding of two facets of vigilante violence. First, vigilantism is basically "negative"; that is, the essential aim is to suppress, or

45. Numerous articles have been written about the Jewish Defense League, including Roy Bongartz, "Superjew," *Esquire* (August 1970); Walter Goodman, "Rabbi Kahane says: 'I'd Love to See The JDL Fold Up. But—'," *New York Times Magazine* (November 21, 1971); and John Peterson, "Camp Builds Cadre of Street Fighters," *National Observer* (July 28, 1969). In addition, the League has produced several pamphlets, such as *"Amacha"—Your People,* and Rabbi Kahane has explained his philosophy in *Never Again!* (Los Angeles: Pyramid, 1971).

even eradicate, any threats to the status quo. Second, vigilante coercion tends to be applied in an ad hoc fashion. Even though the violation of formal boundaries may be supported by substantial segments of the community, vigilantism is disorderly; that is, it inhibits the development of reasonably accurate and stable behavioral expectations.[46]

In general, vigilantism may be initially eufunctional for the stabilization process; but it tends to be dysfunctional over the long run.[47] The short-run gains of establishment violence accrue from controlling the process of mobilization and its attendant strains. The longer term costs relate to the negative nature of vigilantism; that is, though it may buy time, it cannot replace formal political institutions and, indeed, it is probably antithetical to their growth.

In order to stabilize a situation characterized by vigilante (and dissident) violence, a regime can pursue two alternative courses. First, the boundaries defining the legal use of coercion can be expanded in an attempt to absorb and "legalize" the vigilantes. In this fashion the demands for increased regime effectiveness in controlling challenges to the existing distribution might be placated. Additionally, by co-opting some of the more moderate vigilantes, the regime may be able to control the extremists more effectively. Second, a regime may address some of the underlying causes of the dissident challenges in an attempt to mollify some of these latter groups without seriously threatening the established groups.

Neither strategy guarantees success. The attempt to routinize repression depends on the regime's capabilities and the relative power position of the groups being coerced. Although expectations may be stabilized and regularized, thereby correcting the ad hoc nature of vigilantism, the strategy remains essentially negative. A positive course of adaptation may be impossible, however, depending on the extent of the dissident demands and tactics, and on whether the "value pie" is expanding. These observations can be illustrated by examining the problem with reference to the three basic types of vigilantism.

CRIME-CONTROL VIGILANTISM

Crime rate increases appear commonly to afflict a society undergoing rapid social change which erodes previously established communal norms and relations and hinders the development of new ones. These conditions exist in rapidly changing urban areas where relationships are increasingly depersonalized; in frontier regions where the migrant population, though

---

46. Cf. Johnson, *Revolutionary Change,* pp. 8 ff. Samuel P. Huntington defines institutions as "stable, valued, recurring patterns of behavior." See his "Political Development and Political Decay," *World Politics* 17 (October 1965): 386-430.

47. Compare this with the evaluation of charismatic authority in David Apter, *Ghana in Transition* (New York: Atheneum, 1963), p. 303.

dispersed, is also uprooted, and the penetration of the formal system may not be very deep; or in regions disrupted by some social calamity, such as war. Other problems—corruption, inefficiency, or an overly refined system of due process—may also contribute to an increase in crime. Under these conditions, vigilantism may be a temporary substitute for the regular system of law enforcement, until the latter increases its coercive capabilities or the people internalize new system-supporting norms of behavior.

The potential costs of crime-control vigilantism are obvious: establishment violence can rapidly become worse than the crime itself. Punishments tend to be disproportionate; the innocent have little protection; and quasi-criminal elements are attracted to the movement as a semilegitimate avenue for the expression of their antisocial tendencies. In addition, when law enforcement officials participate in the acts of violence, whatever moral validity the formal system of laws retained may be undermined. The course of the South Carolina Regulators amply illustrates both the benefits and the costs:

> The South Carolina Regulator movement was constructive in that it did rid the back country of pervasive crime. Order and stability were at last established after many years of social chaos. But the Regulators were vindictive, and there was a streak of sadism in their punishments. The increasingly arbitrary, extreme, and brutal Regulators bred an opposition movement of "Moderators." Brought to a standstill by the equally violent Moderators and appeased by the Provincial government's provision for district courts and sheriffs, the Regulators disbanded in 1769.[48]

SOCIAL-GROUP-CONTROL VIGILANTISM

Rapid social change is often characterized by increasing demands for participation and services. These demands may exceed the desire and capacity of the formal system either to meet or to suppress them. Group-control vigilantism, insofar as it retards these demands, may buy time to build new institutions to channel or repress them. A partial redistribution of values, which would satisfy at least some of the rising sectors while not seriously alienating established groups, requires time to effect.

When a regime implicitly adopts a program of official group-control vigilantism (e.g., certain forms of terror), additional short-term benefits may accrue. Insofar as the violence is controlled, the regime may gain a useful complement to its formal coercive powers, while not completely abandoning the pretense of legitimacy given by a defined system of due process. The element of control in this subtype means that a regime can more easily manipulate this form of vigilantism, perhaps utilizing it as an aid in the realization of more complex modernization goals.[49]

48. Brown, "The American Vigilante Tradition," in Graham and Gurr, *History of Violence,* p. 159.
49. For a provocative defense of this type of terror, see the conversation between Rubashov and Gletkin in Arthur Koestler, *Darkness at Noon* (New York: Bantam, 1961), pp. 189-90.

Group-control vigilantism involves certain clear risks. The suppression of social groups with rising expectations (i.e., deliberate retardation of their value capabilities) often increases their sense of relative deprivation. Therefore, the potentiality for dissident violence in the future increases, unless these frustrations are alleviated in some fashion.

Nor is the policy of official vigilantism cost-free. In addition to the above risks, the legitimacy of the regime will probably decline over the long run. Moreover, the "vigilance institutions" may begin to usurp control, as the Soviet experience certainly suggests. Finally, though a policy of terror-inspired fear may provide initial impetus to the modernization process, eventually it exhausts rather than motivates people and adds elements of uncertainty and irrationality, which obviate more complex modernization tasks.

REGIME-CONTROL VIGILANTISM

The short-run benefits of regime-control vigilantism with respect to institutionalization probably depend on the relative quality of the leadership or formal institutions partially or entirely displaced. Conditions in Pakistan prior to 1958 appear to provide a classic example of "political decay," and the stabilization initially provided by the military/bureaucratic regime was probably an improvement. Ayub Khan's subsequent efforts to create new institutional patterns, however, must be judged a failure.[50] The inability of a series of military regimes in Argentina either to suppress effectively or to integrate the *Peronistas* after 1955 also illustrates the difference between using vigilante violence for regime control and effective rule. As with other examples of vigilantism, short-run stability may be produced and a particular elite group may initially consolidate its power position. These are largely "negative" gains; viable substitutes for the displaced institutional forms must still be created.

The occurrence of regime-control vigilantism may, however, hinder the process of institution building. Extralegal intervention may give one group a disproportionate advantage, and subsequent institutional development may be asymmetrical. Military/bureaucratic regimes, in particular, often seem to stunt the growth of other, especially representative, institutions, such as parties and legislatures.[51] Additionally, the formal institutions altered or supplanted may have been better than their successors, but may have threatened the position of a very powerful establishment group: the military.

50. Rounaq Jahan, *Pakistan: Failure in National Integration* (New York: Columbia University Press, 1972).

51. For an analysis of the problems of an imbalance favoring the bureaucracy, see Fred W. Riggs, *Administration in Developing Countries* (Boston: Houghton-Mifflin, 1964); for the problems of an imbalance favoring the military, see Eric A. Nordlinger, "Soldiers in Mufti: The Impact of Military Rule upon Economic and Social Change in the Non-Western States," *American Political Science Review* 64 (December 1970): 1131-48.

Finally, a praetorian syndrome may develop to retard institutionalization further.

Vigilantism may, on the other hand, contribute to the survival of certain formal societal arrangements. Like its analogue, political corruption, vigilantism permits conservative "coalitions . . . that could not survive the light of day, government decisions that would set off a public outcry, [and] elite behavior that would destroy many a political career. . . ."[52]

The presence of vigilantes may be functional in mass societies. Vigilantes are more interested in participating in the maintenance of the established order than in protecting due process. For this reason, the vigilante may be the ideal citizen in an unstructured society where there is a direct relationship between leaders and masses. As Samuel P. Huntington has noted, mass societies have a distinctive form of political participation which combines "violent and nonviolent, legal and illegal, [and] coercive and persuasive actions."[53] The vigilante might be comfortable in a society that places a high value on this form of political behavior, and could be a useful agent in helping this kind of system to endure.

CONCLUSION

This chapter has obviously not exhausted the abundant potentialities for additional and more intricate analyses of vigilantism. Yet it should be noted that, although many topics are worthy of consideration, the secrecy imposed by most vigilante organizations and their sometimes ephemeral nature may hinder or thwart scholars wishing to pursue the study of vigilantism. Public exposure is not generally welcomed by those engaged in the extralegal use of coercion.

Among the themes that deserve additional scrutiny are: leadership, followers, ideology, utility, support, and the future of vigilantism. Each of these will be discussed briefly below and further elaborated in the subsequent chapters of this volume.

LEADERSHIP

Very little is known about vigilante leaders, whose identities are often known only by their followers. Nevertheless, it would be valuable to know the various roles, functions, and personal characteristics of these leaders. What qualities help an individual to be an effective vigilante leader and to what extent are ranks in the established order reflected in vigilante organizations? In the case of regime-control vigilantism, it would also be of interest to know

52. James C. Scott, *Comparative Political Corruption* (Englewood Cliffs: Prentice Hall, 1972), p. 2.
53. Huntington, *Political Order in Changing Societies* (New Haven: Yale University Press, 1968), p. 88.

whether or not the characteristics observed in successful vigilante leaders enable them to make the transition from vigilante to administrator of the state. Some well-known American political figures, including Andrew Jackson and Theodore Roosevelt, either participated in or were sympathetic to vigilante movements.[54] Since vigilante leaders are often frustrated members of the establishment, they may find it easier to make the transition to (or back to) positions in the government than would dissidents who historically have been excluded from office. It may well be, moreover, that certain types of leadership are required for the different kinds of vigilantism discussed earlier. Finally, specific kinds of leadership may be needed during the various periods of a vigilante organization's development.

An examination of the personality types of several vigilante leaders might provide some answers to the questions posed. Again, previous work on revolutionary violence might be suggestive. For example, a study based on the model of E. Victor Wolfenstein's *The Revolutionary Personality* might furnish the insights required for an interesting comparison with the more "social-psychological" model developed earlier.[55] Wolfenstein presumes that vigilante and revolutionary leadership are distinct. He declares that "the less an individual is dedicated to radical social change and a total displacement of the ruling class, the less he will be likely to embody the psychological attributes of the revolutionary personality."[56] However, even though the vigilante and revolutionary leader do not have identical goals, they may use similar means; and the reason for the selection of means, rather than goals, may be crucial in determining psycho-political type.

Wolfenstein hypothesizes that the revolutionary "is one who escapes from the burdens of Oedipal guilt and ambivalence by carrying his conflict into the political realm." He further states that the revolutionary's opposition to governmental authority "is the result of the individual's continuing need to express his aggressive impulses vis-a-vis his father and the repressive action of governmental officials."[57]

The vigilante, it might be posited, overidentifies with authority rather than rebelling against it. Basically an authoritarian character, the vigilante perceives the establishment as a punitive father figure and identifies with the aggressor.[58] A harshly punitive father produces an attempt at extreme resolution; the vigilante turns his anger against others who share his own forbidden impulses to challenge authority. He identifies with power to remove himself from the domination of power. This may help to explain why many

---

54. Brown, "Legal and Behavioral Perspectives on American Vigilantism," pp. 123-28.
55. E. Victor Wolfenstein, *The Revolutionary Personality: Lenin, Trotsky, Gandhi* (Princeton: Princeton University Press, 1967).
56. Ibid., p. 21.
57. Ibid., p. 307, 308.
58. This type of personality is discussed in T. W. Adorno et. al., *The Authoritarian Personality* (New York: Harper, 1950).

vigilante leaders who are not members of the system's elite are among the most vehement defenders of the status quo. The vigilante assumes the desired role of the father as protector of home and mother. He threatens interlopers who represent denied aspects of himself.[59]

This analysis may be subjected to several criticisms. It neglects political culture, often using Western, Freudian psychoanalytic categories to analyze non-Westerners; Oedipal guilt, for instance, may not be universal. It ignores particular situations; the demands of a situation rather than personality may provoke an individual to become a vigilante or a revolutionary. This approach also does not account for specific political ideas. It does not explain why someone with the personality described above joins a vigilante group rather than another kind of political movement.

Thus, while Wolfenstein's model is highly suggestive, to understand fully the phenomenology, psychological dynamics, and genesis of vigilante leaders, a more varied approach, including individual, typological, and aggregative analysis, is required. Five classes of variables and their relationships need to be studied. They include: "(1) political behavior itself; (2) situational antecedents of behavior; (3) the different aspects of personality processes and dispositions . . . ; (4) social determinants of personality; and (5) the past and present features of larger political systems that determine many of the basic conditions of the immediate environments within which personality development and political behavior occur."[60]

FOLLOWERS

If little is known about vigilante leaders, still less is understood about their followers. Nevertheless, some impressionistic observations may be offered. First, while the middle classes form the cadres of most revolutionary movements, vigilante organizations seem to be composed of members from all segments of society. Criminal elements may participate in vigilante enterprises for ulterior motives; they may wish to veil their activities or seek a sense of legitimacy. Other marginal members of society may join vigilante groups because of coercion by the establishment or sectors of it. Peasants, for example, may fear that their landlord will punish them unless they please him by lending their services to a vigilante group he supports. As for the bulk of the vigilante rank and file, their commitment is produced by a concern that their

59. In their preliminary research the authors have not encountered a single female vigilante leader. This phenomenon is curious, and requires explanation. Although this approach to the female personality is controversial and has received much criticism recently, Freudians might suggest that a female vigilante leader has not resolved her penis envy and thus desires a male role. The female vigilante follower, therefore, would have achieved resolution and would as a result accept the values provided by men. A sociological interpretation might be more accurate, however. Most societies do not allow women to obtain positions of leadership easily and conservative vigilantes are probably much less likely to alter traditional role assignment than are revolutionaries.

60. Fred I. Greenstein, *Personality and Politics* (Chicago: Markham, 1969), p. 142.

value capabilities are in danger. This feeling of decremental deprivation may affect all but the most humble constituents of a society. This thesis fails to explain why everyone experiencing such anxiety does not join a vigilante movement; nor does it reveal why some vigilantes support the cause with more intensity than others. The degree of decremental deprivation may influence the ardor of vigilantes; but it does not in itself seem to be a completely adequate explication of why some vigilantes are active while others are more passive.

Second, an understanding of the agents of vigilante mobilization might contribute to the knowledge of vigilante group dynamics. Most vigilante movements appear to lack charismatic leadership or a motivating ideology, other than that espoused by the establishment. However, a trigger mechanism, such as an increased crime rate, revolutionary insurgency, or student anti-government demonstrations, often seems to inspire potential vigilantes or galvanize the current membership and stimulate it to become more vigilant. Thus, apparently pragmatism or alarm, rather than idealism or esteem, arouse devotion. Once basic satisfaction is achieved, lethargy results, and membership declines. The absence of charismatic leadership and a compelling ideology, as well as the emphasis on maintenance rather than change, leaves the vigilante group without a force capable of maintaining cohesion. This may be one reason why vigilante groups are generally ephemeral.

It might be profitable to raise some additional questions about the fate of vigilantes. For instance, are they rewarded by the regime for their services? If so, in what manner and under what circumstances? Do the vigilantes feel aggrieved if not commended? How do they adjust if their behavior produces a negative reaction? Do they move toward more dissident-oriented violence?

Additionally, it might be useful to know more about the recruitment of vigilantes and the specific functions they perform within the organizations. There is a need to have more knowledge about their socialization, both before and after they join vigilante groups. Finally, it might be of interest to have more information about mobility within vigilante movements. What kinds of behavior are rewarded and punished? How is discipline maintained within the organization? Do certain talents allow some vigilantes to be more successful than others? Can "underclass" elements ever usurp the original leadership?

IDEOLOGY

Vigilante groups, unlike many revolutionary movements, rarely possess autonomous ideologies; they are dependent for ideological guidance and justification on the prevalent belief system of the establishment they seek to support. It might be argued that vigilantes usually do not have ideologies at all, but only poorly integrated values and attitudes that are not very comprehensive. Apparently vigilantes do not attempt to answer most questions concerning the human condition but instead improvise makeshift justifications that serve to reassure them of the righteousness of the status quo.

The fundamental ideology of the prevailing system is not stated in detail by vigilantes, because it is assumed to be known. Vigilantes are in favor of "what is," and, therefore, they have no need to develop complex explanations of "what ought to be." In this respect vigilante attitudes are much more uncomplicated than those of revolutionaries. If it were not for their fear that their value capabilities were being eroded, vigilantes would have no problems requiring independent ideological guidance.

This assumption that the establishment is being jeopardized is the common characteristic of vigilante political thought. The ideology describes these dangers and attempts to expound the virtues of the vigilantes' utilitarian motives. This helps to account for the often frantic tone of vigilante declarations.

The absence of intellectuals in most vigilante movements is perhaps another reason for the undeveloped nature of vigilante ideology. Apparently activists rather than ideologues participate in vigilante activities. The ideologist is generally a visionary and probably does not find the conservative vigilantes compatible associates. American vigilantes, however, have found sympathetic apologists in the legal establishment.[61]

The primary value of vigilante ideology would seem to be its ability to attract popular support. Therefore, it would be appropriate to assess further the advantages and disadvantages of different kinds of ideological appeals. The form as well as the content of these instrumental invocations to vigilance are related to culture and issues, and should be subjected to cross-national and historical comparison. There might also be some merit in tracing the development of vigilante ideologies. Such an inquiry could disclose some of the internal dynamics of vigilante organizations and, in addition, reveal the levels of decremental deprivation.

UTILITY

The principal goal of vigilantes is deterrence; their tactics consist of threats and sanctions. In this regard, it would be helpful to know how effective vigilantism is as a political tool. The situations in which vigilantes are likely to succeed in obtaining their goals should be more clearly delineated. Are some kinds of coercive control sponsored by vigilantes more productive than others?

Gurr reports that, "a survey of some psychological evidence suggests that negative physical sanctions are at best problematic in their effects on levels of aggression."[62] In this connection it would be helpful to know the consequences of sanctions threatened and imposed by vigilantes in a variety of

61. Brown, "Legal and Behavioral Perspectives on American Vigilantism," pp. 128-44.
62. Gurr, *Rebel,* p. 241.

circumstances. A comparison of responses to vigilante versus official coercive control would also be worthwhile.

The range of vigilante activities seems to extend from subtle and restrained use of force to acts of brutal compulsion and retribution. Violent force may not be used on all occasions, but its future utilization is always implied. It is not clear whether the escalation of violence follows a logical pattern or is determined by the presence of defiance. Whether the degree of fear, despair, or personal interest directly affects the intensity of vigilante violence or the selection of means has likewise not been established.

SUPPORT

The type, source, and extent of support received by a vigilante group are determinants of such an organization's evolution and effectiveness. Vigilantes require material and psychological support, and the absence of one or both may result in dissolution. The source of support may be either internal or external. Internal support may consist of inspired leadership and comradery; external support may be provided by the government or part of it, by the private sector, or by other extralegal organizations. Support may also be direct or indirect. Indirect support by the regime, for example, may simply consist of ignoring the illegal activities of the vigilantes, while direct support may include the provision of arms, training, and funds. At times, support from the populace seems to have limited impact on the development of vigilante groups, although it may significantly affect a regime's attitude toward the vigilantes.

Support from the government is more vital and, in this regard, it might be suitable to ask why a regime turns to vigilantes for assistance. Do governments do so because they fear the vigilantes and do not want to risk opposition by affronting them? Or is it that vigilantes can actually provide some service for the governments? It is known that regimes are not consistent in their support of vigilante activities. For this reason, it is necessary to determine when and why vigilantes have the support of officials.

THE FUTURE OF VIGILANTISM

Some authorities contend that the world is in the midst of a new revolutionary era.[63] The contemporary examples cited earlier in this article suggest that we may be living simultaneously in an age of vigilantism. There is, nevertheless, a need to acquire and order empirical evidence before making such an assertion. The collection of this material is also crucial in order to determine whether vigilante eruptions form a pattern and whether demonstration effects produce vigilante contagion.

It seems unlikely that vigilantism is a passing phenomenon, but when and where vigilantism will arise cannot be predicted with precision. Yet this does

63. Leiden and Schmitt, *Politics of Violence*, p. 212.

not make the following questions any less interesting: Are new types of vigilantism likely to evolve? Are some societies immune from vigilantism? Would the classless society forecast by Marxists eliminate the disparity between peoples' value capabilities and thus signal the demise of vigilantism? If the polarization between rich and poor nations continues or becomes more extreme, will regional or international vigilante wars rage?[64] Will the "greening" of the world or the coming of "Consciousness III" mark the end of the vigilante personality? Is increasing revolutionary rhetoric or the spread of revolution itself likely to cause alarm and thus the expansion of vigilante movements? Are societies permanently affected, once having experienced an episode of vigilantism? Do societies "mature" and overcome their propensity for vigilantism? Are societies more prone to vigilantism during particular periods in their development?

Establishment violence can occur in any society where groups desirous of maintaining their value positions see their capabilities decreasing, primarily due to the apparent ineffectiveness of the government. As an analytical concept, it assumes that there is a recognized sociopolitical order with formalized rules and methods of maintaining its boundaries over time. According to this model one cannot speak of vigilantism where there is no recognized "establishment," where conditions of internal war exist, or where there are no rules governing the application of coercion. Even with these conceptual preconditions, the study of the causes, variety, and consequences of vigilantism can richly complement the existing work on dissident violence.

---

64. Clearly, an "establishment" exists among the nations of the world, but vigilantism on an international scale would necessitate the existence of commonly recognized boundaries regulating interstate relations. Although many observers would deny the meaningful existence of such rules, the double standard often applied by great powers may constitute an example of proto-vigilantism.

Chapter Two

Spontaneous Vigilantism: A Bystander Response to Criminal Behavior

R. Lance Shotland

Recent newspaper accounts have suggested that individuals have begun to react differently to crime.[1] In past years, bystanders' reactions to crime were characterized as apathetic. The most celebrated account of this apathy was the case of Kitty Genovese, a young cocktail waitress, who was murdered in New York in 1964 while thirty-eight of her neighbors did nothing but watch. In contrast, the back pages of newspapers have been replete with descriptions concerning the reporting of suspicious behavior to the police by a neighbor or passerby which ended in the arrest of a burglar or other criminal.[2] Recent newspaper accounts have portrayed bystanders as taking an even more decisive role; i.e., not only have they apprehended suspected criminals, but they have done severe bodily injury to them as well. For example, *The Washington Post* reports:

> . . . in the fashion of a Mack Sennett comedy, twenty-nine cab drivers from the L and M Private Car Service and the No-Wait Car Service chased three men who had robbed and stolen one of No-Wait's taxis.
>
> Alerted over radio by their dispatcher, the cab drivers chased the suspects from 162d Street and Amsterdam Avenue through two boroughs, finally cornering their prey in the Bronx.
>
> There, they collared two of the suspects, beat them and held them until the police arrived. Both were admitted to Fordham Hospital.
>
> One of the drivers, John Mercado, 24, a Vietnam veteran, said after the incident, "We've got to stick together."

1. W. Claiborne, "Vigilantism Increasing in New York," *Washington Post* (September 16, 1973): 1.

2. See *New York Times* (September 2, 1972): 19, column 2; *New York Times* (September 12, 1972): 55, column 2; *New York Times* (November 11, 1972): 1, column 3; *New York Times* (November 26, 1972): 57, column 1.

Again:

> At 4:45 p.m. September 3, Robert Mayfield, 38, was driving his 1967 Cadillac along Morningside Avenue at West 127th Street when he became involved in an argument with another motorist.
>
> According to police, Mayfield became enraged at the taunting of a small crowd, pulled a gun and fired blindly into the crowd, mortally wounding a four-year-old boy and injuring another man.
>
> A woman began screaming, "He killed my baby," and an off duty policeman, Earl Robinson, ran up and ordered Mayfield to drop his gun. Mayfield fired once, hitting Robinson in the chest.
>
> Suddenly, according to Robinson's account, the crowd of bystanders closed in on Mayfield, knocking him to the ground, and kicking him relentlessly. . . . Mayfield was taken to Knicker-Bocker Hospital where he was admitted with cerebral hemorrhage, multiple contusions and internal injuries.[3]

The actions described above shall be referred to as "Spontaneous Vigilantism," defined as the act *by a group of bystanders* of apprehending a suspected wrongdoer and instantly meting out punishment and retribution outside of the normal judicial process. Hence, our discussion does not concern itself with organized vigilante behavior as exhibited by certain groups like the Jewish Defense League or the Ku Klux Klan.[4] Instead, the purpose of this paper is to set forth a theoretical rationale exploring the causes that lead to spontaneous forms of vigilante behavior by people who were formerly carrying out normal daily activities.

Before developing a model concerned with the determinants of spontaneous vigilantism, more should be said about its relationship to the other two bystander reactions to crime: intervention and nonaction. Newspaper accounts suggest that a group of bystanders responds to a criminal act in at least three different ways. These responses can be placed along a continuum which ranges from nonaction at one extreme to spontaneous vigilantism at the other.

As noted in Figure I, each of the points along the continuum represents

Figure 1 Range of Bystander Reactions to Crime

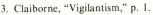

No Intervention	Intervention	Spontaneous
(Nonaction)	(Indirect Action)	Vigilantism
		(Direct Action)

3. Claiborne, "Vigilantism," p. 1.
4. Organized vigilantism may properly be considered a social movement, while spontaneous vigilantism is a product of crowd behavior.

various degrees of action or nonaction on the part of bystanders. The nonaction end of the continuum is characterized by apathetic or nonintervening bystander behavior. No aid is given to the victim of the crime, nor are the police called upon to intervene. In short, the crime is ignored and the victim is left to his own resources. Bystander intervention, in the middle of the continuum, represents behaviors which do not *directly* aid the victim of a crime nor lead to the direct apprehension of a criminal. Instead, it involves calling upon others (such as the police), who are percieved as legitimate and normatively appropriate, to apprehend the criminal suspect. The other end of the continuum is anchored by behaviors which are defined as spontaneous vigilantism. Direct action against the wrongdoer is taken by the bystanders without consulting the police or other authorities. In general, such behaviors are not normatively accepted nor sanctioned by legal institutions.

Intermediate points along the continuum can be described as well. When people intervene in emergency situations, their degree of involvement varies. For example, behavior at point X on the continuum may involve reporting a crime to the police, but in such a manner that one does not identify himself to the authorities and cannot be called upon as a witness in any trial. Behaviors at point Y on the continuum may represent the actual apprehension of a criminal by a group of bystanders but, instead of meting out immediate punishment, they merely contain the suspect until the police arrive. Here direct action is taken that does not violate legal sanctions but is commended by the authorities. Point Z represents behavior that involves a lesser degree of direct action than does Y. For example, a bystander witnessing the occurrence of a crime reports it to the police and attempts to scare the criminal away by shouting for help. No action is taken to directly stop the suspect. In conclusion, bystanders exhibit a whole range of different reactions to crime, only one of which is spontaneous vigilantism.

In the past few years a great amount of research has been performed in order to determine what conditions create no action in comparison to intervention on the part of bystanders.[5] This literature will be used in part to explain the underlying differences between nonaction, bystander intervention, and spontaneous vigilantism. In other words, we will use the two points on the continuum (no intervention—intervention) to help explain the concept of spontaneous vigilantism. Let us now compare the situational milieu of the three basic reactions to crime.

The purpose of bystander intervention, according to Latané and Darley, is to return the situation to the status quo. While no situation can be exactly

---

5. See B. Latané and J. Darley, "Bystander 'Apathy,'" *American Scientist* 57 (1969): pp. 244-68; J. Darley, L. Teger and L. Lewis, "Do Groups Always Inhibit Individuals' Responses to Potential Emergencies?" *Journal of Personality and Social Psychology* 26 (1973): pp. 395-99; A. Ross and J. Braband, "Effect of Increased Responsibility on Bystander Intervention, II; The Cue Value of A Blind Person," *Journal of Personality and Social Psychology* 25 (1973): pp. 254-58.

restored to what it was before the act took place, bystander intervention is not an act of retribution. Spontaneous vigilantism, on the other hand, is an act of retribution and an attempt to ensure the incident does not reoccur. Second, newspaper accounts indicate that all three forms of behavior occur when a number of bystanders are present. Third, all cases of vigilantism recently reported in New York City occurred in high crime areas within an ethnic community or among a community of people (cab drivers). Fourth, the nature of the crime that elicits vigilantism appears to be of the kind that could strike any member of the community; e.g., a man with little provocation jumping out of his car, shooting randomly into a crowd, and killing a little boy; a mugging; a rape; or a stick-up of a cab seen by other cab drivers.

Let us examine some of these points in greater detail. First, as we have previously noted, any of the three reactions may take place when the street is populated with bystanders. What then are the factors that determine which of these bystander reactions will occur? First, the work of Latané and Darley makes it clear that a bystander is less likely to intervene in an emergency if other bystanders are present. These researchers staged the following situation. One or two robbers (who were actually confederates of the experimenter) would enter the NU-Way Beverage Store in Suffern, New York and ask the cashier at the counter, "What is the most expensive imported beer that you carry?" The cashier who was a confederate of the robbers would reply, "Lowenbrau. I'll go back and check how much we have." After the cashier left, the robbers would pick up a case of beer, remark out loud, "They'll never miss this," and then walk out the door, put the beer in their car and drive away. Latané and Darley reported that a bystander was less likely to report the theft when other bystanders were present than when the bystander was alone.[6] Hence, a number of bystanders are likely to inhibit a response to an emergency rather than facilitate "the solution" to it as they do in spontaneous vigilantism.

According to Latané and Darley, bystanders respond in this fashion because of two factors: (1) social influence, and (2) diffusion of responsibility. The former refers to the fact that in unstructured situations people often turn to others for cues concerning appropriate behavior. The cues given off by others act to aid in one's own interpretation and definition of the situation. The bystander's reasoning takes the following form: "if the man next to me isn't helping, perhaps there is nothing wrong." In addition, as Latané and Darley point out, there are various forces existing in any social situation which act to inhibit intervention. If the potential intervenor has misjudged the situation and called the police, the person intervening as well as the victim and alleged perpetrator of the incident may all be extremely embarrassed. It is also possible to violate norms if the intervenor takes direct action and grabs a stranger who had not snatched a woman's purse as the observer supposed.

6. Latané and Darley, "Apathy," pp. 244-68.

These concerns with reacting incorrectly or over-reacting to a situation and possibly losing face may override the concerns people have about the possible victim. Thus social inhibition may prevent them from helping.

The second explanatory concept used by Latané and Darley to describe the reactions of their subjects to an emergency is "diffusion of responsibility." If only one individual is present during an emergency or crime, he carries all of the responsibility for dealing with it; "he will feel all of the guilt for not acting; he will bear all of the blame that accrues for non-intervention."[7] When more than one individual is present, the pressures to intervene do not fall on that one person's shoulders. Instead, the responsibility is shared by all, and as a result each is less likely to intervene.

It is clear from laboratory studies that the diffusion of responsibility factor is important. When the social cues that people pick up from each other are eliminated, one bystander is still more likely to come to the victim's aid if he is alone than if several bystanders are present. For example, Latané and Darley designed an experiment in which they eliminated the subjects' opportunity to observe the reactions of others in an emergency situation, thus eliminating social influence cues. They still found the same effect; i.e., one bystander is more likely to help when he is alone than when several bystanders are present. These results suggest that even when the factor of social influence is eliminated, diffusion of responsibility is strong enough to lead to nonintervening behavior on the part of a group of bystanders.[8] These two factors, social influence and diffusion of responsibility, tend to create bystander nonaction. In that case, can a situation with a number of bystanders lead to vigilante action?

Most emergencies are unexpected and hence often ambiguous. We know that people tend to turn to others for cues about the nature of the situation when the situation itself is ambiguous. Therefore, bystanders are going to turn to others for cues in order to explain the witnessed event (did they just bump into each other or did he lift the man's wallet?). However, criminal events leading to vigilantism do not appear to be ambiguous. When a man jumps out of his car and shoots into a crowd and a woman yells, "He killed my baby," the event is instantly defined for the bystanders. When cab drivers hear over their radios that a fellow cab driver was robbed and his cab was stolen, the event has already been defined for them by their dispatcher. When a man is brought into a police station for questioning because he resembles a police artist's sketch of a rapist, the event has already been defined as a rape of a young girl. The crowds in New York City that have turned to vigilantism had a similar and clarified view of the event. Thus, one of the key factors which determines whether a crowd of bystanders will intervene or remain apathetic rests upon

---

7. Latané and Darley, *The Unresponsive Bystander: Why doesn't he help?* (New York: Appleton-Century-Crofts, 1970), p. 90.
8. Latané and Darley, "Apathy," pp. 244-68.

the degree of ambiguity in the situation. The less ambiguous the situation is, the more likely the crowd is to intervene.

Likewise, in viewing historical accounts of spontaneous vigilantism we find the same high levels of clarity. In 1930, a rash of lynchings occurred in Georgia, Mississippi, Texas, South Carolina, and Indiana. These lynchings were extremely similar to the spontaneous vigilantism that occurred in New York City.[9] The Southern Commission on the Study of Lynching defined a lynching in the following manner:

> whereas a gang murder is premeditated and carried out by a few people in conspiring secrecy from constituted authorities, a lynching is usually *spontaneous* and carried out in a public fashion with scores, hundreds and not uncommonly thousands of eye-witnesses. . . . lynchers operate in the open and publicly defy the law.[10]

Generally, the lynchings occurred in the following manner. First, a crime was allegedly committed. Second, the supposed crime was reported and defined for the community by the victim, associates of the victim, or the authorities as a crime. Third, members of the community decided to launch a "man-hunt," and fourth, members of the community decided to lynch the suspect. For example, Raper reports:

> A young couple, said to have been recently married had been brought to the local store by a passing motorist. They reported that about ten o'clock, just before reaching Wahalak, three Negroes halted them by waving a flashlight, and took forty-five dollars from the man and a wedding ring from the woman (*they also threatened to kill the man and rape the woman*).
> When the couple reached Wahalak the few white people there became very much excited. They called to DeKalb, the county seat, for the sheriff, to Scooba, the nearest town for help to capture the Negroes . . . the Negroes were arrested. . . .
> The Negroes remained in jail at DeKalb until . . . Constable J. J. Dotson of the eastern district of the county started with them toward Scooba for a preliminary trial. When about six miles out, where the road passed through a wood, the mob is reported to have come upon the officers and caught them so completely off their guard that not a shot was fired in defense of the prisoners. . . . the two Negroes were hanged.[11]

If someone had happened to travel down the road and had come upon the

---

9. There are, of course, differences also. Southern lynchings had a strong racial component with blacks serving as the victims and whites as the lynchers. New York's vigilantism does not. In Southern vigilantism a longer period occurred from the time the crime was committed to the time of the lynching than does occur in New York vigilantism. This seems to be a result of the duration necessary for word to get around a rural community so that a mob could gather and of the slower pace of police work in capturing the victim. Moreover, Southern vigilante behavior was more violent, leading to the death of its victims. Southern vigilante behavior, at times, involved more people and at times developed a festive atmosphere.

10. Southern Commission on the Study of Lynching. *Lynchings and What They Mean* (Atlanta: The Committee, n.d.), p. 73. (The italics were added by the author.)

11. A. Raper, *The Tragedy of Lynching* (Chapel Hill: The University of North Carolina Press, 1933), pp. 85 and 86. (The italicized portion was added by the author.)

crime in progress, chances are he would have seen a parked car, four men and a woman. Unless the motorist saw a weapon or some act of violence occurring, the scene would have been ambiguous. Many hypotheses might have come to mind to explain what these people were doing. It is likely that our motorist would have interpreted the situation as a flat tire and decided that there were enough people around to change the tire. Thus he would not have stopped to either apprehend the criminals or help with the tire. If, however, this same hypothetical motorist had been in town when the couple arrived and heard their story, then the event would have required no interpretation on the part of the motorist as it would have already been interpreted for him by the victim.

Again, Raper reports the lynching of a black man named Allen Green on April 20, 1930 in Walhalla, South Carolina. Green was accused of rape and lynched. However, at the pretrial hearing, it became evident that the time span in which the victim was allegedly bound and raped was between twenty-nine seconds and one and one-half minutes. The woman testified that she was not angered by the act. Listening to the evidence should raise some doubts as to the validity of the woman's story. The sheriff indicated that he did not take precautions against the lynching because he thought the man was innocent.[12] Again, the factual evidence leaves one with an ambiguous picture of what really took place. However, the woman's story contained little ambiguity; she and her husband went to the black man's house to buy a mule when she was pulled into the house, her husband was locked out, and she was tied up and raped.

A crowd that turns to vigilantism has a similar and clarified, unambiguous view of the event and agrees upon who is to blame. The unequivocal view of the event does not have to be based on truth or reality. Many people were lynched on the basis of rumors. Rumors, however untrue, provide a clear and unambiguous view of the rumored incident according to Allport and Postman:

> There are few stories that do not have personal and clearly identified victims. And there are few that fail to specify clearly the character of the action or the deed that provides the tenor of the tale.[13]

Several laboratory and field studies have shown that bystanders intervene more often in an emergency when the event is not ambiguous.[14] Hence, the greater the ambiguity of the event, the greater the likelihood that bystanders will look to others to help interpret the situation and thus the greater the

12. Ibid., pp. 263-66.
13. G. Allport and L. Postman, *The Psychology of Rumor* (New York: Henry Holt, 1947), p. x.
14. See R. Clark and L. Word, "Why Don't Bystanders Help? Because of Ambiguity," *Journal of Personality and Social Psychology* 24 (1972): 392-400; R. Clark and L. Word, "Where is the Apathetic Bystander? Situational Characteristics of the Emergency," *Journal of Personality and Social Psychology* 29 (1974): 279-87; R. Shotland and M. Johnson, "Victim and Incident Characteristics of an Emergency," (in preparation).

likelihood that bystanders will be lured into a "conformity of inaction." The greater the clarity of the event, the more likely the bystander will intervene.

Another factor leading to an unambiguous view of an incident is a sense of commonality among bystanders and between bystanders and victims. In viewing the vigilante incidents that occurred in New York City we find that they took place in areas that have a strong ethnic or racial concentration of people. More precisely, out of seventy-one police precincts in New York City, as Table 1 indicates, the precincts reporting incidents of vigilantism ranked first and eighth in concentration of black, non-Hispanic people, and ranked seventh, tenth and eighteenth in their concentration of Hispanic people. Again, from the bystander intervention research we know that if a number of bystanders are present, intervention is more likely to occur if communication takes place between the bystanders that clarifies the situation for them.[15] Communication functions in an emergency to define the situation for the bystanders as indeed an emergency. The literature also suggests that more communication takes place between friends than strangers when an emergency does occur and that friends are more likely to intervene than strangers. Therefore, people of common ethnic or racial origin would be more likely to communicate and clarify their perceptions of the incident for each other than members of a heterogeneous group, and hence would be more likely to intervene.

So far, we have discussed the role that the ambiguity of the event plays in creating either bystander nonaction or intervention. If a bystander has an unambiguous view of the incident, he does not need to look for others to help him interpret the situation. He has interpreted the situation himself, and so will not join in a "conformity of inaction." Bystanders that resort to vigilante activity have a clear, unambiguous view of the incident. However, the explanation developed so far only explores the conditions that lead to bystander action or inaction. We have not explained what leads bystanders beyond the normal legal channels to spontaneous vigilantism.

In order to explain why bystanders should resort to vigilantism, it is necessary to explore the motivational factors that might tempt bystanders to take "the law into their own hands." Table 1 demonstrates that crime is truly a problem in the areas in which vigilante activity has occurred. The police precincts that have experienced vigilante activity have crime rates that are among the highest in New York City. We find that they rank first, second, seventh, ninth, and eighteenth among the seventy-one police precincts in number of robberies per capita. Recently (March 1973), Gallup reported from a national sample that "crime and lawlessness" was an important concern for all Americans. It was high on the list of the "most important problems facing the country today" with 17 percent of the sample listing it. Thus, in a high

15. Latané and Darley, "Apathy," pp. 244-68.

TABLE 1

Population and Robbery Statistics for Police Precincts that Contained Vigilante Activity*

Precinct Number	Percentage of Population that is Black Non-Hispanic	Rank of the Concentration of Black Non-Hispanic People out of 71 Police Precincts	Percentage of Population that is Hispanic	Rank of the Concentration of Hispanic People out of 71 Police Precincts	Robberies per Thousand	Rank of Robberies per thousand of 71 Police Precincts
MS†	4.3	47	11.4	36	93.52	1
7	9.2	35	39.8	7	16.76	18
26	30.4	17	31.7	10	20.44	9
28	93.3	1	4.7	60	62.19	2
30	61.1	8	24.4	18	23.70	7

*Statistics were prepared by the New York City — Rand Institute and *The New York Times* and reported in D. Burnham, "Precinct Crime Compared with People's Age, Wealth," *New York Times* (July 30, 1973): 1.

†This precinct is very different from the others listed in the table. It encompasses mid-town Manhattan including the Time Square area and is basically a business district rather than a residential area. As a result the robbery rate per capita is misleading.

crime area criminal activity should be of paramount concern to the population.[16]

In addition, crimes preceding vigilante behavior have a special quality about them. The crimes by their very nature can touch any member of the community. A mugger can do his work on anyone. The victims of the crime almost appear to be selected at random from the population of the neighborhood. The crime of sexual molestation again has this same quality. While a man might not expect to be molested, he knows that his wife, sister, child, or mother may be. The case of the man shooting wildly into the crowd, perhaps killing any member of the crowd, exemplifies the nature of these offenses. The vigilante taximen are another case in point. In New York it became law that a bulletproof divider must be installed in all cabs in an attempt to stop the robbery and murder of taxi drivers. Drivers refuse to service certain neighborhoods to minimize the possibility of being robbed. The threat of robbery is very real to the cab driver. This constant threat of criminal attack provokes anxiety and is a necessary prerequisite of vigilante behavior. It would be very surprising, indeed, for vigilante behavior to occur in response to a present day bank robbery where everyone is protected from personal loss by insurance (Federal Deposit Insurance Corporation). Similarly, a marijuana smoker is not liable to be victimized by a vigilante attack unless he is perceived as a threat to the community.

In addition to the high anxiety produced by the fear of criminal attack, another necessary prerequisite is the loss of confidence in specialized institutions charged with dealing with the crime problem; i.e., the police and the courts. In a national survey (April 1972), Gallup found that the public most often named the leniency of the law and lightness of penalties as the reason for the high crime rate.[17] Belief in the inadequacies of local institutions to deal with criminal behavior also appeared to be a factor in Southern lynchings. Raper reports:

> Moreover, southern rural communities are generally known to be least policed of any communities in the United States. The general public accepts and relies upon the man-hunt tradition and the lynchings custom.[18]

In addition to the anxiety produced by the nature and frequency of criminal behavior and lack of confidence in traditional institutions, vigilante activity is also a product of frustration. For the purpose of this discussion, frustration can be defined as the blocking of ongoing, goal-directed activity. Miller states that frustration leads to aggression under the correct circumstances.[19] What Dollard, Doob, Miller, Mowrer, and Sears mean when they use the term "aggression" is acts of physical violence, fantasized violence, a malicious

16. "Most Important Problems," *Gallup Opinion Index,* 93 (Princeton: Gallup, 1973), p. 12.
17. "Special Report on Crime," *Gallup Opinion Index,* 82 (Princeton: Gallup, 1972), p. 11.
18. Raper, *Tragedy,* p. 29.
19. N. Miller, "The Frustration-Aggression Hypothesis," *Psychological Review* 48 (1941): 337-42.

rumor, lynchings, etc. Aggression may not occur after frustration if a substitute response is available to replace the blocked one. Eating apple pie when there is no cherry, autoeroticism when there is no partner, a "jilted" lover who marries another soon after the end of his previous relationship are examples of substitute responses. Aggression may not take place because other factors may dominate and inhibit it. Dollard, et. al. suggest that fear of punishment can inhibit the occurrence of aggression.[20] Moreover, when frustration does occur, it may not be directed at the frustrating agent but may be displaced onto a neutral object, perhaps out of fear of punishment. For example, a man who is told that he is not getting a raise probably would not vent his anger on his boss, but may kick his wastepaper basket. Miller and Bugelski used an experimental situation to frustrate human subjects. The subjects were paired with a confederate of the experimenter posing as a real subject and were told they were participating in an experiment on cooperation and competition. During the "cooperation" stage, the confederate caused the subject to fail by bungling his part of the task. During the "competition" stage the confederate caused the subject to fail by competing successfully and by making invidious comparisons. Immediately after being frustrated, subjects were asked to rate a friend who was not present. The subjects who were frustrated rated their friend's personality lower than did nonfrustrated subjects. Since the friends could not be the frustrating agent, Miller and Bugelski concluded that the lower ratings were a product of displaced aggression.[21]

Recently, Milgram and Shotland experimentally demonstrated that frustration can produce criminal behavior, specifically, property crimes. In a letter from a fictitious firm called Television Previews, the authors requested that subjects come to a theater in Manhattan and rate a television program. As a reward the subjects were to receive a transistor radio. The subjects rated the programs at the theater and were given a gift certificate redeemable at one of a number of different firms in an office building in midtown Manhattan. Unknown to the subjects these firms were really fronts for a field laboratory where the subject's every reaction could be observed through closed circuit television. As the subjects entered the appropriate office, they found it empty of personnel. It was furnished with a counter, a charity display on the wall containing over fourteen dollars in bills and change, a telephone, posters, and drapes. On the counter was taped a message. In the high-frustration condition the message was rude; it gave no reason for the empty office and said no more radios would be distributed until further notice. In the low-frustration condition the message was apologetic; it explained that the workers were ill and the radio could be picked up in another office on another floor. Milgram and Shotland found that crime rates could indeed be altered by changing the

20. J. Dollard, L. Doob, N. Miller, O. Mowrer and R. Sears, *Frustration and Aggression* (New Haven: Yale University, 1939).
21. Ibid., pp. 42-43.

level of frustration. In the high-frustration condition 18.7 percent of the subjects stole something from the offices including charity money, ash trays, plants, tools, and other transportable items. In the low-frustration condition, only 2.9 percent of the subjects criminally removed items from the office.[22]

As Table 2 demonstrates, the NewYork police precincts in which vigilante activity has occurred in residential areas are among the poorest areas in the city. Living amid poverty, not being able *to achieve* the material possessions of a middle-class existence because of an inadequate education and discrimination, among other reasons, is a frustrating situation. This frustration then is certainly a possible factor in the production of crime. Moreover, frustration is also an important factor in the creation of vigilantism. As Hovland and Sears point out, it is not possible to be aggressive against a condition.[23] Aggression could be expressed against landlords and merchants, persons that can be seen by the slum dweller as directly blocking goals by not furnishing him with an adequate apartment for his rent, or by selling him inferior goods for his money. According to Hovland and Sears, fear of punishment usually prevents aggression aimed at these individuals.[24] Hence, the aggression will be displaced to victims of spontaneous vigilantism or lynchings because they hold less favorable and protected positions in society and are less likely to be able to mete out punishment. Hovland and Sears supported their hypothesis by correlating a general economic index (Ayres) and the price of cotton (per acre), the staple of the southern economy, with the number of lynchings during the years 1882-1930. They reported negative correlations on the order of .6, indicating that as the economy declined or the price of cotton fell, the number of lynchings went up.[25] In addition, those individuals that participated in lynchings were among the poorest white people in their community.[26] As shown previously, spontaneous vigilantism occurs in the poorest areas in New York. It is exactly these people who would be most affected by the economic pinch of the low cotton prices in the early 1900s or the inflation of the 1970s.[27]

In addition to the displaced aggression, direct aggression is also a factor.[28] The majority of the people that meet with lynchings or spontaneous

---

22. S. Milgram and R. Shotland, *Television and Anti-Social Behavior: Field Experiments* (New York: Academic Press, 1973), pp. 23-28.

23. C. Hovland and R. Sears, "Minor Studies of Aggression: VI. Correlation of Lynchings with Economic Indices," *The Journal of Psychology* (1940): 301-10.

24. The ghetto riots occurring in American cities in the 1960s may be an exception. See Leonard Berkowitz, "The Study of Urban Violence: Some Implications of Laboratory Studies of Frustration and Aggression," *The American Behavioral Scientist* 11 (1968): 14-17.

25. Hovland and Sears, "Minor Studies," pp. 301-10. Using a smaller data set Raper reports a correlation of —.53 between the per acre price of cotton and lynching.

26. Raper, *Tragedy*, p. 30.

27. I recognize that there is a high correlation between poverty, crime, and the racial composition of some areas. I am suggesting, however, that each of these factors contributes to an incident of spontaneous vigilantism.

28. Hovland and Sears, "Minor Studies," pp. 301-10.

R. Lance Shotland

TABLE 2

The Economic Condition of Police Precincts in New York City
in Which Vigilante Activity Has Occurred*

Precinct Number	Median Family Income	Rank of Median Family Income of a Total of 71 Precincts	Percentage of Families with Income Less than $4,000	Rank of Percentage of Families with Income Less than $4,000 from a Total of 71 Precincts
7	$6,399	61	27.6	11
26	$7,920	49	17.4	27
28	$5,648	67	31.1	6
30	$7,567	51	20.2	21

*Statistics were prepared by the New York City — Rand Institute and *The New York Times* and reported in D. Burnham, "Precinct Crime Compared with People's Age, Wealth," *New York Times* (July 30, 1973): 1.

vigilantism are wanted for a crime. Criminal activity by its very nature is a frustrating agent. It blocks the goal of a peaceful, safe life by threatening or harming people or their possessions. The individuals that aroused direct aggression also suffered the effects of displaced aggression. This summation of aggression due to frustration is a major factor in producing spontaneous vigilantism.

The venting of frustration by bystanders does not come automatically; rather, a decision is made. Piliavin, Rodin, and Piliavin suggest that bystanders balance benefits and costs in reaching a decision of whether or not to intervene in an emergency.[29] According to the authors, if the benefits outweigh the costs, the bystanders will intervene. It is reasonable then to assume that those individuals in a position to participate in an incident of spontaneous vigilantism also weigh the benefits and costs before embarking on a course of vigilante behavior. The three authors say that the observation of an emergency creates an emotional state on the part of the observer. This state can range from disgust to rage depending upon the circumstances. The more a bystander can empathize with the victim, the more intense this emotional state will be. For example, a woman is more likely to feel rage at the rape of a strange woman than would a man because she could see herself in the raped woman's place. This emotional state can be reduced by leaving the scene, rejecting the incident or victim as not being deserving of help, or intervening in some manner. The person that embarks on a course of vigilante behavior will be aroused by feelings of rage due to the frustration of having his conception of a safe life upset by the actual crime as well as other displaced emotions. This rage would be more acute because of the random nature of the crime and the bystander's similarity to the person being attacked, reminding the bystander that he could as easily have been the victim. The benefits accrued by participating in spontaneous vigilantism are the reduction of this emotional state and the belief that this act will help make the participant and his community safer. Thus, he lowers his anxiety over the crime rate in his community by taking personal action. On the other hand, the costs for a single person would possibly outweigh the benefits. The possibility of being harmed by the alleged criminal or imprisoned for violating the law himself would inhibit his aggression. However, with a group of people the responsibility would be shared equally; potential costs are diminished while the benefits remain about equal. Spontaneous vigilantism is more likely to occur with a number of people than a single person. Hence, the diffusion of responsibility variable operates very much like a double-edged sword. Not only does the diffusion of responsibility operate in such a way as to inhibit helping because no one bystander feels totally responsible for the fate of the victim, but it also operates so that a person in a group will take more risks and be more likely to

29. I. Piliavin, J. Rodin and J. Piliavin, "Good Samaritanism: An Underground Phenomenon?" *Journal of Personality and Social Psychology* 13 (1969): 289-99.

do injury to another because the possibility of his being held responsible is lowered.

In summary, spontaneous vigilantism as a response to a criminal act may be expected when the following conditions exist:

(1) After a crime has been committed or a rumor exists indicating that a crime has been committed.

   (a) Where the interpretation of the incident is unambiguous and clear.

   (b) Where the opinion of the bystanders or community is unanimous concerning the blame for the crime.

(2) In high-crime areas where crime may be expected to be of special concern to the residents.

(3) Within ethnic areas where people can develop a sense of empathy for one another.

(4) In areas where the population feels that the legal process is inadequate in dealing with the crime problem.

(5) In poverty areas where conditions of goal-blocking or frustration exist.

Chapter Three

The Vigilante Personality

William P. Kreml

What makes a vigilante? Is there one specific type of personality, or are there several types who are prone to join in vigilante activities? It is obviously impossible to define a particular personality who is certain to become a vigilante. We may, however, be able to delineate various predispositions which, when combined with favorable catalytic social and political variables, compel some individuals to participate in vigilante behavior.

This chapter will deal primarily with people who are already engaging in vigilante activities. An attempt will be made to identify the innate personality characteristics of these individuals, taking note of such factors as their location within the sociocultural milieu and of the racial or ethnic makeup of the vigilante groups to which they belong. These social phenomena will be discussed with the view of determining how these variables interact with certain personality characteristics to promote vigilante behavior.

Essentially, our investigation will be divided into four categories: two of these are psychological, one is social-psychological, and the fourth is probably best described as interpersonal in that it seeks to define the essence of certain psychological linkages that are useful to the vigilante in his activities. The true vigilante, even more than most goal-oriented personalities, lives in a state of some permanent psychological tension. His behavior is not fully understood until the larger context of his tension, including his relationships with other members of his culture, is fully explored. Like the rest of us, the vigilante is a purposive being; and though his purposes may sometimes shock us, they are designed by him, either consciously or unconsciously, to fall within a context of acceptability, as defined by those from whom he takes his standards.

We shall begin with the basic question of personality. Imagine first a simple matrix of vertical and horizontal variables to outline the types of psychological traits with which we are dealing. Roger Brown differentiates between two kinds of traits: construct and stylistic.[1] The construct variables, which are the horizontal part of our matrix, indicate what a person believes, i.e., whether his political orientation is right or left. The vertical concept, although not necessarily in a purely orthogonal relationship with the structural variables, are the style variables. This latter category includes personality traits which determine the way a person holds his particular views. For example, there are psychological variables such as intensity, rigidity, and intolerance of ambiguity which do not actually have anything to do with the ideological stance of particular political beliefs, but they give a distinctively qualitative hue to an individual's opinions. While all psychopolitical analysis should include both construct and stylistic elements, a dual approach of this kind is particularly relevant to the vigilante personality (if we may use that term) since a constructural orientation is never adequate, in and of itself, to explain vigilante activity.

We shall look first at the construct variables to see where the vigilante stands in terms of his ideological political orientation. In doing so, we should keep in mind that we will eventually examine violent activity as it relates to the analysis of vigilante behavior. But at this point we will concern ourselves only with the structural psychological variables which can lead someone to believe in conservative political attitudes. These attitudes are located in a place on the ideological continuum where there is a confluence of delineated beliefs of the community. In the same vein, we should keep in mind that the element of violence itself does not necessarily have a relationship with any specific portion of the ideological continuum. As a practical matter, we might agree that somewhat less violence stems from the center of the political spectrum; but we will not attempt to distinguish between the propensity for violence on the part of the right as opposed to the left.

Putting the question of violence aside, we should mention a significant intellectual conflict within the psychopolitical literature before we begin to identify the psychological correlates of vigilante behavior. The human personality is a subtle and complex thing; its study within a political context, thanks to the writings of such pioneers as Harold Lasswell, has only recently become respectable. The issues surrounding the strength of the link between psychological variables, political attitudes, and political behavior, are very much in dispute, as is so often true of the fundamentals of a young subdiscipline. Academics debate among themselves as to how much we understand of the psychopolitical relationship. More significantly, we have been arguing for some time the degree to which individuals within the greater populace exhibit ideological consistency in their political attitudes and behavior. Within the narrow arena of political science, two schools of thought have been in contest over the degree of "rationality" that the common citizen is adjudged to exercise in even such simple matters as voting.

1. Roger H. Brown, *Social Psychology* (New York: The Free Press, 1965), chapter 10.

A group which we shall call the "Michigan" school, consisting largely of such people as the authors of *The American Voter,* maintains that the overwhelming majority of United States citizens do not come to their political attitudes by way of a rational ideological conviction based on closely held personal values.[2] For those who uphold this position, political attitudes are best understood as the result of a wide range of demographic variables, such as Social-Economic Status (SES), ethnic background, region, religion, and the like. These variables, the argument goes, affect the behavior of such a large percentage of the populace that only a few of the very best educated and most aware citizens are capable of achieving a value-oriented congruity between ideological values and political selection of candidate, party, or issue position. Naturally, the psychological correlate of such thinking would be a Stimulus/Response, rather than a Stimulus-Organism-Response psychological model, emphasizing the importance of social, historical, and other external-to-psyche variables, rather than any innate personality traits. Just as naturally, the defenders of this position would argue, the structural psychological variables—those most important in determining political ideology—have little effect on most people's politics.

Yet, even within the framework of political science research, a competing, so-called "Ivy League" school argues that the political ideology of a greater portion of the citizenry is determined in a rational and relatively consistent manner. What this means, of course, is that the structural psychological variables are operating in greater strength than the "Michigan" school would like to admit. The challengers offer stronger support for the S-O-R approach to psychological analysis, because they are essentially arguing that, in spite of the importance of social and environmental influences on the political actor, significant internal factors still remain as crucial determinants of political attitudes. For this school, the personality serves not only as a significant factor in engendering political values, but also as an important screening device, through mechanisms such as selective perception, so that data from the real world are viewed only in light of already well-entrenched personality variables. Advocates of this way of thinking about psychological determinism include Robert Lane of Yale and the late V. O. Key of Harvard. Lane, in his major work, *Political Ideology,* analyzes the political attitudes of a number of middle- to lower-middle-income workers and finds that, although the articulation of political attitudes may be fuzzy and their full comprehension less than perfect, the conscious or unconscious relationship of personality and attitude is a very real phenomenon.[3]

V. O. Key, in his book *The Responsible Electorate,* also takes exception to the "Michigan" school's assumption of value insignificance.[4] He demonstrates that among persons changing their political party allegiance, those who

2. Angus Campbell, et al., *The American Voter* (New York: John Wiley, 1964).
3. Robert Lane, *Political Ideology* (New York: The Free Press, 1962).
4. V. O. Key, *The Responsible Electorate* (Cambridge: Harvard University Press, 1966).

48   *William P. Kreml*

moved to a voting preference more in congruence with their overall values greatly outnumbered those whose shifts in voting patterns moved them farther away from their underlying personal values.

In short, the position of the "Ivy League" contributors is that ideologically oriented values have an impact on people's political orientation and that some relatively static personality variables make a difference, whether consciously or unconsciously, in the political orientations of a significant portion of the population.

We would like to know which of these two views is more valid; for in the study of vigilantism, we need to determine whether or not the basic personality traits that are the seedbed for vigilante activity are either found within some members of all societies or are present only in a very few who have unique psychopolitical orientations. To find this out, and to help us resolve the dispute between the "Michigan" and "Ivy League" positions as to the importance of ideological value congruity, let us begin to examine the kinds of personality traits that seem to show up in the activities of the vigilante. Once we are aware of the crucial personality variables, we may be able to separate the relatively constant variables which carry a predisposition for vigilantism from other variables which may need substantial external reinforcement in order to contribute to vigilante behavior.

CONSTRUCT VARIABLES

In the broad sense of the term, the vigilante is a man of authoritarian personality characteristics. The seminal work on this subject, *The Authoritarian Personality,* is unfortunately marred by methodological and other problems; yet it stands in spite of these as one of the greatest theoretical contributions to the literature of psychology and politics.[5] The major conceptual flaw in the book is its inability to differentiate between structural and stylistic personality variables. Such famous measures as the F (Fascism), PEC (Political and Economic Conservatism), and E (Ethnocentrism) scales stand as combinations of exclusively right-of-center characteristics and other traits which might be found anywhere on the psychopolitical continuum, although probably closer to one extreme or the other.

Four substantive personality traits appear to form the core of those characteristics which correlate with right-of-center political attitudes. The first is a positive feeling toward the concept as well as the exercise of power. The conservative psychopolitical type seems to welcome the direction which comes from higher authorities, while at the same time expecting deferential treatment from those beneath him on some salient ordering of status or rank. The significance of this variable is not the objective existence of such rankings within the society, but the importance that the conservative personality

5. T. W. Adorno, et al., *The Authoritarian Personality* (New York: Harper and Sons, 1950).

attaches to them for his own sense of well-being. In his writings about vigilantes in America, Richard Maxwell Brown stresses the importance of social class and "levels" of a stable society.[6] Yet, Brown is not really drawing our attention to an exclusively sociological or economic phenomenon. Status alone is not enough, for the vigilante must be one who regards the maintenance of appropriate ranking and membership within those levels as necessary to a stable society. Respect must be paid, and people who receive the adverse attention of the vigilante appear to challenge the existing power relationships.

The literature of vigilantism contains numerous prominent references to maintaining established power relationships. In any society, but particularly in one that is undergoing fundamental change, the challenge of new groups or movements frequently leads to vigilante activity. Although newer groups may be concerned primarily with the fulfillment of their own goals, without regard to the effect of their activities on established centers of power, the normal use of social and political power inevitably necessitates a competition between the groups and the prerogatives of establishment units. Thus, Brown writes about American vigilante history as a chronicle of responses to the challenges made against powerful groups. Much nineteenth-century vigilante activity, for example, was directed toward the labor movement; in fact, the origin of the National Guard in some states was largely an effort to curb the unions.[7]

Private detective agencies such as the Pinkertons were part of the same kind of response. In addition, corporate police served to harass and intimidate those who wished to upset the power of the industrial barons. During the Civil War, guerrilla and vigilante bands engaged in a series of low-level, often vicious battles around the fringes of the Confederacy. These confrontations were often a spin-off of vigilante activity within the Confederacy which attempted to suppress slave uprisings and the various strategies to promote the escape of slaves via the underground railroad.

In essence, throughout the history of the vigilante movement, the power of the established forces has been used in order to maintain the rank and privileges of an elite group. The psychological predisposition to utilize power is very much in keeping with the actual need to suppress those who are challenging the status of the elite. A position of social and political power is maintained in great part because of the psychological ease with which power relationships are made understandable and are enforced by the power-oriented personality.

The second structural variable is one of order. The term "law and order" is frequently used by vigilantes as well as by legitimate conservative groups. Law, properly understood, provides its own kind of order—an order which

6. Richard Maxwell Brown, "The American Vigilante Tradition," in Hugh Graham and Ted Gurr, eds., *The History of Violence in America* (New York: Bantam Books, 1969), pp. 168-70.
7. Brown, "Historical Patterns of Violence in America," in Graham and Gurr, Ibid., pp. 60-67.

does not confuse a particular ideology with its enforcement. But for the ideologically oriented personality, something more than that relatively pure philosophy of law is implied. The word "order" within the expression "law and order" is largely a psychological term, since it implies a particular bias on the part of a conservative personality in favor of a society that tolerates few disrupting variables.

To be sure, the vigilante leader is often established in a community business or trade. Thus, he may well have utilitarian reasons for favoring the enforcement of stability. In part, we could classify those reasons as cognitive rather than affective in their true origins. But the desire to go into a stability oriented enterprise, as well as the confluence of the ordered personality's needs with an already existing business need for stability, would only heighten the importance of the order variable.

The early American vigilante tradition, which was carried over into latter-day western American violence, was often directed toward the criminal activities of a variety of bands ranging from common robbers to horsethieves.[8] The economic loss from these adventures was obviously a rational incentive for the formation of vigilante groups. There was a psychological reason as well which Brown refers to in his discussion of certain vigilante groups. In large part, he argues, vigilante activity came as a response to the growing influence of the brigands on the values of the community. In many instances, fear that the younger members of the community would be recruited, if not directly into the outlaw groups at least into an attitude of tolerance for their disreputable way of life, struck hard at the older generations which had firmly established their economic domains, and their community norms.

Clearly, the outlaws were not solely plunderers of wealth. They represented also a challenge to the hard work, thrift, and family life which, of course, strengthened the order of the community. Much vigilante activity occurred in undeveloped, newly settled, or devastated areas of the United States. The insecurities of the conservative personality that felt the need for order were heightened by the difficulties in coping with the social vagaries of such a situation. The South Carolina Regulators, America's first true vigilante movement, were prominent in the wake of the Cherokee Indian War. After that war, much of upland South Carolina lay in ruin, with families broken up and entire communities in disarray.[9] Orphaned adolescents and other socially unlinked individuals formed gangs and engaged in random crime and violence against other citizens. The Regulators succeeded in bringing order to the territory within two years, but their own activities became so odious that the South Carolina Moderators, an anti-vigilante force, sprang up shortly thereafter to quell the Regulators' excesses.

8. Ibid., p. 67.
9. Brown, "The American Vigilante Tradition," in Graham and Gurr, *History of Violence,* p. 158.

A socially unsettled situation was a primary cause of the San Francisco vigilante movement as well. That old and cosmopolitan city was suddenly overrun by a mixture of new residents, including gold rush people and recent American immigrants of Irish and other "undesirable" origins. The virulent vigilante movement which followed, frankly political in its attempts to forestall the rising influence of the new San Franciscans, strove unabashedly for the "reestablishment of the old community structure and its values."[10]

Because the American frontier presented such a wide stage for the formation of new societies, vigilantism found a series of opportunities for action in the wake of newly settled communities. Most Americans who moved westward carried with them their conventional notions of a stable society. They expected to find new economic opportunity well within the confines of their old morality. But their success was confounded by the fact that not all westward-moving Americans were of the same morality. Some were eastern outlaws and malcontents whose activities were soon to jeopardize the dream of the western pioneer. The result of this conflict was that many of the new communities across the Appalachians were forced to undergo a painful reinstitutionalization of an old order. The conventionalities of the former home had to be actively reestablished, and the frequent lack of regular law-enforcement agencies in these new and far-flung territories prompted vigilante action as a service to make the new home a fit place in which to live. Amusingly, the dedication to the "order" in "law and order" was such that virtually all vigilante organizations concluded their attention toward a horsethief or cattle rustler with an appropriate trial, including attorneys for the defendant. The psychological and political commitment to order was to be carried straight through to the throwing of the noose over the strongest limb of the strongest tree!

The third structural variable coincident with conservative political orientations is the rejection of impulse. The conservative personality, like any other, has a degree of natural impulsiveness, a need to express certain psychological or even physiological drives. But the conservative personality handles these impulses differently from other members of the society. His impulses trouble the conservative; therefore, he seeks to control them so that they will never embarrass him.

But the conservative personality is not only concerned with his own conduct; he is also very aware of the conduct of others. Allegedly, the rationale for his concern is that the community needs to have a decorum and regularity in its procedures. Thus, sobriety and nonimpulsiveness must be required of each citizen. His reasons for such an attitude may be little more than those which stem from a psychological motivation, however. At least in part, the conservative personality is responding to his own psychic needs when

10. Ibid., p. 167.

he wishes to suppress the avenues of impulsive behavior within his community. He directs his attention toward such matters as the "corruption of youth" or "the maintenance of community standards" in terms of personal conduct. Yet what he is really doing is attempting to ensure that those temptations do not successfully invade his own conduct.

Thus, the effort to crush any behavior in the community which appears to be morally libertine is in great part an attempt to suppress such impulses within the conservative's own individual psyche. Vigilantism, though violent and emotional as well, may be rationalized by the conservative personality as an acceptable outlet for impulse, and one which is ultimately orderly in its result. Some psychologists talk about a rationalization of this kind in terms of the unintegrated psyche, i.e., a collection of traits and needs which are not resolved into a unified whole. Regardless of whether this kind of analysis is used, the conservative personality, potentially a vigilante when certain other requirements are met, is not willing to accept the disturbing implusiveness of his own personality or of the society in which he lives.

Quite apart from the necessity for order in an unsettled environment, the need to restrict impulse is often found in a more mature society where the possibilities of leisure time may lead some members of the community toward more self-indulgent standards of conduct. To combat this temptation, organizations standing as models for righteous conduct and as sources of manpower are needed to snuff out the opportunities for immoral behavior. Associations such as the Masons used to perform this dual function, holding up a standard of moral conduct for the community, while castigating such groups as the Jews and Catholics on the grounds that the latters' morality was both inferior and threatening to the Protestant culture.[11]

Interestingly, the object of the established hatred can be such that the need for purging the impulses created by certain "outgroups" may even attract members of the outgroups themselves. The San Francisco vigilantes, who were avowedly anti-labor in their attitudes, actually had several laborers among their membership. The Nazi movement, which in many ways had tremendous psychological undertones, incredibly had Jewish members in its early history. The motivation for membership in what would rationally appear to be such an inhospitable association can only be explained in psychological terms. Clearly, the extreme right was appealing to the psychological need for cleansing which comes from suppressing feared impulses. Hitler's appeal resulted in part from his rejection of the new psychology of people such as Freud who had insisted that man was possessed of impulses hidden deeply within his psyche. These impulses had to be denied. Whether it is in an older community going through great change or in a new community whose conservative leaders feel the need to establish the boundaries of permissive behavior, established authority will find that a more

11. Ibid., p. 170.

peaceful order ensues if they suppress the kind of behavior that gives vent to impulses. Once again, impulse is disturbing to the conservative mind; and those elements of the society who permit its expression will be looked upon as potentially dangerous to community morality.

The fourth significant personality trait linked to a conservative political bearing is "anti-introspectiveness." In one sense this is closely related to the repression of impulse, except that anti-introspectiveness covers a full range of internal, sensual feelings. As the conservative personality is unwilling to face his impulses, so, too, he avoids looking at whatever other internal feelings he may have, whether they be as harmless as simple tenderness or as potentially dangerous as extreme anger.

The distinction between the anti-introspective trait and the anti-impulse trait is more than a difference in the inclusion of all relevant internal feelings, however. The anti-impulse trait is directed primarily at internal control—a stifling, if you will, of what is viewed as potentially shameful conduct. The anti-introspective trait is not concerned primarily with control, or even with conduct. It is possibly the most subtle of the four variables, because ultimately it is a fear of the very existence of the individual's own internal self. People who manifest this trait try to take their life's cues from the outside rather than from within themselves; and they wish these external cues to be clear enough and loud enough for the message to ring through and dominate the inner psyche.

Such people, of course, are not contemplative in their own lifestyles. They tend to be individuals of action rather than thought, and are often suspicious of those who seem to lead more leisurely and thoughtful lives. In some ways, their contempt for the contemplative, or less achievement-oriented, individual is both tragic and understandable, for the anti-introspective personality really does not comprehend what the introspective person is doing during those periods of seeming idleness. As the anti-introspective personality is unable to generate internal cues, he must occupy his time with the busy activities of his external life. Naturally, he tends to be what we know as "a man of affairs." Therefore, he is not only psychologically ready to be contemptuous of the contemplative citizen, but he probably has a substantial economic stake in the community which he feels he must protect—even if the method of that protection includes vigilante behavior.

Once again, Richard Brown's analysis of people who have participated in vigilante activity reveals that the nonintrospective personality frequently gravitates toward vigilante behavior.[12] The man of affairs is often like William Tell Coleman, who moved to San Francisco and became a successful importer. When the new citizens of San Francisco threatened him, he was able to organize an expeditious vigilante means of dealing with their intrusions. Another example is Wilbur Fisk Sanders, the prosecuting attorney in

12. Ibid., p. 176.

Montana who dealt vigorously with dissident groups both through and outside the law. Sanders was a man of action and purpose who, once he had established the importance of the predominant social values, went on to become a founder of the Montana Bar Association and one of Montana's original United States Senators.

These examples are not cited to suggest that all men of action and achievement are susceptible to vigilante behavior. But it seems obvious that the vigilante, and particularly the vigilante leader, is often a man in a hurry, who does not wish to be troubled by such ponderous considerations as weighing civil liberties against the security and values of the community.

Interestingly, the attitude toward the life of reflection versus that toward the life of expeditious affairs is well-demonstrated in the method by which vigilante justice is handed out. When functioning properly, the wheels of justice inevitably cost the community a great deal of money. Courts, jails, prosecutors, and law-enforcement people all need to be paid for, and a new community, particularly one under the leadership of aggressive men of affairs, often prefers what is both a cheaper and a psychologically easier method of dealing out justice. Vigilantes have always been prepared not only to apprehend their victims quickly, but also to convict and execute them with little investment of money or time.

In concluding our discussion of the structural psychological variables, let us attempt to focus more clearly on why these variables are the backbone of a discussion on the personality of the vigilante. Clearly, the burden of this chapter is to demonstrate that the tendency toward vigilante activity is not randomly distributed within the population as a whole. Citizens who hold conservative political views are more likely to engage in vigilante behavior; and it has been our task to try to understand what kinds of personality factors enter into this basic value orientation.

We are concerned at the same time with the nature, whether real or perceived, of the elements in society toward which the vigilante directs his anger. We should like to know, in other words, whether the vector of vigilante hostility is psychologically focused not only at its origin, but also at its object. If, in fact, the clarity of focus is significant at both ends of the continuum, this provides additional evidence validating the importance of ideology in vigilante behavior. The next step, then, is to find out whether the personality traits of order, power, anti-impulsiveness, and anti-introspection lead to attitudes that direct themselves against predictable objects of opposition.

Thomas Dimsdale, in his work on the vigilante movement of Montana, describes the objects of vigilante activity as members of the community who were ". . . low, brutal, cruel, lazy, ignorant, insolent, sensual, blasphemous miscreants. . . ."[13] This is an interesting series of adjectives which should be

---

13. Thomas Dimsdale, *Vigilantes of Montana* (Virginia City, 1866), p. 116.

examined on at least two dimensions. The first is exemplified by words which evidence a kind of vertical direction, a matter of status, rank, or achievement. Richard Brown stresses class divisions in a society, asserting that the maintenance of the society is dependent, at least from the point of view of the vigilante, on the maintenance of these divisions. The adjectives "low" and "ignorant" clearly belong to that category of status orientation, while "brutal" and "cruel" are more hazy; the latter could apply across a range of dimensions—whether status, ideological, or something else.

Dimsdale's five remaining terms are of a different nature altogether. If someone is "lazy," "insolent," "sensual," "blasphemous," or a "miscreant," these traits cannot be viewed as a kind of status differentiation. A more value-laden kind of definition for these terms is required. The lazy or insolent in times of rampant vigilante activity were people who, consciously or unconsciously, were perceived as rejecting the Protestant ethic of diligent work and serious attention to the parsimony of life. Those suspected of having a sensual view of life were also discordant elements in the eyes of vigilantes. Lustiness on the frontier may have been acceptable when it was expressed in the proper framework of a rough and ready society surviving on the fringes of civilization. In fact, much of Western vigilantism would hardly have disapproved of such macho-style sexual attitudes. But the term sensuality is both broader and deeper than manly sex alone would imply. It suggests not only a fuller range of human sensitivity, but also a kind of internal communing with matters of artistic or human creativity and warmth. Such feelings, usually enjoyed by someone who is of a contemplative and receptive temperament, are beyond the range of understanding of a vigilante. Finally, Dimsdale uses the two terms "blasphemous" and "miscreants," seemingly to condemn those who are disloyal to the community orthodoxy.

Throughout his discussion of the vigilantes, Richard Brown seems to want to place the burden of understanding on a socio-economic footing; but at one point in his own analysis he mentions the importance of the various anti-vigilante movements that often responded when vigilante behavior became overly zealous. We might expect the core of these anti-vigilante groups to have come from the lower classes, against whom the vigilantes often wrought their havoc. But this does not seem to be the case. Brown himself notes that "[r]espectable men did not join the anti-vigilante coalition because of any great sympathy for the outlaws and lower people."[14] In some cases, the opposition may have been the result of family feuding, but it frequently ran along the lines of partisan political advantage. It was not unusual, Brown notes, to find that "if the leading Democrats were among the vigilantes, the anti-vigilante faction would probably attract the local Whigs."[15] He lists the

14. Brown, "The American Vigilante Tradition," in Graham and Gurr, *History of Violence*, p. 186.
15. Ibid.

56   *William P. Kreml*

Southwest Missouri Slicker conflict between Whigs and Democrats, the Southern Illinois Regulator-Flathead Struggle, in which party identification labelled the "in" and "out" factions of county governments, and the Shelby County, Texas, fight between the different political groupings that preceded and succeeded the Texas Revolution as outstanding examples of social value, rather than economic class, differences in vigilante activity.[16]

In conclusion, then, we can say that, although much of the literature on the vigilante concerns matters which appear on the surface to be economically and even socially stratified, a substantial share of vigilante behavior is indeed value oriented. Our explanation of the structural psychological variable has hopefully been explained in such a way as to underline the importance of value ideology in the study of vigilantism. The personality linkage along the ideological continuum, although a long way from explaining the full range of psychological motivation for vigilante behavior, should lay a groundwork for our understanding of both the personality linkage with value ideology and the sometimes ideological nature of vigilante and even anti-vigilante behavior. We have argued that vigilantes are usually not only people of predictable psychological traits and attitudes, but that their behavior is often directed toward the kinds of opposing behavior and attitudes which we could predict to be natural enemies of the vigilante temperament.

STYLE VARIABLES

We turn now to a different set of concepts that will help us understand better the essence of vigilante behavior. In the final analysis, we cannot be content solely with determining the ideological predispositions toward vigilantism. Very few conservative personalities ever actually engage in vigilante activity, and although understanding the psychological basis for an ideological confluence of conservativism and vigilante behavior is a necessary first step for vigilante analysis, it is hardly a sufficient explanation for something as complex in its origins as establishment violence often is.

Having laid an ideological groundwork for our study, we must now try to find factors which provide an activating agent or catalyst for vigilante activity. We are searching for something which gives an intensity or urgency to a mere ideological position; for without this no political movement—no matter how firmly based in ideological certainty—can ever flower.

To find these activators and signs of intensity, we must look to a different set of psychological variables. Brown calls them "style variables;" he suggests that they are principally concerned with *how* a person holds his views. These style variables are divorced from the structural variables by definition, in that they are specifically concerned not with the ideological basis of beliefs, but with the tone with which people surround their beliefs.

16. Ibid., p. 213.

The primary stylistic variable tells us how tolerant the individual is toward attitudes different from his own. All of us hold certain attitudes; and no matter where the mean of our beliefs may fall on a particular ideological continuum, we must recognize that certain persons are better able to tolerate a broad range of views. Milton Rokeach refers to the closed mind as one with an excess of dogmatism, dogmatism being defined as a quality of resistance to change of opinion about a particular system of beliefs.[17] Rigidity, another variable that Rokeach examines, is again a quality of resistance to change, but in this case resistance to a single belief.

Rokeach has developed "Dogmatism" and "Opinionation" scales to test the openness or closedness of particular belief systems.[18] The dogmatism scale contains almost no political items, but tests instead for the following: attitudes that demonstrate the degrees of differentiation between belief and disbelief systems; those that show the isolation within and between belief and disbelief systems; and other attitudes which demonstrate the relationship between favorable and unfavorable beliefs. The purpose of these items, of course, is to show that the closed mind has a significantly less tolerant attitude toward beliefs not held than does the open mind.

With the truth of this hypothesis largely confirmed, Rokeach turns his attention to determining whether the variable of open-mindedness versus closed-mindedness is in any way related to the left versus right political continuum. He finds that, in areas where ideology is significantly understood, scores of right opinionation are inversely related to scores of left opinionation. Although there may be somewhat greater stylistic intolerance on either the right or the left, it is at least reasonably certain that the stylistic qualities of dogmatism and opinionation are empirically, as well as theoretically, independent kinds of psychological variables.

The question as to whether or not the stylistic variables are truly free of any ideological contamination has probably been best addressed by Hans Eysenck.[19] His interpretation of a number of tests containing both structural and stylistic variables shows that the two variables are, as an actual matter and not simply as a matter of definition, in an orthogonal relationship to each other. Dismissing such possibilities as a *J*-configuration of structural and stylistic variables, Eysenck opts for a *U*-configuration, stressing that both sides of the political continuum are equally prone to having what he calls tough-minded stylistic variables on their side.[20] Eysenck adds to our understanding the fact that, as we move away from the political center, the possibility of the stylistic variables appearing in individual cases increases greatly. In other words, the farther away from the center an individual may be,

---

17. Milton Rokeach, *The Open and Closed Mind* (New York: Basic Books, 1960).
18. Ibid., chapter 4.
19. Hans J. Eysenck, *The Psychology of Politics* (London: Routledge, Kegan Paul, 1954).
20. Ibid., p. 111.

the better the chance that he suffers from the stylistic rigidities which Rokeach subsequently discusses in his work.

Secondly, Eysenck is perceptive in noting that the kinds of stylistic intolerances which Rokeach later explored led the people involved toward a position of high stress, as well as high intensity, in the holding of these views. There was, in short, for the more ideologically oriented personalities, a greater tendency to be rigid, intolerant, and, in fact, even hostile in their attitudes toward other persons. Clearly, then, particularly for those whose ideological position may be somewhat removed from the center, the stylistic variables are very important for our understanding of personality types.[21]

Now that we have identified the structural and the stylistic personality variables, and hopefully placed them in their proper relationship to each other, we shall attempt to answer one of the questions asked earlier. At that time we dealt with the so-called "Michigan" model which repudiates the importance of ideology in the political attitudes of all but a few highly aware citizens, and we explained the essence of the "Ivy League" model of Lane and Key which claims that persons engage in rational political contemplation and decision-making. Their debate has gone on for some time, and although we will not be able to resolve it definitely here, some recent evidence may at least tell us of the constancy of the structural and stylistic variables in the human population. Our question is to what degree certain variables are the result of recurring personality traits that appear throughout the generations. If we can identify these more or less permanent traits, then there is some evidence at least for saying that certain ideological strains run throughout the population, and that, for some portion of the population at least, there will be a rather clear correlation between personality traits and political identifications.

We need to know what kinds of personality traits, particularly as they reflect structural or stylistic variables, may in fact run through different generations and which show some constancy of political orientation. Let us look at two relatively recent pieces of evidence to see if they tell us something about the inheritability of personality traits and the relative permanence of the psychological catalyst toward particular political views.

The first, an article by psychologist Raymond F. Cattell, gives some clue to the idea that our so-called structural variables are more susceptible to hereditary influence than are stylistic variables.[22] Using factor analysis in interviews on 100 test responses, Cattell found that many of the classical theoretical notions of personality were being confirmed. For example, Carl Jung's notion of extroversion/introversion paralleled a three-part factor which came down to a distinction between being (1) aloof versus warm, (2) shy versus venturesome, or (3) practical versus imaginative. Cattell found, too, that a number of other personality traits were significantly determined by

---

21. Ibid., Chapter 6.
22. Raymond Cattell, "Personality Pinned Down," *Psychology Today* (July 1973): 40-46.

heredity rather than by childhood socialization. Generally, these latter traits reflected the kind of dichotomies that we recognize as relevant to ideological considerations.

Cattell's highlighting of extroversion/introversion as a principal trait that appears to be largely inherited is complemented by the work of Irving I. Gottesman.[23] The latter, in reflecting upon the writings of Kasson and Pool and the conclusions of Eysenck, finds that social introversion versus extroversion has often occurred as the most important variable in hereditary psychological analyses. Gottesman's own work was with monozygotic (identical) and dyzygotic (nonidentical) twins. Interestingly, he found that the extroversion/introversion trait was the one most subject to inheritability. Although there is undoubtedly a need for more research, there is now at least a creditable amount of evidence to the effect that the structural variables seem to have greater intergenerational permanence. Thus, we can expect to find—to the extent that psychological variables account for their share of the variance in political attitudes—that the left versus right political dichotomy will continue to exist in similar relative proportions throughout a population. It appears also that the stylistic traits of rigidity, dogmatism, anxiety, intolerance of ambiguity, and other more or less tension-oriented variables that describe *how* we hold our political views are less subject to innate and inheritable causes; thus they are more open to influence from socialization and environment.

This means that the fundamental psychological requirement for vigilante allegiance and behavior—i.e., the personality traits that underlie the predisposition to defend, control, regulate, or mold a particular political community into a conventional well-ordered society—are an inheritable part of the psychological makeup of a certain relatively stable portion of the population. This new information also tells us, however, that the stylistic traits that lead a person to develop the kind of intensity of feeling sufficient to make him decide to engage in vigilante behavior in defense of the conventional community come from some socially created variables which interact with the psyche and thus give full impetus to vigilantism. Early childhood socialization is a well-recognized variable that has an effect on the psyches of all of us. An insecure childhood, where love is conditional, or the atmosphere is tense, or other insecurities abound, is a catalyst to the kind of tension-filled state of mind that, in turn, causes stylistic rigidities in the political attitudes of both conservative and radical personalities. Put another way, the *U*-configuration of Eysenck can be conceptually represented as either a flat *U*, with few stylistic intensities to sharpen the edges of ideological opinion, or it can be a steep *U*, with many stylistic difficulties compounding the results of the ideological beliefs, particularly at the extremes of the continuum.

23. Irving I. Gottesman, "Heretability of Personality," in Daniel N. Robinson, ed., *Heredity and Achievement* (New York: Oxford University Press, 1970), pp. 171-220.

William P. Kreml

TWO ADDITIONAL CATALYSTS

In the final section of this chapter, we shall examine briefly two additional catalysts. Both are functions of the community in which the mature adult finds himself, and both contribute to the tendency to engage in vigilante behavior. We are, in fact, looking for some other-than-psychological variables that add to the insecurities of those who would restore or create a conservative community. The effect of these insecurities is felt largely on the intensity side of our analysis, deepening the frustration of the conservative elements of the population. These variables mean, in short, that certain social or political crises are particularly prone to be catalysts for psychological intensity, especially when they are matched with the structural variables of psychological conservatism and the socialization-type stylistic psychological variables that have already cast the blanket of tension over the potential vigilante personality.

The first of these catalysts is a simple concept known as status insecurity. As stated earlier, particularly in relation to western American vigilantism, the vigilante-prone community is an unsettled place. But the community need not be unsettled solely because of a sudden disruption caused by an Indian war or a new immigration of "undesirable" types. The mere appearance of alleged undesirables in a stable community may be a source of some irritation to established leaders; but an unstable leadership in an already unsettled or unstable community will probably harbor a much more severe attitude toward the disparate elements.

The sociological and psychological literature is filled with studies about the insecurities of the newly won status holder. When the urgencies of this sociological condition are paired with the psychological intensity that comes from the achievement-oriented personality, we can see how severe the anxieties of a new elite can be. We must remind ourselves that, particularly in the newer communities of a place like the American West, the achievers were often from families that had not enjoyed social status back in the East.[24] William Tell Coleman's father had died bankrupt in Kentucky, yet Coleman was a rather recent, but enormously successful merchant in his new home of San Francisco. Wilbur Fisk Sanders was a young, newly arrived inhabitant of Montana, taking up his position of leadership in the Montana vigilante movement at about the same time that he conveniently became the state's prosecuting attorney.

American history provides many prominent names within its vigilante ranks. Both Andrew Jackson and Theodore Roosevelt were on the fringes of vigilante movements in their youths. Leland Stanford, Sr., builder of western railroads, was a member of the San Francisco vigilantes; and several newly

---

24. Brown, "The American Vigilante Tradition," in Graham and Gurr, *History of Violence*, p. 177.

prominent western Senators and other politicians dabbled in vigilante movements in their early lives.[25]

An interesting thread runs through numbers of these vigilante affiliations. Upon investigation, many turn out to be the affiliations of newly rich, newly prominent members of communities who were deeply attached to the new leadership structures that they themselves were developing. The fear of losing recently acquired money and status is always very ripe in the minds of the achiever; and the intensity with which he has worked to achieve his position rarely abates after he has succeeded in his efforts. The achiever still works hard, fiercely protecting what he has recently won. Thus, he is very willing, as well as very much in a position, to organize vigilante movements that attempt to assuage the very status insecurity that his newly won achievement has given to him.[26]

If we have now identified the reason why so much of the leadership of new vigilante organizations corresponds to that of new and unsettled communities, we still need to look at one more catalytic variable in order to determine who follows this kind of leadership. In the law of anti-trust regulation, there is a principle known as conscious parallelism. This denotes a state of corresponding mental attitudes which are not the result of active communication between the parties. Vigilante movements were nearly always short-lived creations, and the organizational rigors of such collections of the citizenry were not very strict. Although the object of contempt was usually clear in the minds of all who participated, the recruitment of subordinate vigilantes and even the planning of particular vigilante activities was often accomplished without the operation of strict lines of authority.

On the surface, this would seem contrary to what we know about right-wing organizations, most of which have strict lines of authority and clear understandings of who their leaders are. But we must remember that the vigilante organization is an outlaw creation, and that even though the line between legal and illegal activities can be blurred very easily within small communities, most vigilante organizations, and particularly vigilante leadership, prefer to remain anonymous in terms of details of membership and extent of operations. Hopefully, the accountability of the leadership is obscured. The best means of ensuring this is to see to it that orders for specific vigilante actions are never given directly, but are simply understood by a process which approximates conscious parallelism.

Not only should communication between leader and follower be concealed; but the lines between the vigilante group and the civil establishment should be hidden as well. Some American vigilante movements have been quite successful at this. The Ku Klux Klan, known as the "invisible Empire," was

25. Ibid., p. 192.
26. Seymour Martin Lipset, *Social Mobility in Industrial Society* (Berkeley and Los Angeles: University of California Press, 1959), pp. 245-46.

62   *William P. Kreml*

specifically created as a secret society, not only to disguise the low membership from which it often suffered, but also to safeguard the membership of certain people in the community.[27] It was always vaguely apparent that police and other law enforcement agencies were either employing Klan members, or that the local sheriff, for example, was working in a kind of tacit agreement with the Klan. Throughout the South, the distinction between the Klan and local leadership was frequently obscured, and anti-Klan groups were often left complaining of instances where they were unable to receive protection either from the police or from an intimidated citizenry.[28]

Even with the original Klan, the lines of communication between a reasonably reputable leader such as Bedford Forrest and his followers could not be maintained. Forrest himself disbanded the Klan in 1869; but the lawlessness which the appeal to Southern restoration had made continued on without his organization.[29]

Occasionally, outright support for the Klan issued from political leadership. The chief of police in Richmond, Virginia, for example, spoke of its virtues; and in other Virginia cities officials openly participated in Klan activities during the 1920s. More often than not, the pursuits of vigilantes like the Klan were approved by a force similar to Herbert Packer's "value system" of crime control.[30] Richard Brown talks about the "legal illuminati" around the turn of the century who were concerned more with the "aim of crime repression" than with the processes of law enforcement. The Shipp affair in Chattanooga in 1906, where a black lynching had the tacit approval of the sheriff when the United States Supreme Court took jurisdiction of the case, may be an example of psychological conscious parallelism between local authorities and a vigilante mob.[31] The collusion of virtually the entire New Orleans leadership cadre in the face of the lynching of the assassins of the city police chief is another instance.[32] And, to prove that even recognition of the linkage between leadership and mob is not necessarily detrimental to continued membership in the elite, there is the case of Joseph B. Wall, a Florida attorney, who, after being described as a "passive" member of a lynch mob, went on to become the first president of the Florida State Bar Association and later president of the state senate.[33]

In each of these examples, leaders, although clearly established within the understanding of all concerned, did not unilaterally organize and initiate the

27. John Moffatt Mecklin, *The Ku Klux Klan* (New York: Russell, 1924).
28. Henry P. Fry, *The Modern Ku Klux Klan* (New York: Negro University Press, 1922, 1969), p. 192.
29. Mecklin, *Ku Klux Klan,* p. 66.
30. Arnold S. Rice, *The Ku Klux Klan In American Politics* (Washington: Public Affairs Press, 1962), pp. 39-40.
31. Brown, "Legal and Behavioral Perspectives on American Vigilantism," in *Perspectives in American History* (Cambridge: Harvard University Press, 1971), 5: 117.
32. Ibid., p. 119.
33. Ibid., p. 127.

activities of the vigilantes. They stood, to some degree, as a more or less silent symbol of what they thought the situation demanded, making it clear at the same time that they themselves would not personally be involved in the dirty business. Rather than thinking that the conservative mind always needs the kind of strict organization and order that we usually attribute to it, we see that the vigilante temperament also permits an authoritarian personality under the tensions of its own status insecurity and stylistic intensity to act on its own in furtherance of what we could identify as establishment goals. Of course, psychological conscious parallelism is not always a factor in vigilante activity; but in circumstances where an "outgroup" is clearly defined and a course of action is salient throughout some potentially active enforcer of community standards, conscious parallelism is a worthwhile psychological tool for understanding the coordination that sometimes goes on between the vigilante, the civil establishment, and law-enforcement agencies.

Our brief discussion of the concept of conscious parallelism leads us to conclude that there are at least four isolatable psychological factors that contribute to the existence and operations of the vigilante personality. The first is a basic conservative psychopolitical orientation. The second is the possession of certain stylistically unbalancing traits through which intolerance and rigidity join the conservative personality. If we add to these the qualities of status insecurity, so often found in the ranks of those with newly achieved wealth and position, plus the not unique, but nontheless useful, vigilante capability of engaging in psychological conscious parallelism, we have a fairly complete picture of the vigilante. He is a conservative personality at heart but, more important, he is a frightened personality, unable to understand the problems that social unorthodoxy, change, and racial or ethical differences have brought upon him.

When activating circumstances of temporary instability and threat occur within a community, persons who possess the kinds of traits identified here often approach the threshold of vigilante activism. The interplay of social stress and certain psychological characteristics of the vigilante personality forge an alloy of vigilante behavior which is ready to wreak vengeance upon the community and its people.

Chapter Four

Vigilantism and Political Theory

Edward Stettner

The topic of vigilantism has not been dealt with explicitly by any important political theorist. Nevertheless, the issues raised in a discussion of vigilantism are, in several regards, similar to the concerns of many theorists. It may, therefore, be of some use to a study of vigilantism to examine the phenomenon in the light of these concerns, and to attempt to bring out some of the underlying assumptions of the vigilante. As almost all political theorists have preferred a "legal" political order and have argued against violent tactics in politics, we shall also be raising some objections to vigilante politics.

CONTRACT THEORY

Perhaps the best way to develop our consideration of the relationship between vigilantism and the concerns of political theorists is to ask what political values vigilantes seek to achieve. Rosenbaum and Sederberg[1] have distinguished different types of vigilantism in their suggested typology, and the distinctions they make are important for this discussion.

The most telling and obvious discussion of a case of crime-control vigilante politics probably occurs in the social-contract theorists, particularly in John Locke's *Second Treatise of Government.* When discussing what they usually regard only as a hypothetical condition of men living outside of government (the so-called "state of nature"), the contract theorists are often taken to be describing a state of anarchy. This is a correct reading of Thomas Hobbes and some others, but not of Locke. Locke clearly assumes that most men in the state of nature will adhere to an established order, the norms of which are grounded in natural law. Some men, however, will not, specifically the

---

1. See chapter one in this volume.

"Criminal, who having renounced reason . . . hath by the unjust Violence and Slaughter he hath committed upon us, declared War against all Mankind. . . ."[2] In the state of nature, men may respond individually to this aggression and violence, or they may organize as an informal group to do so. There is, of course, no generally accepted institution to enforce natural law. To Locke this is a greatly unsatisfactory situation, for he hypothesizes that everyone then has to have the "Executive Power" to enforce the law of nature. The tendency in this situation will be to enforce law in an unfair manner. He remarks: "I doubt not but it will be objected, That it is unreasonable for Men to be Judges in their own Cases, that Self-love will make men partial to themselves and their Friends. And on the other side, that Ill Nature, Passion and Revenge will carry them too far in punishing others. And hence nothing but Confusion and Disorder will follow."[3]

It would seem that any vigilante attempting to justify his course of action must argue that "taking the law into one's own hands" is a satisfactory, or at least the best possible, course of action. For Locke, however, any situation in which even a majority of a community acts outside some explicit political institution is an entirely unsatisfactory situation when measured against any kind of standard for a civilized life. He prefers, instead, to discuss the possibility of constructing a legal order. For Locke, even though men may desire to enforce natural law—or, we might suppose, some other standard of behavior—human frailties will prevent the realization of this objective except through a legal order.

The crime-control vigilante appears to be a case in which "law" and "order" are in fact separated for practical reasons. The vigilante might well wish to have both, but he has determined that he cannot, and has chosen order over law. The vigilante in this case may not be seeking order as his prime goal. He may seek a just society, a free society, an equalitarian society, or whatever. His disenchantment with the regime in practice turns him toward extralegal channels to realize the principles he seeks in his society. Locke's point is that however well intentioned such men may be, however much they intend simply to enforce the Law of Nature against criminals, there are major "inconveniences" to a reliance on extralegal actions. Men will punish excessively, and they will fail to punish themselves or their friends for crimes similar to those for which they punish others. As Rosenbaum and Sederberg argue, the short-run results of crime-control vigilantism may possibly be positive, but the long-run results are not likely to be. Locke expects confusion and disorder to result from any attempt to enforce order outside of accepted political institutions.

2. John Locke, *Two Treatises of Government,* ed. Peter Laslett (New York: Mentor Books, 1965), p. 314.
3. Ibid., p. 316.

DEMOCRATIC THEORY

The social-group-control and regime-control types of vigilantism are perhaps more interesting to consider in light of the concerns of most political theorists. Where the crime-control vigilante may be trying to achieve a variety of political goals, fewer options seem to be open to these other types of vigilantes. Their primary concern is the preservation of their own status or position in society, and of order as the preeminent political value.

The desire to preserve (or, for that matter, to increase) one's own position is, of course, a very familiar one in politics. There is scarcely a political theorist who is not familiar with this aim, and who does not regard it as a necessary part of politics. For example, group theorists, such as Arthur Bentley and David Truman, have elaborated upon the notion of an "interest," which is the shared desire of any group of political actors and which motivates their political activity.[4] This interest may be other-regarding, but much more typically one's own selfish desires form the bases of each person's political "interests." The image of politics projected by the group theorists is often one of considerable disorder. Yet they also suppose that the game has rules in which certain political tactics are considered inappropriate. Even more relevant to a discussion of vigilantism, a view of politics such as Bentley's or Truman's posits certain mechanisms which amount to the establishment of an institutionalized political order. Politics for them entails the conflict of numerous personal desires. Yet these desires must be meshed together into an accepted public policy.[5] This may be only a short-lived accommodation, which will be upset in the next round of political controversy, but without it the society would disintegrate into a state of anarchy.

It would thus appear that vigilantism, particularly of the social-group - control and regime-control varieties, is in important respects an anti-political activity. Group theorists, and many others, see "politics" as the process of accommodation among individuals and groups. Vigilantism attempts to suspend this process and simply to support the status quo and the interests of the vigilante group.

It might be objected here that vigilantism is not anti-political but simply a resistance to being channelled into using "the system" and its "legitimate" means of dissent. It might then be argued that the vigilante is simply using

4. See Arthur Bentley, *The Process of Government* (Cambridge: Harvard University Press, 1967 reprint); David Truman, *The Governmental Process* (New York: Alfred A. Knopf, 1958). For an excellent critique of group theory see Harry Eckstein, "Group Theory and the Comparative Study of Pressure Groups" in Eckstein and Apter, eds., *Comparative Politics: A Reader* (New York: The Free Press, 1963), pp. 389-97.

5. Bentley writes: "In the broadest sense . . . government is the process of the adjustment of a set of interest groups in a particular distinguishable group or system. . . ." *Process of Government*, p. 260. Also: "When we talk about law we think not of the influencing or pressure as process, but of the status of the activities, the pressures being assumed to have worked themselves through to a conclusion or balance." Ibid., p. 272.

force, as, say, a military dictatorship does. To an extent, this is so. Yet it would seem that vigilantism differs in important respects from the conventional use of force in a dictatorship. For instance, vigilantes usually prefer to remain anonymous. Our picture of them (dictated by images of the "Old West") is of a stern group wearing masks who arrive at night, complete their business, and ride off into the night again. The next day they appear to be perfectly normal members of the community, and usually resist any identification as vigilantes. A military dictatorship, on the contrary, is more open. Force is certainly employed, but it is mostly used openly. The use of force may not be precisely "legal," but it is expected and accepted in a real sense. The point of the contrast is that the vigilante attempts to use a mechanism to further his personal "interest" while attempting to deny the same mechanism to others. The give and take, competitive spirit of "normal" politics, tempered by a commonly accepted pattern of behavior, which to a lesser but still important sense may even characterize a military regime, is lacking in vigilante politics.

This point can be amplified by examining David Easton's definition of politics as "the authoritative allocation of values for a society."[6] This definition, probably the most widely used contemporary definition of politics, emphasizes that a formal government is not a necessity for politics to exist. Yet Easton argues that "every society provides some mechanisms, however rudimentary they may be, for authoritatively resolving differences about the ends that are to be pursued, that is, for deciding who is to get what there is of the desirable things. An authoritative allocation of some values is unavoidable."[7] It seems clear that the vigilante does not wish to "resolve" conflicts; he wishes simply to enforce his own desires. The methods he employs are deliberately chosen to frustrate any process of accommodation. Of course, a particular allocation of values *is* thereby guaranteed, but through what we have to call a rather nonpolitical process.

If we can agree that the vigilante attempts to avoid "politics" as much as possible, then it goes without saying that vigilantism is antithetical to any kind of democratic politics, because democratic theory presupposes a competition among different interests. It may be interesting, however, to see precisely how democratic theorists differ from the implicit theory of the social-group - control or regime-control type of vigilante.

Most democratic theorists have stressed the need for some concept of community, some fraternal tie among the members of the society. In Rousseau's *Social Contract* this is stated quite strongly. Rousseau's central problem is to justify abandoning man's natural liberty (again in the hypothetical state of nature) for a rather tight community. Rousseau argues that there are two kinds of reasons for leaving this natural state. "What man

6. David Easton, *The Political System: An Inquiry into the State of Political Science* (New York: Alfred A. Knopf, 1967 reprint), p. 129. See chapter 5 especially.

7. Ibid., p. 137.

loses by the social contract is his natural liberty and an unlimited right to everything he tries to get and succeeds in getting; what he gains is civil liberty and the proprietorship of all he possesses."[8]

Contrast this argument to the vigilante's. In the first place, the vigilante (of the social - or regime-control variety at least) does not really want to give up his claim to what he "succeeds in getting," as his resort to violence to preserve his existing interests shows. Rousseau, Locke, and Hobbes would all argue that such an attitude is self-defeating in the long run. Denial of a community of interests only endangers one's own fundamental interests. Rousseau would also argue that the vigilante does not achieve "civil liberty." What this means is that for Rousseau one of the virtues of the civil society is the sense of community that is fostered—the feeling of caring and being responsible for your fellow men, the fraternity, even the love, created in society. He remarks that "the better the constitution of a State is, the more do public affairs encroach on private in the minds of the citizens. Private affairs are even of much less importance, because the aggregate of the common happiness furnishes a greater proportion of that of each individual, so that there is less for him to seek in particular cares."[9] This feeling of community, and the sense of "freedom" produced by participating in the group, is what Rousseau means by "civil liberty." It is a particular concept of freedom which would not be acceptable to all political theorists.[10] For our puposes, however, we can see that the vigilante is implicitly denying this sense of community which Rousseau desires.

All democratic theorists would not accept Rousseau's stress on fraternity. However, all variations of democratic theory involve another sense of community which the vigilante also denies. This is the quality of tolerance—a willingness to refrain from pushing one's own claims over the desires of a majority of one's fellow citizens, and the willingness to accept them as equals. The legal philosopher, Edmond Cahn, calls this the notion of "Associability." He writes:

> Associability . . . is the quality that fits one to cooperate as an equal in the work of a group or institution. An associate person gives the group its full due by contributing a store of information for its use, submitting his opinions for general consideration, respectfully weighing those of the other members, deliberating before he takes a final position, accepting the group's decision with good grace, and doing his functional share to put it into effect. Associability holds equal men together when they disagree. It prompts the members of a minority party to support laws and measures that the majority may have thrust on them against their interests and inclinations, and it prompts the majority to exercise reasonableness, moderation, and restraint because some day they too

8. Rousseau, *The Social Contract,* in *The Social Contract and the Discourses,* ed., G. D. H. Cole (New York: E. P. Dutton, 1950), p. 19.

9. Ibid., p. 93.

10. See Isaiah Berlin, *Four Essays on Liberty* (New York: Oxford University Press, 1969), especially chapter 3, for a discussion of the different meanings of the concept of freedom.

may suffer the vicissitudes of political fortune and come to occupy the place of a minority. To be associable one must feel respect for his fellow citizens.[11]

It is clear that the vigilante does not possess this quality. In the case of the social-group - control vigilante, we presume that other groups have been gaining more power, prestige, and material rewards in the political system. The democratic theorist insists that everyone in the system must accept this upwardly mobile position of the former out-groups (the groups gaining power), at least if the democratic requirements of free discussion, equal participation, and majority rule have prevailed. Yet by definition the vigilante does not abide by these rules and results. The resort to violence is, of course, a denial of the required democratic processes. More fundamentally, the vigilante renounces the essential quality of associability which the democrat sees as the essential temper of political man. He also refuses to accept the view of men as essentially equal (at least for political purposes) which is a necessary part of the democratic creed.

To sum up this part of our discussion, then, it would seem that vigilantism is in essence a denial of the fundamental perception that many theorists, especially democratic theorists, have of politics. The vigilante believes in asserting his own interest. This virtually all theorists of politics can accept. Further, however, he seems to recognize little or no restraint on this assertion of his interest, and no need to compromise with others. He also recognizes no limitation on the means which may be employed to further his group's interest. A vigilante, by definition, resorts to a secretive sort of violence to maintain his political position. An anti-political, and especially anti-democratic, attitutde is very much evident in vigilantism.

What values, then, does the vigilante hold dear, besides his own self-interest? Only, it would appear, a regard for the status quo as status quo, a regard for order for its own sake. What can we make of this reliance on order?

Order is very difficult to justify for its own sake. It has been highly valued by many political theorists, but usually because order is seen as prerequisite to some other goal. For example, Edmund Burke certainly values order; indeed, Francis Canavan has written that "the central idea in Burke's thought was that of order."[12] Canavan and others argue, however, that Burke desires an orderly society because he sees a social order as a reflection of the natural order of nature. "Behind his conception of the order of society lay always the grand idea of the order of the universe."[13] Others have argued for order because it allows the development of democratic political institutions, or because men

11. Edmond Cahn, *The Predicament of Democratic Man* (New York: Dell, 1962), pp. 164-65.
12. Francis Canavan, "Edmund Burke's Conception of the Role of Reason in Politics" in Isaac Kramnick, ed., *Essays in the History of Political Thought* (Englewood Cliffs: Prentice-Hall, 1969), p. 274.
13. Ibid. See also Peter Stanlis, *Edmund Burke and the Natural Law* (Ann Arbor: University of Michigan Press, 1958) for a similar interpretation. Not all commentators on Burke would accept this argument that he is a natural law theorist.

can thus be sure of their freedoms and rights, whereas disorder creates insecurity and thus restricts the assertion of individual freedoms. Yet it is very difficult to argue that order is good, without asking what kind of an order it is.

Goethe once wrote, "I'd rather commit an injustice than bear disorder."[14] Hobbes' *Leviathan* might be read as an argument for the primacy of order. Still, these examples themselves show the philosophic poverty of the vigilante position. For Goethe also wrote, "From my youth I have loathed anarchy more than even death."[15] And Hobbes certainly attempts to convince us that order is impossible without a sovereign power to promulgate and enforce a legal system. What is paradoxical about the vigilante position is, of course, that it seeks to perpetuate the existing order, but without law and without accepting the actions of the society's political institutions. No political theorist could endorse the vigilante's conception of order given this separation.

OTHER PERSPECTIVES

Our consideration of vigilantism has probably been biased thus far toward a liberal-democratic viewpoint. It may therefore be appropriate at this point to consider briefly how theorists of other persuasions might interpret vigilantism. The theories of the elitists, the Marxists, and the anarchists may have something to say about this confusing phenomenon.

The elitists are best known for their repudiation of classical democratic theory and the claim that every society inevitably develops a "ruling class."[16] Pareto cynically argues: "We need not linger on the fiction of 'popular representation'—poppycock grinds no flour. Let us go on and see what substance underlies the various forms of power in the governing classes.[17] Pareto and the other elitists would certainly claim to be more value-free, more scientific, than previous political theorists. As they saw it, they simply studied political (and social and economic) phenomena as they found them. The use of violence in politics was to be studied along with everything else. In this conviction the elitists accept the use of violence as inevitable, although in their analysis they do not find politics as necessarily characterized by violence in the sense that the Marxists do.

There are some superficial similarities between vigilantism and these elements of the elitist position. A vigilante looking for intellectual support for

14. Quoted in Arnold Brecht, *Political Theory: The Foundations of Twentieth-Century Political Thought* (Princeton: Princeton University Press, 1959), p. 155.

15. Ibid.

16. The group is broad and poorly defined, but certainly includes Vilfredo Pareto, Gaetano Mosca and Robert Michels. See H. Stuart Hughes, *Conciousness and Society* (New York: Vintage Books, 1958), especially chapter 7, for an analysis of the elitists. See also Peter Bachrach, *The Theory of Democratic Elitism: A Critique* (Boston: Little, Brown, 1967).

17. Vilfredo Pareto, *The Mind and Society,* ed., Arthur Livingston (New York: Harcourt, Brace, 1935), 4: 1569.

his position might fasten on the elitists, at first glance, for their claim to value-free analysis, their passing acceptance of violence, and their general repudiation of democratic theory, including the presumption of the equality of men. We might suppose, here, that the typical vigilante would like to think of himself as a "realist," beyond morality in politics, simply out for himself as he presumes that everyone else is, and probably of the opinion that he is better than the average man.

However, the parallel between elitism and vigilantism soon breaks down, nowhere more obviously than in their different theories of social dynamics. One of the most well-known aspects of the elitist theory involves the so-called "circulation of elites." While considering democratic theory in its strict sense a fraud, the elitists do say that the composition of the ruling class changes. Pareto argues that:

> In virtue of class-circulation, the governing *elite* is always in a state of slow and continuous transformation. It flows on like a river, never being today what it was yesterday. From time to time sudden and violent disturbances occur. There is a flood—the river overflows its banks. Afterwards, the new governing *elite* again resumes its slow transformation. The flood has subsided, the river is again flowing normally in its wonted bed.[18]

Mosca, a bit more of a democrat, also notes:

> The democratic tendency—the tendency to replenish ruling classes from below—is constantly at work with greater or lesser intensity in all human societies. At times the rejuvenation comes about in rapid or violent ways. More often, in fact normally, it takes place through a slow and gradual infiltration of elements from the lower into the higher classes.
>
> • • • •
>
> In times more recent, violent and far-reaching renovations of old political classes have sometimes come about through internal upheavals. These would be 'revolutions' proper. They occur when a wide breach opens between a people's official political organization and its customs, ideas and sentiments, and when many elements which would be competent to participate in government are artificially held in a subordinate status.[19]

It seems clear that vigilantism, particularly of the social-group-control variety, would often appear to Mosca or Pareto as an attempt by a former establishment or elite group, now perhaps in decline, to evade being "circulated" out of power. Of course, all vigilantes are not necessarily from declining groups. Indeed, Rosenbaum and Sederberg argue that violence used in an attempt to reestablish a former position should simply be considered reactionary violence and not vigilantism. Yet it would seem that the impetus to engage in vigilantism results from the strong fear that only in this manner can a social position be maintained. A confident establishment group would have little motivation to use the extreme tactics characteristic of vigilantism.

18. Ibid., 3: 1431.
19. Gaetano Mosca, *The Ruling Class,* ed   Arthur Livingston (New York: McGraw-Hill, 1939), pp. 413-14.

In any case, the vigilante's attempt to freeze the power structure of a society would appear to Pareto or Mosca to be a struggle against the inevitable. Certainly neither of them would think it likely (or, for that matter, desirable) that the constant transfer of power should be prevented.

Thus we see that the elitists do not display any great compatibility with vigilantism. They accept violence, but generally see it as the tool of a newly ascending group rather than of the establishment. Both positions repudiate democracy and equality, but the vigilante penchant for order finds no echo at all in the elitist writers. Any justification or sympathetic analysis of vigilantism must be sought elsewhere.

A Marxist could interpret vigilantism in several ways. For instance, vigilante violence might be analyzed as a normal part of the exploitation by the dominant, established class of the under or subordinate class. Certainly the Marxists, even more than the elitists, see violence as a normal part of politics, at least until the proletarian revolution.[20] However, the Marxist analysis of "the State" (the "legal order" in any historical period in which there is exploitation) argues that it is the political institutions themselves which use violence to attempt to perpetuate the status quo. Lenin, for example, writes that "the state is an organ of class *domination,* an organ of *oppression* of one class by another. . . ."[21] He notes that

> A state is formed, a special power is created in the form of special bodies of armed men, and every revolution, by shattering the state apparatus, demonstrates to us how the ruling class aims at the restoration of the special bodies of armed men at *its* service, and how the oppressed class tries to create a new organization of this kind, capable of serving not the exploiters, but the exploited.[22]

In this analysis there would appear to be no need for vigilantism. Or perhaps it might be argued that a Marxist would simply see vigilantism as a sort of supplement to state violence.

Alternatively, the Marxist might interpret a vigilante response as the desperate lashing out of a dominant group which sees that it is losing to others its control of the state apparatus. This interpretation seems appropriate, however, only if the transition from one dominant class to the next is seen as being gradual. The orthodox Marxist view has been that transitions are accomplished dramatically in a violent revolution. Once again, the Marxist analysis tends to see violence as a tactic either of the state or of a revolutionary group, rather than as an establishment group using tactics outside the "normal" political institutions.

It would seem, then, that Marxist political theory really does not focus on

---

20. Indeed, Lenin argues that violence will persist into the stage of history known as the Dictatorship of the Proletariat, and will probably not be eliminated in all its forms until the final stage of Communism. See Lenin, *The State and Revolution* (New York: International Publishers, 1932), especially chapter 1.

21. Ibid., p. 9. Emphasis in the original.

22. Ibid., p. 11. Emphasis in the original.

the phenomenon of vigilantism in any strict sense. As in the case of the elitists, the Marxist analysis is not drawn in such a way that vigilantism can be emphasized. Moreover, the introduction of the concept of vigilantism would complicate the essentially simple view of politics as being composed of two groups, a dominant and a subordinate class. Such an introduction might also question the theory of dialectical historicism in which dominant groups succeed one another according to historical laws.

Normatively (if we can agree that Marxism is normative and not simply "scientific," as its adherents would argue), any attempt to preserve the status quo is of no ethical value, as well as futile. History, for the Marxist, inevitably witnesses the destruction of all established classes until the proletariat is finally triumphant. Any vigilante activity is simply a failure (though perhaps itself inevitable) to accept the inevitable pattern of change; it should not be of serious interest to the scholar in any other terms.

The anarchists' analysis of vigilantism would, in many respects, be similar to that of the Marxists. Although most anarchists do not rely on a simple dominant-subordinate picture of the class structure, they, too, view any existing state as the product of a process whereby one group or class dominates and exploits others. For example, Bakunin writes, "finally one party . . . having vanquished all the others, attains exclusive power and creates *the law of the State.* . . . That is how estates of the realm are created, and the State emerges into the open."[23] In this analysis, violence is seen as a common tactic of the establishment though again the instruments of violence are the state institutions themselves, not some supplementary body. Revolutionary, not vigilante, violence is also considered by many anarchists, especially Bakunin, to be a necessary means of social change.

Like the Marxists, the anarchists tend not to emphasize social phenomena that we might now view as vigilante. The dominant class is usually felt to be unified and to use the state to perpetuate its ends. Extralegal violence in protection of the status quo is simply not stressed.

Anarchist thought is more obviously ethical than Marxist or elitist theories. It is not reluctant to prescribe new political arrangements, which commonly involve the abolition of the state and the establishment of a mutualistic, cooperative society in which it is hoped that human freedom may be maximized and human potential unleashed. This happy picture, from which all sorts of violence are now to be banished, has nothing in common with vigilantism.

CONCLUSIONS

Having now looked at vigilantism in relation to different political theories, what are we to conclude about this kind of politics?

23. Bakunin, *The Political Philosophy of Bakunin,* ed., G. P. Maximoff (New York: The Free Press, 1953), p. 354. Emphasis in the original.

In the first place, it is easy to affirm Rosenbaum and Sederberg's argument that vigilantes are not "ideological." For various and obvious reasons, vigilantes are clearly not interested in stating their position philosophically, in attempting to argue systematically for order and the perpetuation of the favorable status quo. Neither have vigilantes attempted to develop an analysis of society along "scientific" lines. In this they stand in clear contrast to many revolutionaries, the Marxists and anarchists being only two examples. Vigilantism thus shares the common failing of many conservative points of view in failing to make philosophic assumptions explicit. Consequently, this essay has concentrated on how various schools of political thought would analyze vigilantism, rather than on the explicit tenets of vigilantism itself.

It is unfortunate that the vigilante has not made his thoughts explicit more often, as he has a unique and interesting political position. Our survey of different political theories has shown that though some are similar to vigilantism in superficial ways, none is really close. The more common arguments in political theory are justifications of an existing legal order, especially when democratic, and often justifications for the use of violence in effecting social change. Yet the number of examples of vigilantism in practice is not insignificant, as this volume illustrates. The assumption underlying the vigilante position—which we have seen to be an emphasis on order and the perpetuation of the self-interested status quo—need to be argued more explicitly if we are adequately to understand this phenomenon.

It should be admitted, however, that there are good reasons why political theorists have failed to touch very fully on vigilante politics. Much of political theory is ethically inspired. That is, political theorists ("traditional" theorists in particular, and also contemporary democratic theorists) are very concerned to show what the good state would be like. They tend to discuss attractive goals such as justice, freedom, equality, which can be shown to have a positive ethical content. Other questions important to the theorist, for example discussions of proper political institutions and arguments why government should or should not be obeyed, are related to the means of achieving these ends.[24] Vigilantism does not posit ends which are attractive. It is hard to argue ethically for self-interest, or for order qua order. Moreover, the means of achieving these ends, secret violence, is not morally attractive either. Vigilantism is clearly a sickness in the view of traditional theory, a perversion of both the means and the ends of politics as it should be.

More contemporary theorists might be expected to treat phenomena like

---

24. I do not mean to be taken here as arguing that theorists should not be concerned with value questions. These are important in themselves, and are also ultimately inseparable from political analysis. However, an effort should be made to keep different sorts of questions—description, explanation, evaluation—as distinct as possible. An excellent discussion of the nature of political theory is Sheldon Wolin's "Political Theory: Trends and Goals," *International Encyclopedia of the Social Sciences* (New York: Crowell Collier and Macmillan, 1968), 12: 318-30.

vigilantism more fully, but again vigilantism appears as a political sickness, as a perversion of a properly functioning political system. The ethical content in contemporary theory—for instance the group theorists or the elitists, or even the Marxists—is not so obvious as in traditional writers. The contemporary aim is more to construct scientific models of politics which will describe and explain rather than evaluate. These models have a normative attitude inextricably worked into their fundamental perspectives. For example, group theory posits a system which takes diverse interests and works them out into commonly accepted public policy. Elitists claim to find democratic theory a fraud, but their interpretation of the ruling class sees individuals and groups of ability as usually able eventually to rise into positions of power. The normative content of these theories may be less than obvious, but any model which discusses a "functional" political system has some notion of political health and thus some notion of the good political system. Vigilantism is never "functional" in terms of any of the contemporary political models that we have examined.

A study of vigilantism and political theory should demonstrate the necessity for greater understanding of the various ways that political systems fail to follow "scientific models," and how people can fail to embrace what to theorists are often self-evident ethical objectives. Vigilantism should be studied not only for itself, but also in this broader context of dysfunctional political activities.

On the other hand, if we are convinced that political theory can never be free of values and evaluation, can never be ethically neutral, then there is no reason why we should not point out how vigilantism *is* a political sickness. Various normative objections to vigilantism have thus been advanced in this essay.

One last point: This essay has tried to understand the different types of vigilantism by examining the philosophic objectives that seem implicit in their actions. Crime-control vigilantism has been shown to differ quite significantly from social-group - control vigilantism and regime-control vigilantism in that it does not seem limited to arguing for order and the perpetuation of a favorable status quo. Crime-control vigilantism is a practical response to a short-run failure of the legal system to operate "properly." The other types of vigilantism are broader responses meant to supplement or even supplant normal political operations, which may be working too effectively for the tastes of the vigilante group. This is particularly so of social-group-control vigilantism. It may be that these phenomena are too diverse to be studied as simply different types of a single kind of political activity. That, at least, would be a possible conclusion to be drawn from looking at vigilantism from the perspectives of political theory.

Part II:

American Perspectives

Chapter Five

The History of Vigilantism in America

Richard Maxwell Brown

Vigilantism—traditionally defined as taking the law into one's own hands—formed the core of violent American extralegal justice from the late colonial period to the early twentieth century. The first major outbreak of vigilantism occurred in the Regulator movement of the South Carolina back country from 1767 to 1769. Revolutionary Virginia was the scene of a similar movement a decade later when extralegal summary justice upon Tories and outlaws was imposed by hinterland patriots under the direction of a local leading man, Colonel Charles Lynch, whose name eventually became affixed to one of the generic terms of American vigilantism: lynch law.[1]

After the Revolutionary War, vigilantism moved westward across the Appalachians with the pioneers. From 1767 to 1910 there were at least 326 vigilante movements or episodes distributed over practically all of the trans-Appalachian states and a few of the Atlantic states. Known as "regulators"

*This essay is adapted from my prior study, "The American Vigilante Tradition," pp. 121-80, in Hugh Davis Graham and Ted Robert Gurr, eds., *Violence in America: Historical and Comparative Perspectives: A Report to the National Commission on the Causes and Prevention of Violence,* 2 vols. (Washington: U. S. Government Printing Office, 1969), and is based also on my three other treatments: "Legal and Behavioral Perspectives on American Vigilantism," pp. 93-144, in *Perspectives in American History* 5 (1971), reprinted in Donald Fleming and Bernard Bailyn, eds., *Law in American History* (Boston: Little, Brown, 1972); "Pivot of American Vigilantism: The San Francisco Vigilance Committee of 1856," pp. 105-19, in John A. Carroll, ed., *Reflections of Western Historians* (Tucson: University of Arizona Press, 1969); and "The Conservative Mob: Americans as Vigilantes" (unpublished address, Bloomsburg State College History Conference on "Violence in History," May 3, 1973); see, also, Richard Maxwell Brown, *Strain of Violence: Historical Studies of American Violence and Vigilantism* (New York: Oxford University Press, 1975), part III. Graham and Gurr, *Violence in America . . .* (in which "The American Vigilante Tradition" first appeared) has been reprinted in two 1969 paperback editions (Bantam Books, New York; New American Library Signet Book, New York) and in a hard cover edition (New York: Praeger, 1969) under the slightly revised title, *The History of Violence in America.* Because of its readier availability, the hard cover edition is the source for the citations to "The American Vigilante Tradition" that appear in the notes, below, to the present essay.

1. James E. Cutler, *Lynch-Law: An Investigation into the History of Lynching in the United States* (New York: Longmans, Green, 1905), pp. 24-30.

(the predominant term until the mid-nineteenth century), "vigilantes," "slickers," or other names, these 326 organized movements of vigilantism inflicted at least 729 fatalities and levied corporal punishment on thousands of others.[2] Related to vigilantism have been other movements of extralegal violence, including three significant Ku Klux Klan movements: first, the anti-Negro, anti-Radical Republican Klan of the Southern Reconstruction era; second, the national Klan of the 1920s which attacked a variety of targets (immoral, ne'er-do-well whites, especially, but also blacks, Catholics, and Jews); and, finally, the anti-Negro, anti-Civil Rights Klan of the 1950s and 1960s operating mainly in the South.[3] Reflecting the vigilante interest in the maintenance of community order was the White Cap movement which arose first in Indiana in 1887 but soon spread all over the country before declining after 1900.[4] As spectacular as any of these movements was the large, tightly organized Night Rider association which between 1906 and 1909 vengefully swept over southwest Kentucky and northwest Tennessee, raiding towns and abusing individuals in the interest of economically distressed tobacco farmers and serving as a model for later, unrelated night-riding local violence elsewhere.[5] Operating on a grand scale were the ephemeral, unorganized lynch mobs which ravaged the whole nation by the thousands. They were especially evident in the South, from the early 1880s down to the decade of their steep decline, the 1930s. Whites were often the quarry of lynch mobs, but the great majority of such extralegal executions fell upon the vulnerable blacks of the South.[6]

Having noted the existence of Ku Klux Klansmen, White Caps, and Night Riders with their affinities to vigilantism, this essay will focus on the protagonists of traditional American lynch law, organized vigilantes and unorganized lynch mobs. Some measure of the impact of vigilantism is given by the number of fatalities inflicted by this protean institution. The grand total is at least 5459 documented deaths, consisting of the 729 executed by

2. Richard Maxwell Brown, "The American Vigilante Tradition," in Hugh Davis Graham and Ted Robert Gurr, eds., *The History of Violence in America* (New York: Praeger, 1969), pp. 164-65, 174-75, 226, and *passim*.

3. On the first Klan see Allen W. Trelease, *White Terror: The Ku Klux Klan Conspiracy and Southern Reconstruction* (New York: Harper & Row, 1971). For all three Klans, but especially the second, see David M. Chalmers, *Hooded Americanism: The First Century of the Ku Klux Klan, 1865-1965* (Garden City, N.Y.: Doubleday, 1965); see Charles C. Alexander, *The Ku Klux Klan in the Southwest* (Lexington, Ky.: University of Kentucky Press, 1965) on the second Klan.

4. Richard Maxwell Brown, "Historical Patterns of Violence in America," in Graham and Gurr, *History of Violence*, pp. 70-71.

5. James O. Nall, *The Tobacco Night Riders of Kentucky and Tennessee, 1905-1909* (Louisville: Standard Press, 1939); Paul J. Vanderwood, *Night Riders of Reelfoot Lake* (Memphis: Memphis State University Press, 1969); and Robert Penn Warren's significant novel, *Night Rider* (Boston: Houghton Mifflin, 1939).

6. Cutler, *Lynch-Law;* Arthur F. Raper, *The Tragedy of Lynching* (Chapel Hill: University of North Carolina Press, 1938); and Walter White, *Rope & Faggot* (New York: Alfred A. Knopf, 1929), are among the leading authorities.

organized vigilantes (1767-1910) and the 4730 put to death by unorganized lynch mobs (1882-1951).[7] In addition, hundreds of as yet undocumented executions probably occurred, so that a round total of 6000 victims would probably be closer to historical reality. So widely did the epidemic of lynch-law killing rage in the late-nineteenth century that for the period from 1883 to 1898 the number of extralegal executions far exceeded the legal ones.[8]

Part I of this essay is an historical overview of traditional vigilante movements. Part II emphasizes the social-stabilizing effect of frontier vigilantism as a significant agent of community reconstruction in pioneer areas. Part III analyzes the vigilante response to the problems of frontier law enforcement and justice and contrasts the socially constructive model of vigilantism with the socially destructive one. Part IV sketches the transition from frontier vigilantism to neo-vigilantism and notes the recent neo-vigilante phenomenon of neighborhood self-protective patrol groups. Part V delineates the ideology of vigilantism and underscores the symbiosis of elite and popular factors in the institution as well as the favorable attitude to lynch law often exhibited by the late-nineteenth-early-twentieth-century American legal establishment. The conclusion, Part VI, considers the relationship between vigilantism and the broad American tendency to lawlessness.

I

Fundamentally, the pioneer vigilantes took the law into their own hands for the purpose of establishing order and stability in newly settled areas. In the older settled areas the prime values of person and property were dominant and secure, but the move to the frontier meant that it was necessary to start all over. Upright and ambitious frontiersmen wished to reestablish the values of a property holder's society. The presence of outlaws and marginal types, often in a context of weak and ineffectual law enforcement, created the specter and, frequently, the fact of social chaos. A vigilante roundup of ne'er-do-wells and outlaws, followed by their flogging, expulsion, or killing, not only solved the problem of disorder, but also had crucial symbolic value as well. Vigilante action was a clear warning to disorderly inhabitants that the newness of settlement would provide no opportunity to erode the established framework of civilization. Vigilantism was a violent sanctification of the deeply cherished values of life and property.

Because the main thrust of vigilantism was to reinstitute in each newly settled area the conservative values of life, property, and law and order,

---

7. Brown, "American Vigilante Tradition," p. 175, for the vigilante total and Jessie P. Guzman, *et al.,* eds., *1952 Negro Year Book: A Review of Events Affecting Negro Life* (New York: Wm. H. Wise, 1952), p. 277, for the lynch-mob total. The grand total of 5459 includes some double counting of vigilante and lynch-mob victims, but this is more than offset by the uncounted victims not contained in these statistics.

8. Cutler, *Lynch-Law,* chart 1 opposite p. 162.

vigilante movements were usually led by the frontier elite. The duration of vigilante movements varied, but movements which persisted for a year were long lived. More commonly, a vigilante campaign was finished in a period of weeks or months. Vigilante movements (as distinguished from ephemeral lynch mobs) are thus identifiable by two main characteristics: regular (though illegal) organization and existence for a definite (though often short) period of time.

The first American vigilante movement, the South Carolina Regulators (1767-1769), did not occur until nearly 175 years after the first permanent English settlement at Jamestown. The reason for the late appearance of the phenomenon was the slow, orderly pace of frontier expansion. It was well into the eighteenth century before the settlement of the Piedmont region began on a large scale, and at the time of the Revolution the pioneer era of the Piedmont was just coming to a close. With this snail's pace of frontier expansion in the colonial period, it was possible to provide adequate systems of law enforcement and justice for the slowly proliferating pioneer communities. The one exception to the pattern of orderly frontier expansion appeared in the South Carolina back country beyond the lush plantations of the tidewater area.

Recently settled and latterly devastated by the Cherokee Indian War, the disorderly South Carolina back country of the 1760s was typical of later American frontier areas. During the Cherokee War, 1759-1760, so many homes were broken up and so many individuals were killed that the orphaned and homeless became a problem. Many drifted into outlaw bands formed by war veterans who were too restless or brutalized to settle down to peaceful pursuits. Outlaws, runaway slaves, and mulattoes formed their own communities where they enjoyed their booty. South Carolina way stations in an intercolonial network of horse thieves were established. "Crackers" and other frontier "lower people" aided and abetted the outlaws. By 1766 and 1767 the back country was in the grip of a crime wave, and the outlaws were almost supreme. They abducted young girls to be their paramours in the outlaw villages. They tortured and robbed plantation masters and raped their wives and daughters.

Lacking an adequate system of courts and law enforcement, respectable settlers organized as "Regulators" in late 1767 and embarked upon a successful two-year vigilante campaign. Subscribing to articles of organization, the Regulators attacked and broke up the outlaw gangs. The idle and immoral, too, were rounded up by the Regulators, given extralegal trials, and flogged. If thought hopelessly incorrigible, the miscreants were driven from the area. Those the Regulators deemed reclaimable were subjected to a system of forced labor on the plantations of the back country.

The South Carolina Regulator movement was constructive in that it did rid the back country of pervasive crime. Order and stability were at last established after many years of social chaos. But the Regulators were vindictive, and there was a streak of sadism in their punishments. The increasingly arbitrary, extreme, and brutal Regulators bred an opposition movement of "Moderators." Brought to a standstill by the equally violent Moderators and appeased by the provincial government's provision for district courts and sheriffs, the Regulators disbanded in 1769.[9]

Emulating the example of the South Carolina Regulators, the vigilante impulse followed the sweep of settlement toward the Pacific. Eastern vigilantism (that is, frontier vigilantism from the Appalachians to the 96th meridian in the middle of the country) mainly came to an end in the 1860s and focused chiefly upon frontier horse thieves, counterfeiters, and ne'er-do-well white people.[10]

From the 1790s well into the nineteenth century, vigilante activity was general in Kentucky, Tennessee, Indiana, and Illinois.[11] Thereafter, there were four major waves of vigilantism east of the 96th meridian. They occurred in the early 1830s, the early 1840s, the late 1850s, and the late 1860s. The first wave was from 1830 to 1835, largely in Alabama and Mississippi where slicker bands operated against horse thieves and counterfeiters,[12] and vigilantes attacked gamblers and the alleged Murrell conspiracy.[13] The early 1840s included the Bellevue vigilante war in Iowa, the East Texas Regulator-Moderator conflict, the Northern and Southern Illinois Regulators, and the Slicker War of the Missouri Ozarks.[14] The vigilante wave of the early 1840s

9. Richard Maxwell Brown, *The South Carolina Regulators* (Cambridge, Mass.: Harvard University Press, 1963).

10. Brown, "American Vigilante Tradition," pp. 160-61.

11. William Faux, *Memorable Days in America*... [1823] (Cleveland: Arthur H. Clark, 1905), pp. 293-94; John L. McConnel, *Western Characters* (New York: Redfield, 1853), pp. 171-75; William N. Blane, *An Excursion through the United States and Canada during the Years 1822-23* (London: Baldwin, Cradock & Jay, 1824), pp. 233-35; Robert M. Coates, *The Outlaw Years*... (New York: Macaulay, 1930).

12. James W. Bragg, "Captain Slick, Arbiter of Early Alabama Morals," *Alabama Review* 11 (1958): 125-34; Jack K. Williams, "Crime and Punishment in Alabama, 1819-1840," *Alabama Review* 6 (1953): 14-30.

13. Williams, "Crime and Punishment in Alabama," p. 27; Cutler, *Lynch-Law*, p. 99; H. R. Howard, comp., *The History of Virgil A. Stewart* (New York: Harper, 1836); Edwin A. Miles, "The Mississippi Slave Insurrection Scare of 1835," *Journal of Negro History*, 42 (1957): 58-60; David Grimsted, "The Mississippi Slave Insurrection Panic, 1835" (unpublished paper, Southern Historical Association, Atlanta, Nov. 9, 1973).

14. On Iowa, see John E. Briggs, "Pioneer Gangsters," *Palimpsest* 21 (1940): 73-90; John C. Parish, "White Beans for Hanging," *Palimpsest* 1 (1920): 9-28; Harvey Reid, *Thomas Cox* (Iowa City: State Historical Society of Iowa, 1909), pp. 126, 154-55, 165-67; Jackson County Historical Society, *Annals of Jackson County, Iowa* 2 (1906): 51-96. On the East Texas Conflict, see C[harles] L. Sonnichsen, *Ten Texas Feuds* (Albuquerque: University of New Mexico Press, 1957), chap. 1; Lela R. Neill, "Episodes in the Early History of Shelby County" (M. A. thesis, Stephen F. Austin State College, 1950), pp. 77-153, and *passim*. On the Northern Illinois Regulators, see Alice L. Brumbaugh, "The Regulator Movement in Illinois" (M. A. thesis, University of Illinois, 1927), pp. 3, 5-27; and William Cullen Bryant, *Letters of a Traveller*... (New York: George P. Putnam, 1850), pp. 55-68. On the Southern Illinois Regulators, see Brumbaugh, "Regulator Movement," pp. 29-65; and James A. Rose, comp., "Papers Relating to

may have been a response to a shift in outlaw elements (caused by the 1830-1835 vigilante drive) from the lower Mississippi River region of Alabama, Mississippi, Louisiana, and Arkansas to the upper Mississippi area (Missouri, Iowa, Illinois) and to the trans-Mississippi Southwest (east Texas).

The third wave of vigilantism (1857-1859) featured the Iron Hills and other vigilante movements of Iowa, the Northern Indiana Regulators, the San Antonio and New Orleans vigilantes, and the *Comities de Vigilance* of southwest Louisiana.[15] Although they were reacting to local conditions, the movements of the late 1850s may have been inspired by the dramatic example of the San Francisco committee of vigilance of 1856 which was well publicized throughout the nation.[16] The fourth and final wave of vigilantism flared in the immediate post-Civil War period, 1866-1871, with major movements erupting in Missouri, Kentucky, Indiana, and Florida as a reaction to postwar lawlessness.[17]

---

the Regulator and Flathead Trouble in Southern Illinois" (bound typescript in Illinois State Historical Society, Springfield). On the Ozark Slicker War, see James H. Lay, *A Sketch of the History of Benton County, Missouri* (Hannibal, Mo.: Winchell & Ebert, 1876), pp. 46-61; Charles Edward Pancoast, *A Quaker Forty-Niner . . .*, ed. Anna P. Hannum (Philadelphia: University of Pennsylvania Press, 1930), pp. 101-21; J. W. Vincent, "The 'Slicker War' and Its Consequences," *Missouri Historical Review* 7 (1912-1913): 138-45.

15. On Iowa movements, see *The Iowan* 6 (1958): 4-11, 50-51; Jackson County Historical Society, *Annals* 1 (1905): 29-34; *The History of Clinton County, Iowa* (Chicago: Western Historical Co., 1879), pp. 437ff; Paul W. Black, "Lynchings in Iowa," *Iowa Journal of History and Politics* 10 (1912): 151-209; Orville F. Graham, "The Vigilance Committees," *Palimpsest* 6 (1925): 259-370. On the Northern Indiana Regulators, see M. H. Mott, *The History of the Regulators of Northern Indiana* (Indianapolis: Journal Co., 1859); Weston A. Goodspeed and Charles Blanchard, eds., *Counties of Whitley and Noble, Indiana: Historical and Biographical* (Chicago: F. A. Battey, 1882), pp. 33-37, 63-73. On San Antonio, see, among many sources: Dorothy K. Gibson, "Social Life in San Antonio, 1855-1860" (M. A. thesis, University of Texas, 1937), pp. 122-31. On New Orleans and southwest Louisiana, see George A. Ketcham, "Municipal Police Reform: A Comparative Study of Law Enforcement in Cincinnati, Chicago, New Orleans, New York, and St. Louis, 1844-1877" (Ph.D. dissertation, University of Missouri, 1967), pp. 148-50; Harry L. Griffin, "The Vigilance Committees of the Attakapas Country; or Early Louisiana Justice," Mississippi Valley Historical Association, *Proceedings* 8 (1914-1951): 146-59; Alexander Barde, *History of the Committes of Vigilance in the Attakapas Country* [1861], trans. and ed., Henrietta G. Rogers (M. A. thesis, Louisiana State University Press, 1936).

16. The literature on this crucial organization is large. The most complete account, although highly biased in favor of the vigilantes, is in Hubert Howe Bancroft, *Popular Tribunals*, 2 vols. (San Francisco: History Co., 1887); see, also, Richard Maxwell Brown, "Pivot of American Vigilantism: The San Francisco Vigilance Committee of 1856," in John A. Carroll, ed., *Reflections of Western Historians* (Tucson: University of Arizona Press, 1969), pp. 105-19; among the most recent studies are Roger W. Lotchin, *San Francisco, 1846-1856: From Hamlet to City* (New York: Oxford University Press, 1974), chaps. 8-9 and *passim;* and Robert Michael Senkewicz, "Business and Politics in Gold Rush San Francisco, 1851-1856" (Ph.D. dissertation, Stanford University, 1974). On San Francisco's 1851 vigilance committee which preceded that of 1856, see (in addition to the works by Bancroft, Lotchin, and Senkewicz, mentioned in the previous sentence), among many treatments, Mary Floyd Williams, *History of the San Francisco Committee of Vigilance of 1851: A Study of Social Control on the California Frontier in the Days of the Gold Rush* (Berkeley: University of California Press, 1921), and George R. Stewart, *Committee of Vigilance: Revolution in San Francisco, 1851* (Boston: Houghton Mifflin, 1964).

17. On the Missouri movements, see *The History of Johnson County, Missouri* (Kansas City, Mo.: Kansas City Historical Co., 1881), chap. 15; *History of Vernon County, Missouri* (St. Louis:

West of the 96th meridian, vigilantes were mainly concerned with disorder in mining camps, cattle towns, and the open ranges. Repeated strikes of precious and valuable ores in the Sierra Nevadas and Rockies set off rushes that brought thousands of miners and other people into raw new camps and towns. In such places the law was often absent or ineffectual. The result was vigilantism. The other great natural resource of the early West was the grassy rangeland of the Great Plains and the mountain plateaus. The open range system of the early days incited the inroads of cattle and horse thieves who, in turn, attracted vigilante retaliation.

Beginning with the first significant outbreak of vigilantism in the gold-rush metropolis of San Francisco in 1849, and continuing for fifty-three years down to 1902, there were at least 210 vigilante movements in the West. No vigilante movements in American history were better organized or more powerful than the San Francisco vigilance committees of 1851 and 1856. The San Francisco movements had immense impact on American vigilantism in general and on California vigilantism in particular. During the 1850s the San Francisco committees were copied all over the state in the new mining towns (Sacramento, Jackson, etc.) and in the old Spanish settlements (Los Angeles, Monterey, etc.). Of California's forty-three vigilante movements, twenty-seven flourished in the 1850s.[18]

Montana was a most significant vigilante state. It had two of the most important movements in vigilante history: the sanguinary Bannack and Virginia City movement of 1863 to 1865 (which popularized the term "vigilante" in American English)[19] and the 1884 movement in northern and eastern Montana. The latter, led by Granville Stuart against horse and cattle thieves in a human roundup that claimed thirty-five victims, was the deadliest of all American vigilante movements.[20] Moreover, Montana, in its prestatehood period from the 1860s to 1880s, was gripped by a territory-wide

Brown & Co., 1887), pp. 348-49; *History of Greene County, Missouri* (St. Louis: Western Historical Co., 1883), pp. 497-501. On Kentucky, see Lewis and Richard H. Collins, *History of Kentucky*, 2 vols. (Louisville: John Morton, 1924), 1: 198-209; E. Merton Coulter, *The Civil War and Readjustment in Kentucky* (Chapel Hill: University of North Carolina Press, 1926), p. 359. See Wayne G. Broehl, *The Molly Maguires* (Cambridge, Mass.: Harvard University Press, 1965), pp. 239-40, on the Seymour, Indiana, vigilance committee of 1867-1868. On Florida, see Ralph L. Peek, "Lawlessness and the Restoration of Order in Florida" (Ph.D. dissertation, University of Florida, 1964), pp. 91, 105-08, 125-26, 149-50, 216-20.

18. Bancroft, *Popular Tribunals*, 1: 441ff., and the list of California vigilante movements in Brown, "American Vigilante Tradition," p. 219.

19. Thomas J. Dimsdale, *The Vigilantes of Montana . . .* (Virginia City, Mont.: Montana Post Press, 1866); Nathaniel Pitt Langford, *Vigilante Days and Ways . . .*, 2 vols. (Boston: J. G. Cupples, 1890); Hoffman Birney, *Vigilantes* (Philadelphia: Penn Publishing Co., 1929); Barton C. Olsen, "Lawlessness and Vigilantes in America: An Historical Analysis Emphasizing California and Montana" (Ph.D. dissertation, University of Utah, 1968), focuses on Montana.

20. Granville Stuart, *Forty Years on the Frontier*, ed. Paul C. Phillips, 2 vols. (Cleveland: Arthur H. Clark, 1925), 2: 195-201; Michael A. Leeson, *History of Montana: 1739-1885* (Chicago: Warner, Beers, & Co., 1885), pp. 315-16.

vigilante movement whose headquarters were apparently in the capital, Helena.[21]

Texas had fifty-two vigilante movements—more than any other state. There were two important antebellum organizations (in Shelby County, east Texas, 1840-1844, and in San Antonio, 1857ff.), but the majority (at least twenty-seven) were in violence-torn central Texas in the post-Civil War period from 1865 to 1890.[22] Among the other western states only Oregon and Utah did not have significant vigilante activity. Kansas had nineteen movements, Colorado and Nebraska had sixteen each, Nevada had thirteen, New Mexico had eleven, Wyoming had seven, Arizona and Washington had six each, Idaho and the Dakotas had five each, and Oklahoma had four.[23]

Vigilante movements varied in size from twelve to fifteen members (in Pierre, South Dakota) to between six thousand and eight thousand (in San Francisco, 1856), but the typical organization had from one hundred to several hundred members.[24] Considering that the majority of American vigilante movements took place in new frontier localities of sparse population, the typical membership of from one to several hundred underscores the extent to which the community as a whole participated in vigilante action.

The characteristic vigilante movement was organized in hierarchical command fashion and usually had a constitution, articles, or a declaration to which the members would subscribe. Outlaws or other malefactors taken up by vigilantes were given formal (though illegal) trials in which the accused had counsel or an opportunity to defend themselves. The northern Illinois Regulator movement of 1841 provides an example of a vigilante trial. Two accused horse thieves and murderers were tried by 120 Regulators in the presence of a crowd of five hundred or more. A leading Regulator served as judge. The defendants were given a chance to challenge objectionable men among the Regulators, and, as a result, the number of Regulators taking part in the trial was cut by nine. Two lawyers were provided, one to represent the accused and one to represent the "people." Witnesses were sworn, an arraignment was made, and the trial proceeded. In summation, the prosecuting attorney urged immediate execution of the prisoners. The crowd voted unanimously for the fatal sentence, and, after an hour allotted to the two men for prayer, they were put to death.[25] Thus, although the accused were almost never acquitted in vigilante trials, the vigilantes' commitment to the ideals of law and order caused them to offer, by their lights, a fair but speedy trial.

The punishments of whipping and expulsion were common in the early

21. Montana Territory Vigilance Committee, *Notice!* (broadside, Helena, Mont., Sept. 19, 1865); Leeson, *History of Montana,* pp. 303-16.
22. Central Texas vigilantes included those in the counties of Bastrop, Shackelford, San Saba, Mason, Bell Comanche, Coryell, De Witt, Eastland, Gonzales, Hill, Llano, Montague, and Young; see Brown, "American Vigilante Tradition," n. 32, p. 210; pp. 224-25.
23. Brown, "American Vigilante Tradition," pp. 162-63, and appendix.
24. Ibid., pp. 171-72.
25. Brumbaugh, "Regulator Movement," pp. 18-20.

decades of vigilantism, but, as time passed, death—usually by means of hanging—became the customary penalty. Through 1849 there are only eighty-eight documented fatal victims of vigilante action, but in the next ten years 105 persons were executed by vigilantes. About the 1850s the transition in the meaning of the term "lynching" from whipping to killing was occurring. The deathly character of vigilantism, made firm in the 1850s, was accentuated during the remainder of the century. From 1860 to 1909 vigilantes took at least 511 lives. Of the 326 known vigilante movements, 141 (43 percent) killed victims—729 of them. Of the 729 fatalities, 544 (76 percent) were claimed by fifty-nine large vigilante movements. Seventeen of the 141 movements that took lives claimed more than ten, but the tendency was to execute only four or fewer victims, which was the case with ninety-six movements (69 percent of the 141).[26]

As noted above, the trend was for the large movements to kill the most victims, but it was not always necessary for a powerful movement to take a large number of lives. Often a vigilante movement could achieve its aims by executing just a few persons or even only one. The greatest of all vigilante movements (San Francisco, 1856) killed only four men. Two other significant organizations, northern Illinois, 1841, and northern Indiana, 1858, executed only two men and one man, respectively. The fearful example of one or two hangings (frequently in conjunction with the expulsion of lesser culprits) was on many occasions enough to reach the vigilante goal of community stability.

The foregoing figures on vigilante membership and executions reflect only the actions of organized vigilante bands, but significant vigilante activity did not always take the shape of a formally organized movement with officers, trials, etc. By the latter half of the nineteenth century, the ritual-like action of organizing a vigilante movement had been carried out so many times on so many frontiers that to many settlers such formality often seemed an unnecessary delay to swift lynch-law justice. A local consensus in favor of immediate vigilante action without any of the traditional formalities produced instant vigilantism. This was more prevalent in the West than in the East. Many of the "one-shot" vigilante actions in western states resulted from the impulse for instant vigilantism. Instant vigilantism in the West resembled the unorganized, anti-Negro lynch mobs of the South after Reconstruction. In the West it existed side-by-side with the more formally organized species of vigilantism. Instant vigilantism seems to have occurred in all western states but Oregon and Utah and was particularly effective in California. In the Golden State regular vigilante action took 101 lives, but the toll taken by instant vigilantism from 1851 to 1878 was almost as great.[27]

II

In terms of the sociology of the frontier, vigilantism was a major response to the crucial problem of community reconstruction in newly settled areas.

26. Brown, "American Vigilante Tradition," pp. 173-76.

Frontiersmen ordinarily desire new opportunities but not social innovation. Their main desire is to re-create the life they left behind by reconstructing the sort of community from which they came. This is no great problem for communities that migrate to the frontier en masse. There have been some notable examples of the latter. The Pilgrim settlers of Plymouth, Massachusetts and the Mormon migrants to the Great Salt Lake, Utah, are striking cases of "colonized" new communities.

More common, however, have been the "cumulative" communities of inhabitants thrown together helter-skelter by the migration process.[28] The forty-niner generation migrants to San Francisco furnish an example of the cumulative new community. An enormously diverse lot, the San Franciscans were initially united only in their desire to profit from the California gold rush.

Basic to the reconstruction of a community is the reestablishment of the old community structure and its values. To the extent that both are achieved, an orderly and stable new community life will be gained. Although American frontiersmen of the nineteenth century came to the cumulative new communities from all points of the compass and were usually unknown and unrelated to each other, most came from essentially similar American communities. The typical American community of the old settled areas possessed a social structure of three levels: (1) The upper level consisted of eminent business and professional men and affluent farmers and planters. This was the local elite, comprising the community leaders. (2) A middle level, persons of average means, was made up of farmers, craftsmen, tradesmen, and the less eminent professionals.(This industrious, honest middle level formed the core of the community.) (3) The lower level included the upright poor, but also those who were either marginal to or alienated from the remainder of the community.[29]

In but not really of the community (and spurned by it) were ne'er-do-well, shiftless, poor whites. Constituting a true *lower people,* they were viewed with contempt and loathing by the members of the upper and middle levels who could not abide their slatternly way of life, their spiritless lack of ambition for success in regular occupations, their often immoral conduct, and their

---

27. Ibid., p. 166. Bancroft, *Popular Tribunals,* 1: 515-76, for the toll of instant vigilantism.

28. Page Smith, *As a City upon the Hill: The Town in American History* (New York: Alfred A. Knopf, 1966), pp. 17-36, formulates the distinction between colonized and cumulative new communities.

29. The following profile of the three-level American community structure is based upon my own research and recent studies of American society, including Jackson Turner Main, *The Social Structure of Revolutionary America* (Princeton: Princeton University Press, 1965); and for the nineteenth century, Stephan Thernstrom, *Poverty and Progress: Social Mobility in a Nineteenth Century City* (Cambridge, Mass.: Harvard University Press, 1964); Ray A. Billington, *America's Frontier Heritage* (New York: Holt, Rinehart, & Winston, 1966), chap. 5; and Merle Curti, *The Making of an American Community* (Stanford, Calif.: Stanford University Press, 1959), pp. 56-63, 107-11ff., 126, 417ff., 448.

disorganized family life.[30] The lower people were not outlaws but often tended to lawlessness and identified more with the outlaw element than with the law-abiding members of the community. The outlaw element lived on the fringes of the community. In some cases they sprang from the lower people, but frequently they were men of good background who chose the outlaw life or drifted into it. They were alienated from the values of the community, although some occasionally joined respectable community life as reformed men.

A community has behavioral boundaries just as it has geographic boundaries. When a new community establishes its geographic boundaries it must also establish its behavioral boundaries. The latter represent the positive, mutual values of the community.[31] The values which held the allegiance of the members of the three-level community were the linked ideals of life and property. The American community of the eighteenth and nineteenth centuries was primarily a property-holder's community, and property was viewed as the very basis of life itself.

The vigilante leaders were drawn from the upper level of the community. The middle level supplied the rank and file. The lower people and outlaws represented the main threat to the reconstruction of the community and were the main targets of the vigilantes.

In the new communities of frontier America, the lower people and outlaws met the representatives of the middle and upper levels in social conflict. The outlaws and lower people wished to burst their lower-level and fringe boundaries and take over the new communities. In sociological terms the outlaws and lower people constituted a "contraculture."[32] Rejecting the respectable values of life and property, they wished to upset the social structure in which the upper- and middle-level men were dominant. The lack of social bonds in the new settlements was their opportunity. On the other hand, the men of upper-level background or aspirations were determined to reestablish the community structure in which they were ascendant. In this they had the support of the middle-level inhabitants, and with them they mounted

30. On the marginal "lower people" of the South (where they have been labeled "poor whites," "crackers," etc.) see Brown, *South Carolina Regulators,* pp. 27-29, and Shields McIlwaine, *The Southern Poor White from Lubberland to Tobacco Road* (Norman: University of Oklahoma Press, 1939), a literary study. On lower people in the North, see Bernard De Voto, *Mark Twain's America* (Boston: Little, Brown, 1932), pp. 54-58, and George F. Parker, *Iowa Pioneer Foundations,* 2 vols. (Iowa City: State Historical Society of Iowa, 1940), 2: 37-48.

31. Kai Erikson, *Wayward Puritans: A Study in the Sociology of Deviance* (New York: John Wiley & Sons, 1966), chap. 1.

32. J. Milton Yinger, "Contraculture and Subculture," *American Sociological Review* 25 (1960): 629, holds that a contraculture occurs "wherever the normative system of a group contains, as a primary element, a theme of conflict with the values of the total society. . . ." See, also, David M. Downes, *The Delinquent Solution: A Study in Subcultural Theory* (New York: Free Press, 1966), pp. 10-11.

vigilante drives to quell the insurgent outlaws and lower people.[33] "We had whole settlements of counterfeiters, or horse thieves, with their sympathizers—where rogues could change names, or pass from house to house, so skillfully as to elude detection—and where if detected, the whole population were ready to rise to the rescue," wrote James Hall in describing the challenge presented by outlaws and lower people in the early years of Midwest settlement. But, continued Hall, "there were other settlements of sturdy honest fellows, the regular backwoodsmen in which rogues were not tolerated. There was therefore a continual struggle between these parties—the honest people trying to expel the others by the terrors of the law, and when that mode failed, forming *regulating* [vigilante] companies, and driving them out by force."[34]

The danger of a takeover of newly settled areas by the alienated, outcast elements of society as described by James Hall was a real threat in the large region east of the 96th meridian; a threat that was repelled with vigor, and sometimes desperation, by regulator-vigilante movements. Thus, in southern Illinois in the 1840s the "Flathead" element of horse thieves, counterfeiters, brigands, slave stealers, and Ohio River-bottom dwellers triggered a violent Regulator reaction.[35] In east Texas in the late 1830s a similar combine of horse thieves, counterfeiters, slave stealers, and "land pirates" incited a Regulator countermovement.[36] By 1841 a group of outlaw gangs had virtually taken over the Rock River country of northern Illinois until they were challenged by a Regulator movement in that year.[37] For twenty-five years an illicit bandit and blackleg community flourished in the tamarack thickets of the northern Indiana county of Noble. This congregation robbed, murdered, counterfeited money, burned buildings, and debauched the sons and daughters of respectable inhabitants until, at last, two-thousand Regulators rose up and shattered it in 1858.[38]

Whether or not the alleged Murrell conspiracy of the lower Mississippi Valley in the 1830s actually represented a concerted plot of white outlaws to raise a gigantic slave rebellion in the interest of an underworld dominion of the region, the outraged reaction—at times reaching the level of hysterical vigilante activity—of the upright citizens of the fast growing Tennessee-

33. See, for example, De Voto, *Mark Twain's America*, pp. 58-62, and Parker, *Iowa Pioneer Foundations*, 2: 37-48, 247-65.
34. David Donald, ed., "The Autobiography of James Hall, Western Literary Pioneer," *Ohio State Archaeological and Historical Quarterly* 56 (1947): 297-98.
35. On the Flatheads, see Brumbaugh, "Regulator Movement," pp. 28-65; Rose, "Papers Relating to Regulator and Flathead Trouble;" Charles Neely, *Tales and Songs of Southern Illinois* (Menasha, Wis.: George Banta, 1938), pp. 7, 35, 411; and Norman W. Caldwell, "Shawneetown: A Chapter in the Indian History of Illinois," *Journal of the Illinois State Historical Society* 32 (1939): 199-200.
36. Sonnichsen, *Ten Texas Feuds*, chap. 1; Neill, "Shelby County," 77-153, and *passim*.
37. Brumbaugh, "Regulator Movement," pp. 3, 5-27; Bryant, *Letters of a Traveller*, pp. 55-68.
38. Mott, *Regulators of Northern Indiana*, pp. 6-7, and *passim*.

Mississippi-Arkansas-Louisiana region revealed the acute sensitivity of lawful society to the large numbers, aggression, and alienation of the area's outlaws and their confederates.[39] And, as indicated above, the earliest of all vigilante movements, the South Carolina Regulators, was a reaction to the contracultural threat of a disorderly mixture of demoralized Indian-war veterans, "straggling" white refugees, escaped slaves, mulattoes, outlaw horse thieves, and counterfeiters who well-nigh ruled the back country until routed by the Regulators.

In the raw new mining camps, cattle towns, railheads, and open ranges of the West a similar challenge emanated from the professional bad men and outlaw gangs, the blackleg element, and the tireless rustlers and horse thieves. To this challenge vigilantes reacted time and again. Sometimes the members of the upper level in the nascent western communities did not wait for an overt crime outbreak but resorted to vigilantism as a preventive measure and to support the three-level structural pattern. "There is to be a Vigilance Committee organized in the town this evening," Thomas G. Wildman wrote back East from Denver, Colorado on September 8, 1859. "All of the leading men of the town has [sic] signed the [vigilante] Constitution," reported Wildman, "and its object is a good one. . . . It is thought that stabbing and drunkenness will be rampant here this winter, and we think that the rowdies and gamblers will be more careful when they find out that we are organized and that all the first men of the town are determined to punish crime."[40] More generally, the loathing of the upper level men of the West for the contraculture was stated with emotion by Thomas Dimsdale, the noted vigilante author of Montana, who delared that "for the low, brutal, cruel, lazy, ignorant, insolent, sensual and blasphemous miscreants that infest the frontier we entertain but one sentiment—aversion—deep, strong, and unchangeable."[41]

III

Aside from its crucial relationship to the fundamental problem of community reconstruction in newly settled areas, vigilantism was a direct response to the problems of frontier law enforcement and justice. As noted above, outlaws and their lower-level sympathizers headed for the new areas and took every possible advantage of the social disorganization stemming from the pioneer state of settlement and the weakness of the traditional institutions of society and state.

The isolation of frontier settlements intensified the nineteenth-century American characteristic of "localism" as "a natural accommodation to a

39. For sources on the supposed Murrell conspiracy, see note 13, above. Historians tend to doubt the existence of a conspiracy.
40. Letters of Thomas and Augustus Wildman, 1858-1865 (Mss in Western Americana Collection, Beinecke Rare Book and Manuscript Library, Yale University, New Haven).
41. Dimsdale, *Vigilantes of Montana,* p. 116.

frontier country of great distances and poor communications." In a "sparsely settled country with poor communications and people of small means, men naturally sought to bring the administration of justice closer to home." The result in the judicial sphere was the prominence of the justice-of-the-peace court as practically a "neighborhood" court and the multiplicity of courts created on the basis of restricted geographical districts.[42] A facet of this pervasive localism, extralegally, was the proliferation of vigilante movements which, like the justice-of-the-peace and geographical-district courts, were organized on a neighborhood, community basis.

Localism and vigilantism thus responded hand-in-hand to frequently inadequate law enforcement. Throughout most of the nineteenth century, law enforcement was highly localized, pinned down to the immediate vicinity of county seat, town, or township.[43] Poor transportation often made the mobility of sheriffs and other officers only as satisfactory as their horses. A fugitive who gained any sort of lead was difficult to catch. The development of the railroad was a help but was no panacea. The officer was bound to the fixed route of the railroad. Moreover, there were large gaps between railroad lines—gaps into which the fugitives unerringly made. In the hinterland stretches unserved by railroads, the authorities were forced to make their way over poor roads or disappearing trails.

Linked with inadequate law enforcement was an uneven judicial system. Through fear, friendliness, or corruption, juries often failed to convict the criminal. Sometimes the accused were never even brought to trial, because in the early days the lack of jails (or their flimsy condition) made it nearly impossible to prevent escape. The judicial system presented numerous opportunities for manipulation by outlaws who could often command some degree of local support. Whenever possible, outlaws would obtain false witnesses, pack juries, bribe officials, and, in extreme cases, intimidate the entire system: judges, juries, and law-enforcement officials.[44] Deficiencies in the judicial system as such were the basis of repeated complaints by frontiersmen who made the familiar point that the American system of administering justice favored the accused over society. The guilty, they charged, used every loophole to evade punishment.[45]

Compounding the problems of the immobility of law enforcement and the deficiencies of the judicial system was the genuinely heavy financial burden

42. Localism is the concept of James Willard Hurst, *The Growth of American Law: The Law Makers* (Boston: Little, Brown, 1950), pp. 39, 92-93.

43. See, for example, Anthony S. Nicolosi, "The Rise and Fall of the New Jersey Vigilant Societies," *New Jersey History* 86 (1968): 29-32.

44. "Uses and Abuses of Lynch Law," *American Whig Review* (May 1850): 461; Pancoast, *Quaker Forty-Niner,* pp. 103-04; Brumbaugh, "Regualtor Movement," pp. 9-11; Dwyn M. Mounger, "Lynching in Mississippi, 1830-1930" (M. A. thesis, Mississippi State University, 1961), p. 9.

45. Richard Maxwell Brown, "Legal and Behavioral Perspectives on American Vigilantism," *Perspectives in American History* 5 (1971): 114-15.

involved in maintaining an adequate police establishment and judicial apparatus in thinly peopled and economically underdeveloped frontier areas. Localities lacked the economic resources to support constables, policemen, and sheriffs in long journeys in pursuit of lawbreakers. A really large expenditure of funds for the chase, capture, jailing, trial, and conviction of malefactors could easily bankrupt the typical frontier county or town. Hence, the economic rationale arose as one of the chief justifications of vigilantism. Repeatedly, vigilantism was praised "as a measure of economy," for it made the costly incarceration and trial of the criminal types unnecessary.[46]

For many a frontiersman, then, vigilantism was a blunt, inexpensive solution to these problems of law enforcement and justice. "We never hanged on circumstantial evidence," reminisced W. N. Byers, a Denver, Colorado vigilante of 1860. "I have known a great many such executions," continued Wildman, "but I don't believe one of them was ever unjust. But when they [the culprits] were proved guilty, they were always hanged. There was no getting out of it. *No, there were no appeals in those days; no writs of errors; no attorney's fees; no pardon in six months. Punishment was swift, sure and certain.*" [47]

In some cases, however, vigilantism appeared where the regular system of justice functioned well. Why did vigilantes sometimes erect a parallel structure of justice when the regular one was adequate? There were three reasons. By usurping the functions of regular law enforcement and justice or duplicating them, the costs of local government were greatly reduced. As taxpayers, the vigilante leaders and rank and file of the upper and middle levels of the community benefited from the reduction in public costs. Second, the process of community reconstruction through the re-creation of social structure and values could be carried on more dramatically by a vigilante movement than through the prosaic regular functioning of the law. A vigilante hanging was a graphic warning to all potentially disruptive elements that community values and structure were to be upheld.

The sort of impression that vigilantes wanted to make on the settlers was that received by young Malcolm Campbell who arrived in Cheyenne, Wyoming in 1868 at the age of twenty-eight. No sooner had he entered the town than there were four vigilante hangings. "So in rapid succession," Campbell recalled, "came before my eyes instances which demonstrated the strength of law [as carried out by vigilantes], and the impotence of the

---

46. On economic problems, see James Stuart, *Three Years in North America,* 2 vols. (Edinburgh: Robert Cadell, 1833), 2: 212-13; Williams, "Crime and Punishment in Alabama," p. 26; Hurst, *Growth of American Law,* pp. 92-93; and James Bryce, *The American Commonwealth,* 2 vols. (London: Macmillan, 1891), 2: 453. On the economic rationale of vigilantism see Brown, "American Vigilante Tradition," p. 183, and "Legal and Behavioral Perspectives," pp. 111-12.

47. James C. Smiley, *History of Denver* . . . (Denver: Denver Times/Times-Sun Publishing Co., 1901), p. 349 (emphasis mine).

criminal. Undoubtedly, these incidents went far in shaping my future life [Campbell became a leading Wyoming sheriff] and in guiding my feet properly in those trails of danger where I was later to apprehend some of the most dangerous outlaws of the plains."[48]

Finally, the vigilante movement sometimes existed for reasons that were essentially unrelated to the traditional problems of crime and disorder. The San Francisco vigilance committee of 1856 is one of the best examples of the vigilante movement as a parallel structure of justice. The San Francisco vigilantes spoke of a crime problem, but examination of the evidence does not reveal a significant increase in crime in 1855 and 1856. The legal authorities had San Francisco crime well under control. Instead, the San Francisco vigilantes were concerned primarily with local political and fiscal reform. They wished to capture control of the municipal government from the dominant political faction of Irish-Catholic Democrats. During their supremacy in San Francisco in the summer of 1856, the vigilantes in effect conceded the effectiveness of the legal structure of crime control and justice by leaving the routine enforcement of the law to the regular police and intervening only in a few major cases. The parallel structure of the San Francisco vigilantes was used to organize a reform political party (the People's Party) and to shatter the Irish-Catholic Democratic faction by exiling some of its leading operatives.[49]

Sometimes the regular and parallel vigilante structures of justice became intertwined. Law-enforcement officials often connived with vigilantes. A sheriff or police chief, while pretending surprise, was in the know when a vigilante force bent on a lynching converged upon his jail. In flagrant cases the law officer had actually helped plan the vigilante onslaught, although appearances were often preserved by a token resistance on his part. It was usually well known in the community, however, that the officer was a part of the vigilante plot.[50]

Whether filling the void created by absent or ineffectual law enforcement, or coexisting in parallel to the regular structure of justice, two models of vigilantism developed: the socially constructive and the socially destructive. According to the accepted aims of vigilantism, the organized movement of lynch law dealt directly with a problem of disorder and then disbanded with an increase in the social stability of the locality. In pragmatic terms (leaving aside the moral issue raised by any extralegal violence) such a vigilante movement had been socially constructive. This, in behavioral terms, was the "good" model of the vigilante movement. The other model, the "bad" or socially destructive vigilante movement, was either flawed from the outset or, more

48. Robert B. David, *Malcolm Campbell, Sheriff* (Casper, Wyo.: Wyomingana, 1932), pp. 18-21.

49. Brown, "Pivot of American Vigilantism," and this essay, below.

50. Brown, "Legal and Behavioral Perspectives," pp. 115-20.

characteristically, encountered such strong local opposition that the result was an anarchic and socially destructive vigilante war.

The socially constructive movement occurred where the vigilantes represented a genuine community consensus. In such cases a decided majority of the people either participated in the movement or approved of it. Vigilantism of this sort simply mobilized the community and overwhelmed the unruly outlaws and lower people. The community was left in a more orderly and stable condition, and the social functions of vigilantism were served. The problem of community order was solved by the consolidation of the three-level social structure and the solidification of the supporting community values.

Although their methods were often harsh and arbitrary, most vigilante movements conformed to the socially constructive model. Of this sort was the prototypical South Carolina Regulator movement of 1767 to 1769, and one of the best examples of the socially constructive model was the northern Illinois Regulator movement of 1841. The northern Illinois movement confronted a classic threat to community order, an aggregation of outlaw gangs in the process of seizing control of the entire area. With the regular government virtually powerless, the respectable leading men (the community upper level), with the help of the middle-level farmers, took the law into their own hands.

Since 1835 the situation in the Rock River Valley of northern Illinois had gone from bad to worse. Several gangs of horse thieves and counterfeiters found the Rock River country a convenient corridor for illicit operations in Wisconsin, Illinois, Iowa, and Missouri. The Driscoll and Brodie gangs had made Ogle and DeKalb counties a virtual fief. The Oliver gang dominated Winnebago County. The Bliss-Dewey-West gang was strong in Lee County, while the leading Birch gang of horse thieves ranged through the whole northern Illinois area. By 1840 the desperadoes were numerous enough to control elections in Ogle County and similarly threaten other counties. One summer the outlaws even went so far as to burn the newly constructed courthouse at Oregon, Illinois.

With conditions deteriorating, a vigilante counterattack was mounted. In April 1841, fifteen "representative men" of Ogle County formed the first Regulator company. In no time at all the counties were dotted with Regulator squads, but the most vigorous were those of Ogle. The Regulators embodied the social, economic, and political prestige of Ogle County. John Phelps was the county's oldest and wealthiest settler and the founder of the county seat, Oregon. Peter Smith combined a bank presidency with the ownership of sixteen hundred acres of land. The farmers who made up the bulk of the movement were substantial property holders; they had taken up government land claims ranging from 240 to 600 acres. These solid citizens brooked no

---

51. Brumbaugh, "Regulator Movement," pp. 3, 5-27; Bryant, *Letters of a Traveller,* pp. 55-68.

opposition to their vigilante movement; they burned the Rockford *Star* to the ground soon after it published an anti-Regulator editorial. On the whole, however, the local elite kept the movement well under control. Having accomplished their purpose in a whirlwind campaign of whipping, hanging, and shooting, the Regulator companies disbanded. With the conquest of the outlaw gangs, social order and stability characterized the Rock River Valley.[51]

The northern Illinois Regulator movement exhibited the major features of the successful frontier vigilante movement. It was well organized, with good discipline, and it subjected its victims to orderly though extralegal trials. With about one thousand members, mass participation of respectable men was the mode, but the movement was dominated, clearly, by the leading men of the area. The Regulators were implacable in their war on the outlaws and undeterred by criticism. Despite the opposition of the Rockford *Star,* no anti-Regulator coalition developed that might have jeopardized the movement, and the outlaw gangs were isolated and broken up. The vigilante leaders desired the bolstering of their position in the upper level of the community, but they did not covet power for its own sake. With the outlaw challenge repelled, peace reigned, and men returned to their regular occupations.[52]

In the socially constructive model, such as the northern Illinois Regulator movement, opposition to the vigilantes was restricted to outlaws and lower-level people who, although often powerful in their own right, could gain no support from the remainder of the community. For vigilantes to be stymied, a broad anti-vigilante coalition was usually necessary. A socially destructive model of vigilantism resulted in anarchy. Without community consensus behind the vigilante movement, strong opposition inevitably arose, and civil conflict flared. The formation of an anti-vigilante coalition almost inevitably condemned the community to a chaotic, internecine conflict between the vigilantes and their opponents.

Respectable men did not join the anti-vigilante coalition because of any great sympathy for outlaws and lower-level people. They were impelled into opposition by things the vigilantes did or stood for. Sometimes two or three powerful local families would join the anti-vigilante movement. In some cases, these families had been carrying on a feud of sorts with leading vigilante families.[53] At times a local political party or faction entered the anti-vigilante movement, because the vigilantes were dominated by the rival party or faction.[54] If the leading Democrats of a community, for example, were among the vigilantes, the anti-vigilante coalition—in the pre-Civil War

---

52. On other socially constructive vigilante movements see Brown, "American Vigilante Tradition," table 5-1, p. 157; n. 91, p. 213.

53. For example, the Turk family (Slickers) vs. the Jones family (anti-Slickers) in southwest Missouri. Lay, *History of Benton County,* pp. 46-61.

54. On the political rivalry factor, see the examples in Brown, "American Vigilante Tradition," n. 93, p. 213.

period—might attract the local Whigs. Political rivalries were often linked to vigilante strife, for in many instances vigilante leaders harbored political ambitions and were not above using the movement to promote their personal goals.[55] Economic rivalries among community leading men were also a factor in vigilante alignments, pro and con. Acute mercantile competition sometimes caused a leading storekeeper to join the opposition if his rival were a vigilante.[56] Hence, personal, family, political, and economic antagonisms accounted for a readymade vigilante opposition in some communities.

At other times vigilante extremism drew into opposition decent men who otherwise probably would not have opposed them. Even the best vigilante movements usually attracted a fringe of sadists and naturally violent types. Often, such men had criminal tendencies and were glad to use the vigilante movement as an excuse to give free reign to their unsavory passions. It was always a problem for vigilante leaders to keep these elements under control, and sometimes a movement was dominated or seriously skewed by these social misfits. Sadistic punishment and torture, arbitrary and unnecessary killings, and mob tyranny marked vigilante movements that had truly gone bad.[57] When this happened many sound and conservative men felt they must oppose the vigilantes, although they probably felt no quarrel with the initial objectives of the movement.

Examples of the socially destructive model did not occur as often as the constructive model, but when they did extremely violent conflicts tended to arise. Among the leading instances were the east Texas Regulators (vs. the Moderators), 1840-1844; the southwest Missouri Slickers (vs. the anti-Slickers), 1842-1844; and the southern Illinois Regulators (vs. the Flatheads), 1846-1850. Occasionally an anti-vigilante coalition arose which, although unable to match vigilante strength, could define the limits of vigilante power because of its potential for calling in outside help. The anti-vigilante Law and Order faction in San Francisco, 1856, played this role. The vigilantes there would have liked to have hanged Judge David S. Terry but did not dare do so,

55. For example, in later years San Francisco's 1856 vigilance committee leader, William T. Coleman, criticized Charles Doane (the vigilantes' grand marshal) for running for sheriff on the People's Party ticket. Coleman felt that vigilante leaders such as Doane should not run for office. William T. Coleman, "Vigilance Committee, 1856" (Mss, ca. 1880, in Bancroft Library, University of California, Berkeley), p. 139.
56. In New Mexico's Lincoln County War of 1878-1879, the McSween-Tunstall-Brewer mercantile faction organized (unsuccessfully) as Regulators against the dominant Murphy-Dolan mercantile faction. William A. Keleher, *Violence in Lincoln County: 1869-1881* (Albuquerque: University of New Mexico Press, 1957), pp. 152-54. Maurice Garland Fulton, *History of the Lincoln County War,* ed. Robert N. Mullin (Tucson: University of Arizona Press, 1968), pp. 137-42ff.
57. This was the case with the east Texas Regulators, the southern Illinois Regulators, and the southwest Missouri Slickers, but there were other movements of this stripe. Even in well controlled movements, the elements of sadism and extremism often crept in in a minor way. The problem was inherent in vigilantism.

for the Law and Order group would have almost certainly obtained federal action against the vigilantes.[58] Similarly, the Moderators in the South Carolina back country, 1769, were not strong enough to overturn Regulator domination, but they did check the movement and bring its excesses to an end.[59]

During the life of the socially destructive model, the moral standing of vigilantes and anti-vigilantes, alike, increasingly tended to be compromised. As the struggle became more violent, the respectable men of the anti-vigilante coalition put a higher premium on the violent talents of the outlaw element with which they otherwise had nothing in common. So, too, did the original vigilantes themselves recruit and acquire a criminal fringe which they put to mercenary use. With the community descending bloodily into chaos, wise and prudent men left if they could. The opposing movements fell more and more under the control of the worst and most extreme of their adherents. About this stage, the desperate neutral residents would beseech state authorities for the intervention of the militia, and the local war would subside fitfully in the presence of state troops.[60]

The Regulator-Moderator war of east Texas (1840-1844) is representative of the degenerate, socially destructive vigilante situation. The scene was the redland and piney woods country of east Texas in the days of the Lone Star Republic. The center of the conflict was in Shelby County. Fronting on the Sabine River where it formed the boundary between Louisiana and Texas, Shelby County lay in an old border area that had never known much peace and calm. In 1840 the Regulator movement arose as a quite honest and straightforward attack on a ring of corrupt county officials who specialized in fraudulent land transactions. The rise of the Regulators was probably inevitable in any case, for the county had long wilted under a plague of counterfeiting, horse thievery, Negro stealing, and common murder and mayhem. Yet the Regulators overplayed their hand, especially after their original leader, Charles W. Jackson, was killed and replaced by a nefarious adventurer, Watt Moorman. Bad elements infiltrated both the Regulators and their opponents, the Moderators, but by comparison the latter seemed, gradually, to be less obnoxious. Although some honorable and level-headed citizens like John W. Middleton stayed with the Regulators to the end, an attitude of wild vengefulness came to be more typical of the band. The early ne'er-do-well group among the Moderators dwindled. As more and more citizens were forced to take sides, many joined the Moderators in reaction to the sadism and vindictiveness of the swashbuckling Watt Moorman, who

58. San Francisco *Daily Town Talk,* August 8-9, 1856; see also Brown, "American Vigilante Tradition," n. 98, p. 214.

59. Brown, *South Carolina Regulators,* chap. 6. Until about the 1850's, opponents of regulators and vigilantes, following South Carolina precedent, were often called "moderators."

60. For an 1850 paradigm of vigilante movements gone bad see "Uses and Abuses of Lynch Law," pp. 462-63.

affected a military uniform and blew great blasts on a hunting horn to summon his henchmen.

The original reasons for the founding of the Regulator movement were all but forgotten. The war became a purpose in itself, a complexity of personal and family feuds that was consuming the area in blood lust. Several attempts to restore peace failed. Complete anarchy was the situation in 1844 when an all-out battle between the two armies of several hundred men each was forestalled only by the dramatic intervention of Sam Houston and the militia. After four years, eighteen men had been killed and many more wounded, and a stream in the vicinity was called "Widow's Creek." The killing of so many leaders and the exhaustion of the survivors no doubt explain why the war was not revived after Sam Houston and the militia withdrew. Ex-Regulators and ex-Moderators warily fought side-by-side in separate companies during the Mexican War, but for fifty years east Texans were reluctant to discuss the episode lest old enmities be rekindled.[61]

IV

Although the era of classic frontier vigilantism was over by about 1900, the tradition did not die. The main tradition of frontier vigilantism evolved into neo-vigilantism. The latter was an application of vigilantism to the problems of an emerging urban, industrial, racially and ethnically diverse America. The transition from the old to the new vigilantism was heralded by the San Francisco Vigilance Committee of 1856. The latter represented a blending of the methods of the old vigilantism with the victims of the new. Many of the features of neo-vigilantism were present in the San Francisco movement of 1856.

Neo-vigilantism was ordinarily urban rather than rural, and that was the case in San Francisco, 1856. The old vigilantism was directed mainly against horse thieves, counterfeiters, outlaws, bad men, and the rural lower people, while neo-vigilantism found its chief targets among Catholics, Jews, immigrants, Negroes, laboring men and labor leaders, political radicals, and proponents of civil liberties. The actions and overtones of the San Francisco movement of 1856 were strongly imbued with the passions and prejudices that came to feature neo-vigilantism.

With a core membership of old-stock, white Anglo-Saxon Protestants, the San Francisco vigilantes of 1856 were ethnically biased; their ire focused on one group, the Irish.[62] The vigilantes were anti-Catholic; their hero and martyr was the anti-Romanist San Francisco editor, James King, and most of

61. Sonnichsen, *Ten Texas Feuds,* chap. 1; Neill, "Shelby County," pp. 77-153, and *passim.*
62. The following interpretation of the San Francisco vigilante movement of 1856 is based upon Brown, "Pivot of American Vigilantism."

their victims of 1856 were Irish-Catholics. Although the vigilante ranks included workingmen and mechanics, there was a distinct class tinge to the 1856 movement. Middle- and upper-class merchants were aligned against the lower-class adherents of the Democratic political machine of San Francisco. Also present was a disregard for civil liberties. The mercantile vigilantes of 1856, angered by the arguments of John Nugent of the San Francisco *Herald* in favor of regular justice, quickly organized an advertising boycott that transformed the *Herald* overnight from the strongest to the weakest of the city's major dailies.

Superficially concerned with a crime problem, the San Francisco vigilantes of 1856 were more fundamentally motivated by a desire to seize control of the municipal government from the Democratic political machine that found the nucleus of its support among the lower-class, Irish-Catholic workers of the city. Basic to the vigilante movement was the desire to establish a business-oriented local government which would reduce expenditures, deprive the Irish-Catholic Democrats of access to municipal revenues, and lower taxes. To a considerable extent, the San Francisco vigilante episode of 1856 represented a struggle for power between two blocs of opposed religious, class, and ethnic characteristics. Thus, the vigilante leadership of upper- and middle-class, old American, Protestant merchants confronted a political faction based upon lower-class Irish-Catholic, laborers. Such were the social and economic tensions that typically enlisted the violence of neo-vigilantism.

The protean character of neo-vigilantism precludes an extensive account of it here; only significant tendencies may be noted. Black Americans have been the objects of three distinct Ku Klux Klan movements over a century-long period going back to 1867.[63] The second Ku Klux Klan broadened its attack in the 1920s to include Catholics and Jews as well as blacks and immoral, ne'er-do-well whites.[64] Immigrants have repeatedly been the victims of neo-vigilantism, one of the most spectacular instances being the lynching of eleven Sicilians in New Orleans in 1891.[65] Another favorite target of neo-vigilantism was industrial laborers and labor-union organizers (many of whom were immigrants) during strikes or attempts to organize.[66]

Political radicals have often undergone neo-vigilante harassment; one of

63. On the first Klan see Trelease, *White Terror.*
64. On the second Klan see Chalmers, *Hooded Americanism;* Alexander, *Ku Klux Klan in the Southwest;* and, on its significant urban aspect, Kenneth T. Jackson, *The Ku Klux Klan in the City, 1915-1930* (New York: Oxford University Press, 1967).
65. John E. Coxe, "The New Orleans Mafia Incident," *Louisiana Historical Quarterly* 20 (1937): 1067-1110; John S. Kendall, "Who Killa De Chief," *Louisiana Historical Quarterly* 22 (1939): 492-530; Brown, "Legal and Behavioral Persepctives," pp. 118-20. The graphic account of the lynching published in the *New York Times,* March 15, 1891, is reprinted in Richard Maxwell Brown, ed., *American Violence* (Englewood Cliffs, N.J.: Prentice-Hall, 1970), pp. 103-07.
66. For example, in 1917 in Tulsa, Oklahoma, vigilantes attacked seventeen I.W.W. members who were attempting to organize oil field workers. *The "Knights of Liberty" Mob and the I. W. W. Prisoners in Tulsa, Okla. (November 9, 1917)* (New York: National Civil Liberties Bureau, 1918). In this incident the police apparently connived with the vigilantes.

the most striking examples was the arrest of thousands of Communists and radicals in the "Red raids" of January 1, 1920.[67] The raids were carried out under the color of law, but the entire enterprise resembled nothing so much as a gigantic vigilante roundup. Proponents of civil liberties have at times fallen afoul of a neo-vigilante spirit manifested in such waves of intolerance as McCarthyism of the early 1950s. The most recent example of neo-vigilantism has been the self-protective patrol groups of the 1960s and early 1970s.

During the turbulent, crime-ridden, riot-torn 1960s, three sectors of the American population became vigilante-prone: (1) Black enclaves, North and South, which felt the need for self-protective organizations against white violence and harassment. The Deacons for Defense and Justice in the middle and late 1960s came to exemplify the neo-vigilante spirit among this portion of the black population. (2) White urban and suburban neighborhoods which felt threatened by a possible incursion of black rioters and looters. The predominantly Italian membership of the North Ward Citizens' Committee (1967-) of Newark, New Jersey emerged as the leading example of this current vigilante tendency. (3) Urban neighborhoods which were beset by crime. The Maccabees (1964-1966) of Crown Heights, Brooklyn, arose as the prototype for this species of vigilantism. Although the Maccabees were mainly white (reacting against black steet crime), similar black organizations have appeared in high-crime black neighborhoods.[68]

These vigilante movements of the 1960s and early 1970s have differed from classic vigilantes in the sense that the former have not ordinarily taken the law into their own hands. Instead, their main activity has been patrol action in their neighborhoods in radio-equipped automobiles (linked to a central headquarters) for the purpose of spotting, reporting, and discouraging criminal acts against the residents of their neighborhoods. Characteristically, these modern vigilantes cooperate with the police, the single major exception to this generalization being the black organization of Deacons for Defense and Justice formed, in part, to deal with white police harassment of black enclaves in small cities of the deep South. Despite cooperation with the police, these movements are in the authentic vigilante tradition, for they are associations in which citizens join together for self-protetion under conditions of disorder and lawlessness. Moreover, these movements, while not taking the law into their own hands, have been commonly viewed as "vigilantes" by their members, the police and the authorities, and the public at large.[69]

67. Robert K. Murray, *Red Scare: A Study in National Hysteria, 1919-1920* (Minneapolis: University of Minnesota Press, 1955). William Preston, *Aliens and Dissenters* (Cambridge, Mass.: Harvard University Press, 1963), contains examples of neovigilante attacks upon workers, immigrants, and radicals. See also John W. Caughey, ed., *Their Majesties the Mob* (Chicago: University of Chicago Press, 1960), pp. 1-25, 100-205.

68. Brown, "American Vigilante Tradition," pp. 201-08.

69. Ibid. See, also, Gary T. Marx and Dane Archer, "Citizen Involvement in the Law Enforcement Process," *American Behavioral Scientist* 15 (1971): 52-72.

V

In its more than two century history, vigilantism has reflected the profound ambiguity that has characterized so much of American life and thought. Indeed, vigilantism is a salient illustration of one of the major paradoxes of American history: the coexistence in American life of significant and apparently contrary elite and popular aspects.

The elite and popular factors, while contradictory on the surface, have flourished in a symbiotic relationship that is one of the crucial social facts of American history.[70] Yet, it has been customary for us to view the elitist and popular aspects of American life as being in conflict with each other, and much of our social and historical analysis has been in terms of the elite-popular dichotomy. While the orientation of most Americans has been forthrightly democratic, it has been a commonplace of our sociological and economic insight to stress elite dominance. In studies of the American local community from the colonial period to the twentieth century, the local elite has been seen in firm control of the community.[71] Elite domination also appears repeatedly in the realm of economics—a recent study statistically documents the assertion that an "unequal distribution of income has been characteristic of the American social structure since at least 1910, and despite minor year-to-year fluctuations . . . no significant trend toward income equality has appeared."[72] Elite ascendancy in politics is also an old story. There seems to be little qualitative difference between the domination of the gentry in late eighteenth-century Virginia politics depicted by historian Charles S. Sydnor and the preponderance in twentieth-century American politics of what we have come to refer to as the "power elite" or the "establishment."[73]

Still, the most thoughtful observers of American life have discerned a no less significant popular element. In his incomparable study of *Democracy in America,* Alexis de Tocqueville contends that the besetting problem of America, the tyranny of the majority, stems from the might of the democratic element. Tocqueville's insight has been borne out time and again,

---

70. A general study of biformities in American history is Michael Kammen, *People of Paradox: An Inquiry Concerning the Origins of American Civilization* (New York: Alfred A. Knopf, 1972).
71. Among many studies see, for example, for the colonial period, Charles S. Grant, *Democracy in the Connecticut Frontier Town of Kent* (New York: Columbia University Press, 1961), which examines the operation of "democracy" in Kent and finds elite domination, and for the twentieth century, the classic community study, Robert S. and Helen M. Lynd, *Middletown* (New York: Harcourt, Brace, 1929).
72. Gabriel Kolko, *Wealth and Power in America: An Analysis of Social Class and Income Distribution* (New York: Praeger, 1962), p. 13.
73. Charles S. Sydnor, *Gentlemen Freeholders: Political Practices in Washington's Virginia* (Chapel Hill: University of North Carolina Press, 1952). C. Wright Mills, *The Power Elite* (New York: Oxford University Press, 1956).

most recently by the power of McCarthyism in the 1950s. And while covert elite domination has usually been the case, a host of ebullient popular movements—the Jacksonian Democrats, Populism, and the New Deal are only a few of many, many such movements—have been a testament to our irrepressible democratic impulse. At the apex of our political system, some of our greatest presidents—Jefferson, Jackson, Lincoln, Wilson, and Franklin D. Roosevelt—have been popular leaders.

The elite and popular dimensions of vigilantism are equally compelling, and the previous analysis in this study has shown that the typical vigilante movement was thoroughly democratic and popular in its base. Certainly, it is questionable that the American people would ever have given their allegiance in any significant way to any social institution that failed to exemplify a commitment to popular values. Vigilantism could never have been such a powerful force in nineteenth-century America without having gripped the minds and emotions of the mass of Americans. This it did through a system of ideas and beliefs that emerged in the entirely popular ideology of vigilantism.

The ideology of vigilantism was grounded in the frontier settlers' strong belief in "self-preservation [as] the first law of society, and the basis upon which its structure [was] built."[74] But vigilantes clearly recognized that their illegal action in taking the law into their own hands, even if in the interest of the higher goal of social order, dealt a blow at legal, constituted authority. This dilemma was resolved by resort to a higher-law justification on the ground of the inalienable right of revolution. Thus, in 1816 and 1817 early Illinois vigilantes were deemed to be "revolutionary tribunals," and in the Acadian region of southwest Louisiana in 1859 a large vigilante movement explicitly proclaimed its character as a "revolutionary movement."[75]

The concepts of self-preservation and the right of revolution were basic, but even more crucial to the ideology of vigilantism was the doctrine of popular sovereignty. One early-twentieth-century commentator on vigilantism notes "that the doctrine of vigilance, as of lynch law in general, is based upon the theory that the people have the right to hold perpetual vigil over all their institutions and to correct, where necessary, abuses and corruption which threaten the security of their lives and property.[76] The justification of popular sovereignty for nineteenth-century vigilantism was frequently cited by

74. Pierce County, Washington Territory, Vigilance Committee, Draft of Compact, June 1, 1856 (Mss in Western Americana Collection, Beinecke Rare Book and Manuscript Library, Yale University, New Haven). See, also, Griffin, "Vigilance Committees of the Attakapas," pp. 153-55; Dimsdale, *Vigilantes of Montana,* p. 107; and *History of Johnson County,* pp. 372-73. More extended discussions of the ideology of vigilantism appear in Brown, "American Vigilante Tradition," pp. 179-83.

75. Thomas Ford, *A History of Illinois from Its Commencement as a State in 1818 to 1847* [1854], 2 vols. (Chicago: R. R. Donnelley & Sons, 1945-1946), 1: 10-11; Griffin, "Vigilance Committees of the Attakapas," pp. 153-55; see, also, Barde, *History of the Committees,* pp. 26-27.

76. *Green Bag* 14 (1902): 291-94. For a discussion of the "doctrine of vigilance" in the nineteenth century see Brown, "American Vigilante Tradition," pp. 179-80.

vigilantes themselves. This was concisely put by the northern Indiana Regulators of 1858 who prefaced a massive drive on local bad people with the statement, "we are believers in the *doctrine of popular sovereignty;* that the people of this country are the real sovereigns, and that whenever the laws, made by those to whom they have delegated their authority, are found inadequate to their protection, it is the right of the people to take the protection of their property into their own hands, and deal with these villains according to their just desserts. . . ."[77]

Just as vigilantism originated in South Carolina in the decade of the 1760s, so did the concept of popular sovereignty emerge in the Revolutionary era and gain legitimacy from its association with our successful act of rebellion against the mother country. Gordon S. Wood, in *The Creation of the American Republic, 1776-1787,* has shown that popular sovereignty was in part the result of the colonists' "long tradition of extra-legislative action by the people, action that more often than not had taken the form of mob violence and crowd disturbance. . . . Beginning with the Revolutionary movement (but with roots deep in American history)," Wood declares, "the people came to rely more and more on their ability to organize themselves and to act 'out-of-doors' whether as 'mobs,' as political clubs, or as conventions," so that by the 1780s the notion of the "sovereignty of the people" was accepted.[78]

The ideology of vigilantism, with its stress on popular sovereignty, self-preservation, and the right of revolution, attracted the mass allegiance of Americans in its popular dimension. At the same time, the institution gained the ardent participation and approval of members of the American elite. The social, economic, and political leaders of the nineteenth and early-twentieth century who directly participated in vigilante activity or strongly encouraged it underlined the elite component of American vigilantism.

Most of these men took part in vigilante movements as young pioneers, but they never repudiated their vigilante service in later life. In fact, they were proud of it. Some of these young vigilantes reached the pinnacle of American political and economic life. Five became United States Senators: Alexander Mouton, Louisiana (1837-1842); Francis M. Cockrell, Missouri (1875-1905); Leland Stanford, California (1885-1893); William J. McConnel, Idaho (1890-1891); and Wilbur Fisk Sanders, Montana (1890-1893). In 1890 four ex-vigilantes (Cockrell, Stanford, McConnel, and Sanders) were serving in the Senate at the same time. Eight former vigilantes became governors of states or territories: Alexander Mouton, Louisiana (1843-1846); Augustus C. French,

---

77. Mott, *Regulators of Northern Indiana,* pp. 15-18.
78. Gordon S. Wood, *The Creation of the American Republic, 1776-1787* (Chapel Hill: University of North Carolina Press, 1969), pp. 319-21. See, also, Richard Maxwell Brown, "Violence and The American Revolution," in Stephen G. Kurtz and James H. Hutson, eds., *Essays on the American Revolution* (Chapel Hill: University of North Carolina Press, 1973), pp. 108-10.

Illinois (1846-1853); Leland Stanford, California (1861-1863); William J. McConnel, Idaho (1893-1896); John E. Osborne (1893-1895) and Fennimore Chatterton (1903-1905), Wyoming; and Miguel A. Otero (1897-1906) and George Curry (1907-1911), New Mexico.[79]

Two distinguished Americans served in the San Francisco vigilante movement of 1856, one at the head of the organization and the other in the ranks. The rank-and-file member was thirty-two-year-old Leland Stanford who, as indicated above, later served California both as governor and senator. As one of the "Big Four" who built the Southern Pacific and Central Pacific railroads, Stanford was one of the notable American capitalists of his time as well as being the philanthropic founder of Stanford University.[80]

William Tell Coleman, the incisive chief executive of the San Francisco movement of 1856, was not only one of the greatest of all American vigilante leaders but also one of the most prominent Californians of the pioneer generation. A great San Francisco merchant, Coleman followed his vigilante service with significant political activity in California and the nation. In 1865 he was a leading, though unsuccessful, contender for election to the United States Senate, while in 1884 the eminent journalist Charles A. Dana of the New York *Sun* pushed Coleman for the Presidency.[81]

Perhaps most striking of all is the approval which two presidents of the United States gave to vigilantism. As president, Andrew Jackson once advised Iowa settlers to punish a murderer by lynch-law action, and as a young man on his western ranch, Theodore Roosevelt sought unsuccessfully (the vigilante leaders feared that the impetuous T. R. might indiscreetly disclose vigilante actions) to participate in the great Montana lynch-law movement of 1884 led by the powerful cattlemen against horse thieves and rustlers. Roosevelt's youthful enthusiasm for vigilantism was no passing fancy.[82] It remained with him until the end of his days. As late as 1915, and after having served as president, he drew a favorable parallel between western vigilantism and his action in taking the Canal Zone away from Panama, and he looked back on the vigilante movement that he had sought to join as being "in the main wholesome."[83]

Theodore Roosevelt's pro-vigilante attitude might seem all the more noteworthy not only because he became president, and thus the chief executive officer in charge of upholding our laws, but also because he was trained in law at Harvard as a young man. An examination of legal and judicial attitudes in late-nineteenth-century and early-twentieth-century

79. Brown, "American Vigilante Tradition," pp. 177, 192-95, where the vigilante activity and background of each man is given.
80. Ibid., p. 192.
81. Ibid., pp. 177, 192.
82. Ibid., p. 192.
83. Brown, "Legal and Behavioral Perspectives," pp. 121, 138.

America reveals, however, that legal training and practice was by no means an inoculation against provigilante feeling.[84] Rather, a host of leading lawyers, judges, and legal writers looked upon vigilantism with a most benevolent eye. One of the most remarkable features of the elite aspect of vigilantism is that those who were professionally sworn to uphold the law, those who were among the most prominent members of the turn-of-the-century American legal and judicial establishment, actually endorsed vigilantism.

These men, some of whom were founders and presidents of their state bar associations, should have been staunch in their defense of due process of law. Instead, their concerns for the tumultuous conditions of American life in the period from the Civil War to World War I and their desires for the repression of crime and disorder were so overwhelming that the result was often outspoken approval of (and sometimes participation in) lynch law.[85]

Among those who expressed approval of vigilantism were H. L. Hosmer (chief justice, Montana, 1864-1868), Henry T. Lewis (associate justice, Georgia supreme court, 1897-1903), and Walter Clark (North Carolina supreme court, 1889-1924).[86] Joseph B. Wall took a leading role in a flagrant lynching at the doorstep of a federal court in Tampa only five years before he became the first president of the Florida State Bar Association in 1887.[87] Two associate justices of the United States supreme court, David J. Brewer (1890-1910) and Joseph P. Bradley (in 1882), expressed qualified approval of lynch law, and another, Stephen J. Field, had adopted some extralegal expedients while serving as a young magistrate in California during the Gold Rush era.[88]

A vociferous provigilante spokesman was Charles J. Bonaparte, an ornament of the eastern legal elite, a leading Baltimore lawyer and progressive reformer who would ultimately serve as President Theodore Roosevelt's attorney general. In an address to the Yale Law School graduating class of 1890, Bonaparte commented on the "much misjudged custom of lynching." In approving tones Bonaparte declared, "Judge Lynch may make mistakes, and his mistakes can be corrected by no writ of error, but if the number of failures of justice in his Court could be compared with those in our more regular tribunals, I am not sure that he need fear the result. I believe that very few innocent men are lynched," Bonaparte affirmed, "and,

---

84. This is the thesis of Brown, "Legal and Behavioral Perspectives."
85. For my behavioral conception of American justice as a spectrum ranging from the legal emphasis on due process of law to the extralegal emphasis on crime control see "Legal and Behavioral Perspectives," pp. 97-100. My interpretation, in turn, draws upon Herbert L. Packer, "Two Models of the Criminal Process," *University of Pennslyvania Law Review* 113 (1964): 1-68, reprinted in revised from in Herbert L. Packer, *The Limits of Criminal Sanction* (Stanford, Calif.: Stanford University Press, 1968): 149-73.
86. Brown, "Legal and Behavioral Perspectives," pp. 128-31.
87. Ibid., pp. 126-28.
88. Ibid., pp. 131-33, 139.

of those who have not committed the past offense for which they suffer, a still smaller proportion are decent members of society."[89]

Eight years later in the *Yale Law Journal*, Bonaparte underscored the close connection between lynching, vigilance committees, regulators, and white caps, and in a sophisticated statement of the rationale for vigilantism noted that "the underlying purpose in all these cases is not to violate, but to vindicate, the law; or to speak more accurately, the law is violated in form that it may be vindicated in substance, its 'adjective' part (i.e., matter of procedure) is disregarded that its 'substantive' part may be preserved." Bonaparte did not rest content with this salute to lynch law but went on (as would Justice Brewer, later, in 1903) to call for changes in legal procedure that would have moved the regular judicial system toward the substance of vigilantism. Bonaparte was attracted to the certainty and irrevocability of vigilante action, and along this line he called for reforms (to him and others they were viewed as reforms) which would have introduced a measure of judicial lynch law into the regular system. He wanted an increase in the number of capital offenses and the automatic imposition of the death sentence upon a conviction for a third "serious" offense; the aim here, said Bonaparte, was the utter "extirpation" of habitual criminals.[90] That a man with such views became the United States attorney general only seven years after expressing them follows in that he was appointed by the vigilante sympathizing president, Theodore Roosevelt. Fortunately, both Roosevelt and Bonaparte were interested in other things by then, and Bonaparte's chief impact as attorney general was not in criminal law but in the economic area of trust-busting.[91]

VI

Despite the existence of some anarchic, socially destructive vigilante movements, the main result of vigilantism was to enhance social stability and order in frontier areas. Thus, in the short-run perspective of frontier development, the paradoxical aim of vigilantism—breaking the law to uphold the law—was gained. This, of course, is a judgment strictly limited to the behavioral impact of vigilantism; it does not consider the ethical and

89. Eric F. Goldman, *Charles J. Bonaparte: Patrician Reformer: His Earlier Career* (Baltimore: Johns Hopkins Press, 1943), p. 32, and *passim*.

90. Charles J. Bonaparte, "Lynch Law and Its Remedy," *Yale Law Journal* 8 (1898-1899): 336, 338-42. On Brewer, see Brown, "Legal and Behavioral Perspectives," p. 139.

91. Goldman, *Charles J. Bonaparte*, pp. 130-31. Another member of the legal illuminati who favored the legalization of a vigilante punishment (whipping) and a Southern lynch-mob practice (castration) was Connecticut's "leading citizen"—Simeon E. Baldwin, a man of immense distinction, who was a Yale law professor, supreme court justice and governor of Connecticut, and the president of the American Political Science Association and other national learned societies. Neither of Baldwin's proposed "reforms" were adopted. See Brown, "Legal and Behavioral Perspectives," pp. 139-44.

moral questions posed by the lawlessness of vigilantism. Moral and ethical considerations are, however, moot in a long-range, historical perspective on vigilantism.

For generations, Americans have been ambiguous in their attitude to law. In some respects, Americans are and have always been a law-abiding people, yet this widespread respect for law has been counterpointed, historically, by deeply ingrained disrespect for law.[92] The key to this apparent contradiction lies in the selectivity with which Americans have approached the law. Going back to the colonial period and the patriotic resistance to the British mother country, "the Americans," observes James Truslow Adams, "had developed a marked tendency to obey only such laws as they chose to obey. . . . Laws which did not suit the people, or even certain classes, were disobeyed constantly with impunity."[93]

The selective obedience to law noted by Adams relates to an American characteristic cited by legal historian James Willard Hurst, our "instrumental" view of the law. This "instrumental attitude" grew out of the necessity of attaining "immediate practical results" in the course of settling a continent. "Our popular assemblies, our free religious congregations, the simplicity of our surroundings, and our need to use . . . government for . . . very tangible operations," writes Hurst, "taught us a matter-of-fact attitude toward government; government belonged to us, and it was an instrument of utility, not an object of awe."[94]

This arbitrary viewpoint toward law is at the core of the American tendency to lawlessness, and it owes much to vigilantism, as Roscoe Pound and others have seen.[95] Thus, the complaint of opponents of vigilantism that if vigilantes "had expended in the discharge of their duties as citizens the same energy and public spirit they displayed as vigilantes, officers could have been elected who would fearlessly and faithfully have performed their duty" is based on the perception of a legal-extralegal dichotomy not shared by vigilantes.[96]

The vigilante stance, with its typically American instrumental approach to law, supported a dual system of legal and extralegal justice—a dual system that rested upon a primary allegiance to the repression of crime and disorder, rather than to the procedural safeguards of the law. Hence, Americans did not

92. See, for example, Alexis de Tocqueville, *Democracy in America* [1835], and trans. Phillips Bradley, 2 vols. (New York: Alfred A. Knopf, 1948), 1: 247-48, 272-87, 319-23.
93. James Truslow Adams, "Our Lawless Heritage," *Atlantic Monthly* 42 (1928): 736.
94. James Willard Hurst, *Law and Social Process in United States History* (Ann Arbor: University of Michigan Press, 1960), p. 287. See, also, Hurst, *Growth of American Law*, p. 4.
95. Roscoe Pound, *Criminal Justice in America* (New York: H. Holt, 1930), p. 64, an outgrowth of Pound's notable earlier study, "The Causes of Popular Dissatisfaction with the Administration of Justice," *Reports of American Bar Association* 29 (1906): part 1; 395-417. See, also, Brown, "American Vigilante Tradition," pp. 199-201.
96. Charles C. Butler, "Lynching," *American Law Review* 44 (1910): 208-09. See, also, the editorial in the New York *National Democrat* (quoted in Brown, "American Vigilante Tradition," pp. 199-201) in opposition to the San Francisco vigilantes of 1856.

feel any less public spirited when they participated in lynch law. Instead, they saw vigilante action as a devotion to duty as important and necessary in its own way as the choice and support of upstanding officials. To many Americans the legal and extralegal were complementary, not contradictory, aspects of a broad fabric of American justice.[97] Usually, Americans left the enforcement of law and the administration of justice to their constituted agents, the legal authorities, but often the people directly assumed these functions as vigilantes.

97. Brown, "Legal and Behavioral Perspectives," pp. 97-100.

Chapter Six

White Collar Vigilantism: The Politics of Anti-Communism in the United States

Edward Schneier

In 1957 John Henry Faulk was fired by wcbs radio. Like thousands of others in the entertainment industry, Faulk was the victim of a political blacklist. Unlike most of his fellow victims, Faulk fought back. With the help of attorney Louis Nizer, he won back both his job and more than 3 million dollars in punitive damages. "This is a story of violence," Faulk wrote in his account of the ordeal, "not violence involving police brutality, lust, or bloodshed, but a more subtle kind of violence—the violence of vigilantism."[1]

Faulk's metaphor seems appropriate. Especially in the 1950s, the symbiotic relationship between government and private groups in support of the status quo closely matched the vigilante mode. Although it seldom involves physical violence, the pattern of these relationships provides interesting insights into the dynamics of vigilantism. McCarthyism is to vigilantism as white-collar crime is to crime in the streets. Its success depends upon cooperative relationships between public and private bodies. Its ideological force derives from conservative responses to rapid social and political change. Its method of enforcing political orthodoxy is almost exclusively extralegal.

This short chapter will examine the gray area between vigilantism and what Becker and Murray call government lawlessness.[2] The cases reported by Becker and Murray indicate some rather striking breakdowns in due process constraints upon the activities of governing officials. The cases below fall into another pattern, illustrating the role of government agencies in the politics of vigilantism. This is not an exhaustive interpretation of the politics of anti-communism in the United States. Rather, it is an attempt to examine through case studies, the dynamics of the relationship between public and private

1. John Henry Faulk, *Fear on Trial* (New York: Simon and Schuster), p. 9.
2. Theodore L. Becker and Vernon G. Murray, eds., *Government Lawlessness in America* (New York: Oxford University Press, 1971).

groups that are supportive of a form of vigilante politics in a modern, democratic society. The particular emphasis here is on the role of government. Regime sanction and support, tacit if not overt, is an important but infrequently explored aspect of the vigilante mode. It is, however, central to an understanding of the politics of American anti-communism.

Senator Joseph R. McCarthy of Wisconsin (whose name some dictionaries now lowercase as an -ism) was the most visible government agent of white-collar vigilantism in the United States. The key government agent in the process was, however, the House Committee on Un-American Activities. HUAC (the commonly employed acronym) was established in 1939, became a standing committee of the House in 1945, and survived until 1975 as the House Committee on Internal Security (HISC). Largely because House rules, in contrast to those of the Senate, forbade broadcast coverage, HUAC for a brief period in the early 1950s lost its center stage position to Senator McCarthy's Senate Investigating Subcommittee. HUAC, however, both anteceded and antedated McCarthy. Its staff was large and experienced, its files mammoth, and its operations essentially free of partisan taint. More importantly for present purposes, HUAC's ties with outside groups, its links into a network of vigilantism, were well-established and continuous.

THE COMMITTEE

Before this network of relationships is examined, the rather unique status of the Committee itself should be made clear. In the official pecking order of House Committees, HUAC/HISC was a "minor" committee. Fewer bills were referred to it than to any other committee, so few that it could hardly be said to have a normal legislative function. Yet since 1945 it employed more than 10 percent of all House Committee staff and used almost 12 percent of the funds appropriated for committee work. It held more than four hundred public hearings, heard testimony from more than 5000 persons, cited more than 150 for contempt of Congress, and published more than 10 million copies of its documents. More books have been written about HUAC than about all other committees of Congress combined.

Changes in personnel, and more importantly in the political context within which the Committee operated, have given it a protean nature unusual in the annals of congressional committee behavior. Created in 1939 as a temporary, "select" committee under the chairmanship of Texas Democrat Martin Dies, the Committee in its early years tended to reflect the idiosyncratic views of its generally conservative members. Some, like Dies, used the Committee as a forum for opposition to the New Deal. "Stalin," Dies wrote in 1940, "baited his hook with a 'progressive' worm and the New Deal suckers swallowed bait, hook, line, and sinker."[3] He used the hearings of the

3. Martin Dies, *The Trojan Horse in America* (New York: Dodd, Mead, 1940), p. 285.

Committee largely as a forum for the expression of this point of view. No clear rules of procedure, no consistent statements of purpose or legislative intent, can be found in the Committee's early operations. Carefully staged and well-executed legislative trials (such as the Nixon-led pursuit of Alger Hiss) ran in tandem with the circus-like atmosphere of the Committee's Hollywood hearings. The Committee jumped from investigations of sit-down strikes to the German-American Bund to the Communist party. Mississippi Democrat John Rankin was allowed to use HUAC as a medium to express his view that "communism is Yiddish."[4] If one appreciates gallows humor, the early hearings of the HUAC deserve careful reading.

In 1950 and 1951 a number of personnel changes dramatically altered Committee operations. Former Chairman J. Parnell Thomas was convicted of dipping his fingers in the till and resigned his seat to join in a Federal penitentiary some of the unfriendly Hollywood witnesses whom he had prosecuted for contempt. Nixon went on to bigger and better things, and two southern Democrats lost their seats. Using the excuse that only lawyers should be appointed to serve on the Committee, Speaker Rayburn removed Rankin and replaced him with the respected Francis Walter of Pennsylvania, who became chairman in 1954. Walter was a reluctant appointee, and his first act as chairman was a move to abolish the Committee and transfer its functions to the Judiciary Committee. He quickly abandoned this plan when the Republican leadership threatened to make un-American activities a partisan issue. Under Walter the Committee became the first in the history of the House to adopt its own regular rules of procedure. Even the Committee's staunchest critics were forced to concede that Walter had brought a sense of order and decency to an operation whose reputation for fairness was not high.

These changes, however, masked a basic continuity and uniformity in the Committee's fundamental role, a role which I hope to show is consistent with the vigilante mode. They also illustrate patterns in the evolution of vigilante movements which, I suspect, can be more universally appled.

The third phase of the Committee's history dates roughly from 1960 to the present. No longer supported by the political culture, as it had been in the 1940s and 1950s, the Committee began to function more and more as an educational body. Formal reports displaced investigatory hearings. Anti-communist propaganda supplanted individualized exposés. This shift from direct action to propaganda, from the punishment of individual deviants to a focus on broader questions of ideology, is not uncommon. Militant groups of both left and right frequently alternate between educational and activist modes. In the United States, for example, the Know Nothings, the American Protective Association, and the Ku Klux Klan were sometimes vigilante groups, and at other times more concerned with education and propaganda.

---

4. *Congressional Record,* 96th Congress, 2nd Session (1950), p. A1010.

The two modes are not mutually exclusive. Vigilantism is basically a form of propaganda warfare, a way of defining and defending an ideology and way of life. But although the Un-American Activities Committee's attempts to promote anti-Communist ideologies and its propagandistic activities on behalf of various rightist causes are of considerable interest, they are only marginally related to the topic at hand. Hence, the case studies upon which this essay draws are primarily derived from the records of HUAC in the period 1950 to 1960.

HUAC AND THE VIGILANTE MODE

Because the vigilante works in defense of the status quo, his activities usually have the tacit support of the regime, or of some part of it. Government officials themselves sometimes resort to acts which might be described as vigilante. Public officials, however, operate under significant constraints. First, they are bound, more than private citizens, by certain rules of the game: procedural and substantive norms, rules, and constitutional doctrines which—if they do not preclude direct punitive sanctions—impose time constraints and delays. Second, the public official in the modern state is constrained by a highly developed and closely defined political division of labor. To protect his own autonomy he must avoid intruding on the political "turf" of others. Third, if the system is democratic, the public official can assure his own continuity in office only by avoiding confrontations with potentially powerful opponents; the elected vigilante can act overtly only against the weak and disorganized.

HUAC was confronted with all of these problems. First, the "due process" constraints were and are substantial. Although the courts consistently refused to uphold First or Fourth Amendment defenses against Committee inquiries into political affiliations and activities, the Fifth Amendment privilege against self-incrimination was both sanctioned and used. More significantly, HUAC, as a committee of Congress, could not serve as prosecutor, judge, or jailer. Those brave or foolish enough to waive the Fifth Amendment defense and rely on freedom of speech or the right to privacy might expect to spend six months to a year in jail for contempt of Congress, and a few (most notably Alger Hiss) could be prosecuted for perjury; but by-and-large the Committee lacked the means of directly subjecting its victims to legal sanctions. Its one early attempt to punish directly by means of legislation was ruled an illegal bill of attainder.[5] Attempts to pass more general bills making subversive activities a crime had limited success.

5. A list of thirty-nine subversives published by the Committee in 1943 included the names of three federal employees. Dies encouraged the House to attach a rider to an appropriation bill forbidding the government to pay salaries to the three. In the case of *United States v. Lovett* the Supreme Court ruled the rider an unconstitutional bill of attainder and unanimously ordered the three reinstated with back pay.

More importantly, the "crime" HUAC sought to exorcise, political heresy, is not easily punishable by Constitutional means. Even if there were a way legislatively to define fellow-traveling as a punishable form of sedition, the statute of limitations protected most of HUAC's victims. Hiss, for example, could not have been brought to court because all of his alleged transgressions had taken place some ten years before the "discovery" of the famed pumpkin papers. Many of those tarred by the Committee had actually done nothing more criminal than to sign petitions calling for an end to Jim Crow in major league baseball.

Second, the Committee consistently confronted problems of overlapping jurisdictions. Even during the brief chairmanship of Harold Velde, an ex-FBI agent, relations between the Committee and the Federal Bureau of Investigation were not close. More significantly, there were certain sacred cows in the government which could not lightly be gored. McCarthy learned this too late. As William S. White perceptively notes, McCarthy,

> was in fact tried not for intellectual crime against the people and the Republic (though this was the charge really debated pro and con among the public) but wholly for his conduct concerning the *Institution* [of the Senate of the United States].[6]

He made two fundamental mistakes. One, he attempted to take on the army, thus confronting an institution powerful in its own right and implying that another powerful institution, the Committee on Armed Services, had been lax in its oversight. Two, as the final resolution of censure read, he had "failed to cooperate with the Subcommittee on Privileges and Elections of the Senate Committee on Rules and Administration. . . ." Thus,

> it was not the hostile press and public that brought McCarthy to his accounting. It was not the Eisenhower Administration. It was not the Republican Party. . . .
> It was the Institution that finally brought him to book—an Institution led, as always in these supreme cases involving its real life, by its Senate types of the Inner Club.[7]

There is an important paradox here. On the one hand, the very complexity of the political division of labor gives the white-collar vigilante his freedom to act. At the same time, the greater the division of labor in society, and the better entrenched its institutions, the less freedom the vigilante has in choosing his targets. Just as law-enforcement vigilantes must be wary of their relationships with the police, HUAC was forced to focus its attention on subversive activities among groups whose political roots were shallow and whose institutional values were vulnerable. It never took on the armed forces, agriculture, business, or the press. Its primary targets were labor and church

6. William S. White, *Citadel* (New York: Harper and Brothers, 1956), p. 126.
7. Ibid., pp. 126-27.

groups which were badly divided within themselves and institutions with little constituency support, such as aliens, civil liberties organizations, civil rights groups, the State Department, and the motion picture industry.

From a political point of view, the Communist Party made an ideal scapegoat. Its real power in the 1930s, reinforced by the power of the Soviet Union in the 1950s, gave the Party an image of puissance not matched by reality. Hannah Arendt in her essay on anti-Semitism in Europe points out the importance of the Jews' failure to gain real power proportionate to the image of power projected to the public: "although individual Jews in high positions remained representative of Jewry as a whole in the eyes of the Gentile world, there was little if any material reality behind this." Thus, Jewry became "an object of universal hatred because of its useless wealth, and of contempt because of its lack of power."[8] The Communist Party in the 1950s was weak, almost nonexistent as a political force. But its image of power was strong, and HUAC assiduously cultivated that image. Witnesses were asked not simply the famous sixty-four-dollar "are-you-now-or-have-you-ever-been" question, but rather (during the Korean War) if they were part of that international revolutionary movement which is now killing our boys in Korea, or, in 1956, if they were part of "this conspiratorial force known as the Communist Party . . . which is the same force that sent the tanks into Budapest."[9]

Whether or not the American Communist Party deserved to be linked in this manner with the foreign challenge of the Cold War is beside the point. What is important is that the Cold War context served to isolate the American Communist, and by implication the fellow traveler, from his natural allies. Organizations and individuals of the more established and powerful left ran like lemmings. The American Civil Liberties Union and the Americans for Democratic Action required loyalty oaths of their members and ran purge trials of their own. The unions "cleaned house." Liberals in Congress sponsored and promoted the Communist Control Act of 1954, and McCarthy was condemned, not for what he was doing, but for his "methods."

Thus the success of HUAC in carrying out its vigilante mission must in no small part be attributed to the climate of public opinion within which it operated. It had, for the times, chosen a perfect scapegoat. More importantly, I would like to suggest that HUAC was given a free hand less because of its popular support than because of its conformity to the rules of the game of the system that Lowi calls interest-group liberalism.[10] To be sure, the popularity of the Committee as measured by Gallup, Roper, and Harris polls was consistently high. Elite opinion, however, was generally negative, and there is

8. Hannah Arendt, *The Origins of Totalitarianism* (New York: Meridian Books, 1958), p. 15.
9. United States Congress, House of Representatives, Committee on Un-American Activities, *Hearings on the Northern California District of the Communist Party, Structure—Objectives—Leadership,* part I, p. 1987. Hereafter all hearings and reports of the Committee will be cited by title.
10. Theodore J. Lowi, *The End of Liberalism* (New York: Norton, 1968).

no evidence to indicate that HUAC's public popularity ran very deep. Subversive activities, as Stouffer shows, were accorded very low salience in public attitudes. Despite its popularity, few people would have cared much one way or the other if HUAC had been abolished or sharply curtailed. However, so long as it confined itself to attacks on groups whose community roots were shallow, and so long as it invaded the policy spheres of no important interest constellations, incentives to curtail the committee were also lacking. The essence of interest-group liberalism is the differentiation of power spheres: farmers make farm policy, educators education policy, businessmen business policy; and, by easy extension of the rule, right-wing anti-Communists make anti-Communist policy.

Part of conventional wisdom with regard to vigilantes is that they are most likely to operate freely in preindustrial societies. The HUAC record (and that of the Federal Bureau of Investigation)[11] suggests the possible emergence of a new type of postindustrial vigilantism, one which waxes in significance as the society becomes more complex. Lowi's model suggests that the growing complexity of society leads to the breakdown of central mechanisms of control: the president cannot control the bureaucracy; Congress cannot (or will not, if you're an optimist) control its committees. Power is delegated and subdelegated. Central decision-making units serve to ratify the decisions of functionally decentralized subsystems, to define new spheres of influence when new problems emerge, and to adjudicate occasional conflicts between subsystems. Without belaboring the application of this model to HUAC, let me simply cite one interesting indicator:

> Of 107 citations for contempt between 1788 and 1943, Congress refused to prosecute 34. . . . Of 226 contempt citations presented to both Houses of Congress by fourteen committees in the period from 1945 to 1957, few were debated in either the House or the Senate and none was defeated. . . .[12]

What makes this rubber stamping of contempt citations (the majority of them brought by HUAC) particularly significant is the growing tendency to refuse to consider the merits of individual cases. In this light, the 1946 citation of Corliss Lamont was a milestone in the history of congressional committees. Representative Vito Marcantonio argued in vain that "the question of what is material to the case should be determined by the House itself, not by a Committee of the House." As Carl Beck has pointed out,

> The point of order raised by Marcantonio was important. This was to be the first time that Congress was to approve a resolution citing an individual for contempt without being fully aware of the circumstances. Such an occurrence makes the committee, not the Congress, the determiner of what information shall be

---

11. On the FBI's use of vigilante techniques see the fascinating and frightening essay by Frank Donner, "Hoover's Legacy," in a special issue of *The Nation* (June 1, 1974): 678-99.

12. Carl Beck, *Contempt of Congress* (New Orleans: Hauser Press, 1959), pp. 185-86.

supplied to Congress. In this manner the proper relationship between Congress and one of its committees was reversed.[13]

HUAC AND THE AMERICAN RIGHT:
THE DYNAMICS OF VIGILANTISM

Despite its autonomy and freedom of action, despite the vulnerability of its targets, HUAC lacked the power to punish. Its ability to convict for contempt depended upon the acquiescence of the courts, and, more importantly, on the willingness of witnesses not to play the Fifth Amendment game. Those witnesses who tried the First Amendment or other defenses lost. However, the Fifth Amendment defense survived. It also produced a ritualization of the Committee's functions which enhanced the importance of outside groups. A whole new term, "the Fifth Amendment Communist," entered the American political lexicon. The legal dynamics of this development were as follows: a variety of court cases had established the privilege against self-incrimination as the only valid grounds for refusing to answer the questions of a congressional committee. A second set of precedents had firmly established the doctrine that to answer the "greater" question waived all Fifth Amendment Rights as to lesser issues. If one admitted, for example, to having been a member of the Communist Party at some earlier time (the general question), one could not cite the Fifth Amendment (or any other legally protected freedom) as valid grounds for refusing to answer questions as to the specifics of one's membership. In particular this meant that one could not refuse to identify others who had sinned with you. Witnesses thus faced a triple Hobson's choice: they could go to jail, they could name names, they could become "Fifth Amendment Communists."

Exposure as a Communist or fellow traveler is not in itself a punishment. Although the Committee could use its powers of subpoena and access to the media to expose alleged subversives, "the success of any hearing . . . is dependent in large part upon the element of cooperation furnished to the Congress and the committee by local agencies of the government, press, radio, and television, and the public generally."[14] Such cooperation was frequently forthcoming.

The best documented instance of such cooperative vigilante activities is the blacklisting in the entertainment industry. Here private groups depended heavily on the Committee and vice-versa. In the entertainment industry, blacklisting was basically a three-step process. Generally it tended to involve the Committee; pressure groups such as the American Legion, Aware, Inc., and the Veterans of Foreign Wars, and the producer or his ad-agency sponsor. Some private groups published lists of their own, but most of these were

13. Ibid., p. 21.
14. *Northwest Area Hearings* (1954), part 8, p. 6600.

derived from the HUAC publications and files, and the Committee lists were, in the final analysis, definitive. By the early 1950s all motion picture studios and all radio and television networks in the United States could be described as

> unanimous in their refusal to hire persons identified as Communist Party members who have not subsequently testified in full before the House Un-American Activities Committee. The studios are especially adamant about not hiring witnesses who have relied on the Fifth Amendment before Congressional Committees.[15]

Cogley found 324 people on the list between 1951 and 1954 who had been "active motion picture workers," but could not find further employment in the industry.[16] The crackdown on radio and television was even more severe. During John Henry Faulk's case against the blacklist, David Susskind testified that he had been forced to submit a list of five thousand potential guests on his show to the advertising agency for clearance; about fifteen hundred came back classified as "politically unreliable."[17]

Although it made many of its participants acutely uncomfortable, the system had a neat efficiency. The Committee stuck to its Constitutional role of investigating subversive activities. It compiled no blacklists, imposed no direct sanctions either on the accused or on those who hired them. Of course, it did publish an annual index of the names of those referred to in its hearings and reports, and its files were in some cases open to concerned citizens; but it maintained no formal blacklist. Nor, for that matter, did the studios, the advertising agencies, or the networks. They all found the idea of a blacklist "abhorrent," and many gave speeches saying so; but neither did they wish to become embroiled in "political" controversies. Hence, when it was suggested to them that the appearance of a certain person in one of their productions might jeopardize its ratings or box-office success, they quite naturally dropped that person from the show. As for the private groups, their role was simply one of calling public attention to the findings of a legitimately constituted committee of the Congress of the United States, and of suggesting that no true patriot would patronize the products of those sponsoring subversive forces.

For a few years, the system provided its own fuel. A blacklisted performer could clear himself only by going before the Committee and naming names. The names were seldom new, but the recantations of household names like Sterling Hayden, Clifford Odets, and Elia Kazan made good copy for the Committee and the system alike. Eventually, however, the well began to run dry. A few of the more talented hold-outs—Arthur Miller and Pete Seeger, for example—managed to survive despite the blacklist; many went into "other" lines of work;[18] hundreds recanted, named names, and were cleared;

15. John Cogley, *Report on Blacklisting* (New York: The Fund for the Republic, 1956), 1: 162.
16. Ibid., 1: 109.
17. Joseph P. Blank, "The Ordeal of John Henry Faulk," *Look* 27 (May 7, 1963): 87.
18. For a poignant and insightful personal experience with the blacklist see Alvah Bessie, *Inquisition in Eden* (New York: Macmillan, 1965).

thousands learned their lesson: if you want to work, keep your mouth shut, don't sign anything, do what you are told.

For the Committee, success was not a problem; HUAC could and did move into other fields. For the private blacklisting organizations, victory over "subversion" meant economic and political disaster. What does a vigilante do when the enemy has been routed and the demon exorcised? The answer, of course, was to create new demons, to extend and amplify the concept of fellow traveler. It was as a by-product of this process that John Henry Faulk's suit against Aware, Inc. and others developed. Faulk, comedian Orson Bean, and newsman Charles Collingswood were "clean" in the old sense of the term. Their sin was to run as part of a middle-of-the-road slate for leadership of the American Federation of Television and Radio Artists. Aware succeeded in banning all three from the networks, but it lacked the immunity of a congressional committee and soon found itself on the losing end of the largest civil judgment ever awarded by an American court.[19]

In Hollywood, meanwhile, blacklisted writers were smuggling their works in under assumed names. When "Robert Rich" won the Academy Award for best screenplay in 1957, he could not be located for the customary interviews; but it was an open secret that Rich and Dalton Trumbo, one of the original Hollywood Ten, were the same person. In 1958 Stanley Kramer waggishly let the cat out of the bag in his pseudonymous employment of Nedrick Young:

> In the opening of *The Defiant Ones* a truck is transporting a group of convicts in a harsh, driving storm. As the windshield wipers bang across the windshield, the credit "Written by Natan E. Douglas, Harold Jacob Smith" is superimposed over the faces of two truck drivers. The driver on the left is Young. The gesture was typically Krameresque, professing a warm liberality to the cognoscenti, and continuing the straight-faced, cooperative attitude should the American Legion be looking on.[20]

HUAC, too, was changing its style. The first publicly acknowledged hole in the blacklist was the employment of Carl Foreman in 1958 despite his refusal to name names. "I wasn't interested," Committee Chairman Francis Walter later explained,

> in getting names from Foreman of people who had already been identified as Communists. I wanted someone who could get up and tell what a sucker he'd been. I thought Foreman was the kind of important man we needed for this, and I think he did a service to the country in his testimony.[21].

19. Faulk never recovered anything near the $3.5 million judgment. The amount was reduced on appeal, and the defendants were unable to come up with more than a small fraction of the reduced amount. Aware went out of business, and supermarket-owner Lawrence Johnson, whose threatened boycotts of various products had sent hard tremors up Madison Avenue just a few years before, emulated some of his victims by taking his own life.

20. Stefan Kanfer, *A Journal of the Plague Years* (New York: Atheneum, 1973), p. 276.

21. Paul Jacobs, "Good Guys, Bad Guys, and Congressman Walter," *The Reporter* 18 (May 15, 1958): 31.

Reflected in Walter's statement is the shift in the Committee's interest from vigilante to educational activities. Having proven that there were indeed "subversives" at large, having proven its power and succeeded in changing both the personnel and the content of the entertainment industry, HUAC was willing to let the blacklist die.[22]

Although formal blacklists were not institutionalized in other sectors of the American economy, similar patterns of cooperation between HUAC and various private groups can be found in the labor movement, in the Protestant church, among civil rights groups, in the area of immigration, and in various other vulnerable sectors of American society. Here again, the analogies to vigilantism are strong. Extralegal punishments, support for the status quo, and the limitations which "due process" constraints placed upon direct government action are all part of the picture. There are, moreover, the same symbiotic relations between private groups and the Committee that existed in blacklisting; the vigilantes could not have succeeded without HUAC's help.

The Committee's role was threefold. As in the case of blacklisting, its cloak of legal immunity and formal powers of subpoena enabled it to make charges and inquiries impossible for private organizations. The following excerpt from an affidavit filed by an officer of the International Union of Electrical Workers (IUE) concerning the IUE's battle with the rival United Electrical Workers (UE) reveals this role:

> Since we were about to have an election in the union we decided at that meeting (with HUAC investigators) that the investigators should summon certain UE leaders to Washington and charge them with Communist affiliation and activities. . . .
>
> (We) presented the investigator with leaflets, photostatic copies of letters and generally what they called documentary evidence on certain UE leaders. . . .
>
> We knew that if we could get the cooperation of the Committee against the UE leaders, it would be easier to defeat them on any issue as well as to defeat them for office.[23]

The union leaders needed HUAC both for its subpoena power—to put the UE leaders under oath and the threat of contempt—and for its immunity from possible libel. In an instance such as this, a second role of the Committee also played an important part. The charges of an official government agency have a great deal more credibility than do those of a private organization. As a conservative clergyman once wrote HUAC chairman Harold Velde:

---

22. Well, not quite. In 1959 Frank Sinatra, reportedly at the insistence of the Kennedy family, abruptly reneged on his announced plans to hire Albert Maltz to write the screenplay for "The Execution of Private Slovik." Pete Seeger was kept off the nation's television screens until late in the 1960s. And, of course, most of the less-talented blacklistees never were able to come back from their years of enforced exile.

23. Reprinted in *Communist Political Subversion,* Hearings, 84th Congress, 2nd Session, 1956, part 2, p. 7584.

Only an outside authoritative agency can convince the rank and file church members of this apostasy and treason of their self-assertive leaders. They cannot believe such duplicity possible otherwise and conservative clergy in the face of theological school and social action pressure and smears are rendered almost helpless to bring about the expose needed.[24]

Finally, the Committee could provide staff resources and expert assistance (at taxpayers' expense) which private groups could not match. It became a mammoth record-keeping operation whose basic stock-in-trade, in the final analysis, was names. "I realize," one member of the Committee told a witness in 1952,

how repugnant it is to the average person to disclose names, dates, and places; but that is the sum and substance of the things we must have if we are to carry this investigation through to a successful conclusion.[25]

The Committee's obsession with names led Chief Justice Warren, in his widely quoted *dicta* in the Watkins case, to condemn what he called "exposure for exposure's sake"[26] It is this aspect of the Committee's work which has most troubled both its critics and its defenders.

The Committee itself, in a rather strange though not atypical flourish of rhetoric, answered the chief justice as follows in its 1960 Annual Report:

Does the Committee on Un-American Activities seek exposure for exposure's sake? No. That is Communist semantics. . . . We must not permit the incident of exposure, necessarily involved in legislative activity, to be degraded by Communist name-calling. . . . Relentlessly, we must continue to breathe down the stiff necks of traitors and enemies within.[27]

Whether or not Warren's opinion was couched in "Communist semantics," as the Committee charged, both the chief justice and most of the Committee's critics have emphasized the illegitimacy of investigations for the sake of exposure in their denunciations of the work of the Committee on Un-American Activities.

The question is an important one with implications extending beyond HUAC to such phenomena as the Senate Watergate Committee, Robert Kennedy's pursuit of Jimmy Hoffa, and Estes Kefauver's investigations of organized crime. The legal issues and civil liberties implications of the exposure function

24. Howard E. Mather, *What Is the Church League of America* (Wheaton: The Church League of America, n.d.), p. 6.
25. Congressman Jackson, *Communist Infiltration of the Hollywood Motion Picture Industry,* Hearings, 82nd Congress, 1st and 2nd Sessions, 1951-1952, part 5, p. 1821.
26. The Court's decision in *Watkins v. United States* (354 U. S. 178 [1957]) was decided on narrow procedural grounds. Warren's eloquent dicta, as those who attempted subsequently to rely upon it discovered, had no legal standing. Walter Murphy's *Congress and the Court* (Chicago: University of Chicago Press, 1962) provides an excellent analysis of the cases in this area and of the political reaction to them.
27. *1960 Annual Report,* p. 137.

have been thoroughly debated elsewhere and will not be rehashed here.[28] The political dynamics of the process, however, have received considerably less attention and are the major concern of this analysis.

HUAC's insistence on the naming of names derived primarily from its role in the vigilante politics of anti-communism, but it had other important and interrelated goals as well. It served as a test of true loyalty, a concrete manifestation of an ex-radical's willingness to renounce his or her past. It served the educational function (in the words of a former chairman) of letting the "people of this country know that there are serpents crawling about."[29] Moreover, it allowed the Committee to expand its mission infinitely. Each new list widened the net of red-tainted individuals and organizations. Their further associations could then serve as the basis for a new round of investigations. The process had a neat and flexible dynamism. On the one hand,

> affiliations with or activities in Communist-front organizations . . . leave the implication that one is in fact a member of the Communist Party or has been, or that he is in fact a sympathizer of the Communist Party or an encourager of Communist Party concepts and objectives.[30]

At the same time, in determining whether or not a group is a Communist front, it is important to ascertain whether or not "its sponsors have a history of extensive services in the Communist Party itself or in Communist front enterprises."[31] Obviously, the process of accumulation is never-ending.[32]

The number of individuals "exposed" by the Committee on Un-American Activities boggles the mind. HUAC employed four basic types of exposure. Best known was the full-dress investigation which began with the public naming of an individual by a friendly witness[33] and concluded with the Committee asking that person to confirm or deny the accusation while under subpoena. Friendly witnesses sometimes supplied the Committee with information concerning many hundreds of individuals, and, of course, the Committee could not subpoena them all. Thus, the second type of exposure

---

28. Among the most interesting and readable of these works are Alan Barth, *Government by Investigation* (New York: Viking, 1955), and Telford Taylor, *Grand Inquest* (New York: Ballantine Books, 1961).

29. Representative Velde, *Hearings Regarding Communist Activities in the New York Area,* 84th Congress, 1st Session, 1955, part 2, p. 235.

30. Staff Director Frank Tavenner, *1951 Hollywood Hearings,* part 3, p. 536.

31. *Communist Political Subversion,* House Report No. 1182, 85th Congress, 1st Session, 1957, p. 13.

32. A superb case study of this process is Walter Gelhorn, "Report on a Report of the House Committee on Un-American Activities," *Harvard Review* 60 (1947): 1194.

33. The Committee employed a number of friendly witnesses as part-time consultants. They were carefully coached and trained before appearing in public, and were frequently called upon to perform their basic routines in six or seven cities. Many made their livings as professional witnesses traveling the circuit with HUAC, McCarthy, and various state investigating committees. On the care and training of a professional witness see Harvey Matusow, *False Witness* (New York: Cameron and Kahn, 1955).

involved the accusation but not the subpoenaing of the accused. The third type was similar to the second in that the accused was not called to testify, but differs in that more information was given by the Committee than just the name. In this type, material from the Committee files was presented to show that a given person had engaged in certain activities. The information printed in the record was not nearly so comprehensive as that given out in the full-dress investigation, yet it went beyond mere presentation of the name. The fourth type of exposure also drew upon the Committee's files, but was not public in nature. Here the Committee simply passed its file material on to a friendly recipient. In most cases these friendly recipients were loyalty-security officers of government agencies who regularly consulted the Committee's files in checking out potential employees.[34] Frequently, however, file materials were made directly available to private groups, to state and local enforcement agencies, and to other interested parties. Any congressman who was friendly to the Committee had access to HUAC's voluminous files (sorted by name) of old clippings from obscure left journals, rumors, hearsay, membership card numbers, cancelled checks, and what have you. These dossiers, numbering in the hundreds of thousands, were popular items for members of Congress with strong anti-Communist organizations in their districts. As one member, remembering the days when Congress encouraged the cultivation of victory gardens, put it: "this beats free seeds all hollow."[35]

No public records of the extent or nature of such uses of the Committee's files are publicly available. Chairman Ichord recently told the House Administration Committee that HUAC had furnished 656 reports to members in 1971, considerably fewer than in the earlier years when the totals reportedly ran as high as 3000. Some of this material was used directly by House members themselves. During the course of debate on the 1956 Civil Rights Bill, for example, Representative Gathings used HUAC material to "expose" the backgrounds and affiliations of eighty-nine people connected with the National Association for the Advancement of Colored People. The aim obviously was not so much to expose the eighty-nine people as it was to discredit the NAACP, but the material came from HUAC's files, and it provides interesting insight into the nature of the material thus conveyed. As Goodman rather dryly notes,

> Anyone who had followed the careers of most of those listed knew that although their battles in the Negro's cause brought them into alliance with Communists now and then, they were neither Party members nor facsimiles.[36]

34. More than twenty-five government agencies regularly consult HUAC files for pre-employment investigations. Such use appears to have fallen off in recent years. In 1967, for example, the Civil Service Commission reportedly used Committee file 288,000 times as compared with 20,000 in 1972. Congressman Harrington, *Congressional Record* (daily edition) (April 1, 1974): H2357.
35. Quoted in Frank Donner, *The Un-American* (New York: Ballantine Books, 1961), p. 123.
36. Walter Goodman, *The Committee* (New York: Farrar, Strauss, and Giroux, 1968), p. 375.

Few uses of the Committee's files have come to public attention. It seems quite plausible to assume, however, that much of it has been passed quietly into the hands of local law-enforcement officials or of private parties. One member of the House Administration Committee defended his support for the Committee's 1972 budget request with the following anecdote:

> I asked for an examination of a certain case . . . and I got a very, very fine report which was not made public by the Committee. . . . This happened to pertain to a very serious situation, and by getting the report . . . we were able to do something in the State of Pennsylvania that stopped something that could have been a lot worse in its final outcome in that State. We were not able to get anything in the Court on the matter, but by enough information given to the right people, we were able to stop something that was a deliberate and well-planned insurrectional move.[37]

Various private groups have claimed special access to the Committee's files. One suspects that the boastful quality of the claims of such inside dopesters may be more self-serving than realistic; yet given HUAC's generosity in those cases that have come to public light, its files do appear to be a major source of information for vigilante groups.[38]

VIGILANTISM IN MODERN AMERICA: A SUMMING UP

On May 12, 1957, the following news item appeared on the front page of the Baltimore *American:*

> A jeering, laughing crowd of about 75 persons demonstrated last night in front of the home of a woman who pleaded the Fifth Amendment when questioned by the House Un-American Activities Committee.

Such overtly intimidating acts have been the exception rather than the rule. The white-collar vigilantism of the anti-Communist movement in the United States has been far more subtle in its methods of discouraging political dissidence.

Physical violence is not a necessary part of the vigilante mode in modern societies. The blacklist destroyed careers, provoked suicides, ruined marriages, forced expatriations, and dramatically altered both the character and substance of the entertainment industry,[39] but no physical intimidation was involved. It was, however, vigilantic. The legal code which gave HUAC the subpoena power, congressional immunity, and the power to sue for contempt served as a necessary operating base, but it played only a minor role in the

37. Hearings before the Subcommittee on Accounts of the House Administration on Budget Requests for 1972. These hearings are available in typescript in the Subcommittee's files.
38. In its Annual Report for 1960 the Committee stated that its files were open to certain private groups; but such statements have not appeared in subsequent annual reports.
39. Kanfer, in his *Journal of the Plague Years,* examines a number of such individual tragedies in detail, and makes a particular strong point of the impact of McCarthyism on the tone and content of motion pictures.

process of punishment.[40] Punishment by publicity derives its effectiveness from extralegal sanctions, that is, "private coercion which exceeds the boundaries of the political system governing its use." Congress was prohibited by the First Amendment, the statute of limitations, and the Constitution's prohibition of bills of attainder from singling out the kinds of individual crimes of heresy which the blacklist punished. It had no power to interfere in the internal struggles for political control of trade unions. It did, however, have the power to expose and thus to initiate, if not to apply, significant sanctions.

In some instances, these sanctions involved the actions of government. The modern state has a growing capacity to punish through the withdrawal of privileges on the expanding list it controls. Thus, those identified as subversives by the HUAC were frequently denied passports, unemployment compensation, government jobs, veterans' benefits, etc. Such denials of service played an important part in the politics of anti-Communism throughout the McCarthy period and beyond, but are best treated, not as vigilantism, but as instances of normal due process or, if you prefer, of government lawlessness. In the loyalty-security operations of local governments and private industries, however, we encounter a gray area that falls somewhere between official action and vigilantism. In 1959, after HUAC cancelled a scheduled round of hearings in northern California, it turned the names and records of a group of allegedly subversive teachers over to their local school boards for appropriate action. In doing so, the Committee, as Goodman puts it, "had taken the role of an adjunct police agency, supplying raw data to authorities with the power to punish."[41] Such obvious denials of due process emulate the vigilante mode, but, since they involve only government organizations, they do not fit the formal definitions set out in this volume. When the employer is a defense contractor or public utility, even this distinction blurs.

The complexity of the modern state makes the dividing line between public and private increasingly difficult to delimit. One of the ironic effects of laws designed to regulate the conduct of private institutions has been to invest in them certain powers of the state. Wages and hours laws, parts of the internal revenue code, or laws requiring security clearances for the employees of certain sensitive industries are typically perceived as restraints upon the autonomy of the corporations in question. They also have the effect of making these corporations quasi-public bodies. A person who is fired as a security risk by the Bell Telephone Company is no less fired than a person who is let go by the government. The kind of vigilantism typified by the blacklist is no less

40. According to one member of the House, "Of 174 contempt citations issued by HISC up to 1970, 142 have failed in the courts." Representative Harrington, *Congressional Record* (daily edition) (April 1, 1974): H2357. Most of these "failures" involved suspended sentences rather than legal findings against the Committee.
41. Goodman, *The Committee*, p. 426.

dramatic in its impact upon individuals than comparable actions by the state, and is all the more insidious because the private group is not subject to similar due process constraints.

McCarthyism worked. As long as there are private groups willing and capable of applying sanctions, punishment by publicity is an effective means of controlling social or political deviance. To succeed, however, it requires a special kind of victim, one who has the image of power without its substance and who depends upon the maintainance of his public standing in order to survive. During the 1950s, John Roche published an article with the provocative title "We've Never Had More Freedom." Roche's thesis is that toleration of divergent opinions was greater even in the McCarthy period than at most earlier points in American history. "What has confused historians looking back at the social and intellectual history of the United States," Roche wrote,

> is the fact that great diversity of opinion indubitably existed in the nation. From this they have drawn the erroneous conclusion that there was toleration of divergent opinions among the populace at large. It is my contention that the diversity of views was a consequence not of tolerance and mutual respect, but of the existence of many communities within the society each with its own rigid canons of orthodoxy.
>
> In other words, if a man looked hard enough, he could probably find a community within the United States that shared his own peculiar views, and joining it, he could help impose his eccentricities on all within reach.[42]

Roche's thesis is intriguing and probably accurate, but the other side of this coin also deserves attention. Precisely because diverse communities of what David Reisman once called "vested heresies" no longer exist, those dissident individuals who are not accorded the increasing tolerance of American society have no place to hide. This is particularly true of those whose occupational skills are not fungible and who depend for their livelihoods on public acceptance of their products or services. Thus, the blacklist was most effective with regard to radio and television where sensitivity to ratings and to sponsors exerted a continuing pressure. It was somewhat less effective in Hollywood where a company town atmosphere encouraged subterfuges and evasions of vigilante demands. And it was weakest with regard to the highly decentralized, less visible, and more independent community of the legitimate theatre.

If actors and writers made good targets, so did union leaders. Public acceptance was an important part of their rule, and alternative occupations of similar status and salary were not open. The elected leader of a bureaucratized union lacks the mobility of the free floating organizer of the nineteenth century who, when ridden on a rail out of one town, would simply move on to another.

42. John P. Roche, "We've Never Had More Freedom," *New Republic* 134 (January 23, 1956): 12.

In contrast to the victims of the 1940s and 1950s, many of HUAC's more recent targets have had less at stake in their public reputations and have proven far more difficult to deal with. The first "bad" hearing, from the Committee's perspective, was its investigation in the early 1960s of the Women's Strike for Peace. Later in the decade, youth groups proved even more difficult. With little at stake in the "straight" world, they were able to treat the Committee's hearings as a form of public theatre and to turn drama into farce.

One cannot underestimate changing climates of public opinion as a force affecting the Committee's work. By 1960 the Communist Party had been virtually destroyed both as a political force and as a legitimate target of public anxiety. The "new left" was not strong enough in itself to arouse intense public anxieties, nor could it easily be linked with an international menace of real proportions. The Committee's desperate attempts to link new left groups with the old Communist Party provided much amusement, but they reflected a universal need of vigilante groups to establish the credibility of the threat they are attempting to meet. The failures of the anti-Communist movement in the 1960s, manifested in the abolition of HISC in 1975, reflect in large part an inability to fan the flames of such fears.

The Committee's failures in the 1960s produced a change in its operating procedures. In its twilight years, formal hearings designed primarily to expose became almost nonexistent. HISC came to rely almost exclusively on friendly witnesses and staff reports for its investigations of the Black Panthers and various youth groups; and the bulk of its recent publications deal with broad themes and concepts rather than individuals. Exposure is ineffective for those who have nothing to hide; the logical alternative for HISC is propaganda.

The line between exposure and propaganda is, to be sure, a fine one. Propaganda is a major objective of all vigilantes. Beyond immediate victims, the vigilante plays to a wider audience which, fundamentally, is the real target. He is warning potential sympathizers to be on guard, and advising the public at large that there are "serpents crawling about." The success of the vigilante then is not measured by body counts, but by more subtle indications of the state of the public mind.

Oceans of ink have already been spilled on the origins of anti-communism in the United States. The Truman Administration's attempts to secure public backing for its foreign policies must be accorded an important role. The unique contribution of HUAC and its allies, however, was to link such Cold War attitudes to domestic politics, a linkage which the Administration did not particularly welcome. Its method of establishing this linkage was to personify an abstract problem. This process of personification, of going to the public and in effect saying "Here's one! There's another! Wow, look at 'em! Didn't we tell you that the threat was real?" forms the key to an understanding of the role of the vigilante in defending the status quo.

The long-range significance of most vigilantism lies in what the Supreme Court has called its chilling effects. The work of HUAC and its allies combined social-control vigilantism and a form of regime-control-vigilantism designed to undermine the power base of another part of the ruling establishment. Despite the presence of some northern Democrats such as Francis Walter, HUAC was predominantly a right-wing organization, and it succeeded in seriously undermining the American left.

In a sense it might be said that the liberal establishment woke up too late to what the Committee was doing. Only when blacklisting exceeded the boundaries of "purposive coercion" described in Rosenbaum and Sederberg's introductory essay was the system struck down. But for a complex, modern society this model is too flat; it needs a third dimension. The field of coercive acts can vary markedly from one policy arena to another. Allowable coercion means one thing when applied to students, another when applied to businessmen; and the tolerance shown for vigilantism varies similarly. Thus, McCarthy's excesses with regard to the army were standard operating procedures with regard to Hollywood.

Had the Truman Administration wished to, it probably could have contained—or, to use a currently fashionable term, "stonewalled"—the Committee. It was allowed to flourish, however, not so much because the Administration liked what it was doing, but because it seemed rather harmless. Let those nuts chase commies in the movies, the Administration in effect said, while we go ahead with the Marshall Plan and the Fair Deal. Keep them busy and maybe they will stay out of our hair.

The Administration made some attempts, through its loyalty-security program, for example, to co-opt the work of the Committee and its allies. These efforts were insufficient to allay the fears of those groups who felt that the government was acting ineffectively. That some of these people were in the government, on HUAC or in certain agencies friendly to the anti-Communist movement (e.g., the Immigration Service and the FBI), neither allayed such fears nor restrained the actions of the viglantes. Government lawlessness is not the same as vigilantism; but vigilantism, as I hope this essay has shown, can and perhaps must in a modern society have the tacit, if not the overt, support of some part of the formal political system.

Chapter Seven

Community Police Patrols and Vigilantism

Gary T. Marx and Dane Archer

In their introductory chapter, H. Jon Rosenbaum and Peter C. Sederberg define vigilantes as those who identify with the established order, yet in defending it resort to means in violation of traditional boundaries. They suggest a typology of vigilantism according to whether its purpose is primarily crime-control, social-group-control, or regime-control and whether participants are private or public persons. A group may, of course, have more than one purpose and this may change over time. This essay focuses on American private groups primarily concerned with crime-control, particularly those who see themselves as victims of crime and/or are critical of the response of authorities to crime.

Americans have responded to recent law-enforcement problems with increased fear, estrangement from neighbors, avoidance behavior, increased receptivity to law-and-order politics, and, as the rising fortunes of the private security industry suggest, increased purchases of protective devices such as better locks, alarms, and weapons.

The above are primarily passive, defensive, indirect, and individual responses.[1] Other more active, aggressive, direct group responses may also be seen. American society has always placed a heavy emphasis on voluntary

*We are grateful to the Urban Institute and the National Institute for Law Enforcement and Criminal Justice for support. The original version of this article first appeared as "Citizen Involvement in the Law Enforcement Process: The Case of Community Police Patrols," by Gary T. Marx and Dane Archer in *American Behavioral Scientist* 15, no. 1 (Sept./Oct. 1971): 52-72 published by Sage Publications, Inc.
    1. For data on individual responses, F. Furstenberg, "Fear of Crime and Its Effect on Citizen Behavior," (Paper prepared for Symposium on Studies of Public Experience, Knowledge and Opinion of Crime and Justice, Bureau of Social Science Research, Washington, D.C., 1972), and J. Conklin, *The Impact of Crime* (New York, Macmillan, 1975).

action and masculinity. It should not be surprising that the country's populist, self-help ethos should have spawned a large number of citizen policing groups such as the Louisiana Deacons, Anthony Imperiale's North Ward Citizens' Committee, the Watts Community Alert Patrol, and the Jewish Defense League.

It is with these groups ("self-defense patrols," "vigilantes," "peace creeps," "security patrols," or "community patrols," depending on the group in question and the political perspective of the observer) that this paper is concerned. It focuses on an organizational response of victims (or at least those who see themselves and their communities as potential victims). Perceived victimization is expanded to include actions of authorities as well as actions of those engaged in traditional crime and disorder.

Relatively little is known about contemporary American patrol groups beyond an occasional journalistic account. There are few answers for such important questions as: In what contexts do patrol groups emerge? What are their natural histories of development? How widespread and enduring are such groups and what are the main types? What are their purposes and practices? What is the nature of their interaction with police, various levels of government, other ethnic groups, and their own presumed constituency? How are they viewed by these various groups? How are they organized? How are members recruited and to what extent are they screened and trained? What characteristics and attitudes do members have, and what factors are involved in their motivation to participate? What theory of police failure do they hold? How does the public view them? What are their consequences for the reduction of crime and civil disorders, feelings of safety, curtailing police abuses, or increasing intra- and intergroup conflict in a community; e.g., within or between ethnic groups or with the police? What are their implications for law enforcement and public policy? This paper makes a preliminary effort to deal with questions such as the above.

COMMUNITY POLICE PATROLS

When public institutions fail to meet felt needs, a number of recurring responses on the part of the communities presumably being serviced may be observed. These vary, perhaps in decreasing order of frequency, from passive resignation or withdrawal, to reformist and radical politics, to efforts to set up wholly new institutions outside the traditional system.

Citizen involvement in law enforcement is not new to the American scene. In earlier periods of American history when people felt that there was too much crime, that their persons or property were in danger, that cherished traditions and values were being threatened, and that regular law-enforcement officials were not coping with the problem, vigilante-type efforts frequently emerged. Counting only those groups which have taken the law into their own hands, a recent account lists no fewer than 326 vigilante movements during the past two centuries of American history.[2]

R. M. Brown distinguishes two types of vigilantism in America. The first appeared prior to 1856 in areas where settlement preceded effective law enforcement. The concerns of this type of vigilantism were primarily horse thieves, counterfeiters, outlaws, and "bad men"—the enforcement, that is, of consensually formulated standards of peace and law.

The emergence of the San Francisco Vigilance Committee in 1856 was the birth of a second form of citizen mobilization, what Brown calls "neovigilantism." Unlike the earlier type, neo-vigilantism "found its chief victims among Catholics, Jews, immigrants, Negroes, laboring men and labor leaders, political radicals, and proponents of civil liberties."[3]

While the first type of vigilantism filled or attempted to fill a discernible void, the second generally emerged where the regular police and legal systems were already functioning, but where alien groups were seen to threaten the established order. Rather than simply enforcing the law, the second type frequently involved political struggles for power, racism, attempts to terrorize would-be criminals, and even the desire to spare the public the cost of the conventional judicial process.

Recent self-defense groups differ from more classic vigilante groups in that they, for the most part, have not killed or taken the law into their own hands. Instead, their primary functions have been the surveillance and protection of their own communities, often as an ancillary group to regular police. Thus, they more closely resemble the early anti-horsethief societies which amplified law enforcement through pursuit and capture, but did not try to substitute for it by administering summary punishments. Recent groups have performed largely deterrent functions and have not usually held street trials or meted out alley justice. But the fact that private citizens have chosen to involve themselves in police work has meant that the issue, if not often the substance, of vigilantism has reoccurred with them.

One of the most important of contemporary self-defense groups, at least in the last twenty years, has probably been the "self-defense guard" which organized in Monroe, North Carolina in 1956. The group's purpose was to protect its members against the harassment and incursive violence of the Ku Klux Klan, long a citizen patrol group of a very different nature. The Monroe group, led by Robert Williams, attracted sixty members and received a charter from the National Rifle Association.

The next widely publicized self-defense group patrolled the Crown Heights area of Brooklyn between 1964 and 1966. The group called itself the "Maccabees," after a Jewish resistance group which fought to curb Syrian

2. R. M. Brown, "The American Vigilante Tradition," in H. D. Graham and T. R. Gurr, eds., *The History of Violence in America* (New York: Praeger, 1969), p. 154.

3. Ibid., p. 197.

domination in the second and first centuries B.C. Led by Rabbi Samuel A. Schrage, the Maccabees of the 1960s numbered 250 volunteer members and used radio-car patrols to report crime and deter potential criminals.

In 1965, a year after the Maccabees organized, a black self-defense group known as the Deacons gained prominence in Bogalusa and Jonesboro, Louisiana. The Deacons fielded armed patrol cars to protect civil rights workers and blacks from Klansmen, white rowdies, and the police. Led by Charles Sims, the Deacons claimed seven thousand members in Louisiana and sixty loosely federated chapters in Mississippi, Alabama, Florida, and the Carolinas.[4] A useful case study of a group like the Deacons is given by Harold Nelson.[5]

Shortly after the 1965 Watts riot, a group of young blacks organized the Community Alert Patrol to observe the way ghetto residents were treated by the Los Angeles Police. The following year, at about the time that Oakland, California rejected a proposal for a police review board, Huey P. Newton organized the Black Panther Party for Self-Defense to inform blacks of their legal rights and to "preserve the community from harm."

The riots of the latter part of the 1960s gave rise to a number of diverse patrol groups. Terry Knopf presents information on nine youth patrols (and notes eleven others) which worked to limit confrontations, arrests, and violence in ghetto areas during the summer of 1967.[6] Ethnically based white groups, such as Anthony Imperiale's North Ward Citizens' Committee and the Jewish Defense League, emerged partly in response to the black riots.

More recently the concept of civilian policing has overflowed the original street patrol model, coming to focus on more limited contexts such as housing projects, rock concerts, and protest demonstrations. According to one estimate, more than eighty-five hundred unpaid volunteers were on "tenant safety patrols" in ninety-three New York City Housing Authority projects in 1970.

METHOD

We have gathered some descriptive information on twenty-eight self-defense groups, using a snowball technique of gaining cases. This information is based on interviews with police and patrol group members, observation, newspaper accounts, and analysis of documents.[7]

4. Ibid., p. 203.

5. H. A. Nelson, "The defenders: a case study of an informal police organization," *Social Problems* 15 (Fall 1967),: 127-147.

6. T. A. Knopf, *Youth Patrols: An Experiment in Community Participation* (Waltham: Brandeis University Lemberg Center for the Study of Violence, 1969).

7. Interviews outside the Boston area were carried out using a semi-structured phone interview. We do not know the extent to which the descriptive material can be generalized beyond these twenty-eight cases. The "patrols" universe is unknown and subject to much fluctuation. Newspaper accounts of such groups are often deceptive and reflective more of the mood behind

SOME DESCRIPTIVE DATA ON TWENTY-EIGHT GROUPS

Race of Members. Of the twenty-eight self-defense groups, seventeen (61 percent) were black. Since the performance of conventional police is probably least adequate and most controversial in black neighborhoods, the disproportionate emergence of alternate institutions there should not be surprising.

Operations. The functions performed by the groups varied. The most common function, characterizing more than four out of ten, involved patrols of their neighborhoods; 39 percent worked to "cool" existing or imminent civil disorders; 32 percent kept their communities under surveillance and were "eyes and ears" for the police; 25 percent, according to police, actively interfered with police arrests and other work; and 21 percent assisted in public education on matters of law enforcement.

Equipment and Weapons. Unlike earlier vigilante groups, a majority of the groups report themselves or are reported to be unarmed. Only two of the groups (7 percent) admitted to carrying guns, though at least four groups (14 percent) reportedly carried clubs. The most frequently reported types of equipment were walkie-talkies and car radios, and 14 percent of the groups (most of which had young members) wore identifying shirts, berets, or jackets.

Chronicity. Slightly over half the groups had routinized their operations. Roughly a third (32 percent) of the groups were active primarily during periods of civil disorder.

Police Departmental Regulation. Police were in communication with about two-thirds of the groups, generally to explain things like the legal limits of citizens' arrests and to give instruction or advice. In at least one city, Boston, police have actually drawn up guidelines for citizen patrol groups.[8] In about one-third of the cases, police issued some form of identification, often in card form, to group members. This was particularly true in the case of groups whose purpose was to reduce, from within, the level of violence in civil disorders.

Attitudes of Police. In the case of 43 percent of the self-defense groups, police officials reported they were glad the groups existed. It is worth noting that this figure is not as high as the police perception of the number of groups which were pro-police (61 percent). In the case of 25 percent of the groups,

---

self-defense groups than of their substance. Some reported groups, upon inspection, turn out to be evanescent, pratically inoperative, and in at least one case, an announced self-defense group was discovered to have membership of one man: the group founder himself. Our twenty-eight cases consist of most of the fully operative general patrols (as against special purpose patrols such as those restricted to one housing project) known to us and our informants in 1970-1971. The actual number of groups is no doubt much larger since some groups, such as the Jewish Defense League (treated as one case here), claim numerous affiliates. We have excluded traditional police auxiliaries.

8. Knopf, *Youth Patrols.*

police officials said they wished that the groups did not exist. Police felt that 36 percent of the groups had improved police-community relations, 29 percent were actually cutting down on crime, and 18 percent had helped to prevent or deflate riots. At the same time, police felt that 25 percent of the groups had "abused their authority," and they reported receiving complaints from other citizens about the groups' operations in 21 percent of the cases.

ANALYSIS: FIVE ORGANIZATIONAL PROBLEMS

In the course of their creation and development, self-defense groups must come to terms with at least five major issues: (1) their relationship to the police and legal system; (2) their legitimacy in the eyes of the communities they wish to serve; (3) the recruitment and management of personnel; (4) the choice of appropriate operations; and (5) the maintenance of resources, incentives, and motivation for the groups' survival.

1. SELF-DEFENSE GROUPS AND THE POLICE

Self-defense groups are heterogeneous phenomena. One of the most important dimensions on which they vary is their attitude toward police. By definition, self-defense groups believe that the police have failed to keep either order or security. But there seems to be an important and dichotomous difference in their *theory of police failure.*

The first type of group sees police failure as attributable to manpower shortages, overlenient local courts, the *Escobedo, Miranda,* and other decisions of the Supreme Court, and simply the rampant increase and encroachment of those they regard as "the criminal element." This first type of self-defense group sees the police as good men overwhelmed from without and handcuffed from within. They see them, that is, as *failures, but not as blameworthy.*

The second type of self-defense group sees the police as part of the problem. In general, the second type of group attributes police failure to what they see as police (1) lack of understanding or any rapport with the communities they serve, (2) arrogant and corrupt behavior, (3) brutality, (4) racism, (5) their role as guardians only of the propertied classes and the status quo. The second type of self-defense group, then, counts the police among those against whom the community must be defended. This second type of self-defense group is intended either as a check on police or as a clear alternative to them. Police are seen as *highly blameworthy failures.*

The relationship of these two types of groups to police may be described as supplemental and adversarial, respectively.

The attitude of a self-defense group toward the police does influence police response to the group (and, as the increased revolutionary perspective of the Black Panthers indicates, subsequent police response and the nature of official labeling, of course, acts back on the attitudes of the group). It might be predicted that police would approve all supplemental groups and allow them to flourish, while opposing and suppressing all adversarial groups. This is often, but by no means always, the case. Thus, for one-third of the groups that police perceived as "pro-police," the opinion was nevertheless expressed that it would be better if the groups didn't exist. There seem to be two mitigating variables: (1) police do not always approve of all supplemental groups because, among other reasons, they say it is bad for untrained citizens of any ideology to "take the law into their own hands," (2) police do not immediately suppress all adversarial groups, partly to avoid trouble and partly because they know that the groups often have a better chance of maintaining order, particularly during active or threatened disorders.

A Typology of Groups.   There are, thus, two important dimensions along which such groups vary: the nature of the group (supplemental or adversarial) and the nature of the police response (encouragement or opposition). When these two dimensions are combined, a useful typology emerges by which groups may be contrasted and analyzed.

In Figure 1, groups from eight cities have been placed in the appropriate cells of the typology.[9]

Figure 1   A Typology of Groups

Police Response

		Encouragement or Noninterference	Opposition or Suppression
SELF-DEFENSE GROUP	Supplemental	TYPE I Cleveland Queens	TYPE II Seattle Boston
	Adversarial	TYPE III Baton Rouge Tampa	TYPE IV Oakland Minneapolis

9. As with any ideal-typical classification, the actual relations between the police and self-defense groups are often more complex than the table implies. For example, in the case of the proposed Boston Mattapan Dorchester Community Patrol, there is a hierarchical split of opinion within the police department. Officials at the superintendent level endorse the patrol, but the head of the department's rank and file Boston Police Patrolmen's Association is vehement in his opposition. There may as well be differences of opinion within a self-defense group over theories of police failure. Even where there is consistency within departments, the police attitude may be ambivalent. Thus, although the Boston Jewish Defense League considers itself pro-police and reports to the local police before going out on patrols, police interviewed appeared to be neutral toward them, approving of their concern over crime but not taking them very seriously.

Type I: Supplemental and encouraged by police. The self-defense groups which fall into Cell I of the typology generally meet police notions of acceptable citizen mobilization. In all cases within this category, *both power and independence are low.* The police exercise complete authority over the organization, its leaders, activities, and members. Typically, these groups either begin as or are transformed into police auxiliaries with jobs such as traffic control or property protection during civil disorders. Most housing project patrols also fall within Type I. Other Type I organizations are of police-supporting citizens' groups. They may establish and publicize "Crime Alert" telephone numbers and patrol streets only to call in bona fide policemen if they sight suspicious behavior or persons, or they may do public relations work for the police.[10] Type I groups are the most numerous, well manned, and stable.

Type II: Supplemental and opposed by police. Police may oppose groups in Cell II on several grounds, in some cases for reasons having little to do with the specific nature of the self-defense group.[11] Instead, police may express a general dislike of amateurs. The mistakes of citizen patrols, like those of private guards, may be seen to give regular police a bad image. Police may resent the hedging in on their monopoly over violence and be wary of anything that smacks of vigilantism. In Seattle, for example, a citizen group mobilized to offer the police help in dealing with a demonstration against the war in Vietnam. The acting police chief declined their offer, saying he had no desire to end up fighting two mobs instead of one. Apparently, Type II groups either change to meet police requirements or fail. Some move into political action on behalf of law and order.

Several departments took a cooptive approach to patrols. A chief in one western city reported:

> When local people start talking about organizing a patrol, the community relations department goes in and invites them to ride in a partol car. At this point the intent is more to educate the citizen than to help us. If the citizen is still gung ho, he is encouraged to join the police auxiliary.

In Cleveland a number of neighborhood patrols were made regular police auxiliaries. This was seen by the safety director as a way of increasing the size of the force while warding off the danger of vigilantism. In other cities some of those who start as private patrollers later join regular auxiliaries.

10. For example, a Community Radio watch sponsored as a "public service program of Motorola Communications and Electronics, Inc." reports that in 700 cities almost 500,000 drivers of two-way radio equipped vehicles are providing emergency information to public-safety agencies. This includes information on "suspicious acts, street crimes, and unusual occurrences."

11. Here it may be useful to differentiate the public police attitude which may be negative from the private attitude of particular policemen. Some members of self-defense groups interviewed reported that regular police envied what was seen as the private patrol's ability to crack heads and get away with it, in a way that police could not. Some patrols routinely have weapons such as mace or metal-tipped plastic clubs usually denied police.

Type III: Adversarial and encouraged by police. Because of their potential organizational contradiction, the self-defense groups in Cell III are of particular interest. Many of these groups are short-lived, and all appear to survive precariously. They and the police are mutually suspicious and resentful, existing in a state of hostile interdependence. Most of these groups are born during riots, and many demand, as a condition of their "cool-it" function, that police withdraw from troubled areas. Withdrawal is seen by the police as humiliating, though sometimes forced by higher authority, and police embarrassment is compounded if the groups are effective. At the same time, members of the "cool-it" groups may suffer a loss of the respect of their constituents, and they may feel (and sometimes say) that they were used as tools to deflate protest and then discarded. During the disorders, cities which have groups of Type III are remarkable studies in struggle for influence between institutional authorities and nascent alternate powers. However, after the disorder, or when all danger of a major conflagration has passed, groups in Cell III tend to collapse. Many cities voted to salary and support "cool-it" groups during and shortly after a riot, but the salaries inevitably dried up, often with the end of summer. At that point, long-standing tensions between the groups and the police often resurfaced, and the groups might move into Cell IV of the typology.

Type IV: Adversarial and opposed by police. The groups in Cell IV of the typology, although relatively small in number, are the most dramatic. Adversarial patrols have emerged among minority groups or where there are concentrations of whites with deviant life styles and dissenting political beliefs, as there are around university communities. Although specific tactics differ, most of the Type IV groups seek to protect their communities from what they see as police excesses by trying to oversee actual police operations or attacking police. In at least two cities, members of a self-defense patrol carried cameras to record police behavior during arrest situations. In another case, a self-defense group listened to police radio calls for the location of complaints likely to result in arrests and then showed up and urged those involved to leave before police arrived.

Police see these groups as among their most dangerous enemies. They say that most of the members have arrest records, that members have searched cars and homes without authority, and that the members themselves are as active on the side of crime and riots as in their prevention. While there may be some or a great deal of substance to the police assessment, it is also true that police surveillance of Type IV groups is intensive. There are many instances of police harassment of such groups, as in the cases of the original Black Panthers of Oakland, when they had active patrols, or the Deacons of Lousiana. Such groups have a volatile natural history. In the case of one Type IV group, 80 percent of its members were reportedly in jail at the time we made our inquiry.

Many groups which end up in Cell IV began in Cell III. Almost invariably, the groups lost the tolerance of the police through efforts to regulate police behavior, thus challenging the absolute supremacy of the police. As an example, the Community Alert Patrol in Los Angeles had applied for (and received provisional approval of) $238,000 in Health, Education and Welfare funds to finance their operations. The grant included $1600 for cameras and tape recorders, and any evidence of police misbehavior was to have been recorded and submitted for the investigation of complaints. The police opposed the patrol, saying they did not need "nonpolicemen to police the police," and funding was halted.

In part, police oppose Type IV groups simply because they are most clearly "anti-police." But Type IV groups are also those which, more than the other three types of groups, carry weapons, use violence to establish their authority, and resist any kind of control over their operations. It might be argued, of course, that these three traits are also characteristic of the police themselves and that such groups come closest to being competitors and alternatives to regular police. A number of police officials reported that their main objection to the Type IV group in their city was that it did things that only police were entitled to do. Although it is difficult to stipulate its content precisely, there is clearly a threshold between civilians and police which no citizens are permitted to cross.

2. Self-Defense Groups and the Communities They Wish to Serve

In part because they raise the spectre of vigilantism, self-defense groups are likely to be attended by controversy. Even in the case of supplemental organizations where communities generally seem to be united in their recognition of law enforcement problems, they are often divided over the appropriateness of the self-defense solution. In the case of adversarial groups, the host communities are even more sharply divided. The difference may be due, in part, to the lack of agreement among citizens as to whether or not the police are a problem to be dealt with, controlled, or exorcised.

For example, in Boston, a proposal to establish a police-controlled community patrol was supported by some black leaders as a vehicle for improving police-community cooperation. But the Boston National Association for the Advancement of Colored People (NAACP) was highly critical and rejected the proposal. An NAACP position paper called for increased numbers of patrolmen, saying that the overwhelming majority of the black citizens in the area wanted adequate and just police protection, not an amateur substitute. Its statement suggested that if crime rose on Boston's Beacon Hill or other equally wealthy parts of the city, the city's response would be augmented police forces. The statement added:

> It is shameful that where Black people in particular are concerned—whether
> they are a majority or minority in an area—officials and leaders leap for short

cuts, ill-designed programs and faulty planning which in the long run render the situation worse than it was in its previous state . . . Citizens throughout the city are entitled to proper police protection; they should not have to rely on a volunteer group to shoulder this responsibility.

Perhaps ironically, the same proposal was attacked by Boston militants. In the *People's South End News* (July 1970), an article opposed the community patrol, saying:

If the power structure can keep the people arguing over (1) more pigs in the community or an unarmed auxiliary police force; (2) and continue to keep racial tensions high, they will never get around to the real issue facing every community. That is, community control of police and the total withdrawal of the present occupying army. . . . It's long past the time to stop fighting each other, and deal with the enemy.

In another example, two community organizers concerned with reducing crime in a housing project in a small New England town sought to encourage residents to organize a self-defense group. The organizers acknowledged that most residents felt the crime problem could be best handled by assigning more police to the project. Yet their hostility to the police and concern that increased regular police would undermine the community's control over their own affairs led them to try to establish a self-defense group.

At least in Boston, and probably elsewhere (particularly in the North), a clear community mandate for any given autonomous self-defense group as an alternative to regular police is likely to be lacking (though considerable support may exist for the general principle of citizen involvement). The absence of a broad base of popular support may explain in part why Types III and IV live precariously and often have a short life.

However great their failings sometimes are, regular police forces still have something of a legal, consensual mandate to operate, though the strength of this mandate no doubt weakens as social class decreases or the proportion of nonwhite citizens increases. Although in practice the controls are often inoperative, there are still some constraints on police behavior by the courts, local officials, and state and federal government. For most self-defense groups, in the absence of a clear mandate from the communities they wish to serve, the problem of accountability is potentially a highly problematic one. Some groups, of course, may claim a community mandate which appears stronger than it really is because of community indifference, lack of awareness of the group, or fear of intimidation by it.

Legitimacy may simply be denied those seeking to play police roles. Though policing by one's peers seems much more desirable than an outside praetorian guard, it may not always work. Neighborhood policemen may be seen as neighbors not police. Thus, in one housing project when an irregularly employed resident with a reputation for inebriation took a job in a tenant's patrol, he found that his efforts to maintain order were met with amusement and retorts such as, "you're old Ernie; you ain't a cop." Or if legitimacy is granted, the appeal to ties of ethnicity, class, generation, or neighborhood may inhibit fair and universalistic behavior by those on patrol.

The legitimacy issue is also complicated by raising the question for heterogeneous areas : "In whose eyes?" Groups are likely to receive greater or lesser support depending on the degree of homogeneity between the racial and ethnic backgrounds (and other social characteristics as well) of the group doing the patrolling, the group it feels it is protecting, and the groups from whom it is seen to need protection. Many combinations in terms of support from the public are possible, and each has a potentially different outcome. A predominantly white patrol group in an area in racial transition is likely to meet more conflict than a black group in an all-black area.

For groups which emerge out of already existing organizations such as a civil defense unit, a minister's association, athletic teams or faculty on the college campus, and community action and service organizations, problems of organization and legitimacy, while present, are likely to be less pronounced.

There also are problems of an operational nature. Most police interventions stem from citizen requests, usually through telephoning. Even if citizens have heard of the group, they may not know how to contact them. The groups are limited to observable behavior in public places.

3. THE RECRUITMENT AND TRAINING OF PERSONNEL

In discussing civilian mobilization around the issue of law enforcement, one police scholar writes:

> Experience has shown that it is not alone the super defenders of hearth and home who clamor for an opportunity to serve. Truculent, disorderly, intolerant, and downright vicious elements also flock to police standards at such time [of crisis], from motives of their own and with objectives foreign to the maintenance of civil peace.[12]

There is, of course, likely to be variation among groups, and differences in the resources available to screen and train personnel, as well as the will to do this. The exact criteria for membership in the patrols are often not formalized and may depend on the whim of a charismatic leader. In Newark, Anthony Imperiale (who supported George Wallace in the 1968 presidential election) claims that he dismisses any member of his group whom he suspects of racism. He notes, "Many people came to us because of my old name as a Negro hater, but we have special details to look out for these people. They're a bigger threat than the black militants."[13]

In 1969 before aspirant members were allowed to patrol with the Jewish Defense League in Boston they were required to have an interview with the

12. B. Smith, *Police Systems in the United States* (New York: Harper, 1960), p. 314.
13. *Christian Science Monitor* (January 16, 1970): 2.

group's psychiatrist (himself an ex-green beret) to screen out sadistic, unstable, or otherwise undesirable applicants.[14] A JDL patrol coordinator reports receiving calls from a number of people, including members of outlaw motorcycle clubs, who wanted to shoot blacks and adds "the line between dedication and screwballs is very close." The "defenders," a group studied by Harold Nelson, requires, beyond a thorough background investigation, that members be married and, to weed out romantics and the inexperienced, that they have served in the military at least six weeks under active war combat conditions. Some adversarial police patrols require nothing more than an oath and memorization of a political party platform.[15]

Little is know about the range of motives that may lead a citizen to join (and stay in) a community patrol group, just as relatively little is known about why people seek to enter regular police forces beyond the quest for a steady job.[16] American police departments that have a relatively thorough selection process (such as Los Angeles, which takes less than 5 percent of those who apply) still face many serious police-community relations problems.[17] It seems likely that self-defense groups, which often experience manpower shortages and which have much less stringent screening or membership requirements, would stand a far greater chance of recruiting people not emotionally (or, in

14. Included in the undesirable category was a social researcher seeking to do participant observation. However, the ability of some people to patrol without the participation interview suggests that it may also have a public relations function.

15. It has been suggested that one factor (in addition to actions of the government) in the increased violence of the Black Panthers in 1969 and 1970 was a relaxation in their membership screening.

16. An additional motivational factor almost always neglected by social researchers either out of good taste, ideology, or the vast distance between them and those they are studying is the careerist implications that can be involved in the emergence of such noninstitutional phenomena. As with most human matters, motivation may sometimes be less pure than it appears. In describing a case, Tom Wolfe notes:

> There was one genius in the art of confrontation who had mau-mauing down to what you could term a laboratory science. He had it figured out so he didn't even have to bring his boys downtown in person. He would just show up with a crocus sack full of revolvers, ice picks, fish knives, switchblades, hatchets, blackjacks, gravity knives, straight razors, hand grenades, blow guns, bazooks, Molotov cocktails, tank rippers, unbelievable stuff, and he'd dump it all out on somebody's shiny walnut conference table. He'd say "These are some of the things I took off my boys last night . . . I don't know, man . . . Thirty minutes ago I talked a Panther out of busting up a cop . . ." and they would lay money on this man's ghetto youth patrol like it was now or never. . . .

Tom Wolfe, *Radical Chic and Mau-mauing the Flak Catchers* (New York: Simon and Schuster, 1970).

17. Perhaps something can be inferred about the greater abuse potential of those rejected by regular police by noting that private security guards, who seem to be higher in the abuse of their powers than traditional police, are often rejected applicants for the regular force. This may also be true of some who join citizen patrols. The leader of a highly publicized group in an eastern city had reportedly been rejected several times in his bid to join the regular police force. He subsequently set up his own.

some cases, morally) suited to policing others.[18] Police folklore suggests that this is the case, although adequate empirical data are not available.

Patrols strive for public approval or official recognition. However, given the characteristics of many of those who become involved, this may be difficult—particularly in minority neighborhoods, where law enforcement tensions are greatest and where many self-defense groups accept for membership men with arrest records. Unfortunately, an arrest record is an ecological fact of life in such areas and need not imply very much about a person's character or potential. It may even be indicative of an ability to relate better than alien police to the young men on the street likely to be engaged in crime and civil disorders. Yet it also may influence the acceptability and image of the group in the eyes of the police and in at least some parts of the communities they wish to serve.

Even where such problems of membership are not present, a related problem reported in several cities involved nonpatrol members impersonating patrol members and using their authority and coercion to obtain personal or illegal ends. In several cities, supposed abuses of patrol members turned out to involve persons pretending to be in the patrol. Loose organization and ill-defined criteria for membership facilitate such impersonation, and the jackets or armbands which some patrols use as identifying symbols are easily obtained. Impersonation is less likely in the case of regular police, given their uniforms, badges, and clear criteria for membership.

4. CHOOSING SELF-DEFENSE OPERATIONS

The operations of many self-defense groups are conditioned by the nature of the precipitating event. Civil disorders, such as the ones in Newark, have given rise to youth patrols attempting to restore calm to their communities as well as to patrols in white areas, such as Imperiale's, concerned with keeping supposed black rioters out. Campus sit-ins have given rise to student and faculty marshalls. Attacks on women leaving church services have led to escort groups. Attacks on civil rights figures have resulted in protective guards, especially in the South. The Oakland Black Panthers' observations of police activities grew out of the police killing of a black. In New York, tenant patrol groups began frequenting poorly lit areas of their housing projects and, in many cases, rode the elevators with otherwise unaccompaned women after a number of apartment and elevator murders. The Boston Jewish Defense League placed guards in front of synagogues after several were burned. A series of closing-time robberies led one group to stay in stores as they were about to close. Children dying from drug overdoses have given rise to anti-drug groups in various cities. Requests from constituents for a certain kind of

---

18. Of course, this type of criticism seems less appropriate where an entire community of people has been excluded from involvement with the official police force, as it is in many southern communities.

service, help with a child in trouble or protection from harassment, can also help define a group's activities.[19]

In other cases an already functioning organization may come to see policing as compatible with its ends. Civil defense groups have given rise to various anti-crime activities. They offer an organizational structure, are neighborhood based, and have an ethos and sense of mission entirely compatible with crime control (this is of course also true of the local male youth, athletic, and fraternal groups which have been involved in patroling). Some groups have emerged from civic, community welfare and development organizations. In one midwestern city a "clean up and beautification campaign" has since given rise to another kind of clean-up campaign involving local groups with a crime-awareness program.

Yet it is one thing to agree that there are problems and quite another to decide what lines of action are appropriate and possible. The role of the citizen patroller is not as clearly defined as is that of a teaching aide or hospital volunteer, and it appears to have basic conflicts structured into it. Although the groups have considerable latitude of choice with regard to operations, their use of weapons is subject to obvious restrictions. Almost no groups admit to carrying guns, although police said that two groups did.

In carrying out their activities, self-defense groups face potentially serious legal problems. They are on patrol; yet they lack the power of arrest and the right to use force granted regular police. There is no intermediary status in American society between the role of citizen and that of policeman. Unless a citizen, however concerned, is deputized or admitted to the low-power police auxiliaries, he can have no law-enforcement powers beyond those of the ordinary citizen. And the citizen's power in law enforcement is severely circumscribed, with potentially serious penalties for its usurpation.

In almost all cities, police errors (and sometimes abuses not stemming from errors) are routinely excused as justifiable, given the margin of error thought to be required in the performance of a dangerous and difficult job. But citizens, even those with police approval, do not receive the same de facto protective blanket. Instead, they are fully liable to tort actions for wrongful death or injury. Given the nature of self-defense operations, it seems likely that those affected by the groups would seek redress if they felt unjustly dealt with.

Although the legal situation is at present ambiguous, it is not at all clear that self-defense groups even have workable powers of citizens' arrest. In general, citizens are not allowed to use force unless it is to defend themselves personally from felonious violence. Short of that, in theory, citizens may not have the power to restrain, hold, or subdue suspects in most criminal behavior. And in

---

19. For example, a woman in an area many miles from where the Boston Jewish Defense League regularly patrols reported anti-Semitic harassment by a gang of local youth. After a "discussion" with a Jewish Defense League delegation, the gang's harassment reportedly stopped.

the case of adversarial groups, even if citizens did have the power to arrest or otherwise restrict police, such power is unlikely to be recognized.

As pressure is brought to bear on them, or the limits and ambiguities of the patrols are realized, some groups rather quickly abandon active patrols in favor of political action. They may move from threats of vigilante action to holding meetings, pressuring the city council, or evaluating the law-and-order record of judges and candidates. The groups or individuals in them may become part of the regular police auxiliary. Well-to-do communities may hire licensed private security guards. Groups that remain with active patrols may seek legitimacy through the concept of citizens' arrest and the right of self-defense and by stressing their support of regular police. They may be very careful to follow all laws. They may publicly stress that their actions are limited to observation and communications. They may be instructed to avoid any confrontation or use of force and simply be a presence. In one city, patrollers are told not to leave their radio cars unless asked to do so by police.

While an emphasis on the supportive and legal nature of a patrol may be conducive to support from authorities and some members of the community, it may alienate others who will more clearly see them as agents of regular police. Herein lies a dilemma. In such cases, to gain community support they must differentiate themselves from police and stress their independence; yet in doing this they may alienate themselves from police, whose support, at least tacitly, they are likely to require. In Watts, for example, members of the Community Action Patrol were accused of being police agents. To allay fears and suspicions that they would "rat" on blacks by reporting crimes to police, a patrol's commander publicly stated that they would not do this. This then further strengthened police opposition.

The role of citizen patrollers tends to lack clarity and there is not much consensus about what it should entail. It is often unclear whom a group is serving, or what actions it should be taking. During a period of civil disorder, for example, are patrollers agents of established authority, third party intervenors serving as a buffer between (or controls on both) antagonists, or are they agents of an aggrieved community? Even if patrollers have clearly defined this issue for themselves, others may not see them in the same way.

Police may see those playing such roles as part of the problem and not grant them the legitimacy promised by higher officials. For example, according to the governor of New Jersey, during the Newark riot black peacekeeping volunteers (supported by the mayor and the state government) "were chased around so much by [law enforcement] people who suspected them as participating in the riot that they had to abandon their efforts."[20] During a Cincinnati riot, police refused to cooperate with black peacekeepers (given badges by the mayor) and arrested them on charges of loitering. A similar

20. Governor's Select Commission on Civil Disorders, *Report for Action* (New Jersey, 1968).

situation regarding the efforts of student and faculty marshalls prevailed during some campus disorders.

On the other hand, police may treat a group which sees itself as a more neutral peacekeeping force (trying to maintain order while remaining a buffer between authorities and an angry community) as if they were merely an extension of regular police. That the groups need at least tacit police support may offer police a means of bargaining for ends they seek. Given the apprehension, prevention, and surveillance goals of police, there appear to be pressures to move neutral buffer groups into more explicit police activities. Thus, in one city in Kansas, the police chief who cooperated in the setting up of a patrol group later tried unsuccessfully to get the head of the group to infiltrate the Black Panthers. In another city a patrol leader was asked to ride with police and point out "troublemakers." In a western city, local citizen "beat committees" are encouraged to write legislators about "laws due to come before the legislature which the [police] department believes would be beneficial, also those which hamper our efforts." Yet, even with police support, broader political changes may greatly affect a group. Thus, in one midwestern city a newly elected law-and-order mayor replaced the police chief and dissolved a citizen's patrol he had helped to sponsor.

Even where a group is clearly able to play a role independent of authorities, some members of the community they wish to relate to will simply see them as auxiliary police, no matter what the group does. Dissenting political ideas and the fact that the group may have some of the same ends and trappings of regular police (paramilitary organization, uniforms, radio cars, walkie-talkies, etc.) for some people are conducive to seeing indigenous patrols as, in principle, indistinguishable from regular police.

The question of how indigenous policing groups maintain (or try to maintain) credibility with those they wish to serve is an important one. One definition adopted by some black adversarial groups is to try and enforce the morality of the dominant society but not to use its institutional means. A frequent appeal by ghetto patrols to disorderly youths was "Come on, we don't want the cops in here." Several patrols were set up by ex-felons, not to aide police, but to try and keep their friends out of trouble. As one activist put it, "the attitude is you don't want to be a policeman; you want to help." A Baton Rouge group's overall purpose is "looking after the people." This includes victims of crime as well as victimizers. In some places part of looking after the latter may mean getting them to cease criminal activity without turning them over to police and courts. Black groups in some areas are seeking to drive narcotics peddlers, thieves, and prostitutes out of their communities without involving regular police.

Legitimacy may also be sought through a spillover effect as the group's operations come to involve less controversial activities. A number of groups had a tendency to expand into traditional welfare activities: ambulance services, free health clinics, free breakfast and lunch programs, job counseling, tutoring programs, all-purpose complaint centers, Little League baseball teams, community oriented business, etc. This may help their image in the eyes of an uncertain community. Social assistance and order maintenance activities raise fewer problems for a group than do efforts at enforcing the law. They can also give the organization new life and purpose.

5. INCENTIVES FOR GROUP SURVIVAL

A large proportion of self-defense groups fail to develop the requisites for prolonged group survival such as with a formal organization having a relatively clear sense of direction and a continuing source of support. Type I organizations appear to be the most permanent. They are also the most bureaucratic and most likely to be able to pay members. The presence of resources as such is not, however, a guarantee of success; they can result in much in-fighting and factionalism as members of a group compete to control what is available.[21]

The existence of other types of groups seems to depend largely on a sudden felt crisis (civil disorder, a particularly horrible crime or instance of police brutality, a rapidly changing neighborhood) or on a charismatic leader. When these conditions are no longer present, such groups tend to disperse. The modeling influence of the media is important here. For example, within six weeks after the first youth patrol appeared during the 1967 civil disorders, at least eight more appeared. As the riots subsided, so did the groups.

For many of the young, lower-status males involved in patrol groups, to be invested with the symbols of authority (armbands, special jackets, badges, identification cards, uniforms, etc.), and to be offered a degree of respect and responsibility usually denied them had great meaning. In the words of one observer, "the uniform helps a lot; it makes a man feel like a big shot." In the initial stages, such intangibles were important motivating factors. Yet, for many people involved in volunteer groups over a period of time, certificates and banquets are of limited effectiveness as motivating devices. Many police interviewed could not understand why citizens would be willing to undertake gratuitously such a job with its hazards and ambiguities.

An unconscientious approach to the task, which characterizes some policemen, may also characterize patrollers. In the case of one tenant patrol in a high-crime project area, some volunteers preferred to stay in the lobbies where it was warm rather than patrol stairwells and elevators where there was danger of attack or encounter.

Beyond the need to cope with a severely felt problem or payment for the work, such self-defense groups may attract members for a variety of reasons,

21. The leader of a successful Boston group sees the voluntary nature of his group as being crucial to its success and reports "money has been the death of other organizations."

such as the desire for novelty, excitement, authority, and machismo. Such needs can be satisfied or frustrated by group operations. The participants interviewed rarely reported encounters, and so their tasks may quickly become routine. While this might be an argument for the deterrent value of patrols, it does not help sustain those whose motivation for joining involves the search for action. An observer of the Newark North Ward Citizens Committee reports, "Actually, though the potential for excitement is most obviously there, the patrols tend to be boring."[22] As of August 1970, after many months of operation, the Jewish Defense League in Boston had not reported any direct encounters with offenders. After three and a half years the founder of a housing authority patrol had not seen anything "really suspicious" and saw the work as "mostly tedious duty." An analysis of a Minneapolis Indian Patrol notes "On a given night they might help no one. They might not observe any arrests nor encounter any police officers."[23] A common theme in a number of accounts was the boring, routine nature of patrols. There is a high attrition rate and in eastern and midwestern areas participation rates drop appreciably in the winter.

Even those groups which develop an organizational structure and are successful in keeping order and reducing crime or perceived police abuse are not assured of continued existence. In fact, under some circumstances, organizational success may even make survival less likely. A weak, disorganized adversarial group may be seen to pose less of a threat to regular police than a stronger group. For example, when a group—through the use of cameras and tape recorders or the threatened use of violence against policemen seen as offenders—begins to make the police feel its presence, strong pressures may emerge for the group's abolition. The success of groups in dealing with crime or disorders may also be seen to highlight the failure of regular police. Though a degree of external conflict may increase a group's solidarity and will to stuggle, political pressure, particularly from police, has disbanded apparently successful programs in a number of cities including Los Angeles, New York, Minneapolis, and Pittsburgh (California).

SOME IMPLICATIONS

The emergence of self-defense groups (along with increases in gun sales, homicide and riot) represent a countertrend to the increasing tendency of the state to monopolize the means of violence and to extend its control ever outward. The twentieth century has seen a decline in American traditions of

22. P. Goldberger, "Tony Imperiale Stands Vigilant For Law and Order," *New York Times Magazine* (September 29, 1968) p. 120.
23. Fay Cohen, "The Indian Patrol in Minneapolis: Social Control and Social Change in An Urban Context," *Law and Society Review* 7 (Summer, 1973): 784.

nongovernmental interference in private violence.[24] The groups represent a return to an earlier less differentiated period of American history.

Max Weber has argued that a major characteristic of the modern state is its ability to claim "the monopoly of the legitimate use of physical force within a given territory."[25] But, compared to highly centralized European countries, this process is much less pronounced in the United States, a country whose Bill of Rights guarantees each citizen "the right to keep and bear arms." Where it exists, the stuggle between citizen patrol groups and the state is part of a broader historical process and the unresolved conflict over the role of force in modern American life.

Beneath the surface of our supposedly monopolistic social control institutions and our beliefs about the legality of government violence and the illegality of private violence, there endures considerable support for violence of a private, noninstitutionalized, and nonbureaucratic character. This draws on populist and frontier traditions. The United States is perhaps unique among industrialized nations in the strength of this sentiment. It is not surprising that such citizen patrols are almost unknown in most European societies. The patrols can be seen as the iceberg tip of America's potential for the private violence that is likely under greatly increased levels of crime and disorder. Indeed, we have not begun to think about the implications of the increase in privately owned handguns by Americans. In the last ten years this has increased from ten million to forty million. Popular films such as *Death Wish* serve to diffuse and legitimate a vigilantism model.

In our survey of citizen attitudes toward patrol groups in the Boston area, a very high level of support was found.[26] Of adults between the ages of twenty-one and sixty-five in the Boston area, *over half* (55 percent of whites; 69 percent of blacks) supported the idea of supplemental citizen patrols. Perhaps even more surprising, *over half* (55 percent of whites and 70 percent of blacks) also supported the idea of groups which try to check up on the police by observing their operations.

If this finding can be generalized to adults between the ages of twenty-one and sixty-five in all American metropolitan areas the size of Boston or larger, it means (conservatively, using the white percentage based upon the 1970 census) that there are more than 12 million Americans who could support supplemental and/or adversarial citizen patrols in their communities. If our findings can be further generalized to adults between the ages of twenty-one and sixty-five in all urban areas, regardless of size, the number of Americans

24. For example, see A. Waskow, *From Race Riot to Sit-In* (Garden City: Doubleday, 1966).

25. H. H. Gerth and C. W. Mills, *From Max Weber; Essays in Sociology* (New York: Oxford University Press, 1961), p. 78.

26. A full report of the survey can be found in our paper, "Picking Up the Gun: Some Organizational and Survey Data on Community Police Patrols," in the proceedings of Symposium on Studies of Public Experience, Knowledge and Opinion of Crime and Justice, Bureau of Social Science Research (Washington, D.C., 1972).

who would support supplemental and adversarial patrols in their communities jumps to more than 42 million.

These perhaps unexpectedly high levels of support for citizen patrols make it interesting to speculate about the potential for vastly more widespread citizen mobilization in America under various kinds of provocation. For example, if crime or riots and social movements were more sustained or perceived as more of a threat than they have so far been, and law-enforcement authorities were unable to restore order, would literally millions of Americans pick up the gun to respond to the perceived threats with private violence?

Alternately, are there acts of police brutality or oppression sufficiently provocative to galvanize adversarial groups in far greater numbers than have been involved before? These speculations raise important, almost Hobbesian questions about the potential of private man to resort to his own violence if society's monopoly of legitimate violence fails to preserve what is felt to be a desirable level of order. Although our research, of course, is far from providing predictions about the levels of vigilantism and private violence under various conditions, a study of existing citizen patrols can help to illuminate the fears and values which support or oppose citizen mobilization.

Self-defense groups raise important questions for public policy as well as for social theory and future research. The present paper is more an effort to raise issues and questions, and to establish a framework for additional research and thought, than a final presentation of results, firm conclusions, or a well-documented, single point of view. We have specified what seem to be two crucial variables, the group's definition of the problem and the police response. An additional differentiating variable might be whether the group arises in a context where in principle and, at least to a degree, in practice (as in the North) law enforcement has a universalistic character, or in areas (as in parts of the South) where a group, such as blacks to a much greater degree, is granted protection neither by, nor from, law-enforcement officials. A related variable might be whether the group primarily seeks protection from crimes which violate widely held legal and moral standards or (as in the case of the Ku Klux Klan) seeks to enforce a particular set of social practices on a community. It may be that little is to be gained in trying to make broad generalizations about such highly varied groups which may share little more than a desire to act on law enforcement issues.

Let us then restrict our focus to the more prevalent and enduring supplemental groups which are concerned with violations of widely held legal and moral standards in a milieu where there is at least an expressed value of universalistic police protection (e.g., parts of the South are excluded). Most of the existing evaluations of such self-defense groups have been based on hunches, impressionistic evidence, deductions from abstract political theory, parallels to earlier periods of American history, and often a goodly dose of ideological self-justification. But, given the limitations on the nature of the available data, what can we conclude about self-defense groups? Perhaps the safest conclusion is how little is known about them.

But next, the most striking feature of the groups we considered involves the large number of organizational and operational difficulties they face—and the related phenomenon of the relatively short lifespan which many groups experience. Many problems are inherent in authority relations, and groups trying to establish new policing institutions face complex problems not faced by regular police, in addition to all the problems facing the police.

Self-defense groups often lack a clear mandate from the groups they wish to serve and their legal position regarding the use of force and citizen arrests is ambiguous. They may have trouble defining their task. The tendency of the groups to lack the resources for recruiting, screening, and training appropriate manpower, and for sustaining motivation beyond that which stems from a deeply felt crisis (and the degree of autonomy some groups have) may contribute to ineffectiveness and abuses. And even if internal problems are solved, the groups may face harassment from police.

Yet the survival and growth of some groups show that these difficulties are not always insurmountable. It becomes important to ask why. Three important factors would seem to be (1) a crisis that continues to be deeply felt, (2) the presence of a charismatic leader, or at least one capable of performing the delicate liaison role between his patrol group, its presumed constituency, and authorities, (3) the emergence of a formally organized group with a continuing source of financial support.

The longest lived groups tend to be those in Cells I and II of the typology developed earlier (supplemental). They are subject to varying degrees of regulation by local government but in return are able to draw on their financial support and legitimacy. Patrols made up of those higher in social position seem more likely to endure. Also relevant to survival and commitment is whether the group is united by more than a common enemy. Does it have an ideology which helps bind members together and tells them what they are *for* as well as what they are *against*? Are patrols only one part of a broader program, as with some black groups and the Jewish Defense League?

EFFECTIVENESS

The effectiveness of self-defense group operations has not been evaluated with any kind of systematic before-and-after data, such as reports of crime, civil disorders, complaints against police, citizen feelings of safety, attitudes toward the groups and the police, and police and group abuses.[27] In terms of

27. For the evaluation of a one-week New York City experiment, G. Nash, *The Community Patrol Corps* (New York: Bureau of Applied Social Research, Columbia University, 1968). It is perhaps unfair, of course, to ask for evidence of the effectiveness of patrols in reducing crime when

the ability to survive organizationally, a majority of groups appear to fail. But while they are operative their consequences can be assessed. Moreover, as will be indicated, the disappearance of a group may not mean failure. One factor inhibiting the evaluation of effectiveness may be competition with regular police. Thus, the police in one large eastern city have refused to release crime data that would permit some assessment of the effect of a large housing authority tenant patrol Many groups have a spontaneous and nonbureaucratized quality not much given to systematic evaluation efforts.[28]

If there is little evidence that marked regular police patrol cars prevent crime, there is even less indication of the success of irregular, often unclearly marked citizen police patrol cars, though they do occasionally relay information to police. Escort services may mean crimes are prevented, though measuring events that don't happen can be difficult. Several informants reported that they thought the main consequence of their patrols was symbolic and participatory, rather than effective in actual reductions in the crime level. However, visible guards patrolling on foot in a limited area, such as an old people's home or a playground, have reduced vandalism and physical assaults. Some civil disorders, enlarged by regular police, have cooled when police were withdrawn and community patrols attempted to maintain order, though in other cases such patrols have seemed to have no effect.

It is interesting to speculate on the several possible relationships between the groups and disorders. At their inception, self-defense groups often tend to be a precipitate following from the perception of violence, injustice, and

---

evidence of the effectiveness of regular police patrols is also lacking. In the case of southern black adversarial groups there is impressionistic evidence that some of the more grievous white offenses have been curtailed. Charles Sims, a leader of the Louisiana Deacons, observes about groups such as his:

> Well, when the white power structure found out that they had mens, Negro mens that had made up their minds to stand up for their people and to give no ground, would not tolerate with no more police brutality, it had a tendency to keep the nightriders out of the neighborhood.

In characterizing the essentially defensive character of his group, he notes, "The nonviolent act is a good act—providing the policemen do their job. But in the southern states . . . the police have never done their job when the white and the Negro are involved—unless the Negro's getting the best of the white man." *National Guardian* (August 20, 1965). See also the case study by H. A. Nelson, "The defenders."

For the North, the case seems less clear. Groups such as the Black Panthers have certainly helped publicize instances of police abuse, and may have served as a threat inhibiting police abuse. However, their activities may also mean a reduction of police protection as police become more hesitant to take action for fear of criticism and in order to avoid troublesome situations.

28. Some of the most interesting patrol action is also likely to be very well hidden given its "by any means necessary" character. For example, recent rumors are that former SNCC workers and street gang members in a vigilante action are moving to rid black communities of drug pushers. Note ten unsolved murders and numerous shootings of suspected narcotics distributors in New York City. *New York Times* (January 23, 1972): 2; also *Newsweek* (September 27, 1971): 75-76.

lawlessness. If the groups do derive from urban disorders and violent crimes, then presumably self-defense groups would deflate as conditions of order and stability are (often as a result of their own actions) reestablished. While some groups such as the Tampa and Dayton White Hats or the Youth Alliance in Boston appear to have contributed to a reduction of civil disorder, some groups of Type IV may have had a reverse effect on general racial conflict and polarization, if not necessarily on civil disorders. At least some self-defense organizations may themselves become independently strong variables in the disorders which were their occasion. Particularly in urban areas, the groups may give organization and sometimes arms to long-standing hostilities between police and citizens. At the same time, those organizations which operate street patrols may bring into direct contact, often without police mediation, populations whose mutual fears and prejudices are currently tempered by distance. On the other hand (as the decline in labor violence associated with the growth of labor unions suggests), organization, through binding potentially violent members and creating collectivities which can negotiate, may actually reduce violence.[29]

Self-defense groups may also have an importance beyond themselves. Citizen mobilization around the issues of lawlessness and crime or police abuse and neglect may be symbolic of broader tensions during periods of rapid transition. For example, the issue of order has face value but can also be a fairly respectable euphemism for preventing a redistribution of power between competing groups in society. Armed patrols organized by minority groups have also been means for facilitating power changes and questioning traditional standards.

One of the more striking things about the patrols is that, relative to what might be expected, there has been so little organized interethnic and interracial violent conflict. Although far more people probably have access to weapons today than in the 1930s, there seem to have been relatively fewer clashes between (as against clashes within groups or between them and the state) ethnic and racial groups. Such groups today, with several prominent exceptions, tend much more to be literally *self-defense* groups prepared and waiting for attack and violations from some other group, rather than making offensive attacks. A factor here may be the *achieved* rather than *ascribed* source of the problem. The issue is defined (at least publicly) not as an ethnic

---

29. In Newark, Imperiale's group maintained contact with black groups, such as that led by Le Roi Jones, and even had a direct telephone link. In considering one event Imperiale observes:

> There was an incident one night, when we were supposed to have done something. The hot line rings. It's Kamil Wadeu Security [Le Roi Jones' Chief of Staff]. Immediately through our radios we dispatch one of our cars, check it out and find it's a fallacy. In the meantime Kamil's people are in the area, checking out the same thing. We dispel the rumor together, before all our people take to the street and start something.

Quoted in Goldberger, *New York Times Magazine,* p. 118.

group but as a problem: crime and disorder. As one observer noted, "Their orientation is antihoodlum not anti-ethnic." As a result many white northern groups have some black members as well, though the reverse pattern seems less prevalent. Several of the more successful patrols (at least judged in organization and endurance terms) are well integrated. But the lack of offensive group violence is also partly a result of the greater inclusion of white groups into the dominant society and their greater stake in it and of increased residential segregation, particularly in the North. In this sense the greater isolation of whites and blacks and the emergence of clearly delineated ethnic areas may ironically serve to reduce conflict, if at a cost to other desired values.

It would be a mistake to look only at the direct effects of civilian policing groups. In a number of cities, the groups have performed critical catalytic functions—suggesting, in some cases, that the groups are used by communities to bargain for what they want in the way of law-enforcement changes. In addition to their face value meaning as alternative institutions, the self-defense groups act as a form of demand on the law-enforcement system. For example, when citizens in Brockton, Massachusetts organized to apply for gun permits to protect their homes from a wave of housebreaks, city officials met to discuss the lack of adequate police protection. In response to the self-defense initiative of the citizens, the chief of police promised to ask the mayor for additional men and for overtime pay to extend the number of police man-hours in the city. Some of the police interviewed in our study welcomed the groups as a citizen's lobby seen as better able than the police to exert pressure on the political system. Beyond increasing police resources, groups in some places have made it easier for police to crack down. The police may argue that unless they are allowed to act quickly, vigilantes will. The possible illegality of both actions, those of police and vigilantes, may seem less important than the need to prevent vigilante behavior.

The bargaining element is also present in the case of adversarial groups. In summarizing the position of the Defenders, Harold Nelson observes, "if police failed to perform their duties, either they would have to be forced to do so, or someone else would have to perform them."[30] Even where a group lacks power to actually do either of these, it may be important in symbolically communicating dissatisfaction with the status quo. The threat of violence from an adversarial group may also increase the acceptability of more moderate protest groups.

The bargaining perspective, of course, enlarges the criteria for evaluating the success of citizen policing efforts. Groups which successfully change police operations as they wish may be thought of as successful, whether or not their patrolling or other activities are long-lived.

Similarly, whatever their objective consequences, some of the groups may

---

30. Nelson, *Social Problems*, p. 130.

increase citizen feelings of security and reduce feelings of isolation. The patrols may be appreciated for listening and at least trying to act on the complaints and fears of those who feel ignored and forgotten by city governments. They may also contribute to a sense of self-worth and responsibility on the part of participants. Members of the larger, often problem-ridden communities the patrols wish to serve may gain pride and a sense of satisfaction in seeing the community organize to help itself. The Maccabees in the Crown Heights area of New York appear to have served as a cohesive force and slowed down the rapid demographic transition of their neighborhood.

Finally, some citizen patrol groups may form a symbiotic relationship with police. We came across occasional hints that group members sometimes did things for police which the latter were prevented from doing, in return for police cooperation or noninterference in the patrol's operations. In one instance, members of a patrol group kidnapped, through their own means obtained a confession, and then turned over to police a murder suspect who had been released earlier for insufficient evidence. The suspect was subsequently charged with the crime. The cooperation which has existed between the Ku Klux Klan and some southern police is well known. While the dimensions and extensiveness of such symbiotic relations are not known, to the extent that supplemental groups consider police as handicapped from within by overzealous concern for the rights of suspects, extralegal criminal investigations and techniques are not improbable.

Citizen involvement in law enforcement, particularly when it involves autonomous groups, is unlike other forms of citizen participation. The stakes are higher; the risk of miscarriage may be greater, and the consequences of abuse or error appear more serious. New institutions such as the Catholic schools of an earlier era and current community schools, or ethnic and racially centered hospitals and welfare organizations, often face, in addition to some of the organizational problems of older institutions, major difficulties in obtaining resources, but they have generally not aroused as much opposition, resentment, and fear as have some of the patrols. What is at stake here is control over the means of violence and coercion that are so central to the organization of the state itself.

Like other efforts for increased citizen participation, the self-defense groups raise issues with inbuilt trade-offs. The enthusiasm of the group members is usually offset by their lack of professional training; the inclusion of some sectors of an urban community can antagonize other sectors; the use of local residents to protect their own communities may mean a sacrifice of the ideal of the disinterested and even-handed peace officer, but a gain in the ability to relate to the community in question.

On a personal note, let us consider our own ambivalence toward such groups, an ambivalence rooted in contradictory aspects of the American value system and the unmet needs of a sizeable proportion of the American public.

First, it is clear that an acceptable level of public security does not exist in many low income communities, and serious conflicts may exist between police and citizens in such areas. Often police are either unwilling or lacking the resources to provide adequate protection. Rigid requirements may preclude many potentially effective local men from joining the force (such as previous arrest records; past history of radical activities; minimum height, weight and age requirements; or the need to be a policeman full-time). Police may also be separated from many of those they ostensibly serve (or at least deal with) by ideological, social, economic, racial, ethnic, religious, geographical, attitudinal, and age factors. Along with this may go a resulting lack of knowledge about, concern with, or sympathy for a community and patterns of hostility and mistrust on all sides. The isolation of police from their constituents is related to the exceptional degree of autonomy and problems of accountability which characterize some departments. The problems of overly rigid, nonresponsive, highly centralized bureaucracies are well known. As attempts to break through and go beyond the exclusive and professionalized provinces of established authority, self-defense groups are analogous to community mobilization around issues of schools, urban renewal, transportation, recreation, and welfare. They may be seen as a special form of the increasing demand for citizen participation in the planning, control, and delivery of the services which affect them. In light of these factors, the groups are not unappealing.

Who, after all, can be opposed to self-defense? In the best of American violent and populist traditions, the groups can be seen to represent action and involvement, self-help, embattled neighbors banding together in a righteous crusade against the dark forces of crime and disorder.

Yet there is clearly another side: the anti-democratic potential of privately organized citizen violence.[31] Mass enthusiasm for direct action in the face of institutional restraints (the law, courts, elected officials, formal police bureaucracy, and procedure, etc.) for many people raises the spectre of the Ku Klux Klan and European fascist groups. The picture of independent armed entrepreneurs patrolling "their" heterogeneous communities is not one that can be unequivocally welcomed.

The rhetoric of vigilantism and threats to "take care of" a given group must be considered apart from a group's actual activities. A group may make threats of an extremist nature without intending to carry them out. Such rhetoric can be an important factor in political struggles. Some groups may

---

31. This is certainly not to deny the same potential and reality in government-organized violence.

have a high degree of control over their members. Yet they may be unable to limit the violent actions of nonmember sympathizers, who, unaware of the functions of rhetoric, may interpret such rhetorical threats as heroic calls to action. The consequences of such groups must be considered in terms of the general climate of opinion they help create.

Even where the threat of actual vigilante type violence is minimal, there is an ambiguity here reflecting a conflict in values not found to the same extent with citizen involvement in other public service bureaucracies. Take for example, the leaflets passed out by a sheriff's office in Oregon which ask citizens "do you know something the sheriff's office in Multnomah County should know?" On the one hand this can be seen as a legitimate appeal for cooperation with authorities for the enforcement of community standards involving the protection of persons and property. Yet on the other hand such citizen involvement can raise the specter of neighbors spying on each other under the benevolent (or not so benevolent) guidance of Big Brother. For many people the negative reaction against police in unmarked cars giving traffic tickets, or plainclothes police making arrests during demonstations, would also apply to the policing actions of private citizens.

There is a second problem as well. The patrols can be seen as a mechanism for perpetuating the second class services that low income people often receive in American cities. As the survey data indicate, support and mobilization for the patrols is found disproportionately among lower status persons. In the event of a felt crisis over crime, middle class people apparently more often effectively press the government for the increased services of outside professional police specialists, or they hire private licensed guards. Lower status people are more likely to try and do the job themselves, or they may have such a solution thrust upon them by city government. In either case, inequality in city services may result.

Patrols organized around a particular ethnic group or class, aside from the chance of increasing interethnic and class conflict, may be based on the erroneous assumption that serious crime is the problem and responsibility of a specific ethnic group or class rather than a public problem and responsibility. The language of universalism, institutional restraints, and municipal responsibility is appealing from a standpoint of political theory and high school civics courses, its anti-patrol implications are obvious. However, it avoids the issue of what a group that feels threatened is to do if the government is unable or unwilling to provide the required services. In the words of one patrol leader, "If the government can't protect us then we have to protect ourselves."

Aside from their use in delimited and focused contexts of internal policing involving order maintenance and assistance (where clearer boundaries and a relatively homogeneous constituency are more likely to exist), as in rock concerts, protest demonstrations, schools and housing projects, it can be argued that the patrols are inferior to more responsible and sensitive regular police who are carefully chosen, trained, and supervised in restructured departments.[32]

Yet matters are unfortunately not so simple. American society has not dealt meaningfully enough with its lack of equality of opportunity, not to mention equality of outcome, and it shows little sign of doing so at present. Continuing high and increased levels of certain types of crime and disorder related to this are to be expected, as are increased citizen demands for security. To judge from the last ten years and the conditions of the cities, more responsible and sensitive regular police are not likely to be forthcoming in adequate supply. In such a context we may be left with the patrols as the better of limited alternatives.

32. Many of the problems and failings of such groups, of course, also characterize some police. However, the issue is not that police are always appreciably better, but that increasing the total amount of abuse does not seem desirable. In addition, although they are often inadequate, there are mechanisms for regulating police behavior.

Chapter Eight

Vigilantism and the American Police

Kanti C. Kotecha and James L. Walker

One of the main functions of criminal law is to define the boundary between behavior that is acceptable to society and behavior that is unacceptable and therefore labeled deviant. The police, who constitute the official agency of the "establishment," are charged, along with their other responsibilities, with maintaining that boundary. In order to perform this function, the members of the police are trained and equipped to use force whenever necessary. This force can range from the actual or threatened use of violence to the mere giving of an order.

Today the use of that officially sanctioned force is being called into question more and more. Almost every day brings some new revelation of police misbehavior. For whatever reasons, police are accused of a variety of transgressions. Police misbehavior can be for good reasons as well as bad. When their reasons are bad, for example personal gain or pleasure, they are corrupt or brutal. When their reasons are good, for example the desire to protect society, then they are vigilantes.[1]

This chapter is by no means an exhaustive study of the topic of police vigilantism. It has four objectives. The first is to define vigilantism in the police context, indicating the resources available to the police for vigilante activity and the peculiarly dangerous nature of vigilantism as compared to other forms of police misconduct. The second objective is to describe the way vigilantism is handled in some recent literature. The third is to give some accounts of vigilantism in a variety of cultural settings. The final objective is to

*The authors gratefully acknowledge the support of the Wright State University College of Liberal Arts in the preparation of this chapter.

1. The descriptions good and bad reflect the preferences of the majority and are relative to the situation. For example, a revolutionary might describe protecting the socio-political order as bad and a sybarite see nothing wrong in maximizing personal pleasure. The values implied are clearly what the authors conceive as the consensus in the United States at this time.

speculate on the impact various police reforms might have on the phenomenon of police vigilantism.

VIGILANTISM BY THE POLICE

It may seem somewhat ironic to speak of police vigilantism. Vigilantism has been defined above as acts or threats of coercion in violation of the formal boundaries of an established socio-political order, but intended to protect that order from some form of subversion. In the American experience it was the shortcomings of law-enforcement agencies that led to the formation of vigilante groups in the first place. Many of the original American vigilante groups were actually coopted or legitimized by state political authorities when they proved useful, efficient, and economical.[2] Now the shortcomings of law enforcement seem to be perceived more acutely by the police themselves. Police vigilantism can be defined as acts or threats by police which are intended to protect the established socio-policital order from subversion but which violate some generally perceived norms for police behavior.

A great proportion of the public treasury goes into law enforcement, and technology bridges the gaps in communication which helped to cause the original American vigilante movement. However, large expenditures and modern communication have not been a panacea. Criticisms of the police for their shortcomings grow apace. The problem with many of those criticisms is that they fail to differentiate between the different types of police misbehavior. There is a tendency to lump all undesirable activities by the law enforcement personnel together under one umbrella concept such as brutality, corruption, or some other such general term. But criticism implies fault and fault implies need for a cure. In order to be effective, a cure must attack a specific problem, separating it from other police problems.

Police vigilantism shares some of the characteristics of those other police problems. It is born of the tremendous frustration that is built into the police enterprise. Part of the frustration comes from role conflict, since the role of the policeman is not clearly defined. The traditional approach to the policeman's role is that it is to enforce the criminal law by apprehending criminals. More modern analysis sees the policeman primarily as a peace keeper who can have little effect on the crime rate no matter how well equipped and trained he is.[3] The role conflict engendered by this situation causes many problems for the police, but does not cause all of them. What form the resulting deviation from

2. Sources for information on vigilantism in general are Patrick Bates Nolan, "Vigilantes on the Middle Border: A Study of Self-Appointed Law Enforcement in the States of the Upper Mississippi from 1840-1880," and Richard M. Brown, "The American Vigilante Tradition," both in *Violence in America: Historical and Comparative Perspectives,* ed. Hugh Davis Graham and Ted Robert Gurr (Washington: United States Government Printing Office, 1969).

3. For a traditional view, see Stuart Palmer, *The Prevention of Crime* (New York: Behavioral Publications, 1973). The peace keeper approach is in James Q. Wilson, "What Makes a Better Policeman?" *Atlantic* 223 (March 1969): 129-35.

accepted behavior takes depends on the other circumstances in the official life of the patrolman or officer.

The resources of the police to engage in vigilante activity are derived in part from the "monopoly of legitimate (domestic) force," sometimes implemented through a weapon. A more important power than his gun is the policeman's discretion in making an arrest or giving an order.[4] The very act of arresting someone is a violent act. It requires physical restraint, humiliating invasion of privacy, and incarceration, if only for the briefest time. The power of arrest is the most powerful resource of the police.

Short of the arrest power, the policeman also routinely gives orders which he expects will be obeyed: orders to move on, quiet down, or disperse. Not all of these orders are within the strict legal authority of the policeman but they can be within that area accepted by society as part of a policeman's discretion. Although the boundaries of that discretion shift constantly, some behavior is clearly within it and some outside.

It is not a "natural thing" for a police officer to engage in vigilantism. Before he can become a vigilante, he must take four steps. First, he must perceive himself as part of the socio-political order he is protecting. This is by no means a universal perception on the part of Americans, and especially Americans from the social classes from which police are drawn. Second, he must perceive that the order of which he is a part is substantially threatened. This means, depending on the circumstances, that he must have either a negative view of the health of the order or an exaggerated view of the forces threatening that order. Third, he must perceive that he has the resources to make a substantial effort against the threat, not by an irrational striking out against someone or something unpleasant but with a calculated effort intended to diminish the threat. This assumes a high level of political or personal efficacy. Fourth, he must be willing to join with others and/or be willing to risk the consequences of engaging in a solitary crusade (although the latter would not be realistic). Perhaps this final condition is the most difficult of all to fulfill because it also assumes that the frustration of the policeman has no alternative outlet such as the opportunity to misbehave for personal gain (i.e., "go on the pad").[5]

Furthermore, the job of the policeman has another built-in limit to vigilante behavior. That limit is time. Vigilantism, at first, must be calculated. Many policemen have little time for reflection. Although this differs from assignment to assignment and place to place, patrolmen usually run from one call to another, missing many of them and generally reacting rather than acting. For example, a family dispute call can be answered in many ways—brutally, stupidly, or even corruptly. A vigilante way of responding is

---

4. A standard work on arrest is Wayne R. LaFave, *Arrest: The Decision to Take a Suspect into Custody* (Boston: Little, Brown, 1965).

5. The phrase is slang for sharing in protection money paid to police by gamblers, bootleggers, etc.

not likely, however, unless and until vigilantism has become a way of life for the policeman, an ingrained mode of behavior which controls all of his reactions. This type of situation is not prevalent yet, although an example of it in one area of the country is discussed below.

An important distinction must be made between vigilante attitudes and vigilante actions. Anyone who has spent time with policemen knows that there is a lot of hostile conversation about social groups and certain types of criminals. One author recounts a radio conversation in Chicago.

> *Police Operator:* "1814, get a wagon over at 1436. We've got an injured hippie."
> *Voice:* "1436 North Wells?"
> *Operator:* "North Wells."
> In quick sequence, there are the following remarks from five other police cars:
> "That's no emergency."
> "Let him take a bus."
> "Kick the fucker."
> "Knock his teeth out."
> "Throw him in a wastepaper basket."[6]

Such attitudes do not necessarily indicate similar actions by the police. Unfortunately, the author does not tell us whether the "hippie" was thrown in the trash or grudgingly taken to the hospital. Perhaps, as one accused felon has said, the admonition should be "watch what we do, not what we say."[7]

POLICE VIGILANTISM IN THE LITERATURE

Although in the past few years official attempts to come up with answers to "the police problem" have been published, these have not dealt with the problem of vigilantism per se. The word is not used in the texts of the reports, nor is the problem mentioned apart from general discussion of police problems which may or may not include vigilante activity. These other problems include the excessive use of force, the abuse of citizens during questioning, and the use of the arrest power for harassment purposes. The publications, while deploring these practices, do not seem concerned that they can take place for a variety of reasons. One report comes close to acknowledging vigilantism. In a section of *The Challenge of Crime in a Free Society,* the report of the President's Commission on Law Enforcement and Administration of Justice, the Commission recommends that:

> Police departments should develop and enunciate policies that give police personnel specific guidance for the common situations requiring exercise of

6. Jerome H. Skolnick, *The Politics of Protest* (New York: Ballantine Books, 1969), pp. 274-75.
7. John Mitchell, former attorney general of the United States, in reply to a question about Civil Rights.

police discretion. Policies should cover such matters, among others, as the issuance of orders to citizens regarding their movements or activities, the handling of minor disputes, the safeguarding of the rights of free speech and free assembly, the selection and use of investigative methods, and the decision whether or not to arrest in specific situations involving specific crimes.[8]

The commission fails to deal with those situations where police orders to individuals, in line with their discretionary authority, are given not because of a department goal or policy but because of the individual policeman's perception of a threat. All the department guidance or clarification in the world can't help in a situation such as this, a vigilante situation.

However, a successor of the President's Commission report, that of National Commission on the Causes and Prevention of Violence, contains some direct references to the problem. One of the task force reports to the commission was written by the sociologist Jerome Skolnick. The report was later published under the title *The Politics of Protest.*[9] In Chapter VII, Skolnick deals with the question of the police revolt against higher authority. The statements of the report are worth quoting at length:

> Attempts by higher officials to avoid occasions for outbursts of militancy illustrate the severity of that problem and place in perspective another manifestation of police militancy—the revolt against higher authority. A well-documented example of this phenomenon has been provided by the commission's Cleveland Investigative Task Force.
>
> The task force has found that, in the wake of the July 23 shoot-out, police opposition to Mayor Carl Stokes and his administration moved toward open revolt. When police were withdrawn from ghetto duty for one night in order to allow black community leaders to quell the rioting and avoid further deaths, police reportedly refused to answer calls, and some sent racist abuse and obscenities against the Mayor over their radios. Officers in the fiftieth district refused to travel in two-man squads, one white and one black, into the East Side. For several weeks after the riot, posters with the picture of Mayor Stokes, a Negro, under the words "Wanted for Murder" hung in district stations. Spokesmen for the police officers' wives organization have berated the Mayor; the local Fraternal Order of Police has demanded the resignation of Safety Director Joseph F. McNanamon; and many have reportedly been privately purchasing high-powered rifles for use in future riots, despite official opposition by police commanders.

Skolnick continues:

> Similar revolts against higher police and civic authority over similar issues have occurred elsewhere. For example, in New York on August 2, 1968, Patrolmen's Benevolent Association President John Cassese instructed his membership, about 99 percent of the force, that if a superior told them to ignore a violation of the law, they should take action notwithstanding that order. Thus

8. President's Commission on Law Enforcement and Administration of Justice, *The Challenge of Crime in a Free Society* (Washington: United States Government Printing Office, 1967), p. 104.
9. Skolnick, *Politics of Protest.*

if a superior ordered that restraint be used in a particular area of disorder (because, for example, shooting of fleeing looters would create a larger disturbance with which his men could not deal), policemen were to ignore the orders.[10]

Jerome Skolnick's description of police activism remains the most cogent and important contribution to official inquiries into police vigilantism. Skolnick had previously described the policeman as an isolated character whose distinguishing characteristics were suspicion and fear of danger.[11] The "activism" reflected in the revolt against higher authority completes the transformation from policeman to vigilante.

Much of the recent literature on the police discusses the problem of vigilantism, though more by indirection than by name. Accounts of police cooperation with civilian vigilante groups and extreme right-wing organizations are the most common occurrences mentioned. The literature covers a very broad range, however, both in quality and subject matter. In three widely reviewed and well-accepted works on the police, the term is not used nor the problem, as such, discussed. Yet an analysis of their content shows a concern on the part of the authors that parallels the concerns of this essay, and for that reason they are relevant. The works are *Varieties of Police Behavior* by James Q. Wilson,[12] *The Democratic Policeman* by George Berkley,[13] and *Police Power* by Paul Chevigny.[14]

Wilson's book chronicles the differences in the styles of a variety of police departments. Essentially a study in bureaucratic behavior, it points out that empirical measures can be developed to describe a given police department, such as Watchman, Legalistic, or Service. This descriptive pattern makes no allowance for vigilantism as such. However, there are several interesting aspects of the findings that shed light on the problem. It becomes apparent, for example, that some styles of police work are clearly more liable to create the necessary conditions for vigilantism than are others. The fact is recognized that the patrolman is forced by circumstances beyond his control to underenforce the law in both the Watchman style and the Service style of police departments. Wide police discretion and limited resources are seen as a fact of life, a reality which is either ignored or not known in the Legalistic style departments. It seems apparent that in the departments where the police are asked to do something that is beyond their means, frustration that leads to vigilante behavior can be expected to grow. Thus, although Wilson does not

10. Ibid.
11. Jerome H. Skolnick, *Justice Without Trial: Law Enforcement in a Democratic Society* (New York: John Wiley & Sons, 1967), pp. 48-49.
12. James Q. Wilson, *Varieties of Police Behavior* (Cambridge: Harvard University Press, 1968).
13. George E. Berkley, *The Democratic Policeman* (Boston: Beacon Press, 1969).
14. Paul Chevigny, *Police Power: Police Abuses in New York City* (New York: Pantheon Books, 1969).

deal directly with vigilantism, his analysis shows that the conditions for its existence are somewhat controllable.

Chevigny is a civil-liberties lawyer. His approach is to build a case, to argue a point. His goal is not to be balanced but to be persuasive. His book is based on a massive amount of carefully researched claims of police misbehavior. Many of the examples of abuses that he discusses are the "tools of the trade" for a police vigilante—the frame, the harassment, the plant, and, the most pervasive abuse according to Chevigny, the distortion of facts in reports and testimony. Although not calling the phenomena vigilantism, Chevigny is concerned about the activities of the policemen who commit these abuses. He sees them as responses to society's hypocritical moral stances. The public, the legislature, and the courts expect the police to do their dirty work while washing their own hands of the matter.

Berkley writes much like a political philosopher. His major concern, in this comparative work on the United States and democratic European countries, is the conflict between police efficiency and democratic procedures. He contends that true efficiency can be achieved only through the democratizing of the police forces. For Berkley, police behavior reflects society, so that the violent and repressive activities of the American police exist only because the American temperament tends toward violence and repression. He points out the initial condition or potential for police vigilantism when he says, quoting Casamayor, that, "The police are outside the public order because they are created to maintain it."[15] Therefore, we must depend on their perception of the health of that order and evaluate their actions in protecting that health.

Different though their interests and approaches are, the same thread runs through all of these three books. That thread is the difference between what the police forces are able to do and what they are expected to do. It is this discrepancy which creates the frustration necessary for police vigilantism.

Yet although all three of these representative works implicitly recognize the possibility of the vigilante problem, each goes its own way in ignoring the consequences. Their prescriptions are too general to afford any assurance that police tendencies toward vigilance will be affected in any way. To Berkley, the key to the "reform of the police" lies on the road to education. He suggests a variety of programs to require a higher level of education for police forces. The lawyer Chevigny, as might be expected, sees the solution to the problem in the judicial system. He feels that strengthening the courts and the federal government will do much to cure police abuses. This program includes improvement of trials, changes in prosecution powers, and increased changes of civil suits against police. Wilson, as a good social scientist, offers no solutions as such. He finds the problems of the police inherent in the job itself. It is mostly society's perception of the job that he sees changing. "The police

15. Berkley, *The Democratic Policemen*, p. 119.

can cope with their problems, but they cannot solve them," is the way he puts it.[16]

It seems clear that the literature examined does not separate the vigilantism of the police from the other aspects of "the police problem." This situation is not a fatal flaw, but it leads to ignorance of what will increase vigilante tendencies and what will lessen them. The present essay is aimed toward eliminating this dangerous ignorance.

A great deal of knowledge about vigilantism can be gained from a study of contemporary fiction. The idea that fiction can be used as a resource is not new. Police fiction must be believable to be successful. It does not have to be totally realistic, but it must be within those limits set by the audience as reasonable. If this is true, then fiction can tell us a lot about the present state of society. It can tell us what is acceptable as within these boundaries. Of course, there are many other factors to weigh, such as the story-telling ability of the writer and the advance publicity for the book, so that acceptance is not meant as any kind of scientific indicator. Caveats aside, there seems to be a rapid development in police fiction. As recently as 1968, James Q. Wilson wrote a movie review for *New York Magazine* in which he lamented that the police stories tended to be concentrated around detectives, who were not typical of the overwhelming number of policemen:

> . . . in considerable measure there are only two kinds of men, and thus two choices—Dan Madigan [the free-wheeling Eastern "gangbuster"] or Joe Friday [the straight-laced, western professional].[17]

Well, things have changed. Of course, Jack Webb is still with us, behind the scenes running the successful "Adam 12" series on television, an episodic adventure of two very young, clean-cut Los Angeles patrolmen, who never swear, are seldom angry, and deal with their jobs in a sort of Disneyland atmosphere where bullets don't kill, prisoners don't resist, and children love the police.

The real mainstream of police fiction has been another Los Angeles product, Joseph Wambaugh. Being a real policeman, rather than a hanger-on as Webb is, may make the major difference. Wambaugh's series of novels and television shows represent reality. Although by literary standards Maupassant and Balzac are not threatened, the public acceptance of the work has been good. Interestingly enough, from our point of view, the hallmark of Wambaugh's work is police vigilance. In both *The New Centurions*[18] and *The Blue Knight*[19] (as well as the movie version of the latter and the television

16. Wilson, *Varieties,* p. 299.
17. James Q. Wilson, "Movie Cops—Romantic v. Real," *New York* (August 19, 1968), pp. 39-41; reprinted in Arthur Niederhoffer and Abraham S. Blumberg, *The Ambivalent Force: Perspectives on the Police* (Waltham, Mass.: Ginn and Company, 1970).
18. Joseph Wambaugh, *The New Centurions* (Boston: Little, Brown, 1970).
19. Joseph Wambaugh, *The Blue Knight* (Boston: Little, Brown, 1972).

series "Police Story"), a recurring theme is the inability of the individual policeman to carry out his mission of protecting society due to lack of support.

In *The New Centurions*, two patrolmen are driving around the city in the "whore wagon," a completely illegal device for harassing and detaining suspected prostitutes. The older, more philosophical of the two compares his present situation to that of a Roman Centurion witnessing the coming of Christianity. "They would have been afraid, I bet . . . ," he says, "[but their] civilization was never in jeopardy." Clearly perceiving that *his* is, he goes on:

> But today the "don'ts" are dying or being murdered in the name of freedom and we policemen can't save them. Once the people become accustomed to the death of a "don't" well then the other "don'ts" die much easier . . . then later the freed people have to organize an army of their own to find order because they learn that freedom is horrifying and ugly and only small doses of it can be tolerated.[20]

The fact that such philosophies are the basis of vigilantism is clearly illustrated in the second of Wambaugh novels, *The Blue Knight*. In this celebration of the tough, old-fashioned patrolman, the character of Bumper Morgan is created. Morgan not only accepts the role of vigilante but also revels in it. He sees engaging in harassment, summary punishment, and even perjury as necessary to keep his beat clean for the decent citizens, yet he expresses contempt for the lack of support those citizens give him in his job. It is clear that Morgan is not just a brute or mindless bigot, nor is he typical of the police force at large. When accused of perjury, he tells the judge that most policemen don't lie, or at most lie only a little. He blames his lie on failing eyesight, the physical inability to keep up with the rising tide of crime. His superiors caution him against his beat procedures, warning him that he is no longer doing police work but is becoming "some kind of character." This character may be called a knight or a centurion. He is also a vigilante. Court decisions, failing abilities, and the death of the "don'ts" have all conspired to force him outside the boundaries of the society he is sworn to protect. When the judge who discovers his perjury warns of the end of civilization if the enforcers of the law operate outside of it, Morgan can only manage the emotional reply that there are people on his beat who depend on him, who look up to him:

> When you're alone out there on the beat, your honor, and everyone knows you're the man. The way they look at you and how it feels when they say "You're a champ, Bumper . . ."[21]

Only time will tell whether the popularity of such fiction is an indication of a change in public attitudes toward police work and whether this will serve to reinforce the police in their pattern of socialization. As these new police approach the younger citizens through television, there may be a generational change in attitudes toward law enforcement.

20. Wambaugh, *The New Centurions*, p. 90.
21. Wambaugh, *The Blue Knight*, p. 231.

An examination of the extent of vigilante activity actually reported in the press does not at first indicate any sort of epidemic. A four year search of the *New York Times* was made of all stories involving police. During the period of March 1969 to August 1973, fifteen cases of police misconduct reported in the *New York Times* fit the definition of vigilantism. This is out of the hundreds of stories concerning police that were indexed. Some of these fifteen were, of course, much more serious than others. They included the tragic murders of several Black Panthers as well as the comic opera performance of some New York officers in dealing with homosexuals. In July 1969, a neighborhood vigilante group, with the cooperation of the police, cut down all the trees in a park so that the gay habitues would go away.[22]

Even accounting for the obvious shortcomings in the count (i.e., New York is only one city, not typical, and most examples of vigilantism would not be reported), the number fifteen is not very large. A better indication of the extent of vigilante behavior as indicated in the new police fiction may be a recent experiment conducted among classes at the police academy of a medium-sized midwest city (metropolitan area of 85,000). In this experiment, 105 members of the police force back for in-service training were shown excerpts on video tape from *The Blue Knight*. The instructor then requested the class to rank the behavior of Bumper Morgan according to the frequency with which they had encountered it in their work. The most vigilant of the videotaped behavior, summary punishment, harassment and such were ranked very highly and openly acknowledged by the officers. Some even named a particular officer, not in the class, who reminded them of Bumper Morgan. Clearly, in the perception of the police, the behavior defined as vigilant by the authors is seen as routine, at least among this urban police group.

VIGILANTISM AND POLITICAL DEVELOPMENT

Both the survey from the *Times* and the police academy experiment, as well as all the fiction, discussed relate to the job of the urban policeman. It must be pointed out that logically it is not only the urban environment that supports vigilante activity. Because the city is an area where a variety of people and life styles co-exist, it is, by definition, more cosmopolitan. As such, it should be less threatened by behavior that is different or deviant. The suburbs, populated by those fleeing the cities, and the rural areas are more homogeneous and are more likely to consist of people who would be threatened by any outside interference in their way of life. Furthermore, the police forces of these areas, being poorly trained, poorly paid, and most importantly, strongly identified with the ethos of the area, are going to be doubly threatened by deviant behavior. Therefore, we would expect greater support for police vigilantism in small suburban and rural areas.

22. *New York Times* (July 4, 1969): 25.

A look at the small changing suburbs shows a cyclical pattern of vigilantism. At first, a small population of relatively homogeneous origins and goals sets up a local government and police protection. The community then meets a threat, perhaps an influx of a racial or cultural group which is deviant from the norm of the town. The police, identifying strongly with the population, engage in various forms of vigilance, including harassment. Eventually the population of the town grows; it becomes richer, perhaps annexed to a larger area, and the police force becomes more professionalized and less identified with the old ethos of the town. Some of the families move on, perhaps to another small suburb, arrange for low-price police services, and the cycle begins anew.

Because the foregoing is cyclical, it does not pose nearly as great a threat as vigilantism that is born of a permanently "closed society."[23] One of the most comprehensive accounts of such a situation is contained in the Mississippi Black Paper. This book is the compilation of the affidavits of people who had been victimized by the police in Mississippi during the great influx of summer civil rights workers in 1965. The book is filled with almost a hundred pages of examples of action or inaction by various police forces which were done in the name of preserving, at all costs, what Hodding Carter refers to in the introduction as "our way of life."[24] The aspect of this vigilantism which made it so dangerous was that it pervaded all walks of life in the society, but used the police forces as its cutting edge. As Carter goes on to say:

> Segregation was unquestioned publicly by all but a few whites and the use of almost any device at hand to preserve (it) was sanctioned by most businessmen as well as rednecks.[25]

The importance of the Mississippi experience to understanding the nature of police vigilantism is shown in Reinhold Niebuhr's explanation of the conflict in his remarks prefacing the affidavits. Niebuhr views the Mississippi experience as a clash between national and local will. The civil rights bills of the federal government were meant as a rejection of the "inhuman customs of local communities."[26] The problem with Mississippi was that it had never truly become a part of the national community. Thus, the strong local identification of the law enforcement apparatus, coupled with the acceptance by the local elites, led to the institutionalization of vigilantism on the part of the police. Admitting that the specter of bigotry and prejudice is by no means absent at the federal level, Niebuhr nevertheless claims that:

---

23. The term "closed society" comes from James Wesley Silver, *Mississippi: The Closed Society* (New York: Harcourt, Brace & World, 1964).

24. *Mississippi Black Paper: Fifty-Seven Negro and White Citizens' testimony of Police brutality, the breakdown of law and order and the corruption of Justice in Mississippi* (New York: Random House, 1965).

25. Ibid.

26. Ibid., p. xii.

... the majesty of the law in the United States as a whole is preserved in no small part by the recognition by state and local communities that the federal government is the final source of law and order.[27]

Although Constitutional law supports the Niebuhr idea, actual practice, up until now, does not. The civil rights laws of the mid-1960s were clear exceptions to the rule that when all is said and done, the federal government can do little to change local law-enforcement practice.

First of all, the type of vigilantism practiced in Mississippi was social-group vigilantism. It violates the Fourteenth Amendment, equal protection of the law. In this area there is probably a broad national consensus against vigilantism. There is no such consensus for crime-control. If anything, it may run the other way. People may be in favor of unleashing the police, if the claims of the congressmen who voted for the Omnibus Crime Bill in 1968 are any indication.[28] Second, despite the Supreme Court's importance in creating a consensus for due process, the decisions of the Supreme Court often precipitate vigilantism. The decisions help (it is hoped) to deter police abuses such as violation of privacy, coerced confessions, and so forth. They add some essential fairness to the judicial process. However, the bulk of vigilance is calculated to circumvent the judicial process altogether. Thus, court decisions do not necessarily affect police vigilantism. Nevertheless, to the extent that vigilantism is controllable by manipulating the organization or structure or training of the police forces (and to the extent that these manipulations can be supported by the federal government and accepted by the local agencies), clearly the national government ethos has a role to play in eliminating vigilantism. Whether such manipulations and controls are possible is the question to which we now turn.

VIGILANTISM AND POLICE REFORM

The theme of this chapter has been that there is a lack of coherent theory concerning the abuses perpetrated by the police forces of the country. This is a special problem at a time when a great deal of thought is being given to changes in the structure, role, and operation of the police forces. With such a muddled view of the defects in the police forces, it would be impossible to predict what the impact of changes of the present forces will be. We are often striking out blindly to correct some evil when the correction will lead to a newer and potentially worse abuse. Since we have isolated one of the abuses of the police, vigilantism, we are now going to suggest what impact a variety of changes advocated by experts may have on this phenomenon.

27. Ibid.
28. See, for example, Richard Harris, *The Fear of Crime* (New York: Praeger, 1971) for the story of this bill.

The first area is education.[29] There is no proof that education makes people any kinder or more law abiding. There is some proof that it makes people smarter. Smarter policemen will not automatically eschew vigilantism as a tactic or practice. As a matter of fact, there is good logic in saying that the increased education may help the policeman have the requisite perceptual talents to be a true vigilante (rather than an ordinary brute). An educated policeman is more likely to be politicized. This is especially true if the increased education is coupled with a complete demilitarization of the police forces. In the military there is a strong tradition of noninterference in the political or civil sphere (except, of course, at the highest levels where the Joint Chiefs of Staff are the senior policy makers and often make political statements and decisions). An educated, demilitarized police force may very well cure some evils of the present situation, but it may pose some dangers of increased vigilantism.

Another reform that is being considered is lateral entry. This means simply that a man may transfer from one department to the same rank in another. Quite clearly, this would tend to lessen the tendency toward vigilantism in at least two ways. First, it would increase the professional self-image of the policeman and remove the pressure to identify with a particular social setting or political system. Second, it would have a tendency to bid up the market in hazardous areas, where vigilantism flourishes, and bid down the market in comfortable departments. The higher pay and status thus engendered in the vigilante-prone areas may very well then lessen the frustration which is a cause of vigilante behavior.

Getting the policeman closer to the community is a catchword which encompasses a whole raft of different reforms—community relations training, beat-walking, decentralization, team policing, plainclothes, community control, and civilian review boards. With the possible exception of the last one, these all may very well increase the risks of vigilante behavior. To explain this statement it is necessary to go back to the concept upon which the reforms are based—"the neighborhood cop." To describe the neighborhood policeman, or the constable or the sheriff or whatever, as close to the people is deceptive. He was, of course, much nearer physically than his successors in the black and white cars patrolling the streets of our cities. Yet, in many ways, the operation of the policeman on the beat depended just as much on a real separation between the people and himself, a separation based on respect (for the uniform, sometimes) and also on fear. The present day policeman is often striving to create this same fear. When it disappears, and the policeman is closer to the people, he will naturally identify more with some groups in the community than with others. Therefore, he may have an overwhelming tendency to support the values of the groups identified with, rather than those

---

29. A review of educational proposals for police are contained in Charles B. Saunders, Jr., *Up Grading the American Police* (Washington: The Brookings Institution, 1970).

considered to be alien or different.[30] This may be the beginning of an accentuation of vigilantism.

Parenthetically, it must be stated that both authors are actively involved in the study and implementation of police department reforms and do not oppose any of the particular changes mentioned. The purpose of this discussion is rather to point out that the reforms are not necessarily thought through in terms of their ultimate effect on the political structure of the society. It is this political dimension, expressed through the concept of vigilantism, with which we are concerned.

Under the rubric of reforms, we come also to the question of the nationalization of the police force, the trend toward federal standards and increased direct federal aid to the agencies administering the police function, the states and the local governments. This trend will help to spell the end of vigilantism if it encourages the policeman to have a wider national goal, a shared professional experience with police in other parts of the country. In recent years, the idea of a national police academy has been suggested. One author, criticizing the idea of a national police academy, has said, "the last thing the present-day American police need is a West Point."[31] Whatever the talents or lack of talents West Pointers have as fighting men is not involved. The importance lies in the idea of professionalism that West Point has historically instilled in its graduates. They are not political operatives, shifting positions with the most recent poll. Therefore, if a national police academy could increase the national outlook of its graduates and depoliticize their police work, a decrease in the pressure toward vigilante activity certainly could be expected as a result.

CONCLUSION

This chapter has been an attempt to narrow the focus of the study of police problems by seeing if the concept of vigilantism is a valuable tool in analyzing police misbehavior. In that regard it is a step away from any attempt to find a single causal agent for all police misbehavior. It is the position of this paper that a separate cause should be looked for in each type of undesirable activity on the part of the police. However, this should not be taken to mean that no theory is possible. General conditions in the police force cause a variety of phenomena. These conditions can be referred to as frustration, low morale, role conflict, or just plain rage. Depending on the circumstances and the time,

30. This conflict over local control versus centralized control is summarized in Elinor Ostrom and Gordon Whitaker, "Does Local Community Control of Police Make a Difference? Some Preliminary Findings," *American Journal of Political Science* 17 (Feb. 1973): 49-50. James Q. Wilson is there quoted as saying that local control will put the police at the mercy of "the most demagogic spokesmen." However, he is not speaking of police spokesmen but rather community spokesmen.

31. Berkley, *The Democratic Policeman*, p. 202.

the manifestations of these conditions will be corruption, brutality, poor performance, vigilantism, or something else. We agree, for instance, with one observer who has noted:

> There is as yet no evidence that both phenomena—dishonesty and harassment—are but two expressions of the same underlying problem, yet a plausible theory of this effect can be devised, and until more is known about the "police problem" in America, it is worth considering.[32]

To Wilson, that problem and the plausible theory he based on it was the morale of the policemen, the failure to find "some consistent and satisfactory basis for his self-conception."[33]

We must also consider that it may be impossible to abolish completely the underlying factors of police work, the role conflicts and the low morale. Therefore, the elimination of undesirable behavior on the part of the law-enforcement agencies will largely be a trade-off situation. The governing body responsible for the police will have to weigh problems and manipulate conditions according to what it sees as the greatest threat. To speak of eliminating all police abuses and creating the perfect policeman may be a contradiction in terms. If this seems an unusually gloomy view of life, it must be remembered that we have come to terms with the necessity of such trade-offs. Undesirable elements can only be minimized in many areas of human endeavor. We routinely tell people with colds to take two aspirins and go to bed, rather than spend the resources for a crash program to cure the cold.

Vigilantism is a type of corruption. It is a corruption of the spirit, a failure of nerve on the part of the police personnel who doubt the ability of the democratic process to work. For this reason, this particular type of problem is more dangerous to society and more difficult to cure. It is not something that increased education or training or pay will help at all. It requires a whole rededication on the part of the society to give the police forces the support that they need to restore their faith in the democratic principles. It is not enough to simply say that the vigilantes will find some outlet for their antisocial behavior, or that it is a class phenomenon, or that it is a matter of mental deficiency or educational gap which can be screened out. The history of vigilantism tells us otherwise. Vigilante groups and activity spring up in response to specific sets of circumstances and die out when the circumstances no longer warrant their existence. Police vigilantism is bound to follow a similar pattern.

---

32. James Q. Wilson, "Police Morale, Reform, and Citizen Respect: The Chicago Case," *The Police: Six Sociological Essays,* David J. Bordua, ed., (New York: John Wiley & Sons, 1967), pp. 137-138.
    33. James Q. Wilson, "The Police and Their Problems: A Theory," *The Ambivalent Force: Perspectives on the Police,* Arthur Niederhoffer and Abraham S. Blumberg, eds., (Waltham, Mass.: Ginn and Company, 1970), p. 294.

Part III:

Comparative Perspectives

Chapter Nine

Comparative Vigilantism: The United States and South Africa

Christian P. Potholm

Although it is an understudied topic, vigilantism is a popular theme in American folklore and an intrinsic portion of the violent side of our cultural legacy.[1] This is particularly the case with tales dealing with the western expansion of the United States. Perhaps the most classic portrait of this genre is to be found in Walter Van Tilburg Clark's famous *The Ox-Bow Incident.*[2] In Clark's novel, enraged citizens of a small town, acting in haste and with little concern for due process of law, seek to "bring to justice" men they suspect of having committed serious crimes. Energized by half-truths and misperceptions and led by a reckless neurotic, a band of them chase, capture, and execute three men they accuse of rustling and murder.

While some of the strands of the story are atypical of many vigilante actions—the executed men are totally innocent, and the vigilantes suffer direct and severe punishments—*The Ox-Bow Incident* is well worth examining for what it reveals about an entire category of vigilante action. In the first place, the vigilantes are not led by riff-raff, but by prominent citizens in the community. And the action takes place in large part because the citizens of the area have lost faith in local law enforcement. They feel that retribution for criminal activity is not assured. They feel that the law is too lenient, too slow, too lax. Justice no longer serves as an adequate deterrent to crime and, as a result, people who live within the law are jeopardized not only by the actions of the lawless but also by the inefficiency of the judicial process itself.

There is also the sense of needed action satisfied by vigilantism. The vigilantes "do something" and ". . . it doesn't take them six months to get

1. For an analysis of the interplay between violence and American culture, see Richard Slotkin, *Regeneration Through Violence: The Mythology of the American Frontier 1600-1860* (Middletown: Wesleyan University Press, 1973).
2. Walter Van Tilburg Clark, *The Ox-Bow Incident* (New York: Random House, 1940).

started either, the way it does justice in some places."[3] In this context, right and wrong become blurred as a passion for action comes to the fore, overriding legal niceties and procedural delays. While some of the more perceptive citizens see how this erodes the very nature of the law, they are unable to counter this societal urge:

> You don't care for Justice. . . . You don't care whether you've got the right man or not. You want your way, that's all. You've lost something and somebody's got to be punished; that's all you know.[4]

In addition to the sociological impetus for revenge, vigilante action also allows anti-social elements to act out their unacceptable behavior patterns under the guise of doing "good." Individuals normally prevented by society from taking out their frustrations and aggressions on their fellows have an opportunity to take action they would be denied in more structured, less fluid times. Sadistic men can seize the chance to behave in ways which would normally put them outside the law, can enjoy the sense of new-found power, and can mete out punishment with the backing of their peers. Those who disagree with the methods and the brutality must acquiesce because of the dynamics of the situation:

> He was too slow and pleasureable for a job like this. Most of us would have had to do it in a hurry. If you have to hang a man, you have to, but it's not my kind of fun to stand around and watch him keep hoping he may get out of it.[5]

Finally, there is the underscored notion of catharsis, not just for the men who participate in vigilante action, but for the entire community. It is as if society were awry, and something must be done to set things right. Once something is done, however extralegal and rushed, the passions so violently expressed die down, and the emotional catharsis of the moment leads to subsequent peace and tranquility, however transitory. Of course, in many real-life situations, the vigilante violence, far from returning the community to peace and order, spurs others to violence, thereby continuing the cycle. For example, during the 1840s, the dramatic and widespread vigilante violence of the East Texas Regulators resulted in substantial counterviolence by the group known as the Moderators. The violence and near-anarchy lasted nearly four years.[6]

For all its successful depiction of vigilantism in the western context, *The Ox-Bow Incident* focuses on what is essentially sporadic, *ad hoc* vigilante action designed to thwart criminality. Obviously, there are other types of vigilante action, in particular the ongoing, systematic, more generalized type practiced by both governments and local establishments. As the editors of this work have suggested in their introduction, we need to examine vigilante

---

3. Ibid., p. 46.
4. Ibid., p. 261.
5. Ibid., p. 215.
6. For a keenly drawn, if essentially descriptive, portrait of the Regulators, see Colin Rickard, *The Gunfight at Blazer's Mill* (El Paso: University of Texas at El Paso monograph, 1974).

action along a "continuum of intentionality,"[7] to grapple with its considerable complexity and to examine some of the fundamental assumptions about its nature.

A number of scholars, including Bruno Bettelheim, have noted that until recently, violence has been ". . . a neglected mode of behavior" from the point of academic inquiry.[8] Despite a recent spate of books and articles, plus several presidential commissions on the general subject of violence, our knowledge of the role of violence in our society has been increasing only slowly. This volume, focusing as it does on the overlooked phenomenon of vigilante violence, seeks to break new ground and to probe analytically the relationship between that violence and the established sociopolitical order.

Toward this end, the editors have broadly defined vigilantism as establishment violence in which individuals or groups who identify with the established order defend it by responding with extralegal and illegitimate use of force.[9] Most useful is their notion that a variety of phenomena fall under the general heading of vigilantism or establishment violence and that these phenomena can be further divided into working typologies. One category is crime-control, in which the vigilantes seek to punish those who seem to have escaped punishment for their crimes, either by a lack of presence of law-enforcement agents or by the miscarriage of the judicial process. This is the most popular conception of vigilante action and the one depicted in *The Ox-Bow Incident.*

Another category is social-group-control, in which action is taken against those who are perceived to threaten the existing social and political order. Extralegal violence is applied to terrorize the minority (or even the majority) group into submission, whether that group is racial, regional, linguistic, ethnic, or political in nature. This form is evident all over the world, appearing most recently in Northern Ireland, Indonesia, Rwanda, and the Sudan as well as in the United States and South Africa, the subjects of this chapter. Finally, there is the regime-control form of vigilante action, in which certain members of the ruling social or political group use violence to stiffen the resistance of the government and, perhaps, even members of the prevailing security apparatus itself, in order to increase their levels of violence against either criminal or revolutionary elements.

In the essay which follows, I intend to explore what I take to be the key elements of the vigilante phenomenon as seen in the United States and South Africa, particularly those aspects which fall into the second, or social-group-control category. Because of the scope of the subject, the paucity of existing

7. H. Jon Rosenbaum and Peter C. Sederberg, "Vigilantism: An Analysis of Establishment Violence," p. 4, (hereafter cited as "Analysis").

8. Bruno Bettelheim, as quoted in Shalom Endleman, ed., *Violence in the Street* (New York: Quadrangle Books, 1967), p. 37.

9. Rosenbaum and Sederberg, "Analysis," p. 4. See also E. V. Walter, *Terror and Resistance: A Study of Political Violence* (London: Oxford University Press, 1969).

works on the subject, and the space constraints of this chapter, my investigation will be suggestive rather than exhaustive. I shall compare and contrast the historical and cultural baggage of each country in order to identify the strands of the societies which help to explain both the type and the frequency of vigilante action. Finally, I shall suggest some tentative conclusions about the nature of vigilantism drawn from these two case studies.

AMERICAN VIGILANTISM

As the earlier chapters in this work indicate, vigilantism in America is a complex and multifaceted subject. A full treatment of the entire subject obviously lies beyond the scope of this short essay, so it will be limited to several salient themes which reoccur in the American context.

The first of these is that vigilantism has had a long and varied history in the United States. It has been ". . . an almost constant factor in American life" from the early colonial period onward, as Richard Brown has indicated.[10] Other authorities have also stressed its endemic quality in the history of the United States.[11] Beginning with the South Carolina Regulators in 1767, there has been a great variety of vigilante movements, sometimes of a local nature, sometimes more widespread. Vigilantism seems to have come in waves, for example during the early 1830s and 1840s and the late 1850s and 1860s. Although we often think of the vigilantes as small groups of men, some of these movements were quite large. More than two thousand Regulators took part in a raid against an outlaw community in Indiana in 1858, and some six thousand to eight thousand people belonged to the San Francisco vigilante committees of 1856. Often "vigilance committees became a matter of course, not only in the West, but also in the East,"[12] with more than 210 movements in the former part of the country and 116 in the latter.[13]

Many of these early vigilante movements fall directly into the Rosenbaum/Sederberg typology of crime-control, and their administration of summary justice enjoyed widespread popular support. Some writers, particularly Richard Brown, have tended to regard this vigilante tradition as "positive" despite the draconian and extralegal methods, because it brought law and order to a chaotic situation. Cheap and sure "justice" undoubtedly appealed to many Americans during the periods of vigilante action.

10. Richard Brown, "The American Vigilante Tradition," in H. D. Graham and T. R. Gurr, eds., *Violence in America: Historical and Comparative Perspectives* (Washington: United States Government Printing Office, 1969), 1: 121.

11. At the same time Richard Hofstadter and Michael Wallace have obviously overstated the case when they declare that vigilantism and lynchings "can be regarded as distinctly American institutions," Richard Hofstadter and Michael Wallace, eds., *American Violence: A Documentary History* (New York: Vintage Books, 1971), p. 20.

12. Robert Bruce, *1877: Year of Violence* (New York: Bobbs-Merrill, 1959), p. 68.

13. Brown, "Vigilante Tradition," p. 127.

The criminal-control type of vigilantism was overshadowed and, to a considerable extent, submerged by its post-Civil War counterpart of the social-group-control variety. In these movements, establishment violence was directed against racial, ethnic, political, and economic groups which threatened the status quo, and as such, it was often aided and abetted by the use of federal troops. In addition to the obvious anti-black movements of the Reconstruction period in the South, vigilantism of the social-group-control type appeared in the mines, railroads, and factories as the fledgling labor movement in the United States became a primary target.

Armed, private militia acted against strikers from coast to coast in the late 1860s and 1870s, with a severe upsurge in violence toward the end of that period. The year 1877 was particularly bloody. Strikes and strike-breaking violence occurred in Baltimore, Pittsburgh, Cincinnati, Philadelphia, Buffalo, and Chicago. Federal troops, which had been used exceedingly sparingly prior to the Civil War, were called into action twenty-five times between 1865 and 1877.[14] Not only were many of these examples of social-control vigilantism establishment promoted, they also tended to be justified in the incipient philosophies of both social Darwinism and capitalism. Toward the end of the nineteenth century, with the spread of social Darwinism, the perpetrators of establishment violence did in fact have a workable ideology involving the "survival of the fittest."[15]

There was a certain amount of reaction to the excesses of vigilantism during the early 1900s, and many state police units were organized by reformers who wished to reduce the level of vigilante violence. Nevertheless, social-control vigilantism selected a variety of targets during the twentieth century. The maturing labor movement, in particular the Industrial Workers of the World (iww), the Communists and other radicals, minority and ethnic groups, and those held to be "un-American," even "un-middle class," were among those attacked.[16]

Some writers, such as Alan Wolfe,[17] have hypothesized a dynamic of repression operative in American history which includes the social-control types listed above but also expands it to cover such seemingly discrete phenomena as McCarthyism and the placing of Japanese-Americans in concentration camps during World War II.[18] Herbert Marcuse would include

14. Ibid., p. 90.

15. This phenomenon would stand as an amendment to the Rosenbaum/Sederberg assertion that vigilante groups rarely possess autonomous ideologies and usually do not have ideologies at all.

16. For a penetrating analysis of the pervasiveness of middle-class values in twentieth century America, see Edward C. Banfield, "The Imperatives of Class" in his *The Un-Heavenly City* (Boston: Little, Brown, 1968), pp. 46-66.

17. Alan Wolfe, *The Seamy Side of Democracy: Repression In America* (New York: David McKay, 1973).

18. For a full treatment of this subject, see Audrie Ginder and Ann Goftis, *The Great Betrayal: The Evacuation of Japanese Americans during World War II* (New York: Macmillan, 1969).

not only these forms but also any preventative counterviolence which acts as an ongoing form of repression.[19] Although these two points of view are considerably exaggerated (Wolfe, for example, would have a difficult time proving that professional football is a form of political repression), they do underscore the notion that violence, and indeed establishment violence, are central themes in American history.

Moreover, they remain prominent features of the contemporary scene. Alphonso Pickney has called this "an unusually violent society," and others have indicated that in terms of the level of violence within the society, the United States ranks fourteenth out of eighty-four nations in terms of frequency of violent events.[20] Certainly the seemingly ubiquitous use of excess force by law-enforcement agencies and private groups against students, blacks, and "leftists" during the 1960s would give anyone pause for thought. The events of May 1968 at Columbia, April 1969 at Harvard, May 1969 at Berkeley, February 1968 and May 1970 at Kent State, January 1968 at San Francisco, April 1968 at Oakland, September 1968 at Denver, July and December 1969 at Chicago, and December 1969 at Los Angeles, plus other incidents too numerous to mention, suggest that in those turbulent times establishment violence was extremely prevalent. Perhaps no single event more graphically illustrates the extent of extralegal violence used as a form of social-group-control than the Chicago police riot in August 1968 during the Democratic National Convention. Police, exceeding any possible bounds of legal authority, ran amok and violently attacked civilians, including hundreds of innocent bystanders. All told, more than eleven hundred civilians were injured, while much of the spectacle was captured on film for subsequent review and verification.

At the present time, it appears that much of the extralegal, establishment-oriented violence is committed by the police themselves, rather than by private vigilante groups. It is thus a matter of considerable interest to examine the extent of societal support for police violence and to analyze the often subtle interplay between society and the men sworn to protect it. The Law Enforcement Code of Ethics for police officers is clear on this point:

> I will never act officiously or permit personal feeling, prejudices, animosities or friendship to influence my decision. With no compromise for crime and with relentless prosecution of criminals, I will enforce the law courteously and appropriately without fear or favor, malice or ill-will, never employing unnecessary force or violence and never accepting gratuities.[21]

If punishment is not a legitimate police function, however, many police regard

19. Herbert Marcuse, "The Movement in a New Era of Repression," *Berkeley Journal of Sociology* 16 (1971): 1-14.
20. Alphonso Pickney, *The American Way of Violence* (New York: Vintage Books, 1972), p. xiii.
21. Ibid., p. 116.

it as such and are willing to use excess or extralegal force in order to act as a more formidable agent of order maintenance.

Like all social groups, the police are influenced by their own perceptions and misperceptions, and successive studies have indicated the extent to which they feel they are acting in both their own and society's defense. They see themselves as engaged in highly dangerous work (some of them very definitely are, but statistically police work is less dangerous than many other occupations, including transportation, mining, contract construction, and agriculture).[22] In fact, policemen are six times more likely to kill than to be killed in the line of duty.[23] They see themselves as engaged in important and difficult work, unappreciated by the general public, beset by hostile forces and unfair critics. They are often astonished and frustrated that some take the side of those they see as threatening the very nature of society.[24] This sense of isolation and anxiety is often reinforced by recruitment patterns, self-selection, and strong in-group norms.[25] For both the police trying to counter them and those bent on the forceful alteration of society, violence often appears "inescapable, reasonable and legitimate."[26]

And, in point of fact, the police have good reason for thinking their excess force in the name of crime- or social-group-control is legitimate:

> For many Americans, there is apparently a thin blue line between order and chaos. Breach it and untold furies lie beyond. The police require unconditional support when they are in combat; sins are understandable and forgivable when they occur in the stress of battle.[27]

That is why:

> Extralegal police actions directed against unpopular targets are unlikely to draw censure or even disapproval from those substantial segments of the American public for whom the police are the good guys.[28]

For example, of more than one thousand respondents to a questionnaire dealing with the extralegal violence used by the police at the 1968 Democratic Convention, only 19 percent thought the police had used too much force, while 25 percent thought they had not used enough.[29] The rest were satisfied that the proper amount had been used or expressed no opinion.

22. Gerald D. Robin, "Justifiable Homicide by Police Officers," *Journal of Criminal Law, Criminology and Police Science* 54 (1963): 225-31.
23. Ibid., p. 150.
24. Robert Coles, ed., "Policeman Complaints," *The New York Times Magazine,* (June 11, 1971): 11-18.
25. Gordon E. Misner, "The Police and Collective Violence in Contemporary America," in James F. Short and Marvin Wolfgang, eds., *Collective Violence* (Chicago: Aldine Atherton, 1972), pp. 343-51.
26. H. L. Nieburg, "Agonistics: Ritual Conflict," in *Collective Violence,* p. 83.
27. William A. Gamson and James McEvoy, "Police Violence and its Public Support," *The Annals of the American Academy of Political and Social Science* 391 (September 1970): p. 98.
28. Ibid., p. 110.
29. John P. Robison, "Public Reaction to Political Protest: Chicago 1968," *Public Opinion Quarterly* 34 (Spring 1970): 1-9.

The connection between extralegal violence by the police and public support for that violence is obviously a matter of great concern. The President's Commission on Law Enforcement and the Administration of Justice (1965), the National Advisory Commission on Civil Disorders (1967), the National Commission on the Causes and Prevention of Violence (1968), and the President's Commission on Campus Disorder (1970) have all touched upon the problem. In varying degrees all have expressed considerable concern about the situation and have offered a great variety of solutions, ranging from changed recruitment and training patterns for police to the more far-reaching suggestions that poverty and racism be eradicated from our society.

I have suggested elsewhere that the reduction of police violence, while a difficult problem, is not insoluble.[30] While this is not the place to reiterate all of those findings, one aspect, the structural and functional overhaul of the basic law enforcement system, is extremely germane to the continuing problem of vigilantism on the part of law-enforcement personnel.

Before dealing with the overhaul of the police, which is necessary to combat their use of extralegal violence, it is important to point out at least three areas of concern which go beyond this aspect but which impinge directly on it.

The first of these is the ubiquity of firearms in American society. While estimates of the number of weapons abroad in the United States run all the way from fifty million to two hundred million (the range of estimate itself shows how little we know about the problem), the most careful recent assessment puts the number at more than ninety million scattered throughout the country in more than sixty million households.[31] Since firearms are responsible for nearly twenty thousand deaths a year (and have killed more than eight hundred thousand people in the United States during this century), they are clearly a major problem in themselves. Moreover, their very presence is a cause for genuine concern for their own safety on the part of police and in no small way contributes to the pattern of police over-reaction on occasion.

As a first step in reducing violence (and in turn, social-group-control vigilantism), many have urged that the American political system should move toward national firearm control legislation, including registration and mandatory sentencing for the commission of crimes with firearms. Virtually every other industrialized society, from Japan to France, Great Britain to the Federal Republic of Germany, has moved toward stringent control over private ownership of guns, particularly hand guns. And all have seen a marked reduction in the incidence of violence within the society.

A second aspect of the situation has to do with the technological means available to the police for response in violent situations. Currently, the

30. C. P. Potholm, "Toward a New Beginning," in R. E. Morgan and C. P. Potholm, eds., *The Police and Law Enforcement* (forthcoming).

31. George D. Newton and Franklin E. Zimring, *Firearms and Violence in American Life: A Staff Report Submitted to the National Commission on the Causes and Prevention of Violence* (Washington: United States Government Printing Office, n.d.), pp. 3-4.

policeman on the beat is severely handicapped by the inadequacy of the range of weapons available to him. Between the nightstick and the gun are few alternatives, so few in fact that the vigorous research to develop nonlethal weapons should be a priority target for law-enforcement agencies in particular and society in general. Although some recent technological developments may lead to such weapons in the foreseeable future, to date, none of the weapons available (the stinger stick, dart gun, ricochet round, telo-active shock repulsor, and the like) has provided the police with a significant alternative to the firearm. In fact, in the wake of the civil disorders of the 1960s, when the police were forced to call on the National Guard and the regular army to restore order, the movement has been the other way, toward the purchase of heavier equipment, including machine guns, rocket launchers, armored cars, and even tanks. The development of a nonlethal repertoire (or even weapons "less" lethal than firearms) could have a most salutary effect and reduce both the level of extralegal violence and its justification.

The third factor which provides substantial impetus for extralegal violence on the part of the police is the low level of deterrence currently provided by the entire law-enforcement and penal system. Virtually everyone, from the offenders to the experts in the field, has concluded that the present penal system in the United States is a gross failure. Eighty percent of all felons are repeaters, and two-thirds of those released from prison return to crime relatively soon. Even more depressing are the statistics on those under eighteen years of age. Half of all serious crimes are committed by this cohort, and the younger the criminal is at his first conviction, the more likely he is to be a repeater. The police are painfully and frustratingly aware of these statistics and their meaning for police work. In addition to the poor results obtained by the penal system, the police are also discouraged by their inability to apprehend even a majority of those who commit crimes. Currently, this is true for several of the major index crimes, most notably burglary. The odds are 50-1 that a person who commits burglary will be caught and 100-1 that he will ever spend a day in jail. Like the cowboys in *The Ox-Bow Incident,* the police often think that there is a better way.

The several *a priori* handicaps outlined above must be considered when any analysis is made of the structural and functional changes which will have to take place in order to reduce the current levels of establishment violence perpetrated by law enforcement officials. In summary, these are as follows: the ubiquity of firearms, the currently available means of apprehending suspects, and the low quality of the entire deterrence and rehabilitation systems. To overlook these factors is to ignore the obvious and justfiable police frustration with the very institutions of society they are serving and to underestimate the forces acting to produce considerable temptation to use extralegal violence.

Yet any overview of the police situation in the United States must inexorably come to the conclusion that much of the extralegal violence is a result of the mechanics of our current law-enforcement system itself. Indeed, "system" gives by far the wrong connotation. There are currently more than 43 thousand law-enforcement agencies in the United States, employing more than 450 thousand persons. Although we tend to associate law enforcement with the large, urban police forces of television fame, in fact, nearly 90 percent of all police agencies in the United States have fewer than ten full-time officers. Overlapping jurisdictions, poor communications, and other severe inhibitions on the quality and indeed the quantity of law enforcement available to any given community make a mockery of the term.

This haphazard, crazy-quilt of overlapping police forces stems from our heritage of local autonomy and an historical aversion to the centralization of power or a national police force. This has resulted in fragmentation of law enforcement in the United States and widely varying modes of enforcing the law and maintaining order.[32] More germane for the purposes of this essay, I consider that it has allowed individual departments to pursue a great variety of forms of extralegal violence, both of the criminal- and the social-group control types. There are almost no institutions to supervise the maze of law-enforcement agencies or to correct local abuses. In addition, police work is one of the few occupations in which discretion is inversely proportional to rank. A patrolman on the beat has considerable latitude as to how he will enforce (or overenforce) the law. Local police forces must engage in wholesale or notorious practices, well publicized by the media, before they are likely to get even intermittent supervision.

Some national supervision of recruitment, training, and ongoing methods of law enforcement seems absolutely critical if we are to reduce the scale of extralegal violence practiced by the police. It seems inopportune to be arguing for a national police system so soon after Watergate and what appears to have been a major attempt to use the most significant national institutions for political purposes. The FBI is itself under both widespread and significant criticism[33] (although I believe that with regard to law enforcement, the FBI is less violent, more disciplined, better trained, and more effective than all but a handful of the major urban police forces). The lack of supervision of the local urban and rural police forces, the haphazard standards and recruitment patterns, and the minimal checks on the activities of the police which skirt the law, all argue for some type of national supervision. As the various presidential commissions have found, many police forces do not even require a high school diploma; over 75 percent do not screen their applicants for emotional fitness; and well over half do not give their recruits any significant training. As a result, "the failure to establish high professional standards for

---

32. James Q. Wilson, *Varieties of Police Behavior: The Management of Law and Order in Eight Communities* (Cambridge: Harvard University Press, 1968).
33. Stephen Gillers, ed., *Investigating the FBI* (Garden City: Doubleday, 1973).

the police service has been a costly one, both for the police and for society."[34] Moreover, major studies have concluded that the police are generally hostile toward blacks,[35] practice widespread brutality,[36] and that with regard to basic civil rights, "no government institution appears so deficient in its understanding of the constructive role of dissent in a constitutional democracy as the police."[37]

In my judgment, we need national supervision of police training, with regularized procedures, common facilities, common courses, and national standards on a variety of levels. This would provide occupational mobility within the law-enforcement profession, something currently lacking except among a small number of the agencies. The police are often the cutting edge of society, dealing with complex situations which may involve decisions about life and death. They are often faced, as the earlier portions of this chapter suggest, with temptations to use extralegal force. It seems incredible that society tolerates such low standards of police recruitment and training, let alone supervision. It is not surprising that "far too many of those charged with protecting life and property and rationally enforcing our laws are not respected by their fellow officers and are incompetent, corrupt or abusive."[38]

We also need drastic changes in police structure and organization to provide greater central control over police operations without eliminating the good features of local autonomy. One suggestion would be to move simultaneously toward national or regional enforcement in certain areas and, at the same time, place greater stress on the ability of the local police to deal with local situations. The National Conference on Criminal Justice recommended that all the police forces in the United States be classified on the basis of the number of their personnel. Class One departments (those with more than 1000 personnel) should routinely assist other classes on a need basis and, to avoid duplication, there should be a series of regional crime laboratories with formally qualified staff to assist departments in need of specialists. Class Six departments (those with fifteen men or fewer) should perform such "generalist" functions as foot patrol and traffic supervision.

Smaller units should be encouraged (and by the withholding of federal funds, pressured) to consolidate their manpower and jurisdictions in order to improve the quality of law enforcement. Joint service agreements, participation in regional facilities, and sharing of specialist personnel were

34. The President's Commission on Law Enforcement and Administration of Justice, *Task Force Report: The Police* (Washington: United States Government Printing Office, 1967), p. 125.
35. The President's Commission on Law Enforcement and the Administration of Justice, *Task Force Report on the Violent Aspects of Protest and Confrontation, The Politics of Protest* (Washington: United States Government Printing Office, 1969), p. 184.
36. Ibid., p. 185.
37. Ibid., p. 215.
38. *Task Force Report: The Police*, p. 125.

highly recommended. Jacksonville, Florida, which merged its police department with the Duval County sheriff's office and Los Angeles county where twenty-eight cities "lease" police services from the county itself, are two examples which indicate the extent to which this process can be implemented on a local basis. These arrangements enable local police communities to pool their resources, avoid duplication, and coordinate anti-crime activities.

There is a considerable need to speed up this process. The various state governments should pass enabling legislation and facilitate the establishment of regional crime laboratories. The federal government could also make judicious use of federal funds to apply pressure on local police forces to conform to the demands of modern crime fighting and to reach higher standards of police behavior. This is not to suggest that there is no place for the local police personnel. Centralization and specialization are required to deal with organized crime, interstate flight, and a wide variety of serious crimes. However, FBI and state agencies are often far less able to cope with the day to day order maintenance and service functions than competent local counterparts.

The adoption of these structural and functional reforms will not entirely eliminate police misbehavior, but it would represent a critical first step toward providing the type of organization which can be better supervised. National standards and ongoing supervision would reduce the likelihood of local police units acting, with or without community support, in an extralegal manner. It would place them, at least to a certain extent, above the swirl of local events and outside the pressures for extralegal behavior. It is a monumental task, but so is running a 220-million-person collectivity which is increasingly industrialized, urbanized, and interdependent. No other industrialized nation in the world attempts to police itself with such an archaic and too often uncontrolled set of agencies. In fact, so bizarre is the present arrangement that one wonders not why there is so much extralegal violence, but why there is not more.

SOUTH AFRICAN VIGILANTISM

Although our knowledge of the process of establishment violence in the United States is rudimentary, we know even less about its occurrence in most other societies, particularly those in the Third World.[39] In the case of South Africa, however, we have a great deal of documentation on its past, present, and, in terms of speculation, its future. A study of establishment violence in South Africa offers some interesting parallels and differences with the patterns observed in the United States.

39. See the pioneering work of Marshall Clinard and Daniel Abbott, *Crime in Developing Countries: A Comparative Perspective* (New York: John Wiley, 1973). I have also touched upon the various roles of the police in "The Multiple Roles of the Police as Seen in the African Context," *The Journal of Developing Areas* 3 (January 1969): 139-58, esp. pp. 148, 149, and 154.

Like the United States, South Africa has had a long and convoluted history, punctuated by persistent violence. With the initial founding of the Cape Settlement in 1652, there was a series of violent clashes, first with the indigenous Khoi Khoi and San people (the latter being virtually exterminated), then with the various Bantu-speaking groups of Africans who were migrating south at the time the Europeans were moving north. For the first few centuries of European settlement, there was an open frontier to the north and a seemingly endless series of clashes as Boer, Bantu, and Briton struggled for supremacy over most of the subcontinent. Violence and conquest were prominent features of the various European and African societies which emerged. It was not until the twentieth century that South Africa was unified under a single government. Even this was only accomplished at a considerable cost of life and property, first during the various campaigns against African groups, such as the Zulu, and later during the Anglo-Boer war of 1899 to 1902.[40]

There is an enormous amount of material dealing with this early period. However, for the purposes of this chapter, I am confining my analysis to the twentieth century after the Union of South Africa was established and its government held sway over all the inhabitants of South Africa.

From its formation, the Union, and later, Republic of South Africa has been ruled by successive governments, each more racially repressive than the last. Its policy has been characterized by a pervasive ethos of white domination, a strong commitment to the use of violence (legal and extralegal), and the denial of basic human rights to three-fourths of the population in order to keep that majority of the population under control. This is not the place for an extensive analysis of the inequities of the social, economic, and political systems of South Africa. Literature fairly bristles with works dealing with this theme.[41] We are concerned here with instances and patterns of establishment violence, particularly that of the social-group-control variety. The Sharpeville massacre of 1961 and the more recent slaughter of

40. The interested reader should consult Eric Walker, *A History of South Africa* (London: Longmans, Green and Company, 1962); Leo Marquard, *A Short History of South Africa* (New York: Praeger, 1968); C. W. DeKiewiet, *A History of South Africa* (London: Oxford University Press, 1967); Monica Wilson and Leonard Thompson, eds., *The Oxford History of South Africa,* two vols. (London: Oxford University Press, 1969 and 1971). Particularly valuable is Leonard Thompson's own chapter, "The Subjection of the African Chiefdoms, 1870-1898," pp. 245-86 in vol. two.

41. Some contemporary assessments of the situation in South Africa include Leo Marquard, *The Peoples and Policies of South Africa* (London: Oxford University Press, 1962); Jordan Ngubane, *An African Explains Apartheid* (New York: Praeger, 1963); Leonard Thompson, *Politics in the Republic of South Africa* (Boston: Little, Brown, 1966); Herbert Adam, *Modernizing Racial Domination: The Dynamics of South African Politics* (Los Angeles: University of California Press, 1971), and his edited work, *South Africa: Sociological Perspectives* (London: Oxford University Press, 1970); and C. P. Potholm and Richard Dale, eds., *Southern Africa in Perspective: Essays in Regional Politics* (New York: The Free Press, 1972).

mineworkers at Carleton at the Western Deep Level Mine in 1973 are two highly publicized examples of South African establishment violence. There are nevertheless many other less publicized instances of excessive and extralegal violence being used to repress those—black, white, or brown—who would alter the status quo.[42] For example, how many of the four thousand Africans who lost their lives in the poll tax rebellion of 1906 were the victims of extralegal violence on the part of the authorities? How many Africans were victims of the widespread violence and abuses of the police and white vigilante groups in the Transvaal region during 1919? Was it necessary to kill 163 Africans and wound 129 more in order to suppress the Israelite church movement during the Bulhoek massacre in May 1921? Did the preservation of the South African way of life demand the slaughter of more than 100 men, women, and children in the massacre of the Bondelswarts.[43]

There were numerous instances of vigilantism in the decades which followed as the white electorate became increasingly concerned over the Communist movement and by a fear that the Africans would demand justice and equality in a society based on injustice and inequality. In June 1929, for example, a white mob attacked and killed labor leaders in Durban. On May 4, 1930, five Africans were killed in liquor raids at Worster. For days thereafter, white vigilantes marauded throughout African and colored areas, attacking persons at will. Authorities were hardly firm in dealing with the vigilantes. One white man who was apprehended after firing a rifle at Africans was sentenced to a fine of five shillings for being in possession of a rifle without a license.[44]

With the coming to power of the National party in 1948 and its increasing implementation of apartheid, many Africans, coloreds, Asians, and even some Europeans sought to resist the harsh new laws designed to segregate even more finally the various races in South Africa. Initially this resistance was passive and nonviolent.[45] The so-called Defiance Campaign of 1952-1953, the Bantu Education boycott of 1954, and the Alexandria bus boycott, for example, were extraordinarily peaceful considering the numbers of persons involved and the provocations by the authorities.

---

42. A fuller treatment is to be found in Edward Roux, *Time Longer Than Rope: A History of the Black Man's Struggle for Freedom in South Africa* (Madison: University of Wisconsin Press, 1966); Peter Walshe, *The Rise of African Nationalism in South Africa* (Los Angeles: University of California Press, 1971); Edward Feit, *African Opposition in South Africa* (Stanford: Hoover Institution, 1967); Albert Luthuli, *Let My People Go* (New York: Meridian Books, 1962); Mary Benson, *South Africa: The Struggle for a Birthright* (New York: Minerva Press, 1969); and Nelson Mandela, *No Easy Walk to Freedom* (New York: Heineman, 1965).

43. Whites who sought to alter the status quo discovered that the government was not averse to using excess force against those who threatened the establishment, regardless of their color. This was especially true during the Great Strike and so-called Red Revolt of 1922.

44. Roux, *Time Longer than Rope*, p. 235.

45. See, for example, Leo Kuper, *Passive Resistance in South Africa* (New Haven: Yale University Press, 1956) and Edward Feit, *South Africa: The Dynamics of the African National Congress* (London: Oxford University Press, 1962).

The government's response was more violent. On May 16, 1958, four Africans were shot dead at Sekukhuneland. On December 10, 1959, eleven Africans were killed and fifty wounded at Windhoek, while on June 17, 1959, at least three Africans were killed in the Cato Manor disturbances. On March 21, 1960, two Africans were killed and forty-nine injured at Langa Near Cape Town.

Perhaps the most graphic example of governmental vigilantism occurred the same day at Sharpeville near Vereeniging. A crowd of approximately 5000 Africans had gathered at a Sharpeville police station, many of them to turn in their passes. Contemporary photographs show smiling men, women, and children, many of them with food and drink. The meeting is rather picnic-like, with sun umbrellas and other paraphernalia of an outing. There are no indications that the crowd is either sinister or threatening, and the police station, surrounded by barbed wire and guarded by armored cars, seems in no danger.

For reasons that have never been clear, the police suddenly opened fire on the crowd. In the slaughter that followed, sixty-seven Africans (including eight women and ten children) were killed. Virtually all of the victims were shot from behind as they attempted to get out of the way of the murderous fire. Subsequent investigations indicated that the police made no attempt to disperse the crowd by peaceful means, nor to warn the crowd that force would be used if it did not disperse. They did not try to use any force other than firearms, but fired at will into the crowd and continued to fire indiscriminately long after the Africans had turned and run. All in all, there was "no justification for the conduct of the police."[46]

Yet, although the Sharpeville massacre caused world-wide reaction and criticism (including an arms embargo by the United States), the stern measures taken subsequently by the South African government enjoyed widespread support within the white community. The government declared a state of emergency, banned the major African organizations, and embarked on a massive crackdown. Tens of thousands of Africans were arrested, and many were held without trial. The various African leaders were incarcerated as the government passed some of the most draconian laws imaginable. The Riotous Assembly Act, the Terrorism Act, the Suppression of Communism Act, and the General Amendment (Sabotage) Act were passed, giving the government broad and sweeping powers to arrest and detain individuals, ban groups, and broadly define what constituted acts against the state.[47]

The African National Congress and the Pan-African Congress, the two

46. Ambrose Reeves, *Shooting at Sharpeville: The Agony of South Africa* (Boston: Houghton Mifflin, 1961), p. 80.
47. One finds an odd juxtaposition of values in all of this. The South African government is almost compulsive about passing laws to provide legal cover for its repressive measures. Yet it steadfastly refuses to grant the bulk of its population participation in the law-making process or to grant them protection under the firm legal order thus created.

major African organizations of the era, went underground during this period, and both turned increasingly toward counterviolence in the face of the repression outlined above. However, the South African security capability remained strong and continued to accelerate. By the end of the 1960s it had far outstripped the ability of those who would even marginally threaten the status quo, leaving the various African organizations in ruins and their leaders in exile or in prison.[48]

The regulative capability of South Africa became impressive indeed. The police force was enlarged to more than 30,000 men with particular emphasis on the counterinsurgency properties of the special branch.[49] The army increased in size to more than twenty-six thousand men with a reserve force of fifty thousand and a further fifty thousand in the part-time commando units. The resulting security apparatus is currently able to provide a degree of societal supervision and control unparalleled in South African history.[50]

In sharp contrast to the fragmented, flimsy structure of law enforcement in the United States, the South African government has at its command a strong, centralized system with continual emphasis on community control and surveillance. From the seemingly fluid situation of the 1950s and 1960s, the South African security apparatus has emerged capable of keeping the lid on society. Although in terms of scale the South African system covers the much smaller 20-million-person collectivity, its tasks of societal supervision are much greater. It must cope not only with a potentially hostile three-quarters of its population but also with goals that demand an extensive commitment to social, political, and economic control.

In controlling the various societal aspects, the South African security apparatus generates one of the largest prison populations in the world relative to its total population. In 1970 and 1971, for example, the prison population exceeded 474 thousand people, 465 thousand of whom were classified as non-European.[51] Nearly 400 thousand of these are in jail for pass law violations (more than 600 thousand are arrested annually). The head of the South African National Institute for Crime Prevention and the Rehabilitation of Offenders indicated that over the last ten years South Africa's prison population has increased by 76 percent, while the total population increase was only 24 percent.[52] Thus, South Africa now has a daily prison average of

48. For a description of this build-up, see J. E. Spence and Elizabeth Thomas, *South Africa's Defense* (Los Angeles: University of California Press, 1966) and Charles Petersen, "The Military Balance in Southern Africa," in Potholm and Dale, *Southern Africa in Perspective*, pp. 298-317.

49. For an interesting assessment of this phenomenon, see Sam C. Nolutshungu, "The Impact of External Pressure on South African Politics: A Theoretical Approach," paper prepared for delivery at the Yale/Wesleyan Conference on Contemporary Change in Southern Africa, April 1974.

50. C. P. Potholm, "South Africa," in *Four African Political Systems* (Englewood Cliffs: Prentice-Hall, 1970), pp. 91-137.

51. Muriel Horrell, ed., *A Survey of Race Relations in South Africa: 1972* (Johannesburg: South African Institute of Race Relations, 1973), p. 85.

52. Ibid., p. 86.

417 per 100,000 population (versus Norway's forty-four, Sweden's sixty-one, Belgium's sixty-three, France's seventy, and Great Britain's seventy-two and a half).[53]

With the increased societal supervision and severe enforcement of the new laws, private vigilante action dropped from its frequency in the 1960s. In the last several years, however, vigilantism and extralegal violence by the police and security forces once again seems on the upswing. During 1972, for example, such organizations as the "Patriotic South Africans for South Africa" and "Scorpio" attacked and tried to intimidate individuals and such organizations favoring a change in the status quo as the Christian Institute, the Students Defense Fund, the National Union of South African Students, and the South African Students' Organization.

Over the last several years, excessive and extralegal violence has been used against a number of students who have urged changes in the status quo. Attacks have been reported on students at the University of Cape Town, University College of the North, University College of the Western Cape, University of Durban-Westville, Transvaal College of Education, University of Natal, Fort Hare, University of Zululand, and the University of Witwatersrand.

One of the more interesting aspects of the South African situation is the different governmental responses to criminal and political activity. Although the government tends to approximate the Rosenbaum/Sederberg social-group-control model quite well, it seems content to tolerate a high incidence of crime in the African urban areas. Of course, where this situation impinges on Europeans, the government is more willing to devote its scarce resources to fight crime, but generally, it is quite lax in the African areas.

Such a strategy might seem to be contradictory, but in terms of the maintenance of the political system this high crime rate may actually be seen to support the system and help maintain the status quo. It helps to deflect African frustration and aggression away from political activity and toward "commercial" crime. It also forces Indians, Chinese, and other non-European groups to look to the system for protection from Africans. Moreover, it increases the willingness of Europeans to accept the harsh legal system in the political area in order to keep the lid on society and prevent "lawless" Africans from coming to power. From the government's point of view, of course, there is an ironic self-fulfilling prophecy in much of this. In Soweto, the huge sprawling African location near Johannesburg with nearly one million persons, while the Europeans maintain a strong presence during the day, at night they leave the task of order maintenence to approximately seven thousand African police who do not have firearms. The government is then able to point to crime statistics in Soweto to "prove" how lawless Africans are.

---

53. Ibid.

CONCLUSIONS

Several hypotheses emerge from this introductory glimpse at the phenomena of vigilante action in the United States and South Africa.

First, vigilante action, of all three types, is more likely to occur during periods of social flux. Rural to city migration, immigration, threats to the social, economic, and political order all seem to generate a greater incidence of vigilante action than "normal" times. At such fluid times, the security apparatus often seems ineffective in fulfilling the new demands of the dominant group for the maintenance of the status quo (whether this involves reduced lawlessness, fewer threats to the ruling elite, or harsher punishment for those who break the laws of society).

In South Africa, the 1950s and early 1960s spawned greater vigilantism than the late 1960s, and similar patterns seem to be indicated in the United States. Thus, if the security apparatus is functioning effectively, there is less need for private groups to do more than encourage the law-enforcement community. By the same token, if the security personnel are satisfied that they can accomplish the job within the framework of the law, they are less likely to go outside that law. Turmoil, by intensifying conflicts and misperceptions concerning their origins, puts increasing pressure on would-be vigilantes, both in and out of uniform, to take action.

Second, because of its relation to the broader societal patterns, be they economic, political, or international (that is ideological), vigilante action seems to be more reactive than was heretofore indicated. Both in the United States and in South Africa, periodic upsurges in vigilante activity seem to suggest that vigilantism is the dependent variable rather than the independent. The rate of vigilante action and its duration also seems tied to specific locations and times. Some run their course rather quickly; others, such as those currently in operation in Northern Ireland or during the 1950s in Colombia, may take a good deal of time to wear themselves out. This brief study also suggests that while particular vigilante groups may be ephemeral, vigilantism itself is not.

Finally, as Graham Allison has so aptly put it, "where you stand depends on where you sit."[54] So it is with vigilante action. Literature suggests that vigilante action is generally popular. While excesses are deplored, they tend to be overlooked in direct proportion to the extent of the perceived threat to society. Many South Africans find torture excusable if the victim is a "terrorist". Many Americans find police violence against students justified because they show a "lack of respect for this country."

The population as a whole, however, is important in judging the extent of support for particular vigilante action. During the turbulent 1960s, it seems

---

54. Graham Allison, *Essence of Decision: Explaining the Cuban Missile Crisis* (Boston: Little, Brown, 1971).

clear that significant portions of the total population supported various forms of establishment violence. Therefore, one can conclude that major segments of the American population support the status quo that violence was designed to protect. In the South African context, such conclusions would not be valid. It is the white community that provides most support for the vigilante excesses of the past decade. It is reasonable to assume that the three-quarters of the population at whom the violence is directed is less enthusiastic about it. Indeed, the seeming quiescence of African revolutionary activity within the borders of the Republic is probably due to the perception that African, revolutionary-sponsored violence will be inundated by European establishment violence and counterviolence. Further research may thus well uncover evidence that an individual's support for vigilante action is in direct proportion to his support for the existing status quo. Such evidence would be particularly useful in determining the leadership of any vigilante group.

Chapter Ten

Black Vigilantism in Cultural Transition: Violence and Viability in Tropical Africa

Ali A. Mazrui

What is vigilantism? In the majority of instances, vigilantism is indeed "establishment violence."

> It consists of acts or threats of coercion in violation of the formal boundaries of an established sociopolitical order which, however, are intended by the violators to defend that order from some form of subversion. . . . When individuals or groups identifying with the established order defend that order by resorting to means that violate these formal boundaries, they can be usefully classified as vigilantes.[1]

This definition presumes that there are indeed formal boundaries of an established social and political order and that there are recognizable procedures and values determining the limits of legitmate coercion. Unfortunately, this is not altogether true in most African countries which are experiencing cultural schizophrenia. The universe of values is conditioned both by the cultural dualism between Africa and the West and by the cultural pluralism implicit in the newly created multiethnic nations. We refer to the intrusion of Western values in African cultures as the phenomenon of exogenous dualism and to the multiplicity of cultures within each African country as the phenomenon of indigenous pluralism.

But this chapter is concerned not only with violence and values, but also with the problems of creating cultural viability in these countries. Most studies of new nations that have paid any attention to the concept of viability have emphasized preconditions for economic viability. Such studies have questioned whether the economic resources of a given country are adequate for it to be an active and creditworthy member of the international economic system without budgetary subsidies from the outside world. A country's

---

1. H. Jon Rosenbaum and Peter C. Sederberg, "Vigilantism: An Analysis of Establishment Violence."

capacity to meet the minimum economic needs of its people and the minimal social services of the twentieth century have been the ultimate criteria of viability in this sense.

This chapter approaches the question of cultural viability less from the point of view of production and more from the point of view of normative integration. A country becomes a genuine political community only when the rules by which it is governed become internalized in the universe of values of the majority of its people. In the abstract, all human societies put some limitations on the exercise of violence. It could even be argued that all human societies regard the act of killing without good cause as immoral. However, the definition of what constitutes "good cause" contains an enormous range of variation. Groups that seek to become one political community should learn to narrow that range and incidence of legitimate homicide, if they are to avoid the constant dangers of communal rioting or at least communal tensions.

Most countries and societies permit the killing of an "enemy" under certain circumstances. How much of an enemy to the Lugbara is an Acholi in Uganda? How much of an enemy to the Kakwa is a Muganda? Under what conditions would it be fair for an Acholi to kill a Lugbara, or a Muganda to maim a Kakwa? In Africa many different societies have arbitrarily been enclosed by the colonial experience into new national entities without adequate preparation for discerning the subtle but fundamental difference between a compatriot and a hostile alien. Much of the violence which has taken place in countries like Burundi, Rwanda, Nigeria, Uganda, and the Sudan has been intimately linked to the tensions of indigenous cultural pluralism along with the fragile distinction between fellow citizen and alien foe.

The difficulties arising from exogenous dualism and indigenous pluralism are further complicated by the different sources of authority. From the point of view of vigilantism and its manifestations in contemporary Africa, the authority of the Seen (temporal) should be distinguished from the authority of the Unseen (spiritual). The authority of the Seen includes the modern institutions of government, the new schools and teachers operating in those schools, the judges and magistrates in modern courts, the policemen in uniform, and the chief in the village drawing a salary from the government rather than deriving legitimacy from dead ancestors.

The authority of the Unseen includes the dead kinsmen of the tribe, the traditions hallowed by age, the mysterious forces of the night, the commanding power of the elements, and the living vitality of the trees, the rocks, and the rivers. The authority of the Unseen constitutes the African concept of the ultimate. It has a good deal to do with Africa concepts of social causation, of the origins of good and bad fortune, and of the sources of failure and success.

When vigilantes "take the law into their own hands" and beat a thief to death in an African village, the vigilantes are enforcing the authority of the

Seen. On the other hand, when vigilantes beat up a man to death in Nigeria or Zambia on the charge that he is capable of making other men sexually impotent through his magic, clearly the vigilantes are enforcing the authority of the Unseen against those who use the power of the ultimate in pursuit of evil and injustice.

Colonialism, while it lasted, sought to transform the authority of the Seen in African societies by forging new institutions and enacting new laws. Christianity, on the other hand, addressed itself to the task of destroying the old authority of the Unseen in traditionalist Africa and replacing it with the alternative authority of a triune Unseen.

On the destructive side, colonialism has been more successful than Christianity. Indigenous institutions of government in Africa have been more decisively destroyed than indigenous belief systems. Parliaments and party buildings in African capitals are monuments to the destruction of an old system of social and political control, rather than genuine symbols of a viable, new alternative order. Modern African government is struggling to find coherence within an institutional void.

Christianity and secular Western belief systems, on the other hand, have far from destroyed older perspectives. The invocation of the spirits, special rites for the dead and the unborn, special bonds of kinship and the fear of violating these bonds, theories of causation based on spiritual factors, and systems of punishment and reward partly based on transcendental convictions have all survived the massive normative challenge posed by missionaries, transistor radios, Western educational systems, and the demonstration effect of the outer world.

Therefore, while the modern institutions of government in African countries are basically a facade to disguise what is fundamentally still a political vacuum, Christianity and the secular belief systems imported from the West are a facade to disguise some resilient cultural continuities. Old institutional structures have been well and truly destroyed in much of Africa, but old normative patterns have managed to change without dying.

Any discussion of establishment violence in defense of a social order must in African conditions make a clear distinction between the fragile imported values operating within a relative political vacuum and the indigenous traditional values still exercising profound influence on African behavior. Let us now explore these different levels more fully.

POLITICAL VIGILANTISM AND THE NEW CIVILIAN AUTHORITY

Although the effect of colonialism has been to destroy almost totally all the major institutions of government of pre-Colonial Africa, the intentions of colonialism were not always so negative. On the contrary, the whole doctrine of British indirect rule presumed that "native institutions" could be saved under gradual modernization and made to serve, first, the purposes of the colonial power and, at least secondarily, the needs of the colonized peoples. Indirect rule was clearly an economical way of ruling millions of people in different parts of the world, and this was one of its chief attractions to the British. In addition, the British political culture has shown a high responsiveness to and respect for tradition, an inclination to accept cultural relativism as a fact of life in the world as a whole. In the words of the Anglo-Irish philosopher Edmund Burke:

> Neither entirely nor at once depart from antiquity. . . . People will never look forward to posterity who never look backward to their ancestors.[2]

British indirect rule, however, was more concerned with preserving traditional institutions than preserving traditional values. The Kabakaship of Buganda, for example, was more important than the specific marriage customs of the Baganda. Yet the institutions Britain wished to see preserved were destroyed more effectively than some of the customs to which the British were fairly indifferent. The universe of indigenous organizational forms fell under the weight of modern political parties, Western judicial systems, new military technology, and the growth of presidential power. On the other hand, in spite of the British indifference or hostility while colonialism still held sway, the patterns of family life, kinship solidarity, and belief in supernatural forces have all demonstrated resilience.

Even in northern Nigeria, where British indirect rule was most successful and where the "native institutions" of the emirates survived so convincingly into independence, the future of those institutions has been increasingly in doubt since the political reorganizations initiated in 1966. There has been no doubt about the future of the local customs and belief systems, which again have demonstrated a resilience beyond all expectations.

One major consequence of institutional fluidity in tropical Africa is the imminence of violence. The values intended to govern the newly imported political institutions have in most cases not been adequately internalized. The scramble for power and the competition for resources were therefore bound to deteriorate often into dangerous confrontations. Vigilantism becomes a tempting recourse for the regime, or the political party in power, or the supporters of the regime or party.

Vigilantism by youth-wingers of the ruling party has been a feature of politics in many African countries, at least until the military captured power. Young political enthusiasts often resorted to different methods of intimidation in order to harass members of opposing parties or other recalcitrant groups. The Young Pioneers in Nkrumah's Ghana were both a vanguard of party mobilization and a potential instrument of political

---

2. See Edmund Burke, *Reflections on the Revolution in France,* T.H.D. Mahoney, ed., (New York: Liberal Arts Press, 1955).

Ali A. Mazrui

vigilantism. Recalcitrant institutions, ranging from the University of Ghana to the rumps of former opposition parties, were at times harassed by the Young Pioneers.

Youth-wingers in both Malawi and Zambia have been known to terrorize those who were less than politically faithful. When Simon Kapwepwe, once a close friend and colleague of President Kaunda of Zambia, decided to break from the ruling party and form a party of his own, he and many of his supporters were humiliated and at times intimidated by the youth-wingers of the ruling party. Moreover, the government used other methods of pressure and coercion as well. Supporters of President Hastings Banda of Malawi have also used a wide range of violence against recalcitrants, ranging from burning their farms and houses to casting spells of doom on them and their families.

In the first few years of Uganda's independence the youth-wingers of the Uganda People's Congress were often active on different fronts. Juvenile political vigilantism became to some extent a resource which different members of the ruling party sought to control and manipulate. Certainly the competition for the position of secretary general of the Uganda People's Congress in 1964 was affected by the issue of who controlled the youth-wingers and whether he could be trusted as a result. John Kakonge lost the secretary generalship to Grace Ibingira in spite of the support which Kakonge had among the youth of the party. It might even be argued that to some extent Kakonge lost the position because of the youthful enthusiasm behind him. The previous twelve months had revealed both the strengths and hazards of juvenile political enthusiasm. Asian traders had been intimidated for not hanging photographs of the new rulers of Uganda in their shops, and clashes between youth-wingers of different parties had caused concern. A European editor of one of the Uganda daily newspapers had even been kidnapped by youth-wingers to protest a racialistic cocktail party which other Europeans had been accused of holding to lament the demise of the empire.

In both Zanzibar and mainland Tanzania juvenile vigilantism has adopted the cause of "decency in dress." In October 1968 some girls wearing miniskirts in Dar es Salaam were manhandled by members of the Tanzania African National Union (TANU) Youth League. Riot police had to be called in to handle the youths. A resolution (entitled "Operation Vijana") had been proposed to ban miniskirts, wigs, and tight trousers from Tanzania with effect from January 1969, but younger members of the ruling party thought January too far away and embarked on measures to speed up the change.

The Afro-Shirazi Youth League in Zanzibar soon endorsed the move by their sister organization on the mainland. In a resolution marking the close of a three-day seminar, the Afro-Shirazi League pledged that it would work resolutely to eliminate such remnants of foreign culture in their country. Behind these resolutions was the memory of the Kariokoo market place, Dar es Salaam a few days earlier when youth gangs "arrested" girls wearing miniskirts and tight dresses and humiliated them, until riot police carrying guns and tear gas dispersed the huge crowds.

In a way, the excessive enthusiasm of the young militants helped to promote greater toleration in Tanzania toward those who fell below these rigorous standards of "decency." Although the Tanzanian Government itself was at times prepared to be indulgent, women in Dar es Salaam and Zanzibar soon learned to recognize the risk of juvenile vigilantism regardless of the regime's toleration. Many TANU youth-wingers saw the attack on mini-skirts as a partial attack on the cultural guise of capitalism. A combination of socialist radicalism and nationalist militancy increased their potential youthful action in pursuit of decency in attire. Juvenile vigilantism against wearers of miniskirts has also occurred in other African countries, including Malawi, Uganda, and Ethiopia.

As for vigilante action by African governments themselves, this was at times given the paradoxical guise of legality. The idea of a preventive detention act was a great invention for circumventing the legal process. On the one hand, the preventive detention act was a measure passed into law by a national assembly, and therefore it had the guise of constitutional legitimacy. On the other hand, every preventive detention act was a method of enabling an African government to resort to extraconstitutional pressures in defense of its own political order. A preventive detention act released the regime from the constraints of normal procedure so that the jails and even the police could be used for disguised political vigilantism.

Kwame Nkrumah of Ghana was for some time a symbol of the new political order in post-colonial Africa. He was also the first to use official instruments of law enforcement for purposes of disguised political vigilantism. The preventive detention act which Nkrumah passed in Ghana was widely imitated in different parts of Africa.

When Julius K. Nyerere used it in Tanzania, he at least was profoundly sensitive to the moral paradoxes involved in such legislation. Nyerere could see that the preventive detention act was a method of using the law to circumvent the law. Many innocent people could be locked behind bars, sometimes for years, on the suspicion that they were out to subvert the political system. How rigorous a distinction would actually be made between legitmate political dissent and unlawful political subversion? If subversion was indeed being attempted, why not use the ordinary courts of law?

And yet Nyerere argued that at certain times the risks for a society were too great to allow full legal rights for individuals. There might be a real plot to subvert a political system without adequate evidence recognizable in a court of law. The reality of the potential danger was not necessarily negated by a lack of legal evidence. On the contrary, the very efficiency of the plotters in eliminating the possibilities of legal evidence might constitute the most telling aspect of the danger facing the nation. With clear reluctance and moral unease, Julius Nyerere followed the path made by other African leaders—and proceeded to use the law for circumventing the law. Because African countries hovered constantly on the brink of political vacuum and seemed still far from adequate cultural viability, recourse to extraconstitutional methods of countersubversion seemed inevitable to many leaders and their supporters.

Preventive detention was much more efficient as a method of controlling individuals than as a system of disciplining whole groups of people. Nations which are not yet culturally viable might at times require rigorous group control. Certainly in situations where particular communities are obstinately separatist, constantly preparing for the great day of secession, a preventive detention act is not enough. The act may succeed in putting individual leaders of that community behind bars. If every detainee must be handled individually, however, these methods of political control become unwieldy.

Under these circumstances, there is a temptation to declare a "state of emergency," especially if the community is geographically concentrated, and the state of emergency can be declared selectively and confined to that area. Milton Obote of Uganda maintained a state of emergency in Buganda from 1966, when the Baganda attempted a rebellion against the central government, until 1971, when his government was overthrown in a military coup. A state of emergency makes feasible a wide range of actions akin to political vigilantism. It becomes a legal umbrella for many extra-constitutional acts of intimidation and violence. Indeed, many individual Baganda leaders were arrested, not under the preventive detention act, although that was already on the books, but under the powers of the state of emergency.

The determination to give such an umbrella of political carte blanche the guise of careful constitutionality was carried to the extent of requiring that the state of emergency be solemnly renewed by Parliament every six months. Obote's government followed this procedure meticulously, going before Parliament at the prescribed time to ask for a renewal of these special powers against the Baganda. Since Obote had at the same time been emasculating Parliament and reducing it to a legislative cipher, the renewal of those powers every six months was automatic. The umbrella of political vigilantism received a new leease of operation with monotonous regularity. Until their attempted rebellion, the vigorous cultural identity of the Baganda had been a central aspect of Uganda's difficulties in pursuing cultural viability. A deep cleavage had persisted between the Baganda on one side, and the rest of the cultural groups on the other. There were indeed subcleavages among the other groups themselves, which later became even more bloody than anything experienced between Baganda and non-Baganda in the twentieth century. Nevertheless, for much of the period under Obote, the Buganda question looked as if it would remain a central problem in the nation's struggle for political and cultural viability. The state of emergency permitted Obote's government the flexibility to invoke different forms of political vigilantism as a method of bringing the Baganda to heel.

The most important state of emergency in Kenya's history has been the one which accompanied the Mau Mau insurrection, which lasted for nearly a decade. The British and the settler regime in power in colonial Kenya, like others, used the law to circumvent the law. The state of emergency was a carte blanche for a wide range of vigilante activities, primarily against the Kikuyu, Embu, and Meru.

Since independence, a ministate of emergency was declared by President Kenyatta's government in October 1969, following violent anti-regime demonstrations among the Luo in Kisumu during the presidential visit. The president's bodyguard, perhaps a little trigger-happy in a tense situation, opened fire, killing a number of people and wounding many others. Not long afterward, the government moved decisively against its political opponents. The opposition party, the Kenya People's Union (KPU), was banned. Its leaders, including Mr. Oginga Odinga, were arrested and detained. Kenya moved towards a de facto, one-party system once again. The very fact that the opposition party, in spite of aspirations to become nation-wide, had deteriorated into a primarily Luo party was itself another illustration of the strong tendency of politics in Africa to degenerate into ethno-cultural confrontations. The issue of national viability was once again at stake.

Since then, the KPU leaders in Kenya have been released, and Oginga Odinga has rejoined the Kenya African National Union (KANU). No law has yet been passed in Kenya against the formation of rival political parties. Yet President Kenyatta has been known virtually to encourage vigilante action against those who might be plotting to form new parties. In a speech given on Madaraka Day, to mark the attainment of internal self-government, Mzee Kenyatta drew attention to reports he had received about a new party to be formed in time to compete for elections in 1974. Instead of declaring the introduction of a new law to ban the formation of rival parties, Kenyatta strongly implied that extralegal actions would be brought to bear on those who wanted to form such parties. The sanctions against them sounded strong enough to warrant the term of vigilante action. When Mzee Kenyatta talked about creating rival organizations to KANU, the President was publicly legitimizing vigilante action.

POLITICAL VIGILANTISM UNDER MILITARY RULE

The syndrome of the political vacuum and the lack of cultural viability affect not only relations between political parties, or between political leaders, but also relations between soldiers and civilians. The politicization of the armed forces in independent Africa is one major consequence of that situation.

The increasing use of coercion by politicians soon after independence was the beginning of the militarization of African politics. One president after another, either under the guise of a preventive detention act or the more encompassing state of emergency, began to use the threat of force as a method of suppressing dissent. Authoritarianism was legitimized as a quest for discipline, and the very concept of discipline helped to militarize African political systems. In some African countries the armed forces were openly used to intimidate political opponents. In other cases the armed forces were more subtly cultivated for the same ultimate ends.

As this process got under way, political vigilantism also grew. A qualitative change did nevertheless take place in many African countries when the soldiers took over power. Vigilante action to support a civilian regime emerged as qualitatively different from vigilante action to maintain military rule. The domain of private initiative by soldiers once they were effectively in power was in most cases much wider than anything ever before attempted by African politicians.

The image of soldiers as men of "action," as well as the myth of discipline as a necessary ingredient in military behavior, tended to encourage the circumvention of formal procedures and the direct implementation of decisions swiftly arrived at. The actual governmental institutions have not taken such decisions to circumvent procedures. Individual soldiers, almost at any time and place, could convert themselves into units of vigilante action. In many African countries a single soldier equipped with a gun has often acted on his own initiative, in order to enforce some presumed value of the new military regime. This is quite apart from action involving violence or the threat of violence taken privately in pursuit of personal interest.

In Africa the tendency of military regimes to expand the arena of vigilantism has been reinforced by the equally strong tendency for crime to increase following the first military coup. African governments are fragile and deficient in legitimacy at the best of times. The problem is compounded when soldiers overthrow the first civilian government. The restraints in the society as a whole suffer new pressures under the demonstration of a government overthrown. Criminal elements in the society receive a new boost of optimism and self-confidence, and, at least for a while, they become even more daring in their acquisitive adventures.

In 1964 there was not even a full-blooded military coup in Tanganyika to set the criminal element loose into the streets of Dar es Salaam in broad daylight. The soldiers, in what later became mainland Tanzania, staged a mutiny rather than a coup, and demanded better pay and better working conditions rather than political power. In the shadow of the mutiny, President Julius Nyerere went into hiding, and for a short while it was not clear who was in command in the country. The very challenge of the armed forces became a trumpet of encouragement to other lawbreakers. In a matter of hours shops were looted, major streets became vulnerable to highwaymen, and a new wave of insecurity pervaded the community. A number of people were killed and many more wounded. The soldiers' challenge to established authority which caused this sudden rise of criminal activity in Dar es Salaam soon also led to vigilantism by the soldiers to control the lawlessness and to restore order independently of the civilian government.

It was not until January 25, 1971 that East Africa had its first military coup. This was Amin's coup in Uganda. When Amin's army took over, *kondoism,* or robbery with violence, had already reached high proportions in Uganda. In desperation, Obote's government had even made robbery with violence a capital offense— to the consternation of those who feared that it would only increase murder as a way of eliminating all witnesses to a robbery.

Following the coup, in the wake of instability and uncertainty about the survival of legitimate authority, *kondoism* rose even more sharply. There was also some suspicion that members of the Intelligence Department of the Obote regime, stripped of power and disgraced following the coup, used the firearms they had acquired earlier for new purposes. Old informers became new *kondos* as they took to gangsterism and armed thuggery.

Even more significant from the point of view of this chapter is the manner in which the military regime then sought to reclaim a monopoly of the legitimate use of physical force. On March 18, 1971, the government issued two decrees giving powers to the armed forces to search houses and other buildings, vehicles, and aircraft and to take possession of vehicles, stolen property, and dangerous weapons. The campaign was designed, in the words of the attorney general, to "stamp out the scourge of *kondoism."* The Armed Forces (Powers of Arrest) Decree gave members of the armed forces and prison officers power to arrest people for an offense against public order, or an offense against other individuals, or an offense relating to property.

> In simple terms the offences listed are the sort of offences committed by *kondos.* For example, armed robbery and armed attack on defenceless members of the community. Members of the armed forces and prison officers are given power to search houses and other buildings and motor cars and aircraft if they have reason to believe that a person who is to be arrested is in any of those places or anything stolen may be found in such places. They may also take possession of vehicles, stolen property and dangerous weapons. . . .[3]

This decree merely put into official form a trend toward vigilantism by the armed forces which was already underway. Soldiers were already serving as self-appointed policemen in certain areas of Kampala, often performing needed jobs of law enforcement. Burglaries in the city had been increasing and

3. Statement by the Attorney General, *Uganda Argus* (Kampala), March 19, 1971. These powers were extended indefinitely by a new decree issued in October 1972. In a related context I have discussed the Uganda Army's attempt to deal with *kondoism* in "The Lumpen Proletariat and the Lumpen Militariat: African Soldiers as a New Political Class," *Political Studies* 21 (March 1973): 2-3.

thieves were now working in larger and better organized groups. For a while the armed forces played a much needed interventionist role against a background of rapid social disintegration.

The events in Uganda, as in Tanzania in 1964, illustrate how a military challenge to civilian authority could at first let loose further disintegrative tendencies, resulting in increased crime, and how this in turn would compel the military to extend the boundaries of vigilantism by individual soldiers wherever they might be in the country.

In Uganda's experience the vigilantism by the soldiers later took more ominous political forms. To be publicly denounced by General Amin was to be exposed to acts of vigilante elimination by those who took the General's denunciation as a cue for action. It was as if every time the general publicly criticized an individual, he was interpreted to mean: "Will somebody rid me of this man?" The murder of an English archbishop (Becket) in a cathedral, following a similar instigation by an English king, has symbolically hovered over many Ugandans in the shadow of similarly fatal vigilante action in their own society.

Many Ugandans have "disappeared" as a result of such action. Officially, the government denies all knowledge of the whereabouts of such persons. Some have later been found floating in the waters of the Nile; others are reported as murdered in the notorious Makindye prison. Vigilante action is sometimes taken directly by the government, while it publicly denies all knowledge of such action. The results of the military coup in Uganda include this staggering expansion of political vigilantism. At some stage the distinction between political vigilantism and political anarchy becames thin indeed. Which values are being protected by the vigilante action and which values are being destroyed are central questions in the grand dialectic between vigilantism and anarchy in Uganda. Is Uganda culturally and politically viable any more? Once again violence, values, and viability interact in a tense historical process.

In such a situation a second coup is always in the cards. Such a second coup would itself become a vigilante move to control the excess of prior vigilantism.

In Africa as a whole, since independence, the first military coup has tended to be basically redistributive, accompanied by rhetoric legitimizing regime-control. The rise of soldiers to ultimate positions of power might not necessarily lead to a redistribution of economic resources, but it certainly is a redistribution of political power. The better educated civilian rulers in Africa, urbanized and substantially Westernized, begin to decline politically, giving way to less literate warriors. The first coup in Africa south of the Sahara is therefore always a moment of political redistribution, not necessarily followed by economic redistribution.

The first coup in Arab Africa, on the other hand, has often resulted in the redistribution of both political power and economic resources. The Nasser revolution in Egypt, the Qaddafy takeover in Libya, as well as the Algerian revolution, are all cases in point.

The Aboud coup in the Sudan in 1958 was barely redistributive, even politically. The Sudan had to wait until the Numeiry coup more than a decade later, separated by a period of civilian government, before political and economic redistribution could be undertaken by the soldiers.

In non-Arab Africa the second coup has been either ethnically redistributive or a case of vigilante action aimed at controlling the military regime itself. The second coup in Nigeria in 1966 was ethnically redistributive. Ultimate power was seized from the Ibo and put in other ethnic hands. The smaller communities of the north entered the stream of political power as a result of the second coup.

By the 1970s, following the end of the civil war, the question arose whether the soldiers would return to the barracks in 1976 and help to restore full civilian supremacy. On behalf of the military, General Gowan, the Head of State, had indeed promised such a return, subject to the completion of certain jobs by the military regime and to the emergence of viable political parties in the meantime.

Many in Nigeria believe that Gowan himself was sincere in that promise, but that any attempt of his to fulfill that promise would run a serious risk of a third coup to prevent it. Not all the soldiers were enthusiastic about relinquishing political power and permitting the country to be once again ruled by politicians. Would the opponents of civilian restoration go to the extent of threatening a third military coup in Nigeria? Would the threat force Gowan to postpone civilian restoration? Or would the threat actually result in Gowan's overthrow?

On balance, there is indeed a clear possibility that some sections of the armed forces will take vigilante action to control Gowan's regime and prevent a fundamental change in the political arrangements of the country. The threat of a military coup might once again be invoked as a mechanism for regime-control in Africa.

VIGILANTISM AND THE AUTHORITY OF THE UNSEEN

Just as the threat of a military coup might force the military government to remain united in defence of its own established order, so other threats in other circumstances could force an ethnic community to remain united in defense of its own privileged position. Vigilantism directed toward social-group-control need not always deal with groups which are challenging the privileged community. Vigilante action is sometimes designed to increase the solidarity of the dominant group, rather than disrupt or penalize the competitors. In Kenya in 1969, there was some vigilante action by the Kikuyu against the Luo, as well as by the Luo against the Kikuyu. The latter was a challenge by outsiders against the incumbents in power; whereas the Kikuyu initiatives against the Luo were moves by the establishment to control a competitive group. A third type of action concerns us in this part of the essay. This was vigilante action by the Kikuyu against the Kikuyu as a method of enhancing Kikuyu solidarity.

Tom Mboya was the Minister for Economic Planning and Development, Secretary General of KANU, and the leading Luo in the government. Partly because of Mboya's assassination by a Kikuyu in July 1969, and partly because of the eruption of violence in the heart of Luo land in October of that year, the Kikuyu establishment began to sense the possibility of an ethnic confrontation with the Luo. President Kenyatta's car was stoned when he attended the services in honor of the assassinated Luo minister. And when the president's bodyguard opened fire on Luo demonstrators in Kisumu, the possibility of a violent eruption between the Kikuyu and the Luo became serious.

Against this background, the Kikuyu invoked the authority of the Unseen in a bid to consolidate Kikuyu cohesion. Oath-taking in Kikuyuland broke out, and each Kikuyu who took the oath swore absolute loyalty to the principle of keeping the House of Mumbi in power. The oath-taking was, for many in Kenya, reminiscent of the old Mau Mau days. In that struggle to recover tribal lands and rights from the European intruders, many Kikuyu undertook to fight and kill, on pain of their own destruction by the forces of Unseen authority.

In order to give the authority of the Unseen extra persuasive power, oath-taking among the Kikuyu in times of a crisis of this kind has used a number of awe-inspiring devices and rituals. They range from standing naked with one's penis placed against the thorax of a goat to the sacred utilization of menstrual blood for maternal symbolism. A whole atmosphere of ominous unseen powers was thus created to render the oath-taking more compelling, and the threat of sanctions more believable.

We know far more about the nature of oath-taking among the Kikuyu during the Mau Mau emergency than we know about the oath-taking in 1969. This is because the government of Kenya under Mzee Kenyatta naturally wanted to minimize publicity and discussion about events in the heart of Kikuyuland. What is clear is that oath-taking in such circumstances constitutes the invocation of the powers of the Unseen, utilizing ritual awe to strengthen allegiance.

This chapter mentions earlier that Christianity had less success in destroying older belief systems than colonialism had in destroying older political institutions. Christianity has, nevertheless, profoundly influenced important segments of African societies. Among the Kikuyu the tension between ancestral belief systems and the new norms of the Christian religion has escalated in times of peril. Certainly the period of the Mau Mau insurrection was one of acute discomfort for Kikuyu Christians in the shadow of the eruption of older beliefs and values. Many Kikuyu Christians had no difficulty combining some elements of Christian sensibilities with some elements of Kikuyu ancestral norms; but other Kikuyu Christians were profoundly disturbed.

The 1969 oath-taking in Kenya, again increased the tensions between Kikuyu Christianity and Kikuyu ancestral culture. Some Christian Kikuyu leaders spoke up against oath-taking and suffered painful ethnic ostracism as a result.

Both in 1969 and during the Mau Mau emergency it was clear that, in the ultimate analysis, ancestral beliefs would triumph against Christian sensibilities in times of ethnic peril.

Militant Kikuyu vigilantes often demanded the oath-taking by force. Men were captured and taken forcibly to the ceremonies of loyalty. They relied for full compliance on the new initiate's fear of the authority of the Unseen once he had been released. This was indeed political vigilantism, but with a difference. In this case the authority of the Seen, in the form of President Kenyatta's government, was strengthened by its followers through the invocation of the authority of the Unseen. Supernatural forces were being politicized.

This was also an instance in which social-group-control was exercised within the privileged group itself, rather than against its competitors. In this we have the phenomenon of collective autocontrol by the Kikuyu.

Meanwhile, a cultural organization was being created known as GEMA—the Gikuyu, Embu, and Meru Association. In the cities, and especially in Nairobi, this organization was normally social and cultural, rather than political. It helped individuals who had just arrived in the city, organized parties for the group, provided an umbrella for wedding festivities, and occasions for communal dialogue. By 1973 and 1974 knowledgable circles in Nairobi were suggesting that GEMA was also a potential vigilante group should Kikuyu leadership be seriously endangered nationally. This cultural group could then become rapidly politicized and used either to control Kikuyu competitors or, more likely, to enforce solidarity among the Kikuyu, Embu, and Meru related tribes. Rumors in Nairobi were widespread that GEMA had already started to be used for soft vigilante purposes, sometimes to intimidate potential opponents of Kikuyu leadership, and at other times once again to consolidate the principle of loyalty to that leadership among these three related ethnic communities.

Whatever the truth concerning GEMA, whatever the answer to the question of whether it is a cultural organization with considerable vigilante potential, it is a fact that Kikuyu culture has in the past been mobilized to support political ends. Ancestral values have been politicized in defense of ethnic interests for many years from the old debates about female circumcision in the 1920s to oath-taking in 1969.

THE CURSE ON WHEELS

Across the border in Uganda another type of vigilantism, partly linked to a belief in the powers of the Unseen, continues to hold sway in the streets. Unlike the potential role of GEMA, the roadside vigilantism of Uganda is spontaneous, not organized. It concerns the response of Ugandans to road accidents. It is a widely understood dictum of discretion that if a driver knocks down a person on the road in Uganda, he does not stop. He drives on to the nearest police station and reports the accident. But what if the person hit needs the kind of attention which could be facilitated by immediate transportation by the driver to the nearest hospital? What if he should be bleeding so seriously that he may bleed to death?

The imperative of social discretion in Uganda still remains that the driver who knocks down a pedestrian should proceed to the nearest police station and not attempt to take the injured person to the nearest hospital. The advice that the driver should proceed to the nearest police station comes from the police themselves.

What universe of perception lies behind the response of villagers who, on witnessing a car hitting a pedestrian, attempt to drag out the driver and beat him, sometimes to death? Why do they make no attempt to assess whether it was not the pedestrian's fault? Even if confronted with the evidence that the pedestrian was drunk and pushed himself in front of the car in a manner which left the driver no chance, the rural people would still descend upon the man in the driver's seat and wreak vengeance.

The explanation may have three different levels. It may have a class dimension, signifying a basic antipathy between the world of the poor pedestrians and the world of the affluent motorists. The second level of explanation may concern African concepts of accident and the problems arising therefrom. The third level of explanation concerns the issue of statehood, and even of national identity, when the driver who is being threatened or brutalized by villagers comes from an area of the country different from that of the villagers. This last aspect sometimes equates an automobile with a lethal weapon—and the crowd's vengeance becomes virtually the equivalent of a military response.

The class dimension may be there in a somewhat vague and unconsolidated fashion. There may be a suspicion that those who sit behind wheels acquire the deadly arrogance of mobility and pay inadequate respect to the rights of those who have to walk the earth for the necessities of life. The reaction of the ordinary people to an accident may not be conscious resentment of the affluent motorist and his seeming carelessness toward those who do not own cars. The prejudices may be almost instinctive against these symbols of affluence when they inflict harm on the less fortunate. More often than not, the enraged crowd does not stop to ask whether the victim of the accident might not himself be affluent, or whether the driver of the car might not be an employee who is even poorer than the man he has knocked down. It is not precise facts about the individuals concerned that animate the excited crowd. It is the symbol of mobile power incapacitating a piece of human ordinariness walking on its two legs.

The second level of explanation concerns African concepts of chance and responsibility. This again touches the concept of the Unseen. Can it ever be an accident when a car knocks down a man? The question of moral responsibility for one's acts in the African universe of ideas may be intimately related to the behavior of the crowd on Entebbe Road in Uganda when it descends upon an erring motorist. Was the motorist simply an instrument of evil perpetrating injury or death on some other person? In Christianity, problems of individual responsibility arise when issues of free will and its limits are discussed. In certain schools of Protestantism the issue of predestination, implying a negation of chance in human action, has recurrently posed questions about the limits of human accountability.

The omniscience of God is sometimes interpreted in a way which precludes individual free will. If God, even before He created the driver, knew that the driver would kill a man on Kampala Road on such and such a date in such and such a century and yet nevertheless put life into that being who was destined to kill on Kampala Road, did not God's foreknowledge in the act of creation help to determine that accident in advance?

If all human evil is part of a grand design, are the evils of this world not to be punished? Should those who cause death, suffering, and injuries be allowed their freedom simply because they are instruments of bigger forces? Or should they nevertheless be punished as part of the same grand design?[4]

African ideas of chance and moral responsibility are, of course, sharply different from more familiar theological tangles within Christianity, though there are areas of overlap. In African belief-systems not all enemies are human and worldly. On occasion a society has had to declare war on invisible regiments and supernatural foes.

Mysterious forces causing death and injury are multiple in their origins within African belief-systems, but the very complexity of the causes of evil and injury has tended to create a profound ambivalence about the concept of accident and chance. If the driver was an instrument of evil forces should he be

4. This section of the paper concerning roadside vigilantism has borrowed heavily from the author's previous paper "Civic Violence and Political Violence in Uganda and the United States," presented at the Seventh World Congress of the International Sociological Association, held in Varna, Bulgaria in September 1970.

punished nevertheless? Is the driver an agent of an invisible supernatural army?

At times, issues of class differentiation overlap with issues of mysterious forces at work behind an accident. Interviews carried out in East Mengo in July 1970 revealed a persistent suspicion that cars which caused accidents are under a curse. But who cursed the car? A particular car could have been cursed by the man farther back on the roadside who tried to stop it for a lift and was ignored by the driver. Stopping cars for rides is a widespread custom in Uganda—perhaps more so than in some other African countries because many taxis are indistinguishable from private cars. The authorities have made little attempt to control private taxis, and many a rural traveler stands by the roadside signalling almost every oncoming car in the hope that it will either give him a lift free of charge or charge him the accepted taxi rate. The interviews conducted in East Mengo in Buganda revealed a feeling of resentment about cars which do not stop even to explain why they cannot give a lift. The reaction of the wouldbe passenger who is ignored by the roadside is at times to curse the car and the driver.[5]

When people therefore see a car involved in an accident, they sometimes conclude that the driver has been cursed for the discourtesy of leaving needy passengers by the roadside. The driver becomes suspect, a man over whom hangs a curse of the Unseen, and the sin behind the curse was that of arrogance. Class antagonism and primordial suspicions interact in such instances.

There have been reports of drivers in Uganda who were beaten after a car accident that hurt no one but themselves. These are situations where a car overturns or hits a tree, and the driver still suffers some degree of brutalization from onlookers. Such instances are far fewer than those of collective beatings when a driver has hurt someone else. Nevertheless, the suspicion about a car traveling under a curse, furthered by the belief that the curse was earned by the arrogance of the driver, has often resulted in aggressive predispositions among the rural people towards the motorist.

The class dimension seems to have deeper roots in Uganda than in Kenya. One possible reason is that until relatively recently very few Africans in Kenya owned cars. In the 1950s if one saw an African driving a car in Nakuru, or Nairobi or Mombasa, it was, on the whole, safe to assume that the African was an employed driver rather than the owner of the car. The black man behind the wheel was therefore not a specimen of the haves in arrogant disregard of the have-nots. He was an employee, often no better off financially than the fellow African he might knock down on the road.

The phenomenon of car-owning Africans in Uganda is much older. A fairly affluent middle class existed in Uganda when the bulk of Kenyan Africans were peasants, minimum-wage employees, or squatters on other people's

5. These interviews were conducted on behalf of the author by Baganda informants.

farms. The assumption that the black man behind the driver's wheel might well be the owner of the car has made sense in Uganda for a long time. The class assumptions about arrogance could be vindicated way back in the 1940s and perhaps even earlier. In Kenya, however, the phenomenon of car-owning Africans belongs basically to the late 1950s and 1960s. There are a number of reasons why civic violence of this kind is rarer in Kenya than in Uganda, but the relative newness of affluence in Kenya, as compared with the longer established class differences in Uganda, might be a relevant factor behind the different behavior of rural people in the two countries when accidents occur.

The third level of explanation to account for attitudes in Uganda to automobile accidents is more explicitly political. It arises in situations where the driver is clearly from a different regional or ethnic group than either his victim or the crowd surrounding him, or both. Once again the issue of cultural viability is tested. The accident becomes in some important respects another instance of a declaration of war on the neighborhood. The 'foreigner' has come blundering into a community and has injured or even killed a member of that community. People in such areas sometimes have an understanding that when someone valued has been hurt, it is disloyal to begin by investigating where the blame should go before rising in his defense. If a relative is fighting with a foreigner, it would not make sense to inquire who started the fight. Ultimate manliness as related to loyalty demands an instinctive response on the side of one's own people. Relatives should first fight together to repel the enemy or avenge the harm he has inflicted, before they sit down, in retrospect, to assess the real causes of the conflict.

The same reasoning applies to the situation of a man finding his brother killed on the roadside by a driver. He should not go around asking questions. His first priority should be to inflict punishment on his brother's killer. Questions follow later.

The reason why this type of response is fundamentally political is because it signifies the fragility of national identification and cultural viability. A person from another area or another tribe is considered sufficiently foreign to be exposed to ruthless vengeance. The process of national integration in Uganda must, of necessity, aspire to transform these attitudes. It must seek to rehumanize an erring motorist from another tribe in the eyes of those he has offended.

There is no real equivalent of this kind of vigilantism in countries like the United States. Of course, in contemporary America the car has ceased to be a symbol of affluence and has become what it should always have been—a mode of transportation and convenience. Virtually every family owns at least one car. And farmers by the roadside thumbing rides are to be seen only if their own vehicles have broken down. Moreover, the primordial belief in Unseen supernatural armies, though by no means absent in American history, has not usually taken the form of suspecting the behavior of vehicles. Superstitions about haunted houses, and even curses following the fortunes of a family (like the Kennedy curse), are by no means rare. However, American superstitions, in spite of the tremendous mobility of the country, seldom concern wheels.

The automobile has come to Africa at a period of primordial values. The great gulf between the technology of the automobile and the belief-systems of tribal communities may help to explain the differences between Africa and the Western world with regard to this kind of vigilantism.

But it was not simply cattle and land that were stolen in primordial wars. It was also women. One more challenging difference between Africa and the Western world is the balance of value between the security of property and the sanctity of sex. It is to these dimensions that we must now turn.

ON SEX AND SOCIAL CONTROL

The history of vigilantism in the United States includes a high proportion of action taken with regard to sexual offenses. This is especially true of lynching as a form of white vigilantism against a presumed black threat in the southern states of America.

What sexual lynching in the United States has in common with certain types of vigilante action in black Africa is, quite simply, the fear of impotence. This fear in the two societies takes drastically different forms, however. Formerly in the South of the United States, and today in South Africa, the fear of sexual impotence is closely linked to the fear of political impotence. White men's concern about inadequate sexual performance in comparison with that of black men becomes inseparable from their concern about continuing white political hegemony. It is a clear case of the authority of the Seen defending itself against socio-sexual uncertainties.

The fear of impotence in Africa, on the other hand, is less clearly politicized, though it still often bears some connection with wider issues. Early in 1974 a passenger was getting off a bus in northern Nigeria. Let us call him passenger A. A number of others were alighting at the same time. Suddenly passenger B, who was in front of passenger A, turned around in apparent consternation and accused passenger A of having touched him on the shoulder with a view to rendering him sexually impotent. The situation deteriorated very rapidly, as the rest of the nearby crowd took the side of passenger B and then moved toward fatal vigilante action against A. The accused was beaten to death on the spot.

On a Saturday morning in the spring of 1930, in Leeville, Texas, a black man was accused of having raped the white wife of his white employer. For his own protection, the accused was put in a vault room in a court house. A mob set the courthouse on fire. The Rangers, or police, and everyone else got out, but the black man remained in the vault room while flames raged outside. The mob managed to obtain dynamite and blew a hole into the vault. The white vigilante leader entered. A few minutes later a dead body, black, was thrown out with the shout, "Here he is!"

The crowd went wild with enthusiasm. "Take him to Niggertown, take him to Niggertown!" The body was tied behind a car, and five thousand people, yelling, singing, and howling, made a procession behind the car. Some versions of the story say that a leader of the mob helped himself to a blade, and ceremoniously cut off the male organ of the dead man when the crowd got to "Niggertown." There is no dispute about the cremation itself.

> The crowd gave a mighty cheer as flames enveloped the Negro's body. Little boys pointed to the Negro and made suggestive comments as the trousers burnt off. Men whispered to each other and laughed aloud. The body was still in a semi-crouched position as it dangled from the chain. The heat caused great blisters and welts to rise upon the flesh as it began to burn. The air was filled with the acrid odour of burning meat.[6]

A country officer who knew the case thoroughly expressed the belief that the woman encouraged the black man, and the love-making was interrupted by her five-year-old child. This frightened the mother and made her adopt the rape story.

Quite a number of those whites who believed that the black man was encouraged by the white woman did not necessarily regard the black man as innocent. Encouragement from a white woman established the guilt of the woman; it apparently did not detract from the guilt of the black man. Lynchings have happened in situations where there was clear evidence that the black man was responding to an invitation.

The incident in northern Nigeria and lynchings of the kind just described shared the fear of impotence, differently defined. In the case of the Nigerian incident, an ethnic factor was also present. Passenger A, who was accused of an attempt to render passenger B impotent, belonged to a minority group which was somewhat resented in the north. The severity of the vigilante action was due to two factors: first, a general acceptance by the crowd that to cause impotence was indeed a heinous crime, and second, the crowd's resentment of the community to which the accused belonged. Sexual and political factors in northern Nigeria interacted, just as they had interacted forty years previously in Leeville, Texas when a black man was lynched by an indignant white mob.

The whites in the United States assumed, and behaved on the assumption, that what every black man wanted most was to possess a white woman. Gunnar Myrdal's classic work, *An American Dilemma,* first published in the 1940s, includes what he calls "the rank order of discrimination." Myrdal interviewed white southerners and asked them to list in order of importance

6. See Hadley Cantril, *The Psychology of Social Movements* (New York: Wiley & Sons, 1967 reprint), pp. 94-103.

what they thought black people wanted most. The order which was formulated by white southerners was the following:

1. Intermarriage and sex intercourse with whites.
2. Social equality and etiquette.
3. Desegregation of public facilities, buses, churches, etc.
4. Political enfranchisement.
5. Fair treatment in the law courts.
6. Economic opportunities.

Myrdal then turned to the black people themselves to inquire what their ultimate ambitions were and in what order of priority. Their ambitions were the same as those attributed to them by white southerners, but with one fundamental difference: the black people listed those ambitions in the reverse order of priority.[7]

The long-held assumption by whites that sex was more important to the black man than economics did have some self-fulfilling impact for a while. Large numbers of blacks were at one time profoundly affected by the taboo which surrounded interracial sexuality. But the black man's preoccupation with interracial mating was not the cause of white sexual fears; it was an effect of those fears. Preeminent among those fears was probably the fear of being sexually out-performed by the black man precisely because of the presumption that sex was his most compelling drive.

> The sexualization of racism in the United States is a unique phenomenon in the history of mankind. . . . While the Negro is portrayed as a great "walking phallus" with satyr-like potency, he is denied the execution of that potency, he is denied the most precious sexual image which surrounds him—the white woman. . . . The white man's self-esteem is in a constant state of sexual anxiety in all matters dealing with race relations. So is the Negro's because his life, too, is enmeshed in the absurd system of racial hatred in America.[8]

The fear of impotence in Nigeria has links with the authority of the Unseen. The power of sorcery and the efficacy of a curse were taken for granted in the crowd that beat a man to death beside a bus stop. The ethnic difference between the accused and the accuser lent extra credibility to the charge. Issues of the Seen interacted with the shadow of the Unseen—and a man died. In Leeville, Texas, on the other hand, the issues were more directly concerned with political power in the here and now, as well as sexual power in comparative perspective.

Popular wrath against sorcerers suspected of causing impotence has manifested itself elsewhere in Africa in modern times, from the towns of Nigeria to the villages of Malawi, from the farms of Uganda to the mines of South Africa. The fear of physical impotence is immediate and literal among

---

7. Gunnar Myrdal, *An American Dilemma* (New York and London: Harper and Bros., 1944), pp. 60-61.
8. Calvin C. Hernton, *Sex and Racism in America: An Analysis of the Influence of Sex on the Race Problem* (New York: Doubleday, 1965), p. 7.

many African communities; the fear of sexual deficiency among whites in the southern states of America and South Africa is psychological and often directly political.

Further differences between the attitude of traditionalist black Africans and contemporary whites are linked to further cultural differentiations. Rape, for example, is an offense treated with greater horror among white Americans and white South Africans than among blacks. Except in the case of an attempted causation of impotence, sexual offenses are treated with greater severity in the United States than in most indigenous African communities. On the other hand, the violation of the rights of property is often treated with greater anger in African communities than in the United States. There is surprising evidence the Ugandans tend to be more angry with those who violate the rights of property than do Americans. Vigilante groups in contemporary Uganda treat suspected thieves with fatal ruthlessness.

Interviews conducted in the capital of Kampala confirm findings in many rural communities. Rape seems to arouse less horror than robbery and to result in fewer cases of vigilante activity. Both rape and robbery are regarded as wrong, but the anger aroused by the two forms of deviant behavior, and the extent to which the community as a whole is involved, varies significantly. To steal a bicycle is the equivalent of raiding for cattle, because both involve an attempt to take away the goods *forever*. However, rape is not an attempt to take away a woman forever. There is less finality in rape than in either theft or sexual impotence.

Rape against a minor does cause considerable indignation all over Africa. Even then, however, the punishments, though sometimes severe, are seldom fatal when collectively inflicted. The culprit may be flogged and disgraced, but he is not usually beaten to the brink of death.

A major difference between rape and robbery is the degree to which they are regarded as crimes against the community in an African society. Robbery is clearly interpreted in many Ugandan communities as a declaration of war on society. Rape, on the other hand, is interpreted at worst as a challenge against the husband, or the parents of the woman, or at most her family. The punishment may indeed sometimes result in the death of the rapist, but it is a punishment inflicted by the immediate relatives of his victim. In African situations the fear of rape and the fear of impotence are distinct phenomena, to some extent serving as foils to each other. In white communities in the United States and southern Africa, the rape complex and the fear of impotence are mutually reinforcing anxieties.

In African situations, rape is an illegitimate assertion of manhood, while impotence is a tragic denial. Rape symbolizes the excesses of virility, while impotence by definition is a deficiency in masculinity. Rape violates culture while affirming biology; impotence denies both biological and cultural expectations. By finding her attractive the rapist affirms his victim's womanhood; but by violating her wishes he insults her rights as a person. Impotence, on the other hand, when deliberately inflicted on a man by sorcery or by modern medicine, is both a personal and sexual affront. Rape is an act of the moment, an incident; impotence is a continuing condition, and potentially final. Rape as an act of impregnation has links with procreation and creativity. Impotence, by ending a man's capacity to bear his kind, is more clearly destructive.

Vigilantism, as a relatively spontaneous response to social hazards, is more easily provoked in Africa against threats of potency and fertility than against threats to chastity. Among white people, on the other hand, rape and impotence are intermingled fears. The husband fears the possibility of being out-performed by the rapist of his wife. Because of the more inhibited and distorted sexual mores of white cultures, the man might never again be able to make love properly to his raped wife. The ghost of previous experiences might in its own way interfere with his sexual capacity.

And where racial issues are at play, rape and the fear of political impotence become even more interlocked. The hegemony of white South Africa is partly deemed to depend on separating the races sexually. The Immorality Acts on the statute books of South Africa bear continuing testimony to that profound dialectic between the fear of sexual deficiency and the dread of political decline in racialistic systems.

Finally, there is vigilantism in relation to circumcision in those African societies which uphold that tradition. The pace of urbanization in the modern period has sometimes resulted in creating cultural distance between the newly urbanized and their kinsmen in the villages. Townsmen who come from tribes which circumcise might not bother to arrange the circumcision of their urban-born children. The custom has declined in urban areas among members of at least some of the communities which circumcise. This decline has sometimes resulted in vigilante action by militant traditionalists who force certain members of their own communities to be circumcised even if rather late. In Uganda the Bagisu, especially, have been known over the years to kidnap urban kinsmen from the streets of Kampala or Jinja, tie them up, and forcibly have them circumcised, in some cases at a rather advanced age.

Circumcision among such people is not directly linked to the fear of impotence, although it is often regarded as a method of enhancing masculinity. While impotence is a fall from virility, circumcision is a rise in masculine stature. It is often regarded as symbolizing the grand transition from the sexuality of the adolescent to the sexuality of the adult.

In addition, circumcision is connected to the status of a warrior. In the words of Satish Saberwal in his study of the Embu of Central Kenya:

> A boy's circumcision marked his transition from the culturally disvalued role of a boy (*Kavici*...) to the culturally valued role of a warrior (*Mwanake*...). The warriors held the boys in some contempt, and thanks to their superiority with

weapons as well as their corporate strength, the warriors exacted a measure of deference from the boys. . . . The uncircumcised boy went to the dances but was allowed only to observe, not to dance. He was also prohibited sexual access to *airitu*. . . . In Embu society a *muiritu* (pl. *airitu*) was a clitoridectomised, unmarried woman, free to go to dances and welcome suitors into her mother's kitchen for a night.[9]

In the old days, the privileges enjoyed by the circumcised made it worth every boy's while to undergo the ceremony. But for the newly urbanized in the twentieth century, it was relatively easy to live comfortably and well, especially with women from other communities, without undergoing the ordeal of circumcision. Vigilante action by the more militant traditionalists has therefore emerged in some cases as the only answer to ensure enough loyalty to their ancestral duties.

Curiously enough, the warrior factor is still symbolically present in the minds of the Bagisu when they kidnap uncircumcised kinsmen. Because of the link between circumcision and warriorhood, a refusal to be circumcised is the equivalent of draftdodging, a reluctance to make oneself eligible for full military duties in defense of one's community. In modern conditions, such duties now are purely symbolic, yet the vigilantes hunting for the uncircumcised still see themselves as, to some extent, out to arrest deserters and draftdodgers. The fear of collective political impotence is certainly present. In a country still profoundly unviable in ethnic and cultural terms, the vigilantes attempt to ensure that their tribe has its full component of eligible warriors.

CONCLUSION

Against a background of the authority of the Seen and Unseen, this chapter has illustrated a wide range of vigilante activities in contemporary Africa in the context of institutional fluidity and cultural continuity. The Euro-Christian impact on Africa destroyed African traditional institutions and left a substantial political vacuum. Yet, that impact was much less successful in destroying African belief-systems and normative predispositions. Indigenous conceptions of the ultimate and of the powers of the Unseen have survived the influence of Christian concepts of transcendence. Old religions and new political systems have interacted. Hence, vigilantism in Africa ranges from the fear of opposition parties to the dread of impotence, from the declaration of a state of emergency to the agony of enforced circumcision.

9. Satish Saberwal, *The Traditional Political System of the Embu of Central Kenya,* East African Studies, 35 (Nairobi: E.A.P.H. on behalf of the Makerere Institute of Social Research, 1970), pp. 17-18, and n. 2 on p. 46.

Chapter Eleven

"Pariah" Communities and Violence

Fred R. von der Mehden

Establishment violence has normally been directed either against groups without great political power or against those in open conflict with the regime in control. *Pariah* or *parasite* communities in Afro-Asia have been the targets of violence in both the colonial and post-independence years. Yet, these ethnic minorities have usually dominated the economies of their host countries and have generally taken care to work within the system, at least publicly.[1] This study is an effort to analyze the scope and types of violence related to *pariah* communities and then to concentrate upon factors responsible for conflict. Of particular interest will be the interaction of perceptions and political-economic roles as they reinforce dominant community antagonism. Violence can be engendered by tensions that develop over the actual role of antagonists, but violence directed at a particular community may equally reflect perceived attributes which are stereotypical or to be found primarily among the most prominent members of the target group.

THE SETTING

By *pariah* community we mean ethnic minorities, primarily Chinese and Indian, which are not indigenous to their host country but have established themselves as part of the economic and social system over several generations. The size of these groups varies to a considerable extent from country to country. The most significant *pariah* communities in the postwar period have centered in Southeast Asia and East Africa. In Southeast Asia they are represented primarily by the Chinese and Indians, although Vietnamese compose an important group in Laos, Cambodia, and Thailand. The Chinese are the most ubiquitous minority and are found in every state and colony. As can be seen by Table 1, percentages of the total population vary from less than

---

1. It has been a traditional joke in Southeast Asia that the Chinese have the largest collection of flags in the region, one for each government that might come into control of the state.

TABLE 1.[2]

Ethnic Chinese in Southeast Asia (Census Figures in Ordinary Type; Estimates in Italics)

	Chinese		Total Population	Chinese	Total Population
	1931 or circa	1947	1947	1960	1960
Burma	*194,000*	300,000	17,000,000	350,000	20,662,000
Siam (Thailand)	*445,000* (1929)	2,500,000	17,359,000	2,670,000	26,257,916
N. Vietnam				55,000	*15,916,955*
S. Vietnam	*418,000* (French Indochina)	850,000 (French Indochina)	27,000,000	800,000	*14,214,000*
Cambodia				*350,000*	*5,347,000*
Laos				*35,000*	*1,805,000*
Federation of Malaya	*1,704,000*	*2,615,000* (Malaya)	*5,849,000*	2,552,276	*6,909,009*
Singapore				1,230,700	*1,634,000*
Sarawak				*236,473*	*744,529*
North Borneo		220,000	878,000	*104,542*	*454,421*
Brunei				*21,745*	*83,877*
Indonesia	*1,233,000* (1930)	1,900,000	69,000,000	2,690,000	93,506,000
Portuguese Timor				*5,000*	*517,079*
Philippines	72,000 (1933)	120,000	19,511,000	*181,626*	*27,087,685*

1947 Total		1960 Total	
Ethnic Chinese	8,505,000	Ethnic Chinese	11,282,362
Total (all races)	156,597,000	Total (all races)	215,139,471

2. Victor Purcell, "Chinese Society in Southeast Asia," in *Southeast Asia,* John McAlister, ed. (New York: Random House, 1973), p. 378.

1 percent to over 35 percent, averaging approximately 5 percent. They are principally from the southern Chinese provinces of Kwangtung, Fukien, and Kwangsi, although considerable variation in language and custom is apparent.

Indians in Southeast Asia have historically been concentrated in Burma and Malaysia, with small numbers living throughout the region. Prior to World War II the Indian population of Burma was 1,017,825 (6.7 percent of the total population), but after a massive evacuation in the face of the Japanese invasion the number fell considerably. Although many returned after 1945, there were only 600,000 (4 percent) in 1953.[3] A decade later, government moves to nationalize the economy further reduced the number by about 25 percent. The Indian population of Malaya was 735,038 (8.7 percent) in 1957.

Vietnamese minorities in Southeast Asia are significantly smaller than their Chinese and Indian counterparts and are more confined to Indochina and northeast Thailand. In Cambodia they totaled approximately 394,000 in 1962 but dropped to an estimated 165,000 following the fall of Sihanouk in 1970 and the resultant conflict.[4] Prior to efforts to repatriate Vietnamese to North Vietnam between 1959 and 1964, there were about 130,000 in northeast Thailand. Some 45,000 were repatriated before the escalation of the war in Vietnam stopped the program. An estimated 20,000 to 30,000 Vietnamese civilians are in Laos, aside from a probably equal number of North Vietnamese military.

The Asian and Arab communities of East Africa have been the major targets of violence, the most publicized of which have been the Indians (including Pakistanis). Although they do not compose the high percentages of the total population found in Southeast Asia (see Table 2), the Indians and Arabs in East Africa settled mainly in urban centers such as Nairobi,

TABLE 2[5]

	Indians	Arabs	Total Population
Kenya (1960)	174,300	38,600	6,550,700
Tanzania (1957)	81,500	65,000	9,092,466
Uganda (1959)	83,000		5,770,000

3. See R. Hatley, "The Overseas Indian in Southeast Asia: Burma, Malaysia, and Singapore," in *Man, State and Society in Contemporary Southeast Asia,* Robert Tilman, ed. (New York: Praeger, 1969), pp. 450-66.

4. For the Vietnamese minority, see Peter Poole, "The Vietnamese in Cambodia and Thailand: Their Role in Interstate Relations," *Asian Survey* 14 (April 1974): 325-37 and *The Vietnamese in Thailand* (Ithaca: Cornell University Press, 1970).

5. In part from D. Morrison, et. al. eds., *Black Africa* (New York: The Free Press, 1972).

Zanzibar, and Kampala. The numbers of both communities have fallen considerably since independence.

TYPES OF VIOLENCE

Three basic types of vigilante violence have been directed against these communities: government instigated, government approved but not directed, and spontaneous popular. Independent states in the regions concerned have long employed legal, nonviolent means of controlling their nonindigenous Asian minorities, either through prohibiting them from participating in various economic, social, and political activities or by providing special rights to the dominant community. In the former case, nonindigenous Asians have been refused permission to participate in various professions, maintain schools in their language, live in particular parts of the country, become citizens, own land, etc.[6] More drastically, they have been forced to leave countries in which they have lived for generations by governments seeking to place the economy and jobs entirely into indigenous hands. General Idi Amin followed this course against the Indian minority in Uganda during the 1970s as did General Ne Win in Burma in the 1960s (when approximately 177,000 Asians left the country under its nationalization program), although in neither case was physical violence an important element. Malaysia is the foremost example of the special rights pattern through which the politically dominant Malay majority has received high quotas in government and industry jobs and education, obtained subsidies, training, and other favored treatment in order to compete with Chinese and Indian businessmen, and has otherwise benefited from "affirmative action" programs.

Vigilante-type violence by governments publicly directed against *pariah* communities has been rare, political leaders preferring to be more discreet. It has been more common for governments to reinforce or to participate clandestinely in spontaneous popular actions. The latter pattern is difficult to prove, and evidence must be largely anecdotal. Two examples in which governments have been rather obviously involved in directing or participating in vigilantism were the assaults on the Vietnamese population in Cambodia in 1970 and executions of Thai arsonists. In the Cambodian case, a combination of spontaneous popular demonstrations, locally directed military assaults, and government propaganda efforts were responsible for the deaths of thousands of Vietnamese (the exact number will probably never be known, but it was at least five thousand, and some charge two hundred thousand). While the catalysts for the killings were the fall of Prince Sihanouk, antipathy

---

6. For a good review of Thai laws dealing with Chinese businessmen, see Joann Schrock, et. al., *Minority Groups in Thailand* (Washington: Department of the Army, 1970), pp. 164-66. The best book on the Chinese in Thailand is G. William Skinner's *Chinese Society in Thailand* (Ithaca: Cornell University Press, 1957).

toward North Vietnamese and National Liberation Front forces in Cambodia, and the killing of Cambodians in South Vietnam, the bases for these activities went much deeper. As I have noted elsewhere:

> In sum, the Vietnamese in Cambodia formed a distinct communal group who were perceived to have undesirable personal characteristics and who held economic positions that put them in direct conflict with the Cambodian population. . . . Class divisions thus exacerbated traditional antipathies between the communities.[7]

The events in Thailand were more obviously government initiated, and may be classed as coercion beyond normal limits. Over the years, Chinese businessmen in Southeast Asia have allegedly burned their businesses prior to Chinese New Years in order to collect the insurance. To discourage this practice, and probably to gain the support of the populace, the military leader of the government, Marshal Sarit, personally rounded up, held summary judgment, and executed five Chinese businessmen. As Frank Darling has noted, "Sarit's actions against the Chinese arsonists were generally popular with the Thai public because of traditional animosity toward this alien class."[8]

A pattern far more frequent than direct government initiation of violence has been tacit approval of violence instigated by the dominant populace or taking advantage of general unrest to act against common enemies. This is different from the Cambodian case in that the government claims that it is simply maintaining or reinstating order. Violence of this type has erupted throughout Southeast Asia and, to a lesser extent, East Africa. Every state in these regions has experienced riots or mob action against Indian or Chinese minorities in which individual governments have either not interfered or have used repressive measures against the minority under the guise of order maintenance. Two examples of this pattern are the anti-Chinese riots in Burma in 1967 and the conflict following the Malaysian elections in 1969.

The Burmese confrontation developed after young Chinese students demonstrated, wearing Maoist badges and extolling the Proletarian Cultural Revolution. Following attacks by these students on photographers and some teachers, Burmese and Indian mobs broke into Chinese schools and the Chinese Embassy, where one diplomat was killed and eighteen injured. Mobs later killed over fifty people in the Chinese section of Rangoon, and demonstrations took place in other towns. The Burmese government appeared to tacitly support the mobs, arresting Chinese students and establishing a program of vilification against Maoism throughout the country.[9]

7. Fred R. von der Mehden, *Comparative Political Violence* (Englewood Cliffs: Prentice-Hall, 1973), p. 58.

8. Frank Darling, *Thailand and the United States* (Washington: Public Affairs Press, 1965), p. 195.

9. See John Badgley, "Burma's China Crisis: The Choices Ahead," *Asian Survey* 8 (November 1967): 753-62.

An even more violent conflict arose in May 1969 in Malaysia following elections in which the Malay-dominated ruling Alliance Party suffered major losses at the polls. Although the Alliance remained the majority party, members of both the majority Malays and minority Chinese looked upon the elections as a possible turning point in the long Malay domination of the country's politics. The Chinese opposition marched in celebration of their successes, but the Malays began mob action that included killing, burning, and looting of Chinese stores and residences. Targets ultimately included both races but were primarily Chinese. Violence was primarily concentrated in the cities where the Chinese population was largest, and the final death count was between 196 (the official count) and 700.[10] There have been unsubstantiated charges that the riots were instigated by Malay politicians, but there is little doubt that the primarily Malay police and military concentrated their energies upon Chinese activities and did not effectively control Malay violence. In both of the aforementioned examples the government tacitly supported popular vigilante violence.

The final type of vigilante violence perpetrated against *pariah* communities is spontaneous activity employed by the dominant population of the community without government instigation or support. Thus, this pattern is only establishment violence broadly defined. The Chinese and Indian communities of Asia and Africa have been targets of this type of vigilantism since the colonial period when such conflicts were considered as antithetical to the peace and order of the colony. For example, anti-Indian riots in Burma in the 1930s were rigorously dealt with by British authorities, who gained the enmity of nationalists by strong measures against the rioters.[11] As late as 1974, Japanese, and later Chinese, were attacked in Indonesia during and after a visit by Japanese Prime Minister Tanaka. This had the earmarks of past violence against *pariah* groups, except that this time government reactions support the view that the mob action was not desired by Indonesian leaders who believed it to be embarrassing both to the country's international image and to domestic order.

Note should also be made of violence employed by the majority population against a *pariah* community that is in fact the government and economic establishment. This happened in Zanzibar in 1964 when the majority African populace rose against their Arab rulers, reportedly killing 2000 to 3000 and forcing out thousands of others. In this case the minority had gained control of the establishment and suppressed the majority only to be deposed by revolution.[12] The major part of this study will concentrate upon the reasons

10. The best study of these events is by F. Gagliano, *Communal Violence in Malaysia, 1969* (Athens, Ohio: Ohio University Center for International Studies, 1970).
11. Burma, *Final Report of the Riot Inquiry Committee* (Rangoon: Government Printing Office, 1939).
12. von der Mehden, *Political Violence*, pp. 63-64.

24 *Fred R. von der Mehden*

why *pariah* communities have been targets of the aforementioned types of vigilantism.

SOME CAUSAL FACTORS

Antagonism against *pariah* groups results from the combination of roles played by the nonindigenous Asians and perceptions held about them by the dominant community. We can pinpoint three roles that have been important causal factors:

1. Economic role.
2. Collaborator with colonial governments.
3. Silent partner to political leaders.

ECONOMIC ROLE: The economic role of the *pariah* communities is widely recognized. Throughout most of Southeast Asia and East Africa they have been the economic middlemen, composing high percentages of the shopkeepers, money lenders, small-scale food processors, theater owners, and petty tradesmen. The Chinese involvement in commerce has been duly noted by students of Asian culture. In a study published in 1960, Donald Willmott comments that "it can safely be assumed that from 75 to 80 percent of all fairsized retail stores in Semarang are owned by Chinese."[13] J. Gullick's book on Malaya of the 1960s notes that "the Chinese are the dominant elements in local commerce, large and small."[14] James Hendry, in his analysis of a Vietnamese rural community, found that Chinese in the mid-1950s dominated that area's buying, shipping, milling, and distribution of rice.[15] Statistics presented by the Malaysian government in 1973 show Chinese dominating partnerships, individual proprietorships, and other noncorporate business.[16] The Vietnamese in northeast Thailand and Cambodia have played an economic role similar to the Chinese, often competing with them in the market place. The author's own observations in one northeast Thai town found that the bulk of the shops and truck gardening was controlled by members of the Vietnamese minority.

Indians in East Africa and Southeast Asia (particularly Burma) developed along the same lines. Prior to World War II, Indians in Burma were the beneficiaries of large-scale alienation of debt-ridden land and were the most ubiquitous traders in the colony.[17] Regarding Africa, one author writes:

> By 1910 the scene in East Africa was more or less set. Administrative and agricultural development were thought to be European occupations; trade and craftsmanship were relegated to Indians; and Africans were encouragee to work

---

13. Donald Willmott, *The Chinese in Semarang* (Ithaca: Cornell University Press, 1960), p. 42.
14. J. Gullick, *Malaya* (New York: Praeger, 1963), p. 20.
15. James Hendry, *The Small World of Khanh Hau* (Chicago: Aldine, 1964), p. 144.
16. Malaysia, *Mid-Term Review of the Second Malaysia Plan* (Kuala Lumpur: Government Printing Office, 1973).
17. See Hatley, "The Overseas Indian."

in the European agricultural system and to supply cheap labor in the towns. . . .
The picture did not substantially alter in the next forty years.[18]

Indians controlled trade in Uganda to a greater extent than was normal for
pariah communities. In 1966 wholesale trade receipts were 4.6 percent
African, 73.6 percent Asian and the rest European.[19] In Zanzibar the Arabs
and other Asians dominated both the urban and rural economies. The Arabs
owned more than two-thirds of the large plantations and Asians the rest until
the revolution. In urban areas, 95 percent of the upper-class was composed of
Arabs and Asians.[20]

It would be inaccurate to presume that the *pariah* groups were composed
entirely of the economically powerful or that all of the region under study was
economically under their control. It should be noted that in most countries a
high percentage of nonindigenous Asians have been workers, not tradesmen.
In Malaysia a large proportion of the Indian population works on
plantations, and the mean monthly income of urban Chinese and Indians in
1970 was still only slightly more than US $150.00.[21] Prior to the war in Burma,
95 percent of the scavengers and sweepers were Indian as were 47.5 percent of
the unskilled and semi-skilled workers.[22] In Thailand, Hainanese Chinese had
large numbers specializing in semi-skilled occupations.

At the same time, the *pariah* groups were not totally ubiquitous in
Southeast Asia and East Africa. Many rural areas did not have the Chinese or
Indians controlling the economy, and in East Africa the Indians were largely
urban bound. For example, Hendry notes that in his area of Vietnam the
stereotype of the Chinese controlling the economy was not accurate.[23] And in
Indonesia they were forced out of some rural areas. However, a more
important challenge to the stereotype of the *pariah* monopoly over the
economy is the fact that in most countries it has been the European
community which has dominated the upper echelons of the economy. In the
Philippines, one commentator notes that economic power was really held by
three groups, American companies, Chinese professionals and businessmen,
and a dozen Filipino business "giants."[24] Malaysian statistics show that two-
thirds of the share capital in the modern sector is owned by foreigners.[25] In

18. H. S. Morris, *The Indians in Uganda* (Chicago: University of Chicago Press, 1968), p. 11.
19. Jack Parson, "Africanizing Trade in Uganda: The Final Solution," *Africa Today* 20
(Winter 1973): 62.
20. Michael Lofchie, *Zanzibar: Background of Revolution* (Princeton: Princeton University
Press, 1970), p. 64.
21. Malaysia, *Mid-Term Review,* p. 4.
22. Louis Walensky, *Economic Development in Burma, 1951-1960* (New York: Twentieth
Century Fund, 1962), p. 35.
23. Hendry, *The Small World,* p. 138. As well, Gerald Hickey found Chinese in his village to be
marginal to the local society. Gerald Hickey, *Village in Vietnam* (New Haven: Yale University
Press, 1964), p. 235.
24. David Chang, "Current Status of Chinese Minorities in Southeast Asia," *Asian Survey,* 13
(June 1973): 593.
25. Malaysia, *Mid-Term Review,* p. 82.

Thailand, in 1960, only ten of the fifty largest businesses were owned by Chinese. In the colonial world it was the citizen of the metropolitan power that was the major economic beneficiary.

This entire pattern of *pariah* control has been seriously challenged in the post-war period. Asians and Africans have been forced out of East Africa in the past fifteen years, as have been the Indians in Burma. Draconian laws in Indonesia have severely limited Chinese business activity and, as previously noted, many were driven out of rural areas and into the cities. Violence attended each of these actions, although in different degrees of intensity. Only in Thailand, Malaysia, and Singapore has there been no serious diminishment of economic position.

The relationship of the economic role of the *pariah* community to violence is rather obvious. The majority community continuously finds its day-to-day economic dealings are with these nonindigenous Asians. As the aforementioned Filipino commentator observes, "the average successful Chinese businessmen and shopkeepers are resented and discriminated against because they are numerous and spread throughout the country" and thus "closest physically to the average poverty-struck Filipino."[26] When recession hits, it may be necessary to go into debt to the Indian or Chinese with the danger in some areas of the loss of land and livelihood. In some places the rich of the *pariah* community seek to hide their wealth by not conspicuously consuming, but, as we shall see, the perception of the rich *pariah* businessman leads to envy and develops a view that he is sucking the blood of the people. This fear and jealousy of the populace exacerbates feelings and increases communal tensions until the point at which the government gives the sign that it will not hinder pogroms or is momentarily too weak to maintain order. The economic catalyst may be a poor crop year and increased debt, a nationalist boycott of foreign goods such as that which precipitated violence in Uganda in 1959, or the act of an individual member of the minority. At times there have been efforts to destroy the books or other means of ascertaining debts. There have been actions akin to the "commodity riots" that struck the United States several years ago, with groups looting minority-owned shops in order to obtain desired goods and to "pay back" the store owner.[27]

Nationalism has furthered tensions between the communities as the nonindigenous Asian has been termed a foreigner stealing from the people. Where there have been efforts to drive foreign capital from the country as a means of gaining national control of the economy, the Asian has suffered with the European. The most obvious examples of this pattern have been in Uganda under Amin, Indonesia under Sukarno, and Burma under Ne Win. The fact that many nonindigneous Asians were reluctant to take up

26. Chang, "Current Status," p. 593.
27. Morris Janowitz, "Patterns of Collective Racial Violence," in H. Graham and T. Gurr, eds., *The History of Violence in America* (New York: *New York Times,* 1969), pp. 412-44.

citizenship in the country in which they were residing was underlined by nationalist politicians.

COLLABORATOR WITH COLONIAL GOVERNMENTS: Generally, the *pariah* communities were not viewed with approbation by colonial regimes. In some colonies they were necessary to work plantations, docks, railways, and mines where the local population was not available or was unsuitable. But often they were strongly disliked. For example, one government commission in 1919 complained that the Indians in East Africa were hygienically unclean and that their "moral depravity is equally damaging to the African. . . . The Indian is the incentive of crime as well as vice. . . ."[28] However, there were other cases where the colonial government employed nonindigenous Asians in the bureaucracy, largely due to their training and expertise. Thus, Vietnamese were used in the civil service in Laos and Cambodia, Indians were employed in the Burmese police, and Chinese found themselves in government positions that demanded professional and technical competence. To the local nationalists, this tainted the *pariah* groups with collaboration with the imperialists. In Uganda some Asians recognized this danger since "their commercial skills and the place they had built for themselves in the civil service and in clerical and professional occupations laid them open to envy, dislike and possible eviction."[29] In addition, some of the leaders of these minorities feared that the success that they had enjoyed under the colonial system would be lost if the nationalists came to power. Others followed the traditional apolitical pattern of the Asian entrepreneur. Both attitudes were attacked by nationalists who condemned them for being foreigners in spirit and anti-nationalist in action.[30]

The result of this division between the nonindigenous Asians and the nationalists was further reinforcement of the endemic dislike of these *pariah* communities. In East Africa, political leaders referred to the lack of nationalist sentiment among the Asians and Arabs in demanding their ouster, while in Indochina antagonism toward Vietnamese civil servants fed the violence directed against the entire minority group. In Burma, pictures of Indian policemen allegedly attacking religious leaders during the anti-Indian riots of 1938 were used in nationalist newspapers.

SILENT PARTNER TO POLITICAL LEADERS: Finally, some of the relationships established between the minority communities and postwar political leaders and organizations have increased tensions. Noteworthy in this area have been the "extralegal" contacts with government officials on the one hand and

28. Carl Rosberg and John Nottingham, *The Myth of "Mau Mau" Nationalism in Kenya.* (New York: Praeger, 1966), p. 39. A few years later the European community formed a "Vigilance Committee" to meet the dangers of the Indians. Although armed, the whites did not act at that time.
29. Morris, *The Indians,* p. 176.
30. Many Chinese also joined nationalist movements in Southeast Asia, and during the interwar years the Indians were leaders of the movement to gain more freedom in East Africa.

alleged support of subversive elements on the other. In the first instance, these minorities have found it difficult to use regular political channels due to restrictive laws, leading them to seek to employ more clandestine and extralegal means to gain government protection and support. For this reason, corruption often surrounds the dealings of these groups. As James Scott has observed:

> Where a minority is discriminated against and its political demands are regarded as illegitimate by the governing elite and the general population, its members may feel that open pressure-group action would expose them to attacks from more powerful groups. . . . It would be foolish, even suicidal, for these so-called "pariah" capitalists to seek influence openly as an organized pressure group. A healthy regard for their property and skin alike impels them to rely on payments and favors to strategically placed power-holders.[31]

There is considerable evidence of Chinese, in particular, seeking protection from public officials in Thailand and Indochina. During post-war military regimes in Thailand it was normal for Chinese businessmen to put civil and military officials on boards of directors, providing protection for the minority and monetary rewards for the establishment.[32] While this protection system lasted, there were no major pogroms directed against the Chinese. Yet, the belief that members of the *pariah* community are receiving special privileges through their wealth is strong in these countries and leads to anger and frustration within the lower- and middle-classes of the majority culture.

Ironically, while some members of the minorities were being accused of corrupting politicians and bureaucrats, others were under fire for dealing with enemies of the state. In northeast Thailand the Vietnamese community was indicted for aiding insurgents in the area, and stringent government efforts to control their activities were supported on the basis of national security (by their own admission most Vietnamese in the northeast were pro-Hanoi, but there is little evidence that any major sector of the community aided the Thai rebels). In East Africa, General Amin accused the Indians of collaborating with enemies of his regime, and after one abortive coup the Indian leadership found it necessary to publicly deny complicity.

The Chinese in Southeast Asia have found themselves in the most difficult situation in this regard. The public and supposed clandestine relationship between the Peoples' Republic of China and local communism has made suspect the loyalty of the entire minority as governments have accused local Chinese of aiding insurgents. As well, the traditional loyalty, and in many cases citizenship, which Chinese have held with their motherland became dangerous when the Peoples' Republic openly called for revolution against governments in Southeast Asia. This relationship has been used as an excuse

31. James Scott, *Comparative Political Corruption* (Englewood Cliffs: Prentice-Hall, 1972), p. 25.
32. For an interesting analysis of this pattern, see Fred Riggs, *Thailand: The Modernization of a Bureaucratic Polity* (Honolulu: East-West Center Press, 1966), pp. 242-310.

for anti-Chinese violence in Indochina, Malaysia, the Philippines, and Indonesia. The worst and most obviously government-supported examples have taken place in Indonesia during the large-scale killings of 1965 to 1967. Most of those killed during this period were not Chinese, but Indonesian Communists. Yet, for example, in Kalimantan (Borneo) allegations by the government of collusion between the Chinese and Communists, the participation of young Chinese in local insurgency activities, and the breakdown in Sino-Indonesian diplomatic relations "rendered every Chinese in West Kalimantan an object of official suspicion as well as a legitimate target of endemic, popular anti-Chinese sentiment."[33] One result was that when Chinese insurgents were involved in attacks in the area, the Dyaks carried out indiscriminant killings of hundreds of Chinese. This was only one of many similar incidents in Indonesia during those years, some openly encouraged by government, others tacitly supported or not forcibly discouraged, and some prohibited.

These aforementioned roles reinforced one another and led to stereotypes of the *pariah* community as rich, avaricious, corrupt, politically opportunistic, subversive at worst and apolitical and anti-nationalist at best and, overall, unwilling or disloyal citizens. As we have noted, these minorities have not been homogeneous, including as they do individuals of different classes, customs, loyalties, and political opinions. Yet, the stereotypes have remained powerful.

PERCEPTIONS OF THE PARIAH

In analyzing the perceptions which underscore this type of ethnic hostility, three beliefs will be spotlighted:

1. That there is a congruence of class and ethnicity.
2. That personality attributes of the minority groups make them superior or inferior to the dominant culture.
3. That customary habits of the *pariah* community put its members outside the national culture.

I have speculated elsewhere that political violence is likely where communal groups are believed to be of different economic classes (class broadly defined):

> Among causal situations, one of the most volatile would appear to be the *perception* of a communal group that it is being economically or socially subjugated by another primordially based class. The word "perceived" is emphasized because it is the contention here that there need be no objective economic or social difference so long as the politically active element of the lower class perceives, or chooses to perceive, that it is being kept in an inferior position.[34]

33. Justus van der Kroef, *Indonesia After Sukarno* (Vancouver: University of British Columbia Press, 1971), pp. 111-12.
34. von der Mehden, *Political Violence,* p. 56.

There is little doubt that the majority community and many of its leaders perceive that the nonindigenous Asians dominate the economies of their countries and strongly resent the fact. The general population has failed to recognize basic differences within the minority groups and has tended to blame economic difficulties on the entire *pariah* community. This situation is exacerbated by the traditional tendency of Chinese, Indian, and Arab expatriates to enter into commerce in societies where such activities have been of low status within the dominant culture. Worsening this situation has been a new interest in business among young Asians and Africans, who see the entrenched position of the *pariahs* as an obstacle to advancement. In spite of the fact that an economic dichotomy in occupations does not exist and old patterns are changing, when economic troubles arise, violence often ensues. For example, in the Indonesian case,

> This division has led many politically articulate Indonesians to believe that the Chinese are profiting from the present situation while the Indonesians become increasingly worse off. Small wonder, then, that the most recent anti-Chinese activities (spring 1963) were attacks by urban youths on Chinese properties.[35]

This pattern of ethnic-class conflict has been repeated between the Protestants and Catholics in Northern Ireland, Hutus and Tutsis in Rwanda, Ibos and other tribes in Nigeria, and has symbolized relations between the *pariah* communities and the dominant culture in Southeast Asia and East Africa.

Underlying much of this antagonism are sets of perceptions as to the personality attributes of the different communities. To oversimplify, members of the *pariah* groups tend to view the majority culture as composed of people who are lazy, unskilled, and not overly bright, while the dominant culture looks upon the Chinese, Arabs, and Vietnamese in particular as money oriented, clever, and hard-working. Both attitudes are reinforced by the close family units of many minorities who maintain their language, customs, and business contacts within the group. We have the most information about Chinese who argue that locals do not fit into their business practices because of lack of skills and knowledge of the commercial *lingua franca* (Chinese);[36] or because they are not good workers. Thus, one hears comments that, "Filipinos usually do not work hard and are unreliable compared to Chinese employees;"[37] or the comment of a well-educated Chinese, "We shouldn't feel superior. But we do."[38] A more systematic example of Chinese superiority appeared in a set of interviews of 214 Chinese students from Hong Kong and Southeast Asia. When asked the feelings of those of Chinese descent over

35. Mary Somers, *Peranakan Chinese Politics in Indonesia* (Ithaca: Modern Indonesia Project, 1964), p. 56.
36. Many businessmen the author interviewed in Malaysia in 1973 held similar views of the majority community.
37. Chang, "Current Status," p. 594.
38. Willmott, *Chinese*, p. 95.

thirty years of age regarding local culture, way of life and race, the reply was that the Chinese,[39]

Maintain a very high degree of superiority	43.92%
Maintain a minor degree of superiority	22.42%
Seriously despise local race, culture, or way of life	21.96%
Slightly despise local race, culture, or way of life.	20.09%

Public articulation of these views has only added to conflict.

Evidence of stereotypes regarding *pariah* groups are both anecdotal and systematic. Any resident of Southeast Asia or East Africa has heard comments such as, "They are dirty," or "They're very sharp. Even the poor ones—they too will be rich someday. . . . They will do anything for a profit,"[40] or "It is widely believed that the Chinese are achievement-oriented, industrious, opportunistic, avaricious, and are sharp businessmen."[41] In a more systematic fashion, Alvin Rabushka interviewed 500 persons in two Malaysian cities and found that "non-Chinese-Malays and Indians—portray the Chinese as intelligent and ambitious, placing these attributes in first and second place."[42]

Indian stereotypes are more mixed in characterization. On the one hand, commercial elements are perceived as having the general characteristics of the Chinese while, overall, this minority is given very low marks in terms of cleanliness and self-reliance. Gayl Ness comments that estate Indians in Peninsula Malaysia "are generally considered to be low in mental ability, lacking in self-reliance and achievement orientation,"[43] while Rabushka reports that in his survey, "non-Indians stress lack of cleanliness of Indians most emphatically."[44] These twin-threads of lack of cleanliness and commercial ability and avariciousness have been the most important elements of the stereotype in East Africa and Burma.

The characteristics of wealth, opportunism, tightly-knit family-based organization, ambition, opportunism, and cleverness given to the *pariah* communities have reinforced the frustrations of the more assertive members of the newly independent states. They have incited jealousy, envy, and fear resulting in violence not only against those who fit the stereotype but also against the entire community. Thus, governments in Burma, Indonesia, Uganda, and Zanzibar have sought mass eviction from their countries. In Burma, antagonism was generated by both the economic position of the Indians and disdain for their personal habits.

This brings us to the final point that perceptions of the social habits of the

---

39. Chang, "Current Status," p. 602.
40. Willmott, *Chinese*, p. 96.
41. Gayl Ness, *Bureaucracy and Rural Development in Malaya* (Berkeley: University of California Press, 1967), p. 46.
42. Alvin Rabushka, "Racial Stereotypes in Malaya," *Asian Survey* 11 (July 1971): 716.
43. Ness, *Bureaucracy*, p. 46.
44. Rabushka, "Racial Stereotypes," p. 716.

minorities are often believed to be in conflict with cultural norms of the majority. We have observed that Indian minorities have been viewed as unclean, but other groups have been tainted with spiritual uncleanliness. The fact that *pariah* communities have often been of different religions from the dominant culture also heightens tension, particularly when religion is an important element in local nationalist ideology. Thus, there have been Islamic reactions against the Chinese in Malaysia and Indonesia, Buddhist Cambodian antagonism toward the predominately Catholic Vietnamese, and Burmese Buddhist conflict with Moslem Indians. Where Islam has been the religion of the dominant culture or *pariah* group, tensions have been highest, while in Thailand and Vietnam, where this is not the case, assimilation has been easier and mob violence generally less. For example, in Indonesia, "in the Moslem view, a solution to the minority problem can only come with the conversion to Islam."[45] The fact that leaders of the Indonesian Moslem parties have at times been traders in competition with Chinese merchants shows that other issues have been present. However, the difference is more than one of religious loyalty with economic and political underpinnings.

The sumptuary habits and religious laws of the conflicting communities offer ready bases for differentiating people and opportunities for dispute. Integration of communities is inhibited by the fact that Chinese in Moslem Malaysia and Indonesia eat pork, Moslem Indians in Burma eat beef, Indians in East Africa retain their traditional clothing, and that marriage and inheritance laws between Moslems and Buddhists are fundamentally different, etc. It is not surprising that religious and traditional festivals of the *pariah* communities are often the targets of violence.

We should not conclude that all of these groups have been unassimilatable. The Chinese in Thailand have shown a remarkable ability to fit into Thai life, tending to take Thai names, divest themselves of Chinese clothing, and accept other attributes of Thai culture. In Burma the Chinese were looked upon as coming from common stock and called "cousin" in Burmese. In this case, antipathy toward the Indians directed mob violence more in that direction until the Cultural Revolution. In other countries efforts at assimilation have not been so successful, particularly in East Africa and the Malay states where differences are greater and intermarriage less frequent.

CONCLUSIONS

In sum, we have highly visible minority communities, often with different racial, sumptuary, religious, and customary attributes. They include within their numbers unusually high proportions of the commercial and professional leadership of the respective countries. Further, in order to protect themselves

45. Somers, *Peranakan Chinese,* p. 52.

and their wealth, members of these *pariah* groups have sought support from colonial administrations, corruptible politicians, and foreign governments. Finally, the dominant culture has developed stereotypes of the entire community which tend to portray all of the minority in the guise of its most visible elements. The aforementioned roles and reinforcing stereotypes have made the *pariahs* frequent targets for governments seeking control of their own economies and scapegoats to explain away difficult problems. This situation became more dangerous to the minorities as nationalism increased after the war and the independent states were unable to meet the goals articulated at the time of independence. The majority population on its part has seen the *pariahs* as obstacles to their advancement, the explanation for their frustrations, and a continuously visible dominating economic class. The reactions to all of these factors has all too often been vigilantism.

Chapter Twelve

Vigilantism in Northern Ireland

Richard Ned Lebow

The gunman casts a long shadow in Ireland. Images of Fenians, the Easter Uprising, or the grim Irish Republican Army (IRA) assassin in trench coat stalking his victim through the streets of Dublin come readily to mind. The Irish revolutionary has long been immortalized in song and film. However, little is sung or written of the Irish anti-revolutionary, a less romantic but far more effective figure who continues to shape the destiny of modern Ulster.

Anti-revolutionary violence in Ireland has traditionally been either social-group-control or regime-control vigilantism. The former is directed against groups which are competing for and/or advocating a redistribution of values within the system. The latter is directed against the political establishment in an attempt to make the "superstructure" into a more effective guardian of the "base."[1] Social-group-control violence has been a fairly constant phenomenon in Ireland for the last eight hundred years, increasing in times of political agitation and economic distress. Regime-control vigilantism has been marked in two periods during the twentieth century, between 1912 and 1920 and again after the emergence of the Catholic civil-rights movement in 1969. In the first instance vigilantes succeeded in preserving the political and economic status quo throughout most of Ulster by forcing a partition of Ireland. The outcome of the current struggle still hangs in the balance.

THE HISTORICAL BACKGROUND

In Tudor and Stuart times the English colonial elite in Ireland, usually referred to as the Ascendancy, was concentrated along the eastern coast of Ireland, especially in the cities of Dublin and Cork. Few soldiers, settlers, or administrators lived in the western, more rural part of the country. They were gradually reinforced during the seventeenth and eighteenth centuries by retired soldiers and civil servants who received large grants of Irish land as

1. See the introductory theoretical essay in this volume by the editors.

recompense for their services to the Crown. By 1800, four-fifths of the land of Ireland was in the hands of the Ascendancy, among whom were a powerful class of landed gentry allied to the Tory party in England. The Anglo-Irish elite as a whole did not feel Irish in culture, religious association, or politics. The gulf separating them from the native Irish was similar in most respects to the division between colonists and natives in other European colonial outposts.

Given the geographic concentration of the Ascendancy, as well as its numerical inferiority—never more than 10 percent of the total population—the government continually sought to strengthen the power of its loyal forces by encouraging British colonization of the more rural areas. The most ambitious and successful scheme for colonization was implemented in Ulster which, at the beginning of the seventeenth century, was the least British of Ireland's four provinces. Anxious to break the hold of Gaelic culture, the government chartered the "Plantation of Ulster" and offered large grants of land to "undertakers" who were to recruit and finance settlement. The city of London, for example, undertook to plant the county of Coleraine in return for extensive economic privileges. Derry was renamed Londonderry (although Catholics and many Protestants still refer to it as Derry), and large tracts of land were set aside for colonization by Londoners. However, it proved more profitable to lease the land back to the original inhabitants at high rents. While this policy was acceptable to English investors, it was unsatisfactory to the government because few native Irish were driven from the province. True colonization was successful only in eastern Ulster, beyond the Bann River, where large numbers of Scots, anxious to resettle for both religious and economic reasons, emigrated to Ireland during the seventeenth century. Ulster thus came to resemble a patchwork quilt composed of Presbyterian Scots-Irish, Catholic natives, and, above them both, a small Anglo-Irish elite. The Scots-Irish, distinct in both religion and culture from the native Irish and from the Anglo-Irish, became a third force in Irish politics and ultimately came to hold the balance of power between the other two opposing factions.

Throughout the seventeenth century the Scots-Irish supported the British government because of the religious passions of the time and their very real fear of the Irish. By the end of the eighteenth century, however, the beginnings of industrialization and the ensuing economic transformation of Ulster threatened to disrupt the alliance. Ulster Protestants, mostly independent farmers, small businessmen, and merchants, suffered from the same narrow mercantile policy that led to rebellion in America (an insurrection that found considerable support in Ireland). Some Ulstermen, irked by these economic restrictions and fired by the radical zeal of the times, concluded that the real interest of Ulster Protestants lay in alliance with the emerging Catholic middle-class against the Ascendancy and the British government. This sentiment was by no means limited to a few intellectuals and was partly responsible for the rebellion of 1798 and later for the widespread Protestant support of Catholic Emancipation, achieved in 1829.

The dream of a united and independent Ireland in which communal differences were secondary to the political and cultural bond of Irish nationality motivated many Ulster Protestants, among them the great Irish nationalists Henry Grattan, William Smith O'Brien, and Charles Stuart Parnell. But for the majority of Ulster Protestants religion remained the dominant issue. This ancient passion, aggravated by working-class competition with Catholics for jobs and housing, kept the masses of Ulstermen loyal to the Crown and adamant in their opposition to Irish-Catholic demands for reform, home rule, independence, and later, union with the Republic.

By 1820, the relaxation of the Penal Laws, together with the industrial development of Belfast and Dublin, led to the growth of a small but articulate Catholic middle-class. Their leaders, shrewdly exploiting the widespread peasant discontent, pressured Westminster for reforms aimed at improving the Catholic position. Emancipation (1829), which had permitted Catholics to hold political office (though at the price of disenfranchising the masses), led to demands for disestablishment of the Church of Ireland (achieved in 1869), land reform (1870 and 1881), and Home Rule (Home Rule meant the repeal of the Act of Union of 1801 and the restoration of an Irish parliament). The agitation for these reforms was ultimately based on a threat to escalate rural violence, but was in practice generally limited to peaceful demonstrations and parliamentary appeals. The British response to Irish demands was a mixture of repression and minimal concession that served only to undermine the position of moderate Irish leaders. It helped to foster the development of revolutionary nationalism characterized by such groups as Young Ireland (1840s), the Fenians (1860s), and later, Sinn Fein (literally, "We Ourselves"). These organizations rejected any form of assimilation into British culture or political life and espoused national independence, which was to be achieved by revolution if necessary.

PARTITION

Despite the rise of revolutionary conspiracies, the Catholic moderates appeared to maintain the upper hand in the struggle to win public support. The Irish Parliamentary party, which controlled most of the Irish seats in the House of Commons, sought to hold the balance of power between the two British parties and to trade their votes for Home Rule. These efforts met with success when William Gladstone, dependent upon the Irish for a majority, agreed to introduce Home Rule in 1886. The Home Rule Bill offered only a minimal measure of self-government. Nevertheless, it aroused strong opposition within Gladstone's own Liberal party as well as united opposition from the Tories. It also evoked the threat of violent resistance by Ulster Protestants. The bill proved so divisive that Gladstone was deserted by a faction of his own party which crossed the aisle to join the Tories, now reconstituted as the Unionist party. Gladstone persisted, only to have the bill defeated in the House of Lords. A second Home Rule Bill, introduced in 1892, fared no better, and the idea was not resurrected again until 1910 when the Liberal government, led by Herbert Asquith, once again became dependent upon Irish parliamentary support, this time in its struggle to reform the House of Lords. In return, Asquith introduced the third Home Rule Bill in April 1912, the first to have any real chance of success because in the interim the veto power of the Lords had been curtailed. The introduction of the third Home Rule Bill proved to be the curtain raiser to a drama that threatened to destroy the very fabric of the British Constitution.

Still reeling from their bitter defeats over the Lloyd George budget and the reform of the House of Lords, the Tories saw Home Rule as a further threat to the diminishing prerogatives of their class. The Tory leadership decided to fight it, by extraparliamentary means if necessary. Their strategy was to encourage resistance in Ulster and, by raising the specter of civil war in Ireland, to coerce the government into dropping its support for the controversial measure. Much to the shock of Asquith, Bonar Law, leader of the Unionist party, went so far as to declare, "If Ulster resists by force, they [will] have the wholehearted support of the Unionists."[2] Although the Liberals dismissed the suggestion of resistance as bluff, Ulstermen were very serious and implemented measures required to make their threat a credible one. Under the forceful leadership of Edward Carson, a Dublin lawyer, Ulster Protestants collected more than fifty thousand signatures of individuals pledged to resist Home Rule by force. Carson also organized the Ulster Volunteer Force (UVF), a paramilitary force of about one hundred thousand men. The UVF drew its recruits from the Orange Lodges, received financial support from leading Belfast and London businessmen, and, in a dramatic coup, circumvented the British ban on the importation of weapons by landing thirty-five thousand German rifles and five million rounds of ammunition. By the end of 1913, Carson had both an army and shadow government which stood ready to take over the province on the day the government attempted to enforce Home Rule.

The threat of rebellion in Ulster was serious enough, but what shook the government to its core was the revelation that the British Army was deeply implicated in the conspiracy. Asquith was outraged to learn from Sir Henry Wilson, director of Military Operations, that 40 percent of the officers were likely to defect to the side of the rebels in the event of civil war. Unknown to Asquith, both General Wilson and his superior, Field Marshal Roberts, were

---

2. A. T. Q. Stewart, *The Ulster Crisis* (London: Faber, 1967), p. 57.

closely connected to the Orange cause and assisted Carson by suggesting names of retired officers to staff and train the UVF. They also supplied the force with advance intelligence about the government's plans for military moves against Ulster.

The UVF's successful defiance of the government aroused both the envy and militancy of the nationalists, who hastened to make their own military preparations. In October 1913, James Larkin and James Connolly organized the Irish Citizen Army. Dedicated to the creation of a worker's republic, the leaders of the force considered national independence the first step toward this goal. A second force, the Irish Volunteers, was organized by Catholic nationalists associated with the Gaelic League and the Gaelic Athletic Association, both of which were hotbeds of nationalist sentiment. The Volunteers had no clearly defined policy, but the Irish Republican Brotherhood, forerunner of the IRA, soon captured control of the force and envisaged it as the shock troops of the coming revolution.

The threat of civil war in Ireland, with the army and Unionist party supporting the rebels, was not a situation Asquith regarded with equanimity. To forestall chaos, all the more disturbing in light of the deteriorating international situation, Asquith, David Lloyd George, and Winston Churchill sought out the leading protagonists and tried to arrange a compromise Home Rule Bill acceptable to all parties.

The most obvious compromise involved some kind of special status for Ulster. This had been envisaged by Thomas Macaulay as far back as 1833 but was first seriously mooted by Joseph Chamberlain in the 1880s when he ironically employed the idea of partition to demonstrate the impracticality of Home Rule. Partition was now resurrected by Churchill and Lloyd George as a possible means of averting civil war. However, the nationalists, laying claim to all of Ireland, found the idea unacceptable as did the Ulster Protestants for whom it meant betrayal of their fellow Unionists elsewhere in Ireland. Asquith nevertheless pursued the compromise scheme and in March 1914 persuaded the reluctant John Redmond, leader of the Irish Parliamentary party, to agree to an amendment of the Home Rule Bill. This stipulated that any Ulster county, by a vote of its parliamentary electors, could exclude itself for six years from the new Ireland after which it would be automatically brought in. Carson, speaking for the Unionists, flatly rejected the compromise. "We do not," he declared, "want sentence of death with a stay of execution for six years."[3] As the crisis deepened, it became clear that Ulstermen were willing to sacrifice the rest of Ireland to the nationalists but would not budge with respect to Ulster. Asquith nonetheless incorporated the amendment in his bill, which was close to passage in the Commons in the early summer of 1914. At this juncture, King George, sympathetic to the plight of

3. J. C. Beckett, *The Making of Modern Ireland* (New York: Knopf, 1966), p. 432.

the Unionists, initiated a final attempt at mediation. He called a conference of opposing leaders and asked them to consider the possibility of permanently excluding Ulster. The nationalists would not agree, and the conference broke up on July 24. Passage of Home Rule and the expected civil conflagration were forestalled only by the outbreak of war on the continent in August.

Both Carson and Redmond pledged full support to the war effort and agreed to a compromise by which Home Rule became law but was accompanied by an act of suspension delaying its implementation for the duration of the conflict. The UVF was incorporated into the British Army and sent to France, where it was all but destroyed in two days of savage fighting on the Somme in July 1916. The Irish Volunteers also requested incorporation into the army as a regiment but were rebuffed by the War Office. Despite this affront, thousands of Irish nationalists enlisted in the British Army and Navy and fought in all theaters of the war. However, the more militant nationalists wanted independence, spurned Redmond's "collaboration" with Britain, insisting on independence, not limited self-government. They rose in rebellion on Easter Sunday, April 23, 1916, quickly captured the center of Dublin, and Padraic Pearse proclaimed a republic from the steps of the General Post Office. The government, commanding only twelve hundred troops in the vicinity of the city, hastened to bring in reinforcements. A week of merciless artillery bombardment forced the surviving rebels to surrender.

The Easter Rebellion marked a turning point in modern Irish history. Future Irish leaders, committed by the sacrifice of the rebels, could not settle for anything short of independence without invoking widespread resentment and loss of support. This became readily apparent in the first general election held after the war in December 1918. Sinn Fein, the political front of the Irish Republican Brotherhood, captured seventy-three seats. The Unionists won twenty-six, and the Irish Parliamentary party was reduced to a mere six seats. The newly elected nationalists ignored Westminster and convened instead in Dublin, where in January 1919 they proclaimed a republic. The revolutionary government gradually asserted its control over most of Ireland. The Volunteers, reorganized as the Irish Republican Army, carried out assaults against the remaining British bastions of authority in Ireland, and effective British rule was soon limited to Ulster. The Unionists responded by reorganizing the UVF. With the B Specials, a Protestant militia financed by the British, it was sufficient to overcome nationalist resistance in the North.

British policy was at first marked by confusion and a fear of alienating the United States, where the Irish cause had received strong congressional support. However, Lloyd George, head of a coalition government that depended upon Unionist support, soon felt compelled to reassert British authority in Ireland. He approved the imposition of martial law and dispatched troops to shore up the Royal Ulster Constabulary. By mid-1920, the pattern of ambush and counterattack had escalated into a full-scale civil war, and Lloyd George, in need of more soldiers, created two special armies, the Auxiliaries and the infamous Black and Tans, so named for their uniforms.

The war was essentially a struggle between two poorly controlled forces, each trying to disrupt the communications and morale of its opponent. The British government, faced with the choice of systematically conquering Ireland, which meant political suicide at home, or abandoning publicly proclaimed war aims by negotiating with the rebels, chose the latter course. A truce was concluded in July 1921, as a preliminary to treaty negotiations.

Prior to the truce, Lloyd George had tried to effect a political settlement by enacting a new Home Rule Bill (the Government of Ireland Act, 1920) which became law in December of that year. The act, which became the fundamental law of Northern Ireland and from which de jure partition may be said to date, divided the island into "Northern Ireland," comprising six of the nine counties of Ulster, and "Southern Ireland," the remaining twenty-six counties. Each was to possess a bicameral legislature and a responsible ministry. The supremacy of the Westminster Parliament was to be preserved, and both Irelands were to elect representatives to it. Partition was not envisaged as permanent, and reunification could be effected by a simple vote of the two parliaments to merge. The act also authorized the creation of a Council of Ireland, to be composed of representatives from both legislatures, to regulate national issues and to act as a possible bridge to reunification. The council was stillborn.

The Ulster Unionists disliked the surrender of their coreligionists to a Catholic government in the south but were won over by the realization that Protestants would have a clear majority in Northern Ireland and the promise that Ulster would not be incorporated into the rest of Ireland without its consent. When elections were held in Northern Ireland in May 1921, Unionists won forty of the fifty-two seats in the lower House. They promptly organized a government with Sir James Craig as prime minister.

A PROTESTANT STATE FOR A PROTESTANT PEOPLE

In theory the border between the two Irelands was designed to separate Protestant Unionists from Catholic nationalists. In practice it was an attempt to make Northern Ireland as large as possible without sacrificing a working majority of Protestants. Of the nine counties of Ulster, only four—Armagh, Antrim, Down, and Londonderry—had Protestant majorities. Lloyd George imposed a boundary that awarded the counties of Tyrone and Fermanagh and the city of Londonderry to the Unionists as well. Both counties contained Catholic majorities, and the city of Londonderry was 65 percent Catholic.

Northern Ireland therefore included a Catholic minority of 34.5 percent, a large enough minority to trigger the insecurities of most Protestants. These insecurities were further aggravated by the fact that the Catholic population was concentrated along the long border with the Free State. This frontier, roughly equivalent to the old county boundaries, was hardly a viable frontier and is probably the most permeable border in the world—especially for northerners who cross it en masse every Sunday because their own pubs are closed. It is 256 miles long, or three times the distance as the crow flies between Newry and Londonderry, the cities at either extremity. By way of comparison, the longest distance in the entire island is only 300 miles! Running through the middle of villages and crossing and recrossing major communication routes, it is traversed by more than two hundred paved roads and is almost impossible to secure. The British Army has never been able to seal it off from terrorists.

The Protestant fear of a Catholic minority with ready access to their compatriots was reflected in the crescendo of sectarian violence that accompanied the creation of Northern Ireland. In the first few months of 1920, vigilante groups began to patrol the streets of Northern cities and towns. Captain Basil Brooke (later prime minister) was active in organizing and coordinating the activities of these vigilantes and unsuccessfully pleaded with the British government to issue the men sufficient arms to engage the IRA. Instead, the vigilantes used UVF weapons stockpiled before the war. The UVF was itself reconstituted and with other vigilante groups carried out pogroms against Northern Catholic communities. Large sections of the Falls Road were burned out, and numerous Catholics were expelled from Ulster.

In September 1920 the British government decided to organize the Ulster Special Constabulary, in part to facilitate their control over Protestant vigilantes. Three classes of Constabulary were created: the A Specials to serve full-time, the part-time B Specials, and the C Specials to be available in time of emergency. The first two classes were armed and were, in theory, to act under the supervision of the Royal Irish Constabulary (RIC). By midsummer 1922 the Special Constabulary consisted of fifty-five hundred A Specials, nineteen thousand B Specials, and seventy-five hundred C Specials.[4] Most of the recruits were drawn from vigilante associations and Special Constabulary officers that even when well-intentioned, were often unable to curb the sectarian excesses of their troops. The B Specials were especially notorious. They encouraged mobs to attack Catholic quarters of northern cities and in 1921 initiated a policy of reprisal murders against Catholics. In 1922 ninety-seven people were murdered in Belfast alone, and the city was placed under a curfew which was not lifted until December 1924. In the course of the violence more than seven hundred northerners were killed, nearly one thousand seriously wounded, and more than twenty-five thousand Catholics were driven from the country.

Northern Protestants had a comfortable majority of 2 to 1 in Ulster, and by

4. Sir Arthur Hezlet, *The B Specials* (London: Stacey, 1972). This book has a pronounced pro-B Special bias but nevertheless contains useful information.

1924 the regime had demonstrated its ability to maintain security against threats from within and without. Given this success it would have been wise policy to make some conciliatory gestures toward the Catholic minority in the hope of securing its tacit acceptance of the regime, if not ultimately its active support for the system. Instead, the Unionist party did just the opposite. It actively fostered distinctions between Protestants and Catholics and attempted to stimulate Protestant fears of the minority. The new prime minister, Sir James Craig (later Lord Craigavon), declared Northern Ireland to be "a Protestant Government" with "a Protestant Parliament for a Protestant People." Catholics, he asserted, would be "tolerated" if they obeyed the laws.[5] Neither Craig (1921-1943) nor his successor, Lord Brookeborough (1943-1963), made any attempt to integrate Catholics into the political or economic life of the country. Nor was any effort made to extend to them even the meager quality of services Unionist politicians brought to Protestant voters.

The decision to build a Protestant state is best understood as a function of the peculiar political and economic structure of Northern Ireland. During the nineteenth century, Ulster had undergone rapid industrial development, most of it concentrated in the northeast where the growth of the linen and shipbuilding industries had transformed Belfast into a major metropolis. Between 1821 and 1901, the population of the city had mushroomed from 37,000 to 249,000. Much of the new population consisted of Catholic laborers from beyond the Bann, and later from the South, who were attracted by the prospect of steady work. The Belfast industrialists, facing a severe labor shortage, welcomed the new emigrants, and most Protestants, prospering by reason of the boom, at first showed little animosity toward their Catholic coworkers.

The rapid industrialization of the province spurred the growth of a predominantly Protestant middle-class and a large, mixed working-class which gradually asserted itself under the banner of trade unionism. Working-class leaders sought to advance the political and economic interests of their class by uniting Protestant and Catholic workers in trade unions and challenging the absolute power of the industrialists and gentry. The Tory elite sought to preserve its prerogatives by fostering sectarian strife among its opponents. The economic recession in the last decades of the century which led to increased competition for jobs and housing—sedulously fostered by the Unionist elite—and the challenge of three Home Rule Bills, each of which led to considerable communal rioting, appeared to crown the elitist efforts with success. By the turn of the century, Protestant middle-class support for Catholic rights was restricted to a small minority of intellectuals, and on the other hand the emerging Labour party had made few inroads among

5. Nicholas Mansergh, *The Government of Northern Ireland* (London: Allen and Unwin, 1936), p. 240.

Protestant workers. The Orange Lodge, financed by Belfast industrialists and dedicated to the preservation of Protestant supremacy, had become the dominant institution of the Protestant working-class. Fearing the imagined horrors of Catholic power (Home Rule equals Rome Rule) and jealous of their marginal advantages over Catholics, Protestant workers ignored their real economic interests and supported the Unionist party.

Until the end of World War I, the North enjoyed some prosperity, but partition, civil war, a series of major strikes, and a general decline in the market for Belfast goods led to a twenty-year economic decline. Unemployment (of insured workers) rose from 18 percent in 1923, the first year of real peace, to 25 percent by 1926. After a brief resurgence in the later 1920s, due to a short boom in the linen industry, production again declined and unemployment averaged 25 percent throughout the 1930s. Worst hit of all was Londonderry, which to this day remains the most depressed city in the United Kingdom.

Unwilling to initiate radical economic reforms, yet politically dependent upon the Protestant working-class, the Unionist leadership sought to sidetrack any challenge to its power by maintaining and fostering sectarian conflict. The postwar depression, which further aggravated the struggle for jobs and housing, facilitated this strategy of divide and rule. In 1932, for example, Protestant and Catholic workers began to collaborate in demands for greater unemployment benefits and better housing. Worker demonstrations led to bitter fighting with the police. The government, anxious to diffuse this threat and to destroy any possibility of working-class solidarity, gave prominent support to the Ulster Protestant League which was dedicated to "persuading" all good Protestants not to employ Catholics or to work with them. Although the League relied primarily upon economic sanctions, it was not averse to employing outright coercion to compel employers to give preference to Protestants. Sir Basil Brook (later Viscount Brookeborough), declared: "Many in the audience employ Catholics but I have not one about my place. Catholics are out to destroy Ulster with all their might and power. They want to nullify the Protestant vote, take all they can out of Ulster and see it go to hell."[6] Similar rabble-rousing by Lord Craigavon and other Unionist leaders had the desired effect, and the bitterness of Protestant workers was turned against fellow Catholic workers, culminating in three weeks of "Paddy-bashing" and sectarian rioting in Belfast in July 1935.

Wartime prosperity and British subsidies somewhat eased the economic plight of the North. The British Treasury, which contributed millions (close to £400 million in 1974) to pay for a high level of social benefits, in effect, permitted the Unionist regime to circumvent meaningful reform. Westminster also provided incentives to attract industry to the North. Nevertheless, the

---

6. Ibid.

unemployment rate in the postwar years has hovered around 8 percent as compared with 1.7 percent in Great Britain.

Among insured Catholic workers the unemployment rate was closer to 15 percent.[7] Moreover, pronounced differences in living standards are apparent among those fortunate enough to be employed. In 1969, only 4 percent of those with an income of at least £2000 per annum were Roman Catholic, a function of continuing discrimination. In many firms, especially family businesses, there is a strict policy against hiring Catholics. In other enterprises, Catholics are restricted to jobs on the lowest rung of the economic ladder. The Belfast shipyards, for example, are the largest single industry in the city and employ more than ten thousand workers, only four hundred of whom are Catholic. In private enterprise, Catholic workers earn 20 percent less per capita than their Protestant compatriots. Until very recently the pattern of discrimination was even more striking in the public sector.[8]

The depressed state of the economy and the differential living standard between Protestants and Catholics had certain advantages for the regime. It not only gave Protestant workers, fearful of losing their marginal advantages over Catholics, incentives to support the Unionist party but also forced numerous unemployed Catholics to leave the North in search of work. Given the high Catholic birthrate, 28.3 per thousand, the Protestant majority has been maintained only through Catholic emigration, which has been twice that of Protestants. Despite Protestant fears of becoming a minority, the relative size of both communities changed only slightly in fifty years.[9] Thus, Unionist politicians have come to view economic development as a double-edged sword, and Ulster remains the poorest area of the United Kingdom.

While sectarian conflict kept Ulster Protestants loyal to the Unionist party, the regime employed both constitutional and extralegal means to ensure that Catholics, unalterably opposed to the status quo, remained powerless and largely quiescent. One of the most important devices in this respect was the rigged electoral system which facilitated fifty years of uninterrupted Unionist rule. Until 1970, elections to Stormont (the regional parliament) and to local governmental bodies were governed by a complicated franchise designed to

---

7. The difference can be explained in part as the result of a conscious governmental effort to concentrate industrial development in the northeast, the area of densest Protestant settlement. Between 1945 and 1966, 217 new firms (100 with one-third funding from the British government) were established in the six counties, but only twenty of these were located west of the Vann and only seven in Londonderry, the largest Catholic city in the North.

8. For statistics on discrimination, see Denis P. Barritt and Charles F. Carter, *The Northern Ireland Problem: A Study in Group Relations,* 2nd ed. (London: Oxford University Press, 1972) and Harold Jackson, *The Two Irelands: A Dual Study of Inter-Group Tensions* (London: Minority Rights Group, 1971).

9. The percentage of Roman Catholics in Northern Ireland since partition is as follows: 1911 (34.4 percent), 1926 (33.5 percent), 1937 (33.5 percent), 1951 (34.4 percent), 1961 (34.9 percent), and 1971 (35.2 percent). Given unchanging birth rates for both communities, the earliest the Catholics could become a majority is 2010.

inflate the Protestant vote and reduce the Catholic. In addition, corporations, overwhelmingly Protestant, were, under certain conditions, entitled to nominate up to six extra voters. In local elections, subtenants, lodgers, servants, and children over twenty-one living at home were deprived of the vote. About 250,000 adults, the majority of them Catholic, were thus disenfranchised. This was a significant percentage of the electorate because in 1967, for example, the total role of eligible voters (for internal elections) was only 694,484.

Equally important was the use of the gerrymander to guarantee Protestant domination of county councils. The most extreme example of this was in Londonderry. In 1966, the city had 14,325 Catholic voters and only 9235 Protestant voters. But housing segregation, informally enforced throughout much of the North, had the effect of concentrating almost all the Catholic voters in the Bogside and neighboring Creggan Estate which in turn were constituted into one huge Catholic ward. Each Protestant ward, containing many fewer voters, nevertheless sent the same number of councillors to the County Council, giving the Protestants a majority of 12 to 8. The Unionist majority on the council maintained residential segregation, provided better public services to Protestants, and, most importantly, guaranteed preferential treatment to Protestants with respect to jobs and housing. This was true of most county councils in the North.

The Stormont regime also controlled its minority through the application of what Catholics call "law and Orange Order," so named because the Royal Ulster Constabulary (RUC) has traditionally drawn most of its recruits from the Orange Lodges. The RUC and the part-time militia, the B Specials, were the military arm of the Unionist party. Both forces were well-armed (the Specials were finally disbanded by the British government in 1969-1970) and over the years showed little compunction about using their weapons. The Specials were especially active during the almost farcical IRA bombing campaigns of 1938-1940 and 1956-1962. Otherwise, they intimidated nationalist voters during elections, and individual Specials upon occasion engaged in the northern equivalent of "Nigger bopping." On Saturday nights, after a few drinks too many, they would go out and beat up or even shoot a few randomly selected Catholics. The ability of the police and Specials to intimidate Catholics was vastly facilitated by the Civil Authorities (Special Powers) Act (Northern Ireland), 1922, renewed annually until 1933 when it was made permanent. The Special Powers Act (finally revoked by Prime Minister Heath after the imposition of direct rule) permitted the suspension of habeas corpus and sanctioned indefinite internment without trial. It empowered the government to suspend freedom of the press, search buildings and arrest people without warrant, restrict personal movement, reverse the onus of proof in trials, and dispense with holding inquests on dead bodies. The only safeguards rested with the judiciary. Yet, with the exception of the first Lord

Chief Justice of Ulster, who was a Catholic, the bench has been overwhelmingly Protestant and Unionist and supportive of the regime's intimidation of Catholics.

THE COLLAPSE OF STORMONT

On March 24, 1972, the British government ended five decades of Unionist rule by assuming direct control over the affairs of Northern Ireland. The suspension of Stormont resulted from its inability to stem the escalating spiral of communal conflict which had already led to the deaths of several hundred people. The British government itself had made the reemergence of serious communal discord all but inevitable by including a substantial Catholic minority within the borders of Northern Ireland at its inception and giving the Unionist regime a blank check on the exercise of internal political power. Fifty years of repression bred only mutual fear and hatred which, given the proper stimulus, finally exploded.[10]

Conditions favorable to such an upheaval were manifest by the early 1960s. The most significant development was the gradual improvement in the economic condition of the Catholic community and the corresponding emergence of a Catholic middle-class. The roots of the Catholic economic transformation can be traced to the Labour victory in the British election of 1945. The new government was anxious to effect a redistribution of wealth in Britain and introduced educational and welfare reforms designed to raise the standard of living and improve the mobility of working-class families. The Unionist regime was hardly in favor of educational reform, national health, or increased welfare benefits; nevertheless, it was compelled to introduce such legislation in Northern Ireland by reason of the "step-by-step" principle which committed Stormont to keep pace with important British legislation in return for noninterference by Westminster in the internal affairs of Northern Ireland. The application of this principle resulted in the gradual extension of the British welfare state into Ireland and, most importantly, in the introduction of a system of national insurance conferring the same benefits received by unemployed workers elsewhere in the United Kingdom. Pensions, allowances, and National Health, largely financed through a complicated system of grants from the British Treasury to the Northern Irish government, were also introduced. By statute, no religious discrimination was permitted in the dispensation of funds and services, and the legislation thus had the immediate effect of considerably alleviating the economic plight of the Catholic

---

10. For an analysis of Northern Irish politics both prior to and after the imposition of direct rule, see Richard Ned Lebow, "Ireland," in Gregory Henderson, Richard Ned Lebow, and John Stoessinger, *Divided Nations in a Divided World* (New York: David McKay, 1974), pp. 196-265 and Richard Ned Lebow, "Civil War in Ireland: A Tragedy in Endless Acts?" *Journal of International Affairs* 27 (Autumn 1973): 247-60.

community. These reforms reduced the pressure on Catholics to emigrate. Other measures, most notably the Education Act (Northern Ireland), 1947, encouraged them to seek upward mobility.[11]

The emergence of a Catholic professional class and intelligentsia renewed Catholic pride and self-respect and heightened the community expectations of upward mobility. However, these expectations were thwarted by pervasive discrimination against Catholics in all areas of economic and political activity. The resultant frustration and anger, particularly acute among university graduates, gave impetus to the emerging civil rights movement. It is important to note that these developments occurred in an international environment sensitized to anti-colonial struggles and followed the full-blown emergence of the civil rights struggle in the United States. Northern Irish-Catholics, closely linked to the outside world by the media, were profoundly influenced by these events, especially the struggle of black Americans to achieve racial equality.

The first civil-rights demonstrations were organized by the Northern Ireland Civil Rights Association (NICRA), founded in 1967. The association was an unwieldy alliance of Catholic groups and Protestant individuals, many of them with divergent goals but united by a common opposition to Unionist repression. The member organizations agreed upon a six-point program calling for one-man-one-vote in local elections, reform of gerrymandered districts, laws against discrimination by local government, allocation of housing on a points system, repeal of the Special Powers Act, and the disbanding of the B Specials. Despite Unionist threats, the first civil rights march in June 1968 was a huge success, and, to the astonishment of the organizers, more than 4000 people participated. Significantly, the demonstration closed with the crowd singing "We Shall Overcome."

The second demonstration, in Londonderry on October 5, turned civil rights into a mass movement. The police, armed with batons, attacked the demonstrators at Craigavon Bridge. The public reaction in Britain, where the march had been televised by the BBC, forced the Labour government to intervene in Irish affairs for the first time since partition. Prime Minister Terence O'Neill was called to London where Harold Wilson threatened a "very fundamental reappraisal" of the government's relationship with

11. Prior to the Education Act, only 5 percent of all schoolchildren received any public support, and almost all of these were enrolled in state (Protestant) schools. No money was mandated for nursery schools or medical services, and books and paper were provided for only one child in ten. The Catholic community was most directly affected by the lack of support; most Catholic parents had been unable to afford educating their children beyond the primary grades. The Act of 1947 committed the state to pay all teachers' salaries in both state and voluntary (Catholic) schools as well as 65 percent of the constuction and maintenance costs of these school systems. The percentage was later increased, and the minimum age for completion of schooling raised to fifteen. Additional legislation opened higher education to Catholics by requiring universities to be nonsectarian. The proportion of Catholics at Queen's University, Belfast, the most prestigious school in the North, rose from 5 percent in 1947 to 22 percent by 1960.

Ireland.[12] O'Neill returned home and, on November 22, unveiled a package of five reforms which, if enforced, promised to meet the demonstrators' demands.[13]

The civil-rights marches provided the catalyst for the emergence of Protestant vigilante groups dedicated to preserving the political-economic status quo in Ulster. The strategy of these groups was two-fold: to intimidate Catholic demonstrators and to generate greater insecurity among Protestants by escalating communal conflicts, thus undermining support for moderate Unionists willing to make concessions to the Catholic community. In 1969, their immediate objective was to bring down O'Neill's government.

The most prominent of the early vigilante groups was organized by the Reverend Ian Paisley and his pompous comrade in arms, "Major" Ronald Bunting, "Commandant" of the Ulster Protestant Volunteers. Bunting was fond of exhorting his troops with sermons on the "religion of love" and the "evils of Rome" prior to confrontations with Catholics. Paisley and Bunting organized counterdemonstrations at numerous civil-rights activities and, on January 2, 1969, directed the attack on NICRA marchers at Burntollet Bridge, outside of Londonderry. The marchers, nevertheless, continued into the city where they were again attacked by a Protestant mob. That evening, the police, many of whom were drunk, lost all pretense of impartiality. Removing their identification badges, they joined in an attack on the Bogside where the mob smashed windows, broke into houses, and beat up the inhabitants. For all practical purposes, this pogrom put an end to the era of civil-rights marches and ushered in a more violent kind of confrontation.

The rioting succeeded in eroding Protestant support for the moderate O'Neill. His administration collapsed four months later, the direct result of a bombing campaign initiated by the Ulster Volunteer Force, a new Protestant terrorist group which had no relation to the former organization of the same name. In April 1969 the UVF blew up post offices and utilities, including the pumping station that provided water to Belfast, but made it appear to be the work of the still largely defunct IRA.[14] The government, taken in by the ploy, declared a state of emergency and mobilized the B Specials, provoking even

12. Despite this threat, no plans were made for such a contingency, and the cabinet was apparently convinced that O'Neill would somehow survive. One senior minister later reflected: "If anyone had told me that we would let O'Neill fall to be replaced by someone further to the Right, and that he in turn would be replaced from the Right—well, I would not have believed it."

13. O'Neill promised to initiate a points system to ensure the allocation of housing solely on the basis of need, to bring in a bill to appoint an ombudsman, and to establish some kind of machinery for investigating charges of discrimination. He further promised to reform local government and with it the franchise, and to dismiss the gerrymandered Londonderry Borough Council and replace it with a Development Commission on which Catholics would be fairly represented. The last measure was the only one ever to materialize.

14. Samuel Stevenson, self-styled "chief of staff" of the Ulster Volunteer Force, was later placed on trial for the bombings and pleaded guilty, giving evidence against other members of the Force who had pleaded not guilty.

more violent confrontations between Catholics and aroused Protestants. O'Neill was summoned to London and ordered to placate Catholic opinion by implementing the principle of one-man-one-vote. Caught in a crossfire between his irreconcilable British and Irish constituencies, the prime minister resigned. The new government, led by James Chichester-Clark, was forced to include more militant Protestants in the cabinet.

Chichester-Clark's unwillingness to implement O'Neill's reform package brought Catholic demonstrators back onto the streets in June. This led to sporadic fighting throughout the early summer and culminated in a week of violence in August that threatened to engulf the country in civil war. The Irish Republic mobilized troops along the border, and Harold Wilson felt compelled to send in the British Army to restore order to both Belfast and Londonderry. The army, at first welcomed by the Catholic community, was cleverly used by the Unionist government to enforce repressive measures against Catholics.[15] The deterioration of army-Catholic relations facilitated the reemergence of the IRA, dormant since its abortive terror campaign of the 1950s. In March 1971 both branches of the IRA commenced a bombing campaign. The official IRA agreed to a cease-fire in May 1972, but the Provisional IRA campaign has continued to grow in intensity.

In retrospect, it is apparent that the political culture of Northern Ireland was so fragile that the civil-rights demonstrations set in motion a chain of events that destroyed the political system within the course of four years. The marches, aimed only at securing reform, triggered a violent Protestant response. This in turn radicalized Catholic opinion and led to more far-reaching demands. At the very core of the problem was the terrible dilemma faced by Unionist politicians. The party had maintained power for fifty years by first inciting, then exploiting, Protestant working-class fears of the Catholic minority. This aroused extreme Protestant passions, making it impossible for any Northern Irish prime minister to espouse reforms without

---

15. The most dramatic of these measures was internment, a gamble that proved to be the single most disastrous throw any British prime minister has ever given to the shaky dice of politics in Ireland. Heath envisaged internment as a kind of surgical operation in which the British Army would arrest the command structure of the IRA, destroying their capability to sustain the bombing campaign. Instead, Brian Faulkner, Northern Irish prime minister, used internment to silence as many political opponents as possible, whether or not they had any connection with the IRA. The Royal Ulster Constabulary prepared a list of 500 names of which, by their estimate, only 120-130 were suspected gunmen. Another 300-400 were classified as IRA sympathizers. The rest were neither gunmen nor sympathizers but Catholic politicians, to be arrested because they were deemed to be less troublesome behind bars. The British Army wanted to arrest only 150 people, all suspected gunmen, but their recommendation was overruled. In the early morning hours of August 9, 1971, the army, acting as Faulkner's agent, set out to "lift" 450 people. By evening, 342 persons had been arrested, many dragged from their beds in the middle of the night. They were held without charges, an action permitted under the Special Powers Act. Ultimately, 1576 suspects were lodged in several detention camps on the outskirts of Belfast. Internment triggered off severe and sustained Catholic rioting throughout the North and, more than any other single act, served to increase Catholic support for the IRA.

opening himself to a devastating political attack from more militant
Unionists. Concessions thus became the equivalent of political suicide, as the
careers of O'Neill and Chichester-Clark attest, but repression, as Chichester-
Clark's successor, Brian Faulkner, demonstrated, proved to be equally
disastrous because Unionist rigidity led to the rapid growth of the IRA and the
escalation of the Provisional IRA bombing campaign. The gunmen on both
sides set the stage for a possible civil war and forced the direct intervention of
the British government.

THE UNIONIST DILEMMA

With the imposition of direct rule, William Whitelaw was appointed
Secretary of State for Northern Ireland. Whitelaw attempted to restore a
degree of tranquillity to the province by reaching a truce with the IRA and
restoring a regional assembly based on the principle of power sharing between
Catholics and Protestants. The British government also began to channel
increasingly large sums of money into the North in the hope of reducing
unemployment, a major cause of communal tension. The search for a lasting
truce proved illusory, but Whitelaw was surprisingly effective in temporarily
restoring regional government to the North.[16]

The demise of Stormont and the imposition of direct rule confronted
Unionists with four basic policy options:

1. Noncooperation with the British government in the hope of restoring Stormont and with it Protestant supremacy.
2. Agitation in favor of complete integration of Northern Ireland within
   Great Britain.
3. Agitation in favor of independence for Northern Ireland.
4. Cooperation with moderate Catholics and non-Unionist Protestants
   in a reformed regional assembly—the proclaimed objective of the
   British government.

Brian Faulkner, Unionist prime minister upon the suspension of Stormont, was the most important Unionist leader to opt for power sharing
with Catholics. His advocacy of this position represented a total about-
face for Faulkner, formerly associated with the more extreme wing of the
Unionist party. While prime minister, he had been the guiding force behind internment which, more than any other single act, polarized the
Protestant and Catholic communities and prompted the escalation of violence that forced Heath to impose direct rule.

Faulkner's reversal, heralded by his cautious acceptance of the British

16. For a discussion of Unionist politics during the period of power sharing, see Richard Ned
Lebow, "The Unionist Dilemma," *The Irish-American Review* 1 (April 1974): 24-29.

White Paper on Northern Ireland in March 1973, was condemned as sheer opportunism by his critics, but applauded as a courageous act of realism by his supporters. Regardless of his motives, Faulkner appears to have realized that power sharing was the only practical policy to pursue in order to preserve regional autonomy and with it a degree of Unionist power in the North.

Faulkner did his best to persuade Northern Protestants that cooperation with both moderate Catholics and the Republic was the only sure way of maintaining the influence in London necessary to prevent a total sell-out of Ulster to the Republic. In the process he obtained significant concessions in the tripartite negotiations leading to the creation of the Council of Ireland (the Sunningdale Agreement). Great Britain pledged not to alter the status of Northern Ireland without the consent of its inhabitants and promised to contribute more funds to the depressed economy of the province. The Republic, whose constitution lays claim to sovereignty over all thirty-two counties, made an historic pronouncement recognizing Northern Ireland to be part of the United Kingdom. Prime Minister Liam Cosgrave further affirmed that this status could not be changed unless a majority of Northerners wished to do so. Cosgrave also promised to step up measures in the Republic against the IRA and cooperate more closely with Northern police authorities to suppress terrorism.

While unable to abort the Council of Ireland, Faulkner succeeded in somewhat limiting its powers and making all important actions dependent upon the unanimous vote of its members, parliamentarians to be drawn from the Assembly in the North and the Dail in the South.

These negotiations, completed in late December, cleared the way for the creation of the Northern Ireland Executive, a coalition government of Protestant Faulkner Unionists, nonsectarian Alliance members, and predominantly Catholic Social Democratic and Labour Party delegates in the reconstructed regional assembly. On January 1, 1974, the Executive assumed power with Brian Faulkner at its head.

The phasing out of internment, the introduction of proportional representation, power sharing and, above all, the Sunningdale Agreement, were viewed with the deepest suspicion by militant Protestants. At the very least these developments promised to alter the political-economic status quo to the perceived disadvantage of the Protestant working-class. At the worst, they were interpreted by many Protestants as the prelude to Northern Ireland's incorporation into the Republic of Ireland.

The anti-power sharing sentiment of the Protestant organizations was expressed through the Ulster Vanguard, created by William Craig in February 1972 to act as spokesman for the panoply of Protestant militant groups such as the Orange Order, the Ulster Special Constabulary Association (retired B Specials who run gun clubs throughout the North), the Loyalist Association of Workers (first organized among Belfast dockers), and the Ulster Defence

Association. Vanguard mounted a campaign to bring back a Stormont with even greater powers and, failing that, independence. Craig has cited the example of Rhodesia and has frequently mooted the use of violence as a proper means of achieving either goal.

Power sharing is also anathema to the Democratic Unionist Party, organized by the Reverend Ian Paisley in 1970 to oppose any concessions to the Catholic minority. Prior to direct rule the DUP was the second largest Protestant party in Stormont. Paisley, who has close ties to Enoch Powell, is opposed to independence and favors instead the complete integration of Northern Ireland into Great Britain.

Finally, power sharing is opposed by the majority of regular Unionists. The anti-Faulkner faction emerged dominant from the party split caused by Faulkner's acceptance of power sharing, and the former leader was expelled from the party in January 1974. Harry West was subsequently elected chairman and, together with Vanguard and DUP, set up the United Ulster Unionist Council (UUUC) to coordinate the three parties' efforts to destroy the Executive. They achieved their objective in May 1974 by means of a strike that paralyzed the province. The British government proved reluctant to use troops to break the strike, and the coalition Executive collapsed. The demise of the Executive had the expected effect of further polarizing opinion in the North, precluding any renewed attempt at power sharing in the near future.

Following the collapse of the Executive, the three dissident Unionist factions announced plans to merge into a new political party in order to work for the restoration of a Protestant-dominated regional assembly and greater representation in Westminster, a state of affairs totally unacceptable to all shades of Catholic opinion. The Loyalists warned that rejection of their demands by the British government could lead to civil war.

The Loyalist threat to commence military operations is made credible by the existence of the Ulster Defence Association and the Ulster Volunteer Force, the shock troops of Protestant militantism.

The Ulster Defence Association (UDA), which rapidly increased its membership in the aftermath of direct rule, is well armed by reason of its close ties with the Ulster Defence Regiment (organized in 1970 to replace the Special Constabulary) and draws its recruits primarily from the Protestant working-class. Estimates of its strength run as high as fifty-three thousand which, if correct, would make it a far greater threat to British authority than the IRA in any military confrontation.

The philosophy of the UDA is a rather primitive form of anti-Catholicism. The organization makes no distinction between the IRA, moderate Catholic politicians, and the Catholic Church, all of whom it perceives as out to destroy Protestant liberties. In a recent statement, Sammy Doyle, UDA press officer, asserted, "The enemy of the Ulster Protestant and the Protestant faith is the I.R.A. Provos, aided covertly by the Roman Catholic Hierarchy. While the present violence on the part of these enemies continues unabated, the U.D.A. will continue to carry out the function for which it was created: the defence of the Protestant people and the preservation of the Protestant faith."[17]

In keeping with this policy, the UDA has continually pressed the British government to take more strenuous action against the IRA even if this provokes violent confrontations between the army and the Catholic community. In July 1972, for example, the UDA erected its own "no go" areas and declared its intention to maintain blockades in Protestant areas until the army occupied similar Catholic sanctuaries. This the British did on July 31, and the army-IRA clash, which UDA surely hoped to provoke, failed to materialize. The UDA has also engaged in counter terrorism, and, while documentation of such charges is naturally difficult, it is generally believed that the organization has assassinated Catholics suspected of being members or supporters of the Provisional IRA. The organization has also participated in attempts to drive Catholics out of Protestant or integrated areas of Belfast. In July 1972, for example (the yearly intimidation always reaches its peak in the summer months), threats to Catholic tenants and homeowners were so widespread that Whitelaw's Public Protection Agency was helpless to render effective assistance, and more than five thousand dispossessed Catholics sought refuge in the Republic.

On several occasions the UDA has clashed violently with the British Army, resulting in deaths on both sides. These clashes have led to a serious deterioration of army-Protestant relations, similar to that which occurred in the Catholic community following earlier army-IRA confrontations. Like the IRA, the UDA has complained bitterly of army brutality. In the Shankill Road section of Belfast, for example, UDA officers have recently made the same sort of allegations against the paratroopers that once came only from Catholic districts. They claim harassment: houses searched with frustrating frequency, members beaten, children questioned, and women insulted. At this point, the UDA would like to see the army withdrawn from Northern streets. However, since the organization has refrained from major military operations, it is allowed to operate openly and legally throughout the North.

By way of contrast, the Ulster Volunteer Force, the other major Protestant paramilitary organization, is not only more radical in its politics but until recently was also proscribed by the British government. There is nevertheless some overlap in membership between the UDA and UVF, although each has its own territory and relations between them are characterized by respectful jealousy.

Members of the UVF admit that "they turned to violence as a result of feelings of fear, insecurity and powerlessness" and that their military actions have been directed primarily against the Catholic community. For several

17. *Irish Times* (February 5, 1974): 9.

years prior to the November 1973 cease-fire, the UVF bombed IRA meeting places and alleged sources of finance, engaged Republic gunmen during sectarian confrontations and robbed businesses, banks, and armories for funds and weapons. One brigade officer interviewed proudly asserted that the UVF and its associated groups have been responsible for 97 percent of all the Loyalist violence in the North during the last four years.[18] Another officer explained:

> By bombing the heart of Provisional enclaves we attempted to terrorize the nationalist community into demanding that the Provisionals either cease their campaign or move out of the ghetto areas. By bombing business premises and other such properties which we had reason to believe were terrorist meeting places or sources of revenue, we believed that we could force the Provisionals out of business, or at least cause a drastic reduction in their operational activity. By attempting to eliminate Provisional activists and "Backroom boys"—a very hard task; even for the security forces—we hoped to crack their morale and destroy their chain of command.[19]

The UVF denies any involvement in sectarian or political assassination. However, individual members of the Force engage in such activities, and several have been convicted of sectarian murders. The UVF has also threatened "military action" against the British Army, in particular the Third Parachute Regiment, accused of harassing Protestants in the West Belfast area, but has so far refrained from large scale confrontations with security forces.

Since the November truce, the UVF has concentrated on political action. Its leaders have met, in their own words, "with every shade of political opinion who would speak to us" and subsequently have held education classes and "teach-ins" for their membership. These political contacts included spokesmen for Sinn Fein (Gardiner Street), the political front of the Official IRA, and UVF leaders have expressed public support for Sinn Fein's federal solution to the Irish problem.[20]

The UVF's flirtation with Sinn Fein highlights one of the more paradoxical aspects of the Irish situation, the many areas of agreement between working-class Protestant militants and both branches of the IRA. Sectarian suspicions aside, the UVF and IRA oppose the prevailing power structure and perceive both traditional Unionists and prominent Catholic politicians as men who, the UVF asserts, "have used the fear of their co-religionists as stepping stones to power and are prepared to bolster up the present undemocratic system of

18. Interviews with UVF members; see also an anonymous article by a UVF brigade leader in the *Sunday News* (Belfast) (February 3, 1974).

19. See *Combat* (April 19, 1974), the recently launched organ of the Ulster Volunteer Force.

20. Many observers believe that the agreement between the two otherwise antagonistic organizations is merely tactical and designed to facilitate the withdrawal of the British Army after which Protestant and Catholic gunmen would be free to fight it out among themselves for control of the province.

government forced upon the people of Ulster by the British Government."[21]

In early 1974, many UVF brigade commanders actually expressed the view that Northern Ireland's problems were the result of "fifty years of sectarian indoctrination by the Unionist leadership" designed to prevent collaboration between Protestant and Catholic workers. In a recent official publication the organization declared that it has "a new outlook on life" and no longer views Ulster "through the eyes of sectarian bigots and gunmen," but "as Ulstermen who now see that life in Ulster can only be enjoyed to the full by the creation of a new society based on the unity and sovereignty of the ordinary rank-and-file Ulster people, Protestant and Catholic alike."[22]

If some of the UVF leadership has undergone an apparent conversion—how deep a conversion it is difficult to assess—the majority of the membership holds less sophisticated and more sectarian views. The majority clearly favors ending the cease-fire and abandoning efforts to reach a detente with the Republican movement. This divergence of opinion touched off an internal struggle for power between the so-called "moderate" and "proloyalist" factions. In April 1974, supporters of the more militant faction assassinated James Hanna, a member of the UVF delegation that traveled to Dublin in December for secret talks with political representatives of the Official IRA. The proloyalist faction appears to have gained the upper hand and, at the present time (June 1974), the UVF is threatening to end its five-month's cease-fire "with swift and devastating" effect unless the Provisional IRA halts its bombing campaign.[23]

While engaged in political activity, the UVF has not neglected military organization and declares itself ready to repel any enemy incursions into Loyalist areas. In December 1973, the Force participated in the organization of the Ulster Army Council, an umbrella organization of paramilitary groups, among them the Ulster Defence Association, the Loyalist Defence Volunteers, and the Red Hand Commandos. There are unpleasant rumors circulating in Belfast that the Council is preparing for a concerted terror campaign. The recent upsurge of murders may well mark the beginning of this campaign. However, it is more likely that these killings were the work either of individual members of the UVF attempting to force a termination of the cease-fire or of still other terrorist groups which have proliferated since 1972. Most of these groups, like the (Protestant) Avengers, for example, are composed of a few people who meet in backrooms to plan sectarian assassinations. Finally, it should be noted that the upsurge in lawlessness and the corresponding inability of the police and army to maintain order have encouraged mentally disturbed individuals, both Catholic and Protestant, whose motives are

21. *Combat* (April 19, 1974).
22. Ibid.
23. *Combat* (April 26, 1974).

nonpolitical, to engage in murder. Some of the worst atrocities, killings, and mutilation of retarded individuals and children, for example, have been the work of such individuals.

Whatever happens in the near future, it is clear that the police and the Army are unable to control either Provisional IRA or Loyalist violence, and neither community of gunmen show any signs of looking for peace or a new detente. Moreover, it is apparent that the Labour government is contemplating eventual withdrawal of the British Army from Ulster, their presence being costly and increasingly unpopular with the British electorate.[24] Given the failure of power sharing, such a withdrawal would be likely to trigger a full-scale civil war.

CONCLUSIONS

There is a certain symmetry to Irish politics. Twice in the twentieth-century Protestant vigilante groups have raised the specter of civil war in order to deter the British government from radically altering the status quo in Ireland. On the first occasion, the vigilantes met with partial success. Lloyd George, dependent as he was upon the parliamentary support of British Unionists, sought to salvage what he could for the Unionist minority in Ireland through partition. The partition, in effect, gave Unionists a new lease on life by making them a majority within a separate northern state. However, by separating the six counties of Ulster from the rest of Ireland, and by including a substantial Catholic minority in the new political unit, the British government ensured that the conflict which had brought Ireland to the brink of civil war in 1914 would ultimately be resumed on a smaller geographic scale. Thus, partition, like other halfway measures that preceded it, failed to resolve the key issues of discord in Ireland, merely postponing their resolution to a later date.

Unionists are currently attempting to replay the prepartition scenario in the hope of forcing the British government to restore Protestant political supremacy to the North. While they succeeded in destroying the Executive, it is unlikely that the British can be coerced into restoring a Protestant regime. The political considerations that facilitated the success of the Unionists in 1914-1920 are not present in 1974.

Unionist demands in 1914 were widely supported throughout Britain. Public opinion was strongly anti-Irish, and the Tory party, as noted earlier, gave overt support to the Ulster Volunteer Force. So did the British army and the king. The unwillingness of both political parties to coerce Ulster Protestants was determined by more than feelings of sentimental affinity. Control of Ireland was deemed a strategic necessity in any naval confrontation with Germany, a very likely possibility in the early summer of

---

24. The government publicly hinted at withdrawal in April 1974.

1914. The near success of the U-boat campaign during World War I reinforced British perceptions of their need to maintain bases in the North, bases which played an extremely significant role in the Battle of the Atlantic in World War II. In addition, Northern Ireland, prior to 1914, was an economic asset. Her linen trade and ship-building industry made important contributions to the British economy. None of these conditions hold true today.

To begin with, Northern Ireland is a serious drain on the British Treasury. The Exchequer contributed close to £400 million to Northern Ireland in 1974, exclusive of the cost of maintaining a significant military presence in the province. This is an expense that the depressed British economy can ill-afford. Nor, in the age of air power and nuclear submarines, is Northern Ireland still indispensable to British security.

More importantly, the Loyalist cause finds little support in Britain. Enoch Powell and Ulster Protestant immigrants aside, the British people appear to have little interest in Irish affairs aside from their concern about the violence. The rash of bombings in London in 1973 galvanized this sentiment, and most people express equal indignation with the tactics of both sides to the conflict. Public opinion, moreover, has become extremely restive about the Army's continuing presence in Ulster, where several hundred soldiers have been killed since August 1969. Polls reveal that the overwhelming majority of the electorate favors withdrawal of the Army despite the widespread realization that such an action would probably trigger civil war. In the words of one porter interviewed by the *Observer,* the government "should pull out the plug and sink the bloody lot of 'em."[25] If the situation deteriorates to such a point that Loyalists begin shooting at British soldiers, this sentiment will become even more pronounced and the British Prime Minister will face a difficult decision. To evacuate the army would remove the last effective restraint on the gunmen, but to maintain an active military presence and engage in a costly three-cornered struggle for control of the province would be political suicide at home. Most observers believe that the government would be inclined to pull out the troops and wash its hands of the situation.

If the British Army pulled out, the Loyalists would attempt to reestablish a government and conceivably declare independence. The Provisional IRA, supported by large numbers of Catholics, would resist Protestant supremacy by force, prompting the UDA and UVF to go after the Provisionals. Bloody pogroms, especially against the relatively unprotected Belfast Catholics, would certainly result. Thousands of Ulstermen would flee the country, Catholics to the Republic and both Catholics and Protestants to Britain. The Republic can hardly be expected to remain a bystander in such a conflict, and public opinion would probably force her intervention. Even assuming that the Republican army were capable of occupying the province, the UDA and UVF

---

25. *Observer* (London) (February 6, 1972): 7.

would retain effective control of Protestant urban enclaves and wage guerrilla war against the Irish army of occupation. The present situation would thus be reversed, with the UDA and UVF playing the role of the Provisionals (and far more effectively) and the Republican army substituting for the British.

The above speculation is, of course, only one of many possible scenarios, but it nevertheless reveals with dramatic impact the dilemma currently confronting the British government. All the major parties to the conflict appear to be locked into historically determined roles from which the British have been unable to encourage significant deviation. As a result, civil war is a likely possibility. Even more tragically, civil war would itself still not produce resolution of what is likely to remain one of the most intractable conflicts of the twentieth century.

Part IV:

Conclusions

Chapter Thirteen

Vigilante Politics: Concluding Observations

Peter C. Sederberg and H. Jon Rosenbaum

The term "vigilante" was originally used to denote a particular pattern of American frontier violence: that designed to impose some sort of order on a fluid and disrupted social situation. The principal thrust of this volume has been to demonstrate that vigilantism is not a geographically fixed, historically specific phenomenon. On the contrary, in chapter 1 we suggest the general conditions which seem likely to encourage vigilante violence and argue that it is not confined to any one place or time. The essays by Professors Shotland and Kreml (chapters 2 and 3) go further in describing the social psychological context which stimulates a vigilante response and the type of personality likely to engage in such acts. In Part II, the panorama of American vigilantism is presented, from Professor Brown's historical survey to contemporary cases of police violence. Finally, in Part III, establishment violence is shown to be a global problem in this age of social discord. Indeed, examples of vigilantism outside of America could be extensively multiplied.

We believe, therefore, in the significance of establishment violence and its need to be studied along with the related problems of dissident violence and normal, or "acceptable," regime coercion. We are fully aware, however, that this volume is only a preliminary step toward systematic crossnational and crosstemporal analysis. The multiple talents of our contributors have served to identify some conceptual ambiguities in our initial efforts to "stretch" the idea of vigilantism to cover what appeared to be all the relevant cases of establishment violence. Consequently, in this concluding chapter, we identify, if not completely resolve, some of these problems. We hope that by doing this, further research will be stimulated. Second, we address the ethical problems in studying, as well as engaging in, vigilante acts. Finally, in keeping with the current popularity of prognostication, we speculate about a number of "alternative futures" in the development of vigilante politics.

CONCEPTUAL PROBLEMS

MICRO AND MACRO ANALYSES

One of the recurring challenges of social scientific analysis is to bridge the gap between systemic explanatory frameworks and individual behavioral responses. In chapter 1 we set forth some hypothesized determinants of the magnitude of establishment violence in a society. Essentially, we argue that increases in the level of frustration with regime ineffectiveness, combined with a culture of violence and an inability of the regime to defend its own prerogatives from vigilante incursions, contribute to a rise in the level of vigilante violence. Nothing is directly said about those who participate in this kind of activity or whether some people might have a greater propensity for vigilante violence. The essential argument is that, in a given population, the amount of vigilante activity will rise as these systemic factors intensify.

Professor Kreml adopts the obverse perspective. He asks what type of personality is prone to vigilantism. He suggests four "structural" and two "stylistic" traits which, combined with certain intensifiers, are associated with the vigilante personality. In effect, Kreml attempts to identify who is most likely to engage in vigilantism in a given systemic context.

The two perspectives complement one another. People possessing a strong positive orientation to power, a high need for order, and a fear of their own impulsiveness are more easily distressed by the appearance of government ineffectiveness than are those who demonstrate these traits to a lesser extent. The stylistic factors of dogmatism and rigidity make it more difficult for people to tolerate stressful situations; rather, they are strongly driven to resolve their tension in some fashion.

David Schwartz, in a study of alienated political behavior, argues that people respond differently to such tension.[1] Some choose the relatively passive paths of either "withdrawal" or "ritualism" (i.e., continuing to follow the forms of prior behavior even though no longer believing in their efficacy). Others tend to the more activist alternatives of "reform" or "revolution," which in this case refers to any resort to unacceptable physical coercion, whether creative, preservative, or restorative in purpose. A strongly anti-introspective personality, Kreml's fourth structural trait, would seem more likely to choose an activist method of resolving the anxiety-producing situation. Reform, such as attempting to strengthen governmental enforcement capabilities, would not be vigilante in nature, but such reforms take time and may not be fully satisfying, especially as the frustration over perceived government ineffectiveness increases. In a culture which rationalizes the use of violent self-help, the anti-introspective personality

---

1. David C. Schwartz, *Political Alienation and Political Behavior* (Chicago: Aldine, 1973), especially pp. 3-28.

would be further encouraged to engage in a more activist response to the frustration. Schwartz mentions a number of other personality factors which encourage activist behavior, including high energy levels and relative psychological comfort with one's anger (people who fear their own anger are more likely to withdraw from their environment than attack it). Both of these qualities also seem likely to correlate with anti-introspectiveness.

Schwartz identifies two other elements which serve to complete the portrait of the vigilante personlity. First, he argues that the activist must feel relatively invulnerable from reprisals. Certainly, as regime boundary maintenance capability declines and social support for the vigilantes increases, the participants in establishment violence will feel less threatened by the possibility of countermeasures. Second, Schwartz suggests that the activist will probably have a low need to be reintegrated into the polity. This trait is of less significance to vigilantes than it is to dissident activists. The vigilantes believe they are the established order, and they attempt to reintegrate the polity with themselves.

Although the complementarity of the micro and macro approaches outlined above appears quite strong, the correspondence is not perfect. First, though these traits may generally be associated with one another, there is no obvious reason why an individual should manifest all of them with the same intensity. One could conceive of an order-prone personality who is not particularly anti-introspective and would thus be inclined to more passive behavioral responses to frustration. Alternatively, a person could strongly manifest all four structural characteristics, but also possess a greater tolerance of frustration. The extent to which these factors associate with and reinforce one another is a fruitful subject for future research.

Second, it seems useful to conceive of each of these traits in terms of a threshold, and different people probably have different thresholds. As the systemic sources of frustration intensify, more people reach their threshold and become available for some type of alienated behavior. A person may have a different threshold for each trait. Another area for research, then would be to develop an aggregate measure of the propensity to engage in vigilante acts. In this way it may become possible to empirically link the intensity of the systemic factors encouraging vigilantism to the percentage of the population prone to vigilantism at any given level. Related to these efforts would be an attempt to determine whether these traits will be manifested regardless of culture.

Finally, although Kreml labels the structural personality traits as "conservative," not all psychological conservatives identify with the established order. Many reject it and find their need for power rankings and order fulfilled in a dissident political community. Indeed, the "conservative" personality may provide the organizational backbone of every significant revolutionary movement, as well as the personnel of vigilante groups. Thus, though all vigilantes may possess these personality traits, not all "vigilante" personalities will necessarily participate in establishment violence.

All these considerations indicate that the synthesis of psychological and systemic perspectives is not an easy task. Hopefully, the suggestions outlined above will provide the basis for further refinements in this area.

DEFINING COERCION AND VIOLENCE

The idea of physical force or coercion has been central to political analysis at least since Machiavelli's Prince manipulated it to gain and maintain power and Hobbes' Natural Man bound himself to a sovereign authority in order to escape the constant threat of bodily harm. Despite its importance, the concept often lacks precision which causes some problems for our study. Perhaps the most fundamental of these concerns the observer's own ethical and emotional involvement with the phenomenon. It is difficult to escape some kind of personal reaction when studying the use of force in social relations, except through a process of intellectual abstraction which is probably akin to dehumanization. This problem will be further discussed in the section on ethics and vigilantism.

The concept of coercion generates certain definitional difficulties as well. In order to discuss vigilantism, we developed a number of distinctions. First, we limit "coercion" to those acts which are intended to damage another person or his value position, thereby excluding such dilatory uses as the "force" of someone's personality or persuasive "force." Second, we distinguish coercive acts according to their intensity and purpose (creation, maintenence, and restoration). Third, we argue that every established social system defines certain laws and norms, or boundaries, which approximately delineate between acceptable coercion and unacceptable violence. Although these boundaries favor the status quo, usually some limits are placed on the exercise of maintenance coercion. We do not accord the state a monopoly on "legitimate" coercion, at least in the conventional sense, for some acts of private coercion may lie within the limits of acceptability. Rather, we believe that in contemporary political systems the state plays the primary role in demarcating these boundaries.

We think this analysis helps to clarify the use of the concept, but it is not without difficulties. A number of contributors, particularly Professor Mazrui, indicate the problem created by conflicting norms within the same system; for example, what was acceptable "self-help" in a traditional society may no longer be so in a modernizing political order. Alternatively, coercion that is tolerated or even supported in a regional subsystem (e.g., Klan activities in the South) may be deemed violence in the context of the national system. Since the definition of violence depends on making this distinction, conflicting norms can present a significant problem. Generally, we believe that it is reasonable to resolve such clashes in favor of the more general authority making a plausible jurisdictional claim. In the cases cited above, the proscriptions of the nation state would be given precedence over those of either regional or traditional loyalties. Another possible decision criterion would be that the more restrictive norm or law takes precedence. Public authorities can commit vigilante acts by violating the rules to which they are formally bound. If no limits are placed on the exercise of state coercion, then the regime itself could be considered vigilante. These qualifications still leave an area of ambiguity as the restrictiveness of the rules will differ from system to system.

A second problem arises in determining the purposes of the perpetrators of violent acts: are they attempting to preserve, restore, or create? As noted in our introductory chapter, we believe that some account of purpose must be made in order to distinguish between revolutionaries and reactionaries, much less identify cases of "conservative" violence. Purposes, however, are not always easy to detect and classify and often tend to merge with one another. Some of the cases discussed in this collection are borderline in nature and could be judged as either revolutionary or reactionary rather than vigilante in nature.

Finally, the concept of coercion as intentional damage covers a wide range of acts from the mild to the intense. Professor Schneier notes that the coercion exercised during the McCarthy era was fairly subtle, blacklisting and job loss rather than murder and mayhem. He questions whether our model includes such subtleties. We believe that it does, though disguised coercion does raise problems of detection. In the case of the victims of cold war scapegoating, the damage, though indirect, was fairly obvious and inflicted without regard to a basic boundary of the American political system—that of due process.

There is, however, a related difficulty: that of determining what sorts of acts are damaging. In part, this will depend on cultural norms. Professor Mazrui points out that vigilante violence in Africa can be a response to the perceived damage inflicted by witchcraft. The believed ability to curse someone with impotency becomes a coercive threat to which a violent response may be given. Moreover, in a complex society, interdependence may make sophisticated coercion difficult to detect at all. For example, the vast store of information held by both private and public organizations could be used to cause significant damage without the victim or the observer ever being able to identify exactly what is occurring.

These kinds of vagaries could probably be uncovered through a close examination of any conceptualization about the functioning of society. Despite the problems at the peripheries, we think that in most cases the purpose of the act will be clear and its acceptability within a given context will be easily determined.

DEFINING THE ESTABLISHMENT

In order to decide whether a specific act of coercion is intended to maintain the established order, one must first define the contours of the establishment. As we suggested, the members of the establishment need not constitute an elite; rather, these are people who prefer things as they are and look with suspicion on any proposal for significant change, whether of a creative or restorative sort. Yet as the adjective "significant" suggests, change is a matter of degree, and citizens may be more or less attached to the status quo. The exact point where an act becomes creative or restorative, rather than preservative, constitutes another area of judgment. Many cases are clearly one or the other, but some are borderline, such as Klan activity or certain of the community police patrols studied by professors Marx and Archer.

Another obstacle in identifying establishment violence emerges when there appears to be more than one establishment. Often, this will be associated with conflicting norms on what is excessive coercion. We noted this problem with respect to the Allende regime in Chile. Who represented the establishment during this era? The peasants who siezed the holdings of large landowners, or the owners who resisted them?

Again, Professor Mazrui suggests that a dual establishment often exists in African countries, as seen in the competition between the modernizing heir to the colonial government and the traditional authorities. He also introduces a further complication in the "establishment" of the "unseen" world and lucidly suggests some of the ways in which the seen and the unseen worlds interact. Finally, as the study of Professor von der Mehden implies, in some Asian and African countries one could argue that there are two establishments: one dominating the economic system and the other prevailing in the social and political orders. Are attacks on the former by members of the latter more "creative" than "preservative" in purpose?

In most cases of crime- and social-group-control vigilantism, the establishment reacts against clearly dissident elements, and the appelation "vigilante" is easily applied. In the examples cited above, and most cases of regime-control vigilantism, one faction of the establishment appears to be attacking a rival element. The purpose, then, is not simply to maintain, but to enhance the attacking group's value position. This objective is not clearly revolutionary or reactionary in nature, though it might conform to the meaning of "revolution from above;" nor is it "pure" vigilantism. In this instance, Professor Stettner's objection to the diversity of the phenomena included in the model is well taken.

Notwithstanding these problems, we think that the analysis and typology of vigilantism refines the usual classifications of political violence, though we are not so arrogant as to assume that further improvements could not be made. Many of the cases of intraestablishment violence discussed in this volume seem to be illuminated by the hypotheses advanced under the rubric of vigilantism, but additional refinement is required.

The Problem of Ideology

An apparent contradiction has also arisen in various discussions of vigilante ideology. We suggest that vigilantes are unlikely to develop "autonomous" ideologies. To adopt David Riesman's categories, they are not "inner directed" by a strong and highly developed system of personal norms. On the contrary, vigilantes tend to be "other directed," taking their values and behavioral cues from the prevailing political culture.[2] Professor Kreml develops a similar analysis, adapting the concept of "conscious parallelism" to explain correspondences between the values of the vigilantes and those of the dominant members of the community. Taking a somewhat more philosophical stance, Professor Stettner agrees that vigilantes do not appear to make either a systematic statement of their social and political ends or a "scientific" analysis of society—both characteristics commonly associated with the term ideology.

In seeming disagreement with these views, Professor Brown not only repeatedly speaks of the "ideology" of the American frontier vigilante, but he also goes on to develop its major principles. These, he argues, consisted of the right of revolution, self-preservation, and the ideal of popular sovereignty, which together justified taking the law into one's own hands. He adds that the vigilantes received further intellectual rationalization from some jurists.

This confusion results, in part, from different meanings assigned to the term "ideology." Political scientists, perhaps overinfluenced by the proliferation of apologias and programs of the revolutionary left, usually associate the word with explicit, comprehensive, systematic, action-oriented statements of values and interpretations. As the status quo is established, the values and assumptions supporting it are often left unelaborated because they have been well-absorbed by the members of the establishment. Revolutionary action, because it seeks to change the status quo, must develop a more explicit rationale. This does not mean that it would be impossible to develop a conservative ideology or that the absence of such a statement means that there are no values or ideas motivating vigilante action. Professor Brown, then, seems to be using ideology in a somewhat looser sense when he identifies the core principles of vigilante behavior. Even the defense offered by Charles J. Bonaparte (later to become Attorney General under Theodore Roosevelt) does not appear to be comprehensive enough to constitute an ideology in the more restricted sense. Nevertheless, this does not mean that it would be impossible to write a "vigilante manifesto." The major components of such a document, however, would most likely consist of a systematization of the contents of the dominant political culture.

2. David Riesman, et al., *The Lonely Crowd* (New York: Doubleday, 1956), pp. 28-40.

PARTICIPANTS

In developing a typology of vigilantism, we divided the possible participants into "private" and "public" persons. The latter category gives rise to the phenomenon of "official vigilantism." This may produce some misunderstanding, for vigilantism is usually conceived of only in terms of private self help when the official agencies of rule enforcement have failed in some way.

In defining vigilantism we found it necessary to discuss the limitations placed on the use of coercion in social relations. These limits obviously apply to private persons, but they also regulate the behavior of political authorities. When individuals acting in their official capacity violate these boundaries, we can speak of official vigilantism. We believe that this distinction is essential, especially when comparing the activities of off-duty policemen who participate in the Brazilian "death squad" with cases of police violence such as those discussed by Professors Kotecha and Walker. If laws (and customs) are seen to bind the rulers as well as the ruled, then the possibility of official vigilantism exists.

THE ETHICS OF VIGILANTISM

In carrying out our investigations of vigilantism, we have encountered criticisms from both the left and the right. On one hand, we have been condemned for trundling out yet another exaggerated condemnation of the establishment, especially by those who have grown weary of the protestations of activist social scientists. On the other, our efforts to identify the causes and to give a balanced assessment of the consequences makes us out to be apologists for vigilante violence in the view of those activists with whom we are sometimes associated. Often when one is attacked from two opposing sides, there is a somewhat illogical tendency to assert that this proves the validity of the position because it alienates all "extremists." We believe, however, that these criticisms serve to remind us of the value-volatile nature of many, if not all, areas of social scientific analysis.

We would be foolish, and even dishonest, to deny the "subjective" impact of our subject matter, both on us and our readers. It should be clear that the other contributors to this collection are similarly involved in their studies. We do not apologize for this involvement, for we believe that our personal attitudes toward vigilantism are an inseparable part of our knowledge of it. They led us to choose to study the problem in the first place; they maintained our interest in the project; and they informed the interpretation of the information we gathered and the analysis we developed. Our point of view is neither the only one nor the "correct" one. Other scholars may be differently motivated, and we invite those who disagree with our approach or that of any of our contributors to grapple with the phenomenon we have attempted to identify. "Objectivity," if it exists, is not the monopoly of any one social scientist; rather, it emerges out of the dialectical interplay of alternative perspectives.

With these comments in mind, it would be appropriate for us to identify some of our personal reactions to vigilantism before considering more general ethical issues. We must admit to a certain morbid fascination with vigilante behavior. Generally, we are appalled at the abuses which are justified in the name of order and stability, and we approach vigilantism with a presumption of guilt; such acts should be condemned unless it can be demonstrated "beyond a reasonable doubt" that they were justified. In saying this, we are, in effect, admitting that vigilantism may be unavoidable under some circumstances, and we recognize that the conditions which give rise to it sometimes appear to be intolerable.

Vigilantes generally do not commit acts of violence out of complete disregard for all moral and ethical principles; rather, they act because they believe they are justified. This does not mean they necessarily develop an elaborate moral rationale, simply that they see themselves as defending something they hold to be of value. The overused cliche about ends justifying means does not, however, fully satisfy the ethical problem which must be probed more deeply.

The "ends/means" debate disguises two issues: First, some evaluation must be made of the quality of the ends pursued. We note in our introductory essay that this seem to be the fundamental question: What is the value of the order being preserved? Professor Stettner notes that neither the goals of self interest or order qua order seems particularly attractive, but it may be too harsh to say this is all vigilantes are defending. They often appear to be self-serving, but actually may be trying to protect their families and community. Nor is their preferred order just any order. Rather, it is one reflecting certain social norms and values which cannot be automatically dismissed.

These defensive actions, of course, raise the second question: What is the impact of the chosen means on the end? In part, the problem of appropriate means is a matter of simple efficiency. It would be wasteful to inflict needless destruction if the same goal could be reached at a lesser cost. Unfortunately, vigilantism, like other forms of political violence, is not easily assessed in quasi-economic, cost-benefit terms, and the tendency is to err on the side of too much, rather than too little, coercion.

Another, more profound consideration is whether violent means necessarily corrupt the ends, no matter how noble. History provides us with numerous examples of the terrible consequences of good causes perverted by ill-considered violence. It may not be possible to give a definitive answer to this challenge. We believe that coercion, especially coercion which destroys lives, is evil. Its use can perhaps be justified as the lesser evil under some circumstances. This does not make it good. As the Greek tragedians recognized twenty-five hundred years ago, sometimes humans confront choices where all the available alternatives outrage the gods.

If vigilante violence is to be judged the lesser evil, it can be utilized only when all other less destructive courses have been exhausted. The negative consequences of the resort to violence must be minimized, and the vigilante response should be kept proportional to the threat it is repressing. Finally, it must be demonstrated that vigilantism can achieve the desired objective. All this presumes that the objective is worth pursuing in the first place. In our analysis we attempt to identify some of the ambiguous effects vigilantism has on the objectives of crime, social-group, and regime-control. Other contributors have also grappled with this problem. Our own assessment suggests that the effects of establishment violence on the ends pursued may be difficult to determine, and this further complicates the process of ethical evaluation.

One final note: there has been discussion, especially by some of the defendants involved in the Watergate scandal, of the supposed similarity between those who take the law into their own hands and the advocates of civil disobedience. This analogy strikes us as spurious. Civil disobedience consists of the refusal to comply with a particular law which is considered to be unjust, not the self-appointed enforcement of "laws" presumed to be necessary to the defense of the establishment. Civil disobedience, because it affirms the overall system of law while violating a particular part, is nonviolent so as to minimize the damage done to the system. Vigilantism is, by definition, violent, and its perpetrators often show little regard for the impact on the system. Finally, the person engaging in civil disobedience is willing to go to jail for the offense as a symbolic protest. Vigilantes have no intention of willingly submitting to prosecution for their acts. Ironically, the justification for vigilantism, if it can be made, will more closely resemble that for revolution than civil disobedience.

THE FUTURE OF VIGILANTISM

Outbreaks of revolutionary violence have attracted considerable scholarly attention. The studies included in this volume suggest that establishment violence is also widespread in the contemporary world, and it would be tempting to predict that it will continue to be a significant phenomenon for the rest of the century. However, as James Q. Wilson has argued, precise determination of collective violence is difficult since the estimator is dealing with relatively rare events.[3] It may be possible, nonetheless, to identify some of the conditions which might give rise to vigilantism in the coming years. Of

3. James Q. Wilson, "Violence," in Daniel Bell, ed., *Toward the Year 2000* (Boston: Beacon, 1967), p. 278.

course, "traditional" stimulants, such as crime or the activities of *pariah* social and political groups, may also continue to be of significance.

ECONOMIC CONDITIONS: Perhaps the major source of future discord of both a vigilante and dissident nature lies in the performance of the economy. Although many analysts of the "post-industrial" society believe that economic disruptions will be limited in intensity and duration, others believe that declining resources, rising population, and environmental pollution will lead to an economic collapse if growth is not slowed or halted.[4] In a "no-growth" world, economic conflict could intensify, and established groups (or nation-states) might view any proposal for redistribution as a serious challenge to their position. If governments fail to protect their economic position, these groups might be willing to turn to vigilante self-help.

On an international scale, the less developed countries will almost certainly continue to seek a reallocation of world wealth by engaging in collusive agreements to raise commodity prices. If the developed nations feel sufficiently intimidated by this, they may find it tempting to resort to vigorous countermeasures to preserve their standards of living. One melancholy prospector even predicts the possibility of nuclear blackmail as poorer countries acquire nuclear weapons.[5] Again, established nations may give in to these threats or respond with force. Whether interstate coercion could ever be termed vigilante in nature depends on how one evaluates the efficacy of norms governing the use of coercion in international relations. We suggest that the use of coercion by the developed nations to preserve their privileges could be considered "proto-vigilante" in nature.

Even if the catastrophists are proven to be false prophets, other economic changes may lead to a decline in some groups' economic position. Automation may make previously profitable occupations obsolete. The remaining unskilled or semi-skilled positions may be filled by immigrants from less developed countries who are willing to work for lower pay than the native labor force.[6] To complicate matters further, the strike may lose some of its potency in automated industries as supervisory personnel are able to keep the machines going for long periods of time.[7]

Those employed in marginal occupations, finding themselves unemployed or seeing their bargaining position diminish, may have an incentive to engage in defensive violence. Not only will supervisory personnel and immigrant laborers face harassment, but also there may be efforts to sabotage newly

4. Donella H. Meadows, et al., *The Limits to Growth* (New York: Universe, 1972).
5. Robert L. Heilbroner, *An Inquiry into the Human Prospect* (New York: W. W. Norton, 1974), p. 43.
6. Herman Kahn and Anthony J. Wiener, *The Year 2000* (New York: Macmillan, 1967), p. 219.
7. A. F. K. Organski, *The Stages of Political Development* (New York: Alfred A. Knopf, 1965), p. 195.

installed automated equipment. These actions would be on the border between vigilante and reactionary violence.

Finally, in some countries, women and members of some minority groups are being given special consideration in an attempt to compensate for past discrimination. Class, ethnic, or sexual identity has become a major factor in determining who shall be admitted to university programs or given employment. This trend, if sustained, could cause anguish among those who believe that satisfactory performance will assure them and their children a gratifying position in society. The change in the "rules of the game" might cause the disillusioned to turn to vigilantism as they seek to defend their access to rewards they feel they have justly earned.

POLITICAL CONDITIONS

Political status also is likely to change as nations enter the post-industrial age. In the United States, for example, it is already possible to discern the beginnings of what may be a struggle for political power between those who own physical capital and rule industry and the post-industrial professionals who hold positions related to theoretical knowledge, research, and development. In fact, the transition to post-industrial society is creating what one scholar calls three Americas—technetronic, industrial, and pre-industrial—with the pre-industrial sharecroppers, migrant workers, and obsolescent miners constantly becoming more politically impotent.[8] If their political influence begins to erode seriously, those associated with the industrial and commercial establishments may utilize subtle means of coercion to defend their positions, rather than the blatant vigilante tactics often used by those having a stake in pre-industrial society when they confronted an identical challenge.

The political changes that attend the transition to post-industrial society certainly will be more complex than merely a competition between those whose base of power is property, obtained through inheritance or entrepreneurial ability, and those whose base of power is skill, acquired through education. It may also involve a decline in the political status of blue-collar workers and central city dwellers who will vie with the more numerous suburbanites and white-collar workers for political influence.[9]

Moreover, political institutions may be unable to adapt to the demands placed upon them by the broadening of participation created by the growth in education. As Samuel Huntington has stated, ". . . a society that is highly educated and presumably highly innovative intellectually and technologically could be highly conservative politically, not in terms of the values of the

8. Zbigniew Brzezinski, *Between Two Ages: America's Role in the Technetronic Age* (New York: Viking Press, 1970), p. 200.
9. Samuel P. Huntington, "Postindustrial Politics: How Benign Will It Be," *Comparative Politics* 6 (January 1974):h178.

population but of the output of the system."[10] With substantial numbers of people wishing to participate directly in political decision-making, innovation could be stultified in post-industrial societies.

The failure of institutions to respond to novel demands could be a major source of establishment frustration. Institutional decay could just as easily provoke the defenders of the establishment to turn to vigilantism as the failure of institutions to extend to frontier regions did in an earlier era. Clearly, the external stimuli fomenting vigilantism are not confined to any particular stage or period of development.

CONCLUSION

Vigilantism is a form of instrumental violence and requires incentives. The preceding discussion of potential incentives in post-industrial societies is speculative and far from comprehensive. From this account, however, it can be concluded that the superdeveloped countries hardly will be immune from vigilante violence. Indeed, as long as individuals and groups exist who maintain a strong social and psychological identification with the established order, significant challenges to that order will most likely provoke violent resistance.

10. Ibid., p. 177.

Contributors

THE EDITORS

H. JON ROSENBAUM received his Ph.D. from the Fletcher School of Law and Diplomacy and taught at Wellesley College before assuming his present post as an associate professor of political science at the City College and the Graduate School of the City University of New York. He is the coeditor of *Contemporary Brazil: Issues in Economic and Political Development* and *Latin American International Affairs* as well as the author of approximately twenty articles, many of them concerned with Brazilian politics. Rosenbaum has been a fellow or guest scholar at the Brazilian Institute of International Relations, the Woodrow Wilson International Center for Scholars, Harvard University's Center for International Affairs, the Brazilian School of Public Administration, and Columbia University's Institute of Latin American Studies.

PETER C. SEDERBERG is an associate professor of political science at the University of South Carolina. He received his Ph.D. from Johns Hopkins University and has taught at Wellesley College. He is the author of *Interpreting Politics: An Analytical Inquiry.* His articles have appeared in *Comparative Politics, Philosophy of the Social Sciences,* the *Journal of Developing Areas, Asian Forum* and other reviews. A member of Phi Beta Kappa, Sederberg has been the recipient of Woodrow Wilson Dissertation and National Defense Education Act fellowships.

THE CONTRIBUTORS

DANE ARCHER is an assistant professor of social psychology at the University of California at Santa Cruz. He received his Ph.D. from Harvard University. Professor Archer's research interests include the study of interpersonal power and dominance, as well as non-verbal sensitivity.

RICHARD MAXWELL BROWN is a professor of history at The College of William and Mary. In 1968-1969 he was a consultant to the National Commission on the Causes and Prevention of Violence. His publications include *The South Carolina Regulators, American Violence,* and *Strain of Violence: Historical Studies of American Violence and Vigilantism.*

KANTI C. KOTECHA has taught at Rutgers University and Southhampton College of Long Island University and currently is an assistant professor of political science at Wright State University. Before receiving his Ph.D. from the Fletcher School of Law and Diplomacy, Professor Kotecha served as legal advisor to the government of Zanzibar, Tanzania. He has participated in several evaluations of the Dayton, Ohio police department.

WILLIAM P. KREML is an assistant professor of political science at the University of South Carolina. He received his Ph.D. in 1972 from Indiana University and his J.D. in 1965 from Northwestern University Law School.

RICHARD NED LEBOW is an associate professor of political science at the Graduate School and the City College of the City University of New York. In recent years he has been associated in a research capacity with the Council on Foreign Relations, the United States Naval War College, and the Institute of War and Peace Studies at Columbia University. Professor Lebow is author of *Between Peace and War: The Anatomy of International Crisis* and coeditor of *Divided Nations in a Divided World.* He has written numerous articles on Irish politics and currently is political editor of *Am Clamheanh Solius: The Irish-American Review.*

GARY T. MARX is an associate professor in the Department of Urban Studies and Planning at the Massachusetts Institute of Technology. He is the author of *Protest and Prejudice* and editor of *Muckraking Sociology: Research as Social Criticism* and *Racial Conflict.* His research interests at present include the study of racial and urban questions, social movements, and deviance. Professor Marx is a member of the Executive Council of the American Sociological Association and has served as an editor of the *American Sociological Review* and *Social Problems.*

ALI A. MAZRUI is a professor of political science at the University of Michigan at Ann Arbor as well as the director of the African Section of the World Order Models Project and a member of the executive committees of the International Political Science Association and the African Association of Political Science. He is the author of *Towards a Pax Africana, On Heroes and Uhru-Worship, The Anglo-African Commonwealth, Violence and Thought,* and *Cultural Engineering and Nation-Building in East Africa.* Professor

Mazrui also is the co-editor of *Africa in World Affairs* and *Protest and Power in Black Africa.*

FRED R. VON DER MEHDEN is Albert Thomas Professor of Political Science at Rice University. After receiving his Ph.D. from the University of California at Berkeley, he taught at the University of Wisconsin and served with the United States Agency for International Development in Thailand. Among Professor von der Mehden's many published works are *Religion and Nationalism in Southeast Asia, Politics of the Developing Nations, Comparative Political Violence,* and *Southeast Asia 1930-1973.* His articles have appeared in such journals as *Pacific Affairs, Southeast Asia Quarterly, Ayian Survey,* and the *Antioch Review.*

CHRISTIAN P. POTHOLM has taught at Dartmouth College and Vassar College and currently is an associate professor of politica science at Bowdoin College. He received his Ph.D. from the Fletcher School of Law and Diplomacy. Professor Potholm has traveled and conducted research in East, West, and Southern Africa and is the author of *Four African Political Systems* and *Swaziland: The Dynamics of Political Modernization* and is the coeditor of *Southern Africa in Perspective* and *The Police and Law Enforcement.* His articles have appeared in *The Journal of Developing Areas, International Journal, Africa Report,* and many other scholarly reviews.

EDWARD V. SCHNEIER, JR. is an associate professor of political science at the Graduate School and the City College of the City University of New York. After receiving his Ph.D. from the Claremont Graduate School, he served as a legislative assistant to Senator Birch Bayh and a research fellow at the Brookings Institution. Professor Schneier taught at Princeton University and The Johns Hopkins University before coming to New York. He is coauthor of *Party and Constituency* and *Vote Power* and editor of *Policy-Making in American Government.*

R. LANCE SHOTLAND received his Ph.D. from Michigan State University and currently is an assistant professor of psychology at Pennsylvania State University. His articles have appeared in the *Journal of Applied Psychology,* the *Public Opinion Quarterly, Psychonomic Science,* and other journals. Professor Shotland is the co-author, with Stanley Milgram, of *Television and Antisocial Behavior.*

EDWARD STETTNER is an associate professor of political science at Wellesley College. He received his Ph.D. from Princeton University and taught at Rutgers University before coming to Wellesley. Professor Stettner has published in *Polity,* the *Annals,* and other journals and has edited

Perspectives on Europe. At present he is preparing studies of Herbert Croly and Walter Lippmann. Professor Stettner is president of the Massachusetts state conference and a member of the national council of the American Association of University Professors.

JAMES L. WALKER is an assistant professor of political science at Wright State University where he also serves as assistant director of urban studies. Dr. Walker is the author of *Paraprofessionals in Law Enforcement* and several articles on police politics. He received his Ph.D. from the University of California at Berkeley.

Index

Adams, James Truslow, 108
Africa, East. *See Pariah* communities, in Africa, East
Africa, South. *See* South African vigilantism
Africa, tropical, 194-97; authority of the Seen and vigilantism in, 195-96, 207; authority of the Unseen and vigilantism in, 195-96, 205-8, 209-10, 214, 217; exogenous dualism and, 194, 195; illustrations of vigilantism in, 198-201, 202-4, 205-8, 212, 216; indigenous pluralism and, 194, 195; juvenile vigilantism and, 198-99; political vigilantism by civilians in, 196-201; political vigilantism by military in, 201-5; preventive detention acts as vigilantism in, 199-200; roadside vigilantism in, 208-12 (*see also* Africa, tropical, spontaneous vigilantism in; Spontaneous vigilantism); sex and vigilantism in, 212-17; spontaneous vigilantism in, 208, 216; "state of emergency" declarations as vigilantism in, 200-1; vigilante groups, specific, in, 197-98; vigilantism by governments in, 199-201; youth-winger vigilantism in, 197-99. *See also* names of countries under Vigilantism
Afro-American Group Attack Team, 11
Afro-Asia, 218
Afro-Shirazi Youth League, 198-99
Aggression and spontaneous vigilantism, 41, 43
Alabama. *See* Patrol Groups, community, in Alabama; Vigilantism in Alabama
Aliens. *See* Vigilantism: aliens and
Allende, Salvador, 9, 15
Ambiguity: lack of, and spontaneous vigilantism, 36-37, 44
America, vigilantism in. *See* Vigilantism: in America; Vigilantism: in the United States
American Civil Liberties Union. *See* Vigilantism: American Civil Liberties Union and
American Indians. *See* Vigilantism: Indians, American and
American Legion. *See* Vigilantism: American Legion and

American Minutemen, 17
American Protective Association, 112
Americans for Democratic Action. *See* Vigilantism: Americans for Democratic Action and
Amin, Idi, 203, 204, 221
Anarchism, vigilantism and. *See* Vigilantism: anarchism and
Anglo-Irish elite, 235
Anti-Communism: vigilantism and, 110, 111, 113, 122, 125, 127, 128. *See also* Communist party: vigilantism and
Anti-Communist Command of Guatemala (CADEG), 16 n. 40
Anti-Communist Group (GRACO), 16 n. 40
Anti-politics, vigilantism as, 66, 69
Anti-socialism, vigilantism as, 176
Anti-vigilante movements, 96-97, 98. *See also* Moderators
Anxiety in spontaneous vigilantism, 39, 43
Appalachian states, 79
Arabs. *See Pariah* communities, of Arabs; *Pariah* communities, vigilantism towards Arabs of
Argentina, 11, 16 n. 40, 18, 22
Arizona. *See* Vigilantism: in Arizona
Arkansas. *See* Vigilantism: in Arkansas
Armed forces. *See* Vigilantism: military and
Armed Forces (Powers of Arrest) Decree, 203
Ascendancy, 234-35.
Asians. *See Pariah* communities, of Asians
Asia, Southeast. *See Pariah* communities, in Asia, Southeast
Assassinations, political, 17
Associability, vigilantism and, 68-69
Atlantic states, 79
Authoritarian character of vigilantes, 24
Auxiliaries, police. *See* Police auxiliaries
Avengers, 255
Aware, Inc. *See* Vigilantism: Aware, Inc. and
Ayub Khan, Mohammed, 18, 22

Bakunin, Mikhail, 71
Balaguer regime, 16

Baldwin, Simeon F., 107 n. 91
Band, 16, 16 n. 41
Banda, Hastings, 198
Bannack. *See* Vigilantism: in Bannack
Baton Rouge. *See* Patrol groups, Community, in Baton Rouge
Bean, Orson, 119
Bellevue vigilante war, 83
Bengalis, 15
Bentley, Arthur, 66
Berkley, George, 164
Bettelheim, Bruno, 177
Blacklist, 117-20, 124, 125, 126
Black Panthers: and vigilantism, 127, 132, 134, 137, 141, 142, 145, 151 n. 27
Blacks in United States. *See* Patrol groups, community, and blacks in United States; Vigilantism: blacks in United States and
Black vigilantism. *See* Africa, tropical; South African vigilantism, blacks and; Vigilantism: blacks in United States and
Bogalusa, Louisiana. *See* Patrol groups, community, in Bogalusa, Louisiana
Bonaparte, Charles J., 106-7
Boston. *See* Patrol groups, community, in Boston
Boundaries, 5, 29, 89, 194, 264. *See also* Vigilantism: boundaries and
Bradley, Joseph P., 106
Brazil, 10-11, 16, 17, 18
Brewer, David J., 106, 107
Brockton, Massachusetts, 153
Brooke, Basil, 241, 242, 243
Brookeborough, Lord. *See* Brooke, Basil
Brooklyn. *See* Patrol groups, community, in Brooklyn; Vigilantism: in Brooklyn
Brown, Roger, 45-46
Brown Shirts, 16
B Specials. *See* Ireland, Northern, B Specials of
Buganda, 200-201
Bunting, Ronald, 248
Burke, Edmund, 69, 197
Burma. *See* Pariah communities, in Burma; Pariah communities, vigilantism by Burma toward
Busia, K. A., 18
Byers, W. N., 93

Cahn, Edmond, 68
California. *See* Patrol groups, community, in Los Angeles; Patrol groups, community, in Pittsburgh, California; Vigilantism: in California
Cambodia. *See* Pariah communities, in Cambodia; Pariah communities, vigilantism by Cambodia toward
Campbell, Malcolm, 93-94

Canavan, Francis, 69
Carter, Hodding, 168
Catharsis. *See* Vigilantism: catharsis and
Catholics. *See* Vigilantism: Catholics and
Cattell, Raymond F., 58, 59
Chattanooga, 62
Chatterton, Fennimore, 105
Cherokee Indian War, 82
Chevigny, Paul, 164
Chichester-Clark, James, 249, 250, 251
Chicago, 11, 14, 15, 16
Chile, 9, 15
China, 18
Chinese. *See* Pariah communities, of Chinese; Pariah communities, vigilantism toward Chinese
Christian Institute, 191
Church groups. *See* Vigilantism: church groups and
"Circulation of elites," 71
Civil Authorities (Special Powers) Act (Northern Ireland), 245
Civil liberties proponents, vigilantism and. *See* Vigilantism: civil liberties proponents and
Civil rights, 80, 115, 120, 168, 185
Civil society concept, and vigilantism, 68
Civil War, 49. *See also* Post-Civil War period
Clark, James Chichester-. *See* Chichester-Clark, James
Clark, Mark, 16
Clark, Walter, 106
Class, and vigilantism. *See* Vigilantism: and class
Closed-mindedness, 57
Cockrell, Francis M., 104
Coercion, 3-4, 4 n. 2, 264-65
Cold War, 115, 127
Coleman, William Tell, 53, 60, 105
Collingswood, Charles, 119
Colonial period, American, 79
"Colonized" communities, 88
Colorado. *See* Vigilantism: in Colorado
Comando de Represion de Actividades Redicioses, 16 n. 40
Comities de Vigilance, 84
Communal vigilantism. *See* Vigilantism: communal
Communist Control Act of 1954, 115
Communist party: vigilantism and, 101, 112, 115, 118, 122, 123, 127, 179, 188. *See also* Anti-Communism
Community Action Patrol, 144
Community Alert Patrol, 132, 138
Community, concept of: and vigilantism, 67-69
Community police patrols. *See* Patrol groups, community

Community reconstruction, vigilantism and. *See* Vigilantism: community reconstruction and

Community structure, typical American, 88

Community support, and vigilantism. *See* Vigilantism: community support and

Confederacy, 49

Confidence: loss of, in spontaneous vigilantism, 39

Conscious parallelism and the vigilante personality, 61-63

Conservatism: and the vigilante personality, 48-58, 63, 74, 81, 111, 263

Construct variables: and vigilante personality, 48-56, 58, 59

Contract theory, vigilantism and. *See* Vigilantism: contract theory and

Contraculture, 89, 89 n. 32, 91

Costa Rica, 17

Coups d'etat, 17-18

"Crackers," 82

Craig, James, 240, 242, 252

Crime-control vigilantism. *See* Vigilantism: crime-control

Crown Heights. *See* Patrol groups, community, in Brooklyn

Cultural dualism, 194

Cultural pluralism, 194

"Cumulative" communities, 88

Curry, George, 105

Dakotas, the. *See* Vigilantism: in the Dakotas

Dana, Charles A., 105

Dar es Salaam, 198-99, 202-3

Dayton. *See* Patrol groups, community, in Dayton

Deacons, 130, 132, 137

Deacons for Defense and Justice, 101

Death Squadron (Bolivia), 16 n. 40

Death toll, vigilante. *See* Vigilantism: fatalities and

Defenders, 141, 153

Democratic Convention riots of 1968, 15, 180

Democratic party, 18, 55, 56, 100

Democratic theory, vigilantism and. *See* Vigilantism: democratic theory and

Democratić Unionist Party, 252

Deprivation: decremental, 5, 26, 27; relative, 5, 7, 22

Dialectical historicism, 73

Dies, Martin, 111, 113 n. 5

Dimsdale, Thomas, 91

Dogmatism, 57, 59

Dominican Republic, 16

Doyle, Sammy, 252-53

Dualism, cultural, 194

Dualism, exogenous, 194, 195

Dysfunction, political: vigilantism as, 75

East. *See* Vigilantism: in the East

East Africa. *See* Pariah communities, in Africa, East

Easton, David, 67

East Texas Regulator-Moderator conflict, 83, 176

East Texas Regulators, 97, 176

Economics, 93, 97

Economic vigilantism, 12, 15

Egypt, 14, 18, 19, 205

Elitism, vigilantism and, 70-72, 73, 74, 75, 102, 104-7

Embu, 201, 207

Entertainment industry, vigilantism and, 110, 117, 124

Equality, vigilantism and, 69, 72

E scale, 48

Esquadrão da Morte, 10-11

Establishment, 266-67

Establishment violence, 4

Ethics, vigilantism and, 268-70

Ethiopia, 199

Ethnic groups. *See* names of ethnic groups under Vigilantism

Ethnocentrism scale, 48

Exogenous dualism, 194, 195

Extroversion, 58, 59

Eysenck, Hans, 57, 58, 59

Falcons, 16

Fascism scale, 48

Fatalities, vigilante, 80-81, 87, 99

Faulk, John Henry, 110, 118, 119, 119 n. 19

Faulkner, Brian, 249 n. 15, 250, 251

FBI (Federal Bureau of Investigation), 116, 116 n. 11, 128

Fellow traveler, 115, 117, 119

Fiction, vigilantism in, 165-66, 175-76

Field, Stephen J., 106

Fifth Amendment, 113, 117

"Flathead" element, 90

Florida, 84, 132

Fluidity, institutional, 217. *See also* Vigilantism, social flux and

Folklore, vigilantism in, 175

Followers. *See* Vigilante groups: followers in

Foreman, Carl, 119

Forrest, Bedford, 62

French, Augustus, 104

Freudianism, vigilantism and, 24-25, 25 n. 59

Freud, Sigmund, 52

Frontier vigilantism, 82, 83, 86

Frustration and vigilantism, spontaneous, 39-40, 41, 43, 44

GEMA, 207

Genovese, Kitty, 30

Gentlemen (vigilante group), 11
Georgia, 35
German-American Bund, 112
Germany, 16
Ghana, 18, 18 n. 43, 197, 199
Ghetto, 132
Gibson, Kenneth, 13 n. 27
Gikuyu, Embu, and Meru Association, 207
Goodman, Walter, 123, 125
Gottesman, Irving I., 59
Government: vigilantism and, 110-11, 117-18, 120-21, 123, 124, 176, 189, 191, 199-201, 221-23
Greece, 16
Green, Allen, 36
Group theorists, 66
Guatemala, 16 n. 40, 19
Gurr, Ted Robert, 5-7, 9, 27

Halcones (Falcons), 16
Hall, James, 90
Hampton, Fred, 16
Hangings. *See* Lynchings
Hanna, James, 255
Hayden, Sterling, 118
Helena, 86
Heresy, political, 114
HISC (House Committee on Internal Security), 111, 127. *See also* HUAC
Hiss, Alger, 112, 113, 114
History, vigilante: in America, 49, 79-109, 131, 178-80; in Northern Ireland (*see* Ireland, Northern, history of, to 1920; Ireland, Northern, vigilantism in, during twentieth century); in South Africa (*see* Vigilantism: history of, in South Africa)
Hitler, Adolph, 16, 52
Hobbes, Thomas, 64, 68, 70
Hoffa, Jimmy, 121
Hosmer, H. L., 106
House Committee on Internal Security. *See* HISC
House Committee on Un-American Activities. *See* HUAC
Housing project patrols, 136
Houston, Sam, 99
HUAC (House Committee on Un-American Activities), 111-14; exposure and, 121-24, 125; interest-group liberalism and, 115-17; success of, reasons for, 115-17; targets of, 112, 114-15, 126-27; vigilantism and, 111, 112, 113, 115, 117-24, 128
Huntington, Samuel, 23, 272
Hurst, James Willard, 108

Ibingira, Grace, 198
Ibo tribe, 14
Idaho, 86

Ideology: political, 26, 27, 48, 58; vigilantism and, 26-27, 46, 54, 56, 74, 103-4, 179, 179 n. 15, 267
Immigrants. *See* Vigilantism: immigrants and
Immigration Service, 128
Imperiale, Anthony, 13 n. 27, 130, 132, 140, 152 n. 29
Impulsiveness and the vigilante personality, 51-53
India, 13
Indiana. *See* Vigilantism: in Indiana
Indian Patrol, 147
Indians, American. *See* Vigilantism: Indians, American and
Indians, Asian. *See Pariah* communities, of Indians, Asian; *Pariah* communities, vigilantism toward Indians, Asian of
Indians, Mapuche, 9
Indochina. *See Pariah* communities, in Indochina
Indonesia, 16 n. 41. *See also Pariah* communities, in Indonesia; *Pariah* communities, vigilantism by Indonesia toward
Industrial Workers of the World (IWW), 15, 179
Institutional fluidity, 197, 217. *See also* Vigilantism: social flux and
Intensity, 56, 59, 60, 63, 264
Intentionality, 4, 4 n. 3, 177
Interest-group liberalism, 115-17
Interest, political, 66
Internal Security, House Committee on. *See* HISC
International Union of Electrical Workers (IUE), 120
Introspectiveness and the vigilante personality, 53-54
Introversion, 58, 59
Iowa. *See* Vigilantism: in Iowa
Ireland, Northern, 14, 234, 240; B Specials of, 14, 239. 241, 245, 247, 248; history of, to 1920, 234-40; Protestants in, 235, 236, 237, 241, 242, 243, 244, 245, 246, 247, 248, 249, 250, 251, 252, 253, 254, 255, 256, 257, 258; regime-control vigilantism, historically in, 234; social-group-control vigilantism, historically in, 234; Ulster Volunteer Force (UVF) (first) and, 237, 238, 239, 241; Ulster Volunteer Force (UVF) (second) and, 248, 248 n. 14, 252, 253-55, 257, 258; Unionists and, 237, 238, 239, 240, 243, 244, 245, 246, 247, 248, 249, 250, 251, 252, 256; vigilante groups of, 248, 256; vigilantism in, during twentieth century, 240-258
Irish in Ireland. *See* Ireland, Northern
Irish in United States, 99, 100
Iron Hills, 84

Italians, 101. *See also* Sicilians
"Ivy League" school of thought, 47-48, 58
IWW (Industrial Workers of the World), 15, 179

Jackson, Andrew, 24, 60, 105
Jackson, Charles W., 98
Jackson. *See* Vigilantism: in Jackson
Janowitz, Morris, 13, 14
Japanese, 223
Japanese-Americans, 179
Jatis, 13
J-configuration, 57
Jewish Defense League (JDL): vigilantism and, 19, 130, 132, 133 n. 7, 135 n. 9, 140-41, 142, 143 n. 19, 147
Jews. *See* Jewish Defense League; Vigilantism: Jews and
Jim Crow, 114
Johnson, Lawrence, 119 n. 19
Jonesboro, Louisiana. *See* Patrol groups, community, in Jonesboro, Louisiana
Jones, Le Roi, 152
Judges, vigilantism and, 105, 106, 107 n. 91
Jung, Carl, 58
Juvenile vigilantism, 198-99

Kahane, Meir, 19
Kakonge, John, 198
Kampala, 203, 221
Kansas, 86, 145
KANU (Kenya African National Union), 201, 206
Kaunda, Kenneth, 198
Kazan, Elia, 118
Kefauver, Estes, 121
Kennedy family, 120 n. 22
Kennedy, Robert, 121
Kentucky, 80, 83, 84
Kenya, 201, 205-7, 210-11, 220
Kenya African National Union(KANU), 201, 206
Kenya People's Union (KPU), 201
Kenyatta, Jomo, 201
Kenyatta, Mzee, 201, 206, 207
Key, V. O., 47, 58
Khan, Ayub. *See* Ayub Khan, Mohammed
Kikuyu, 201, 205-7
Kisumu, 201
Know Nothings, 112
Kondoism, 203
Korean War, 115
Kramer, Stanley, 119
Ku Klux Klan: vigilantism and, 13, 13 n. 25, 61-62, 80, 100, 112, 131, 132, 149, 154

Laborers, vigilantism and, 99, 100

Labor movements: and vigilantism, 15, 49, 52, 114, 120, 179, 188
Lane, Robert, 47, 58
Laos, 218, 220, 227
Lasswell, Harold, 46
Latin America, 16 n. 40, 18
"Law and order": vigilantism and, 49-50, 51, 65, 86, 129
Law and Order faction, 97-98
Lawlessness, American: vigilantism and, 108-9
Lawyers and vigilantism, 105-7, 107 n. 91
Leaders, vigilante. *See* Vigilante groups, leadership of
Left (political spectrum), 128, 180. *See also* "New-left"
Lenin, Vladimir Ilyich, 72
Libya, 205
Localism, vigilantism and, 91-92
Locke, John, 64-65, 68
Los Angeles, 85, 147
Louisiana, 85, 147
Louisiana Deacons, 130, 132, 137, 151 n. 27
Lower level (social structure), 88-89, 90, 100
Lowi, Theodore J., 115, 116
Loyalist Association of Workers, 251
Loyalist Defence Association, 255
Loyalty oaths, 115
Luo, 201, 205-6
Lynch, Charles, 79
Lynchings: and vigilantism, 35, 35 n. 9, 36, 41, 62, 80, 81, 82, 87, 93, 94, 96, 100, 106, 107 n. 91, 178 n. 11, 212, 213. *See also* Lynch law: and vigilantism
Lynch Law: and vigilantism, 79, 80, 81, 94, 103, 105, 106, 107, 109. *See also* Lynchings: and vigilantism

Macro-analysis. *See* Vigilantism: macro-analysis of
Malawi, 198, 199
Mau Mau, 201, 206, 207
Maccabees. *See* Vigilantism: Maccabees and
McCarthy, Joseph R., 111, 114, 115
McCarthyism, 101, 103, 124 n. 39, 126, 179
McConnel, William J., 104, 105
Malaya, 220, 224
Malaysia, 14. *See also* Pariah communities, in Malaysia; *Pariah* communities, vigilantism by Malaysia toward
Maltz, Albert, 120 n. 22
Mandelbaum, David G., 13
Mao Tse-tung, 18
Mapuche Indians, 9
Marcuse, Herbert, 179-80
Marxism, 70, 72-73, 74
Masons, 52

Massachusetts, 153
Mboya, Tom, 206
Medici regime, 17
Meru, 201, 207
Mexico City, 16
"Michigan" school of thought, 47, 48, 58
Micro-analysis. *See* Vigilantism: micro-analysis of
Middle level (social structure), 88, 89, 93, 95, 100
Middleton, John W., 98
Military and vigilantism, 49, 205
Miller, Arthur, 118
Minneapolis, 147
Minority groups. *See* names of minority groups under Vigilantism
Minutemen, American, 17
"Mission Impossible," 12 n. 23
Mississippi. *See* Patrol groups, community, in Mississippi; Police vigilantism, in Mississippi; Vigilantism: in Mississippi
Mississippi Black Paper, 168
Moderators, 21, 98, 176. *See also* Anti-vigilante movements; South Carolina Moderators
Monroe, North Carolina, 131
Monterey, 85
Moorman, Watt, 98-99
Mosca, Gaetano, 71, 72
Motion picture industry, 115, 118
Mouton, Alexander, 104
Movimiento Costa Rica Libre, 17
Murrell conspiracy, 83, 90, 91 n. 39
Myrdal, Gunnar, 213-14

Nairobi, 220
Nasser, Gamal Abdel, 18
National Advisory Commission on Civil Disorders (1967), 182
National Association for the Advancement of Colored People (NAACP), 121, 138
National Commission on the Causes and Prevention of Violence (1968), 182
National Guard, 49
National Resistance Front (FRN), 16 n. 40
National Rifle Association, 131
National Union of South African Students, 191
Nebraska. *See* Vigilantism: in Nebraska
Ne'er-do-wells, vigilantism and, 80, 81, 82, 100
Negroes. *See* Blacks in United States
Nelson, Harold, 141, 153
Neo-vigilantism, 99-101, 131
Ness, Gayl, 231
Nevada, 86
New Anti-Communist Organization (NOA), 16 n. 40

Newark, New Jersey, 13 n. 27. *See also* Patrol groups, community, in Newark, New Jersey; Vigilantism: in Newark, New Jersey
"New-left," 127. *See also* Left (political spectrum)
New Mexico. *See* Vigilantism: in New Mexico
New Orleans. *See* Vigilantism: in New Orleans
Newton, Huey, 132
New York City. *See* Patrol groups, community, in New York City; Police vigilantism, in New York City; Vigilantism: in New York City
Niebuhr, Reinhold, 168, 169
Nigeria, 14, 197, 205. *See also* Vigilantism: in Nigeria
Nixon, Richard, 112
Nizer, Louis, 110
Nkrumah, Kwame, 18 n. 43, 197, 199
Noble County, Indiana. *See* Vigilantism: in Noble County, Indiana
Noniyas, 13
North Carolina. *See* Patrol groups, community, in North Carolina
Northern Illinois Regulator movement, 83, 95-96
Northern Indiana Regulators, 84, 104
Northern Ireland. *See* Ireland, Northern
Northern Ireland Executive, 251
North Ward Citizens' Committee. *See* Vigilantism: North Ward Citizens' Committee and
Nugent, John, 100
Nyerere, Julius K., 199-200, 202

Obote, Milton, 200-201, 203
Odinga, Oginga, 201
Odets, Clifford, 118
Oedipal guilt, 24-25
Ogle County. *See* Vigilantism: in Ogle County
Ojo por Ojo ("Eye for Eye"), 16 n. 40
Oklahoma. *See* Vigilantism: in Oklahoma
O'Neill, Terence, 247, 249, 250
Open-mindedness, 57
"Operation Vijana," 198
Opinionation scale, 57
Orange Lodge, 243
Orange Order, 251
Order: and the vigilante personality, 49-51, 65, 69-70, 72, 74
Oregon. *See* Vigilantism: in Oregon
Organized National Argentine Movement (MANO), 16 n. 40
Osborne, John E., 105
Otero, Miguel, 105

Outlaws, 82, 86, 89. *See also* Vigilantism: and outlaws

Paisley, Ian, 248, 252
Pakistan, 14, 18, 22
Pakistanis, 220
Pareto, Vilfredo, 70, 71, 72
Pariah communities, 12, 218-21; in Africa, East, 218, 220, 224, 225, 226, 227, 228, 230, 231, 232; of Arabs, 220, 225, 227, 230; in Asia, Southeast, 218, 219, 220, 222, 224, 225, 228, 230; of Asians, 220, 221, 225, 226, 227, 230; in Burma, 220, 221, 224, 226, 227, 231, 232; in Cambodia, 218, 219, 224, 227, 232; of Chinese, 218-20, 221, 224, 225, 226, 227, 228, 229, 230, 231, 232; defined, 221; economic role of, as cause of vigilantism, 224-27; of Indians, Asian, 218, 220, 221, 224, 225, 226, 227, 228, 230, 231, 232; in Indochina, 220, 227, 228, 229; in Indonesia, 226, 229, 230, 231, 232; in Laos, 218, 220, 227; in Malaya, 220, 224; in Malaysia, 220, 224, 225, 226, 229, 231, 232; perceptions of, as cause of vigilantism, 229-32, 233; political roles of, as cause of vigilantism, 227-29; in the Philippines, 225, 229; in Singapore, 226; stereotypes of, 229, 231, 233; in Thailand, 218, 220, 224, 225, 226, 228, 232; statistics regarding vigilantism in, 221, 223; types of vigilantism directed against, 221; in Uganda, 220, 227, 231; in Vietnam, 224, 225, 232; of Vietnamese, 220, 224, 227, 228, 230, 232; vigilantism toward Arabs of, 223; vigilantism by Burma toward, 222, 223; vigilantism by Cambodia toward, 221-22; vigilantism toward Chinese of, 13-14, 222-23; vigilantism, government approved against, 222-23; vigilantism, government initiated against, 221-22; vigilantism towards Indians, Asian of, 222, 223; vigilantism by Indonesia toward, 223; vigilantism toward Japanese of, 223; vigilantism by Malaysia toward, 222, 223; vigilantism, spontaneous against, 223; vigilantism by Thailand toward, 222; vigilantism toward Vietnamese of, 221-22; vigilantism by Zanzibar toward, 223; in Zanzibar, 221, 225, 231
Partido Revolucionario Institucional, 16
Patriotic South Africans for South Africa, 191
Patriots, 79
Patrol groups, community, 101, 129-31; adversarial, encouraged by police, 135, 137, 138; adversarial, opposed by police, 135, 137, 138; in Alabama, 132; in Baton Rouge, 145; and blacks in United States,

132, 133, 142, 144, 151 n. 27; in Bogalusa, Louisiana, 132; in Boston, 133, 135 n. 9, 138-39, 140, 142, 143, 147, 148, 152; in Brockton, Massachusetts, 153; in Brooklyn, 131 (*see also* Patrol groups, community, in New York City); chronicity of, 133; in Cincinnati, 144; constituency support for, 138-40, 148-49; in Dayton, 152; descriptive information on, 132-34; deterrence and, 131, 132; difficulties faced by, 150; effects of, 151-54; equipment of, 133; evaluation of, 149, 150-51, 153, 155-57; examples of, 130, 131-32, 134, 135 n. 9, 138, 140, 142, 144, 145, 147, 151 n. 28, 152, 152 n. 29, 154; in Florida, 132; functions of (*see* Patrol groups, community, operations and); housing project, 132, 136; implications of, 147-49; in Jonesboro, Louisiana, 132; in Kansas, 145; in Los Angeles, 147; in Louisiana, 132, 137; membership requirements of (*see* Patrol groups, community, recruitment and training policies of); in Minneapolis, 147; in Mississippi, 132; in Monroe, North Carolina, 131; motivations of, 141, 141 n. 16, 150; in Newark, New Jersey, 140, 144, 147; in New York City, 132, 147, 154 (*see also* Patrol groups, community, in Brooklyn); in North Carolina, 131, 132; operations of, 142-46, 151 n. 28, 152 n. 29, 153; in Pittsburgh, California, 147; and police, 132, 133-38; recruitment and training policies of, 140-42, 150; in South Carolina, 132; statistics regarding, 131, 132, 133-34, 148-49; supplemental, encouraged by police, 135, 136; supplemental, opposed by police, 135, 136; survival of, 146-47, 150; in Tampa, 152; typology of, 135-38, 150; in Watts, 132, 144; weapons of, 133; whites and, 132, 137, 142, 151 n. 27
PEC scale, 48
People's Party, vigilantism and, 94
Peronists, 22
Personality: inheritability of, 58-59; vigilante (*see* Vigilante personality)
Phelps, John, 95
Philippines, 17, 225, 229
Pickney, Alphonso, 180
Pierre, South Dakota, 86
Pinkerton (detective agency), 49
Pittsburgh, California, 147
"Plantation of Ulster," 235
Pluralism, cultural, 194
Police auxiliaries, 136, 144
Police reform. *See* Police vigilantism, reforms, future and
Police vigilantism, 14, 15, 49, 158-61, 180-82; accounts of, 163, 167-69; Berkley,

George on, 164; Chevigny, Paul on, 164; "closed society" and, 168-69; conditions tending toward, 159, 163, 164, 171-72; defined, 159; elimination of, prospects for, 172, 182 (*see also* Police vigilantism, reforms, future and); extent of, 167; in fiction, 165-66; figures regarding, 167, 181, 183; frustration, causative and, 159, 163, 164, 171; in the literature, 161-67; in Mississippi, 168-69; in New York City, 167; perceptions of police and, 160, 181; reforms, future and, 169-71, 182-86; resources available for, 160; revolt of police against higher authority and, 162-63; role conflict and, 159, 171; rural environment and, 167; Skolnick, Jerome on, 162-63; styles of police work tending toward, 163; suburban environment and, 167-68; support, societal for, 180, 181-82; Supreme Court decisions and, 169; "tools of trade" in, 164; urban environment and, 167; Wambaugh, Joseph on, 165-66; Wilson, James Q. on, 163-64, 172. *See also* Patrol groups, community, and police
Political and Economic Conservatism scale, 48
Political heresy, 114
Political parties, vigilantism and, 94, 96
Political radicals and vigilantism. *See* Vigilantism: and radicals, political
Political theory, vigilantism and, 64-75
Political vigilantism. *See* Vigilantism: political
Politics: defined, 67
Pontiac, Michigan, 13
Popular aspects, vigilantism and. *See* Vigilantism: popular aspects and
Popular sovereignty, vigilantism and, 103-4
Populism, 103, 130, 148, 155
Post-Civil War period, 84, 86
Postindustrial vigilantism, 116
Pound, Roscoe, 108
Poverty and spontaneous vigilantism, 41, 44
Powell, Enoch, 252, 257
Power and the vigilante personality, 48-49, 96
President's Commission on Campus Disorder (1970), 182
President's Commission on Law Enforcement and the Administration of Justice (1965), 182
Pressure groups, vigilantism and, 117
Propaganda, vigilantism and, 112-13, 127
Protestants: vigilantism and, 14, 55, 99, 100, 120. *See also* Ireland, Northern, Protestants in
Psychological characteristics, vigilante. *See* Vigilante personality

Psychopolitical analysis, 46
Psychopolitical literature: intellectual conflict within, 46-48
Puerto Ricans, 11
Punishments, vigilante. *See* Vigilantism: punishments imposed under

Rabushka, Alvin, 231
Racial considerations, vigilantism and, 99
Radicals, political and vigilantism. *See* Vigilantism: and radicals, political
Radio networks, 118
Rank and file. *See* Vigilante groups, followers in
Rankin, John, 112
Rayburn, Sam, 112
Reconstruction era, 13, 80, 87
Red Hand Commandos, 255
"Red raids," 101
Regime-control vigilantism. *See* Vigilantism: regime-control
Regulator-Moderator war of East Texas, 98
Regulators, 79, 86
Religion and vigilantism, 100. *See also* names of religious groups
Revolution, American: vigilantism during, 79, 82
Revolution, right of: and vigilantism, 103, 104
Right (political spectrum), 112, 128. *See also* Conservatism: and the vigilante personality
Rigidity: and the vigilante personality, 57, 58, 59, 63
Rockford *Star,* 96
Rokeach, Milton, 57, 58
Roosevelt, Theodore, 24, 60, 105, 106, 107
Rousseau, Jean Jacques, 67, 68

S. A., 16
Sacramento, 85
Sadism: vigilantism and, 97, 97 n. 57, 98, 141
San Antonio, 84
Sanders, Wilbur Fisk, 53-54, 60, 104
San Francisco. *See* Vigilantism: in San Francisco
San Francisco *Herald,* 100
San Francisco vigilance committees, 84, 85; of 1856, 94, 99, 100, 105, 131, 178
Schrage, Samuel A., 132
Schwartz, David, 262-63
Scorpio, 191
Scott, James, 228
Seeger, Peter, 118, 120 n. 22
Seen, authority of the. *See* Africa, tropical, authority of the Seen and vigilantism in
Self-defense groups. *See* Patrol groups, community

Self-incrimination. *See* Fifth Amendment
Self-preservation, vigilantism and, 103, 104
Self-protective organizations, 101. *See also* Patrol groups, community
Senate Investigating Subcommittee, 111
Senate Watergate Committee, 121
Sharpeville massacre, 187, 189
Shelby County, Texas, 56, 86, 98
Shipp affair, 62
Sicilians, 100. *See also* Italians
Sims, Charles, 132, 151 n. 27
Sinatra, Frank, 120 n. 22
Singapore, 226
Skolnick, Jerome, 162-63
Slavery, vigilantism and, 49, 82
Slaves, 90, 91
"Slickers," 80, 83
Slicker War of the Missouri Ozarks, 83
Smith, Peter, 95
SNCC, 151 n. 28
Social Darwinism, 179
Social flux: and vigilantism, 192
Social-group-control vigilantism. *See* Vigilantism: social-group-control
Socially constructive vigilantism. *See* Vigilantism: socially constructive
Socially destructive vigilantism. *See* Vigilantism: socially destructive
Social stability, vigilantism and, 81, 94, 107
Social structure of American community, typical, 88
Social support and vigilantism. *See* Vigilantism: social support and
Society of the Muslim Brothers, 14, 19
Sociology of the frontier, vigilantism and, 87-91
Sociopolitical order: stabilization of, and vigilantism, 19-23
Soldiers. *See* Vigilantism: military and
South, vigilantism in the. *See* Vigilantism: in the South
South African Students' Organization, 191
South African vigilantism, 186-93; American vigilantism compared with, 177, 187, 192-93; blacks and, 188; examples of, 187-89; groups engaged in, 191; organizations engaged in (*see* South African vigilantism, groups engaged in); whites and, 187, 188, 188 n. 43, 189
South Carolina, 35, 104, 132
South Carolina Moderators, 50, 83
South Carolina Regulators, 21, 50, 79, 82-83
Southeast Asia, 13. *See also Pariah* communities, in Asia, Southeast
Southern Commission on the Study of Lynching, 35
Southern Illinois Regulator-Flathead Struggle, 56

Southern Illinois Regulators, 83, 97
Southwest Missouri Slickers, 56, 97
Soviet Union, 16, 22
Spades Unlimited, 11
Spontaneous vigilantism, 30-44, 221, 223; aggression and, 41, 43; ambiguity, lack of and, 36-37, 44; anxiety and, 39, 43; confidence, loss of and, 39; in continuum of bystander reactions to crime, 31-37; defined, 31, 31 n. 4; frustration and, 39-40, 41, 43, 44; motivational factors governing, 37-44; poverty and, 41, 44. *See also* Africa, tropical, roadside vigilantism in; Africa, tropical, spontaneous vigilantism in; Vigilantism: instant
Stabilization, sociopolitical order: and vigilantism, 19-23, 107
Stalinist terror, 18
Stanford, Leland, 104, 105
Stanford, Leland Sr., 60
State Department, 115
Statistics regarding vigilantism. *See* Vigilantism: statistics regarding
Status insecurity: and the vigilante personality, 60-61, 63
Stevenson, Steven, 248 n. 14
Stimulus-Organism-Response psychological model, 47
Stimulus/Response psychological model, 47
Stuart, Granville, 85
Students, vigilantism and, 180, 191
Students Defense Fund, 191
Stylistic variables: and vigilante personality, 56-59
Subversive activities, 114
Sudan, 205
Suharto, Mrs., 16 n. 40
Susskind, David, 118
Sydnor, Charles S., 102

Tampa, 106, 152
Tanganyika, 202-3
Targets of vigilantism. *See* Vigilantism: targets of
Tanzania, 220. *See also* Vigilantism: in Tanzania
Tanzania African National Union (TANU), 198, 199
Television networks, 118
Tennessee, vigilantism in, 80, 83, 90-91
Tension, 45, 59
Terror, 15, 15 n. 34, 18, 21, 21 n. 49, 22
Terry, David S., 97
Texas. *See* Vigilantism: in Texas
Texas Revolution, 56
Thailand, 18, 222. *See also Pariah* communities, in Thailand
Thomas, J. Parnell, 112

Tolerance: and the vigilante personality, 57, 58, 59, 63, 68
Tories, 79
Tropical Africa. *See* Africa, tropical
Truman, David, 66
Trumbo, Dalton, 119
Turbulence, 180. *See also* Turmoil
Turmoil, 192. *See also* Turbulence
Typology of vigilantism. *See* Vigilantism: typology of

U-configuration, 57, 59
Uganda, 220, 227, 231. *See also* Vigilantism: in Uganda
Uganda People's Congress, 198
Ulster Army Council, 255
Ulster Defence Association (UDA), 251-53, 255, 257, 258
Ulster Defence Regiment, 252
Ulster Protestant League, 243
Ulster Protestant Volunteers, 248
Ulster Special Constabulary Association, 251
Ulster Vanguard, 251, 252
Ulster Volunteer Force (UVF) (first). *See* Ireland, Northern, Ulster Volunteer Force (UVF) (first) and
Ulster Volunteer Force (UVF) (second). *See* Ireland, Northern, Ulster Volunteer Force (UVF) (second) and
Un-American Activities, House Committee on. *See* HUAC
Unionists. *See* Ireland, Northern, Unionists and
Unions and vigilantism. *See* Vigilantism: unions and
United Electrical Workers (UE), 120
United Ulster Unionist Council (UUUC), 252
United States and vigilantism. *See* Vigilantism: in the United States
United States v. Lovett, 113 n. 5 .
Unseen, authority of the. *See* Africa, tropical, authority of the Unseen and vigilantism in
Upper level (social structure), 88, 89, 91, 93, 95, 96, 100
Utah, 86, 87

Value capabilities, 5, 5 n. 7, 7, 9, 22, 26, 27
Value expectations, 5, 5 n. 7, 6-7
Variables, construct: and vigilante personality, 48-56, 58, 59
Variables, stylistic: and vigilante personality, 56-59
Velde, Harold, 114, 120
Veterans of Foreign Wars and vigilantism, 117

Victims of vigilantism. *See* Vigilantism: targets of
Vietnam, 224, 225, 232. *See also* Vietnamese
Vietnamese, 221-22. *See also Pariah* communities, of Vietnamese; Vietnam
Vigilante activities. *See* Vigilantism: illustrations of
Vigilante groups, 50; followers in, 25-27, 89, 93, 100, 105; ideology of (*see* Vigilantism: ideology and); leadership of, 23-25, 25 n. 59, 26, 60, 62, 85, 89, 93, 96, 98, 105, 131, 132, 151; organization of typical frontier (*see* Vigilante movements, organization of); punishments imposed by (*see* Vigilantism: punishments imposed under); size of (*see* Vigilante movements, size of); specific, 10-11, 13, 14, 16, 16 n. 40, 16 n. 41, 17, 18, 19, 21, 22, 23, 82-83, 84, 87, 94, 95, 96, 99, 101, 112, 191, 197-98, 248, 256; support for, 28 (*see also* Vigilantism: community support and; Vigilantism: social support and); trials of frontier (*see* Vigilante movements, trials of); typical frontier (*see* Vigilante movements, characteristic); utility of, 27-28. *See also* Vigilante movements
Vigilante movements, 79, 80, 82-87, 131; characteristic, 86-87; organization of, 86; punishments imposed by (*see* Vigilantism: punishments imposed under); size of, 86; trials of, 86. *See also* Anti-vigilante movements; Vigilante groups
Vigilante organizations. *See* Vigilante groups; Vigilante movements
Vigilante personality, 24-25, 29, 45-63; conscious parallelism and, 61-63; conservatism and, 48-58, 63, 74, 81, 111, 263; construct variables and, 48-56, 58, 59; dogmatism and, 57, 59; impulsiveness and, 51-53, 262; introspectiveness and, 53-54, 262-63; order and, 49-51, 65, 69-70, 72, 74, 262; power and, 48-49, 96, 262; rigidity and, 57, 58, 59, 63, 262; status insecurity and, 60-61, 63; stylistic variables and, 56-59; tolerance and, 57, 58, 63, 68, 101
Vigilantes, 4, 71, 85, 268; prominent persons as, 18, 24, 60, 105, 106, 107. *See also* Vigilante groups; Vigilante movements; Vigilante personality; Vigilantism
Vigilante trials. *See* Vigilante movements, trials of
Vigilantism: in Africa, South (*see* South African vigilantism); in Africa, South and United States compared, 77, 187, 192-93; in Africa, tropical (*see* Africa, tropical; names of countries under Vigilantism); aggression and spontaneous, 41, 43; aims of (*see* Vigilantism: purposes of); in Ala-

bama, 83, 84, aliens and, 115; ambiguity, lack of in spontaneous, 36-37, 44; in America, 10, 11, 79-109, 129-57, 158-72, 178-86 (*see also* Vigilantism: in the United States); American Civil Liberties Union and, 115; American Legion and, 117; American Minutemen and, 17; Americans for Democratic Action and, 115; anarchism and, 70, 73, 74; and anti-Communism (*see* Anti-Communism: Vigilantism and); Anti-Communist Command of Guatemala (CADEG) and, 16 n. 40; Anti-Communist Group (GRACO) and, 16 n. 40; as anti-politics, 66, 69; as anti-socialism, 176; anxiety in creation of spontaneous, 39, 43; Arabs and (*see* Pariah communities, vigilantism toward Arabs of); in Argentina, 11, 16 n. 40, 18, 22; in Arizona, 86; in Arkansas, 84, 91; assassination and, 11, 16 n. 40, 17; associability and, 68-69; authoritarian character of participants in, 24, 48; Aware, Inc. and, 117, 119, 119 n. 19; Ayub Khan, Mohammed and, 18; Band and, 16, 16 n. 41; in Bannack, 85; Bengalis and, 15; blacklisting and, 117-20, 124, 125, 126; blacks in Africa and (*see* Africa, tropical; South African vigilantism, blacks and); blacks in United States and, 11, 13-15, 19, 35 n. 9, 62, 80, 87, 99, 100, 101, 132, 180, 185, 212-13 (*see also* Patrol groups, community, and blacks in United States); boundaries and, 4, 7, 8, 19, 20, 129; in Brazil, 16, 17, 18; in Brooklyn, 101; in Burma (*see* Pariah communities, vigilantism by Burma toward); in California, 85, 87; catharsis and, 176; Catholics and, 14, 80, 99; causes of, 5-9; in Chattanooga, 62; in Chicago, 14, 15, 16; in China, 18; Chinese and (*see* Pariah communities, vigilantism toward Chinese of); church groups and, 114, 120, 121; civil liberties proponents and, 99, 101, 115, 120, 132; civil society concept and, 68; class and, 72, 89, 99, 100, 208-9, 210-11; in Colorado, 86; *Comando de Represion de Actividades Rediciosos* and, 16 n. 40; *Comities de vigilance* and, 84; communal, 12-15; Communist party and (*see* Communist party: vigilantism and); community, concept of and, 67-69; community reconstruction and, 81, 87-91, 93; community support and, 8, 8 n. 13 (*see also* Vigilantism: social support and); comparison between American and South African, 177, 187, 192-93; conceptual problems concerning, 262-68; concluding observations concerning, 261-73; confidence, loss of and spontaneous, 39; con-

servatism and (*see* Vigilante personality, conservatism and); contract theory and, 64-65; cooperation in, by United States government and private groups, 110-11, 117-18, 120-21, 123, 124; in Costa Rica, 17; coups d'etat and, 17-18; crime-control, 10-12, 20-21, 64-65, 66, 75, 92-93, 94, 129-57, 169, 177, 178-79, 184, 266; in the Dakotas, 86; in Dar es Salaam, 198-99, 202-3; Deacons for Defense and Justice and, 101; debtors and, 11; defined, 4, 5, 159, 172, 177; Democratic Convention riots of 1968 and, 15; Democratic party and, 100; democratic theory and, 66-70, 72, 103-4; deprivation and, 5-6; in Dominican Republic, 16; drug dealers and, 11; duration of, 192; in the East, 82, 87, 178; economic, 12, 15; in Egypt, 14, 19; elitism and, 70-72, 73, 74, 75, 102, 104-7; emergency, state of and, 200-1; entertainment industry and, 110, 117, 124; episodes of (*see* Vigilantism: illustrations of); equality and, 69, 72; ethics and, 73, 74, 75, 268-70; in Ethiopia, 199; ethnic groups and (*see* names of ethnic groups under Vigilantism); examples of (*see* Vigilantism: illustrations of); exposure by HUAC and, 121-24, 125; extremism and, 97, 97 n. 57; fatalities and, 80-81, 87, 99; FBI and, 116; in Florida, 84; Freudian approaches and, 24-25, 25 n. 59; frontier, 82, 83, 86; frustration and spontaneous, 39-40, 41, 43, 44; future of, 28-29, 270-73; in Georgia, 35; in Germany, 16; in Ghana, 199; government and, 110-11, 117-18, 120-21, 123, 124, 176, 189, 191, 199-201, 221-23; in Greece, 16; groups engaged in (*see* Vigilante groups); in Guatemala, 16 n. 40, 19; *Halcones* (falcons) and, 16; in Helena, 86; history of, in America, 49, 70-109, 131, 178-80; history of, in Northern Ireland (*see* Ireland, Northern, history of, to 1920; Ireland, Northern, vigilantism in, during twentieth century); history of, in South Africa, 187-91; House Committee on Un-American Activities and (*see* HUAC, vigilantism and); HUAC and (*see* HUAC, vigilantism and); Ibo tribe and, 14; in Idaho, 86; ideology and, 26-27, 46, 54, 56, 74, 103-4, 179, 179 n. 15, 267; in Illinois, 56, 83, 84, 86, 87, 90, 95, 97, 103; illustrations of, 10-11, 13-19, 28, 35, 36, 49, 56, 62, 80, 81, 100, 178 (*see also* Africa, tropical, illustrations of vigilantism in; South African vigilantism, examples of); immigrants and, 99, 100, 120; in India, 13; in Indiana, 35, 80, 83, 84, 87, 104; Indians, American and, 15; Indians, Asian, and (*see* Pariah communities, vigilantism toward Indians, Asian of); in Indonesia, 16 n. 40 (*see also* Pariah communities, vigilantism by Indonesia toward); instances of (*see* Vigilantism: illustrations of); instant, 87 (*see also* Africa, tropical, roadside vigilantism in; Spontaneous vigilantism); in Iowa, 83, 84; in Ireland, Northern (*see* Ireland, Northern); by geographic area (*see* name of area under Vigilantism); Irish in Ireland and (*see* Ireland, Northern); Irish in United States and, 99, 100; Italians and, 101 (*see also* Vigilantism: Sicilians and); Jackson, Andrew and, 24, 105; in Jackson, 85; Japanese, Asian and, 223; Japanese-Americans and, 179; Jewish Defense League and (*see* Jewish Defense League); Jews and, 16, 19, 80, 99, 100 (*see also* Jewish Defense League); and judges, 105, 106, 107 n. 91 (*see also* Vigilantism: judicial system and); judicial system and, 92, 93 (*see also* Vigilantism: judges and); juvenile, 198-99; in Kansas, 86; in Kentucky, 80, 83, 84; in Kenya, 201, 205-7, 210-11; Kikuyu and, 201, 205-7; Ku Klux Klan and, 13, 13 n. 25, 61-62, 80, 100, 112, 131, 132, 149, 154; laborers and, 99, 100 (*see also* Vigilantism: labor movements and; Vigilantism: unions and); labor movements and, 15, 49, 52, 114, 120, 179, 188 (*see also* Vigilantism: unions and); in Latin America, 16 n. 40, 18; and lawlessness, American, 108-9; and lawyers, 105-7, 107 n. 91; leaders of (*see* Vigilante groups, leadership of); localism and, 91-92; in Los Angeles, 85; in Louisiana, 84, 91, 103; lynchings and (*see* Lynchings: and vigilantism; Lynch law: and vigilantism); lynch law and (*see* Lynchings: and vigilantism; Lynch law: and vigilantism); Maccabees and, 101, 131-32, 154; McCarthyism and, 101; macro-analysis of, 262-64; in Malawi, 198, 199; in Malaysia, 14, 222, 223; Marxism and, 70, 72-73, 74; in Mexico City, 16; micro-analysis of, 262-68; military and, 49, 201-5; minority groups and (*see* names of minority groups under Vigilantism); Minutemen, American and, 17; in Mississippi, 35, 83, 84, 91; in Missouri, 56, 83, 84, 97; Moderators and, 21, 98, 176; in Montana, 60, 85, 105; in Monterey, 85; motion picture industry and, 115, 118; motivational factors governing spontaneous, 37-44; *Movimiento Costa Rica Libre* and, 17; by Muslims, 14; narcotic dealers and, 11; National Resistance Front (FRN) and, 16 n. 40; in Nebraska, 86; ne'er-do-wells and, 80, 81, 82, 100; in Nevada, 86; New Anti-Communist Organization (NOA) and, 16 n. 40; in Newark, New Jersey, 101; in New Mexico, 86; in New Orleans, 62, 84, 100; in New York City, 11, 33, 34, 35, 35 n. 9, 37, 41; in Nigeria, 14, 212, 213, 214; in Noble County, Indiana, 90; in the North, 101; northern Illinois Regulator movement and, 95-96; northern Indiana Regulators and, 84, 104; North Ward Citizens' Committee and, 101, 130, 132, 147; Oedipal guilt and, 24-25; official, 12, 12 n. 23, 15, 16, 17; in Ogle County, 95; *Ojo por Ojo* ("Eye for Eye") and, 14 n. 40; in Oklahoma, 86; opposition to (*see* Anti-vigilante movements; Moderators); in Oregon, 86, 87; organizations engaged in (*see* Vigilante groups, specific); organized, 31, 31 n. 4; Organized National Argentine Movement (MANO) and, 16 n. 40; and outlaws, 79, 81, 98; in Pakistan, 14, 18; *pariah* communities and (*see* Pariah communities); participants in, group (*see* Vigilante groups, specific); participants in, individual (*see* Vigilantes); patrol groups and (*see* Patrol groups, community); People's Party and, 94; Peronists and, 22; personality of participants in (*see* Vigilante personality); in Philippines, 17; in Pierre, South Dakota, 86; police and (*see* Patrol groups, community, police and; Police vigilantism); political, 15-17, 196-205 (*see also* Africa, tropical, political vigilantism by civilians in; Africa, tropical, political vigilantism by military in); as political dysfunction, 75; political parties and, 94, 96, 97, 100, 101; political theory and, 64-75; in Pontiac, Michigan, 13; popular aspects and, 102, 103-4 (*see also* Populism); popular sovereignty and, 103-4; postindustrial, 116; poverty and spontaneous, 41, 44; and pressure groups, 117; preventive detention acts as, 199-200; by private persons, 10; prominent people involved in (*see* Vigilantes, prominent persons as); propaganda and, 112-13, 127; Protestants and, 14, 55, 99, 100, 120; by public persons, 10, 11; Puerto Ricans and, 11; punishments imposed under, 80, 81, 82, 86-87, 96, 97, 107 n. 91, 125-26; purposes of, 10, 81, 94; radicals, political and, 99, 100-101, 179; radio networks and, 118; rate of, 192; reactiveness of, 192; regime-control, 17-19, 22-23, 66, 67, 68, 75, 128, 177, 234, 266; revenge and, 176; revolution, right of and, 103, 104; Roosevelt, Theodore and, 24, 60, 105, 106, 107; in Sacramento, 85; sadism and, 97, 97 n.

57, 98, 141, 176; in San Antonio, 84; in San Francisco, 51, 52, 60, 84, 85, 86, 87, 94, 178 (*see also* Vigilantism: San Francisco vigilance committees and); San Francisco vigilance committees and, 84, 85, 94, 99, 100, 105, 131, 178 (*see also* Vigilantism: in San Francisco); Seen, authority of the and (*see* Africa, tropical, authority of the Seen and vigilantism in); self-defense groups and (*see* Patrol groups, community); self-preservation and, 103, 104; sex and, 212-17; in Shelby County, Texas, 98; Sicilians and, 100 (*see also* Vigilantism: Italians and); slavery and, 49, 82; social context of, 6; social flux and, 192 (*see also* Institutional fluidity); social-group-control, 12-17, 18, 19, 21-22, 66, 67, 68, 128, 169, 171, 177, 179, 180, 184, 205, 234, 266; socially constructive, 94-96, 97; socially destructive, 94-95, 96-99; social stability and, 81, 94, 107 (*see also* Vigilantism: stabilization of sociopolitical order and); social support and, 7-8, 180, 192-93 (*see also* Vigilantism: community support and); Society of the Muslim Brothers and, 14, 19; sociology of the frontier and, 87-91; sociopolitical order stabilization and, 19-23; in the South, 35 n. 9, 80, 87, 101, 107 n. 91; in South Africa (*see* South African vigilantism); in South Africa and United States compared, 177, 192-93; in South Carolina, 35, 104 (*see also* Vigilantism: South Carolina Regulators and); South Carolina Regulators and, 21, 50, 79, 82-83, 91, 95, 98; in Southeast Asia, 13 (*see also* names of countries under Vigilantism); in Soviet Union, 16, 22; spontaneous (*see* Spontaneous vigilantism); stabilization of sociopolitical order and, 19-23, 107 (*see also* Vigilantism: social stability and); State Department and, 115; statistics regarding, 79, 80-81, 81 n. 8, 85, 86, 87, 99, 131, 221, 223, 241 (*see also* Patrol groups, community, statistics regarding; Police vigilantism, figures regarding); students and, 180, 191; in Tampa, 106; in Tanganyika, 202-3; in Tanzania, 198-200, 202-3, 204; targets of, 11, 13, 17, 18, 54-55, 79, 80, 81, 83, 85, 86, 89, 91, 94, 99, 100, 110, 112, 119, 120 n. 22, 126-27, 130, 131, 179, 180, 181, 188, 198, 218; television networks and, 118; in Tennessee, 80, 83, 90-91; in Texas, 35, 56, 83, 84, 86, 90, 97, 98, 212-13, 214; in Thailand, 18, 222; turbulence and, 180 (*see also* Vigilantism: turmoil and); turmoil and, 192 (*see also* Vigilantism: turbulence and); typology of,

9-19, 177; in Uganda, 198, 199, 200-201, 203-4, 208-12, 215, 216; unions and, 15, 99, 100, 115, 120, 126 (*see also* Vigilantism: labor movements and); in the United States, 11, 13, 110-28, 178-86 (*see also* Vigilantism: in America); in United States and South Africa compared, 177, 187, 192-93; unorganized, 81 (*see also* Spontaneous vigilantism; Vigilantism: instant); Unseen, authority of the and (*see* Africa, tropical, authority of the Unseen and vigilantism in); in Utah, 86, 87; Veterans of Foreign Wars and, 117; victims of (*see* Vigilantism: targets of); Vietnam and, 224-225, 232 (*see also* Vigilantism: Vietnamese and); Vietnamese and, 221-22 (*see also* Vigilantism: Vietnam and); in Virginia (state), 62, 79; in Virginia City, 85; in Washington (state), 86; Watergate operation as, 18; in the West, 86, 87, 175, 178; white collar, 110-28; White Hand and, 19; whites and, 80, 83, 91, 99, 100, 101, 212, 213 (*see also* Patrol groups, community, whites and; South African vigilantism, whites and); in Wyoming, 86; in Zanzibar, 198, 199, 223. *See also* Neovigilantism; Patrol groups, community; Spontaneous vigilantism; Vigilante groups; Vigilante movements; Vigilante personality; Vigilantes

Violence, 5, 71; defined, 3-4, 264-65

Virginia (state), 62, 79

Virginia City, 85

Wall, Joseph B., 62, 106

Walter, Francis, 112, 119, 128

Wambaugh, Joseph, 165-66

Warren, Earl, 121

Washington (state), 86

Washington, D. C., 11

Watergate Committee, Senate, 121

Watergate operation: as vigilantism, 18

Watkins v. United States, 121, 121 n. 26

Watts, 132, 144

Watts Community Alert Patrol, 130

Weber, Max, 148

West. *See* Vigilantism: in the West

Whigs, 55, 56

White, William S., 114

White collar vigilantism, 110-28; defined, 110

White Hand, 19

White Hats, 152

Whitelaw, William, 250

Whites, vigilantism and. *See* Vigilantism: whites and

Williams, Robert, 131

Wilson, James Q., 163-64, 172

Win, Ne, 221
Wolfe, Alan, 179
Wolfenstein, E. Victor, 24-25
Women's Strike for Peace, 127
Wood, Gordon S., 104
Wyoming, 86

Young Pioneers, 197-98

Youth Alliance, 152
Youth-wingers, 197-99

Zambia, 198
Zanzibar, 198, 199 (*see Pariah* communities, vigilantism by Zanzibar toward; *Pariah* communities, in Zanzibar